FROM PLURALIST TO PATRIOTIC POLITICS

From Pluralist to Patriotic Politics

Putting Practice First

CHARLES BLATTBERG

OXFORD
UNIVERSITY PRESS

OXFORD

UNIVERSITY PRESS

Great Clarendon Street, Oxford OX2 6DP

Oxford University Press is a department of the University of Oxford.
It furthers the University's objective of excellence in research, scholarship,
and education by publishing worldwide in

Oxford New York

Athens Auckland Bangkok Bogotá Buenos Aires Calcutta
Cape Town Chennai Dar es Salaam Delhi Florence Hong Kong Istanbul
Karachi Kuala Lumpur Madrid Melbourne Mexico City Mumbai
Nairobi Paris São Paulo Singapore Taipei Tokyo Toronto Warsaw

and associated companies in Berlin Ibadan

Oxford is a registered trade mark of Oxford University Press
in the UK and certain other countries

Published in the United States
by Oxford University Press Inc., New York

British Library Cataloguing in Publication Data

Data available

Library of Congress Cataloging in Publication Data
Blattberg, Charles.
From pluralist to patriotic politics : putting practices first / Charles Blattberg.
Includes bibliographical references.
1. Political science—Philosophy. 2. Pluralism (Social sciences) I. Title.
JA71.B534 1999 320'.01'1 21—dc21 99-045062

ISBN 0-19-829688-6

1 3 5 7 9 10 8 6 4 2

Typeset by Best-set Typesetter Ltd., Hong Kong
Printed in Great Britain
on acid-free paper by
Biddles Ltd
Guildford and King's Lynn

To my mother
and the memory of my father

וַיֹּאמְרוּ כֹּל אֲשֶׁר־דִּבֶּר יְהוָה נַעֲשֶׂה וְנִשְׁמָע

. . . and they said, all that the Lord has spoken, we will do and (so) hear.

Exodus 24: 7

Thus the hearsomeness of the burger felicitates the whole of the polis.

James Joyce, *Finnegans Wake*

Preface

My country is in trouble. In 1982, then Canadian Prime Minister Pierre Trudeau ushered in a series of constitutional reforms, the most important of which being the new Charter of Rights and Freedoms. The Charter—designed, ostensibly, to give greater protection to the rights of individuals—has not only done little to help Aboriginal Canadians, as well as contributing to a revitalization of the separatist forces in Quebec, but it has also led to what some describe as an exorbitant increase in the capacity of the Canadian judiciary to review and strike down legislation, a role which had previously been limited to jurisdictional matters, themselves rarely insignificant. Many of those who supported this vast expansion of the scope of judicial review and the compromising of parliamentary sovereignty that has gone with it justified doing so by invoking a particular kind of political philosophy, one which conceives of Charter-based judicial rulings as taking place from within a realm of decision-making that somehow transcends ordinary politics. According to this approach, judges' rulings, like those of bureaucrats, can and should be 'neutral' as regards the various conceptions of the good life held by the citizenry. The 'whitecoat' political thinkers behind it—those, that is, who would strive for a neutrality in politics which could be represented by the garb of the natural scientist—can thus be said to have combined with lawyers and judges—the 'blackcoats' of the legal profession—to help ensure that pleading has become one of the dominant forms of discourse in Canadian politics.[1]

If the birth of the Charter can be considered a harbinger of the rise of a certain form of 'neutralist' thought as a major force in Canada, another development, one already long under way in the country's political practices, points to the increasing role of a different approach. As political scientists throughout the Western world have noted, the twentieth century witnessed a decline in the influence of the political party, one coeval with the rise of the interest group and the new social movement, and Canada was no exception in this regard.[2] Political parties, which tend to appeal to the broadest possible constituency by reconciling numerous varied and divergent positions under the rubric of single, more-or-less coherent political platforms, are thus losing their influence to a plurality of pressure groups, each advancing positions on what are often very particular, narrowly focused and sharply distinguished political issues. In pressure group politics it is left to government, and not parties, to make the negotiated compromises, rather than reconciliations, that such groups make increasingly necessary. It is in the writings of 'pluralists' that we find the greatest support (implicit in most cases, explicit in some) for these practices in political thought. As I will argue in this work, both the position they assume within the philosophy of language, as well as their associated conceptions of practical reason, strongly encourage a divisive—as opposed to integrative—politics. Moreover, pluralist politics has, at least in practice, had little difficulty in combining with those developments supported by the neutralist, for pressure groups tend to favour the ability to focus their energies on such concentrated centres of power as the judiciary and the bureaucracy rather than on parties or legislatures. By funnelling their resources into legal funds used to promote their causes in court, pressure groups have found a highly efficient means of carrying out their often narrowly focused campaigns.[3]

It is my contention that, together, these two developments constitute a veritable 'one-two' punch to Canada's body politic, one that is doing serious damage to the health of its political culture, just as it is doing the same to those throughout the West as a whole. For although they each do indeed express something of what we are trying to fulfil in our politics, my claim is that neutralism and pluralism also either contradict certain fundamental features of what is important to us or, when they do not, nevertheless express these in a highly distorted fashion.

When it comes to the world of political thought as distinct from active politics, however, the neutralist and pluralist have been anything but allies. Indeed, as we begin a new century, the mainstream of the discipline in the anglophone world can be described as turning increasingly towards pluralism and away from neutralism. In consequence, many political thinkers may be said to be coming into line with 'common sense', as here, at least in spirit, pluralism has long been pervasive. For when one asks the average non-philosopher the question of what should be done in the face of a moral or political dilemma, one rarely hears talk about the necessity of turning to some neutral, systematic theory for guidance; instead, a great deal is often said about the need to strike a rough 'balance' between the conflicting values involved, about finding the 'trade-off' or 'compromise' appropriate to the situation at hand, and this, as I will show in this book, is the essence of the pluralist's response to moral and political conflict.

It is as a result of these realities of thought and practice that it seems to me particularly important at this time to advance a critique of pluralism and to use it as a means of articulating what I consider a superior alternative, the conception of politics that I call 'patriotic'. In pre-modern times, 'patriotism' was associated with classical republicanism, an ideology which trumpeted the priority of the 'common good' of a city-state or republic. Since then, however, it is the nation which has, for the most part, claimed the loyalty of the patriot. My aim in this work is to proffer a somewhat different meaning for the term, one which evokes a whole philosophy of politics rather than any particular ideology (the latter being always much more programmatic and relevant to specific contexts).[4] And though this conception is one which strives to give due regard to the aspirations of the classical republican as well as of the nationalist, it nevertheless aims to do so without neglecting—as these two tend to do—to assert a significant respect for the individual. It is thus distinct from these two other patriotisms in being *both* modern and political. For it is as much at odds with classical republican politics, which fails to respect the individualism inherent to the modern distinction between the state and civil society, as it is with the 'antipolitical' thrust of many forms of nationalism. What makes many nationalists, as well as the adherents of numerous other ideologies, antipolitical is that they fail to recognize that, in a society in which there is a real heterogeneity of interests, moral or material, amongst its members, it will be necessary to engage in the dialogues of politics to deal with the often profound conflicts that inevitably arise.[5] Like pluralism, but unlike neutralism, patriotism should be considered a '(pro)political' philosophy. That being said, politics as advanced by the patriot is, I would claim, more defendable intellectually than is that of the pluralist, as well as being truer to our common sense, though—and I realize this may sound paradoxical to some—it can call for that common sense to be revised.

At its most fundamental, the critique of pluralism to be presented here rests upon a single idea: that there are at least two kinds of dialogue appropriate in politics, namely, negotiation and conversation. Pluralists, however, seem limited to (a certain conception of) the compromising talk of the former, leaving no place for the reconciliations that can be produced by the latter. As a result they disavow what, to the patriot, should be one of the central aims of politics: progress towards greater truth.

This being, above all, a work of political philosophy, the arguments I will be advancing will take a very general form, and so are meant to be relevant to all of the citizenries present throughout the West. That being

noted, it will, I hope, become quite obvious that patriotism lends support
to different ideologies, and different mixtures of them, in different countries, and so that, at the level at which it is advanced here, it is impartial
as regards the many political, as distinct from antipolitical, ideologies
that are compatible with it. Patriotism as a political philosophy, then, is
meant to be but a general articulation of the many and varied political
cultures that are shared in very different ways by very different citizenries in the West today. As advanced here, it will be supported by a
series of interpretive and trans-disciplinary readings presented in an
essayistic style, this being in line with the (anti-)methodological perspective for which I express a preference. As such, this work will also
constitute a defence of an approach to political philosophy which wholeheartedly rejects that of the dominant orthodoxy in the English-
speaking world, namely, analytic method.

Many friends and colleagues graciously agreed to read and comment
on parts of this work, and I am grateful to them all. In particular, I would
like to thank Jonathan Allen, Sir Isaiah Berlin, Eyal Chowers, G. A.
Cohen, Mark Cohen, Marc Fabien, Simon Hodson, John Horton, Barry
McCartan, David Miller, Daniel Ohana, Tom G. Palmer, Mark Philp,
Raymond Plant, Marie-Anne Solasse, Adam Swift, Charles Taylor, Rod
Tweedy, and Robert Ware.
Two individuals from this list deserve special mention. I will always
cherish the truly wonderful meetings and exchanges I had with the late
Sir Isaiah, from whom I learned a great deal. And yet, this work is to a
great extent a critique of the pluralism that he can be said to have largely
founded. Am I, then, trying to bite one of the hands that have fed me?
To the extent that this is possible in philosophy, I guess I must say that
I am. But it seems to me to be another peculiarity of the discipline that
criticism—and not imitation—can sometimes constitute the sincerest
form of flattery. I offer this work in the knowledge that this is one of
those times.
As readers make their way through the book, it should become
quickly evident that it is to Charles Taylor that my greatest intellectual
debts lie. As a teacher and in his writings, he has provided me with a
powerful source of inspiration. Indeed, I think it would be safe to say
that, where Taylor has been stumbling after the poets, I have been
largely stumbling after him.
A number of institutions provided me with generous support and the
friendliest of working environments. I would very much like to thank
Oxford University's Hertford College and International Office for all
their assistance; the Philosophy Department of the Sorbonne (Univer-

sité de Paris I) for providing me with an alternative perspective; and the Hebrew University of Jerusalem and the Ben-Gurion University of the Negev for research fellowships.

A portion of Chapter 3 of this work was published in a previous form as 'Compromising Zero-Sum Morals', in *Iyyun: The Jerusalem Philosophical Quarterly*, 47 (July 1998), 309–45, and I thank its editors for permission to reprint here.

Finally, my deepest gratitude must go to Michael Freeden, who has been most incisive and supportive throughout every stage of my research, and to Karen Luscombe, without whom this journey would have never even begun.

C. B.

Jerusalem
September 1999

Contents

1

Introduction: Against the Neutralist 'Politics' of Political Theory

The beautiful lull
the dangerous tug
we get to feel small
from high up above

And after a glimpse
up over the top
the rest of the world
becomes a gift shop

The Tragically Hip, 'Gift Shop'

A well-schooled man is one who searches for that degree of precision in each kind of study which the nature of the subject at hand admits.

Aristotle, *Nicomachean Ethics*

I

What does it mean to make a good distinction? By this I want to ask not just that all too familiar 'Where should we draw the line?' but also 'What kind of line should we draw?'. That is, should it be straight or indented, rigid or flexible, solid or dotted? These questions are significant because, as I shall argue in this work, how we answer them connects directly to the matter of how, or whether, we think we can combine those things that we have come to consider as distinct. And this is important since, when what we have distinguished is our values or goods—the things that matter to us—and these have come into conflict, then how we deal with such conflicts is a fundamental part of our moral and political lives.

What we mean by this word 'distinct', then, says a great deal about how we interpret our world and so, when what we are interpreting is a

practical situation, our conception of practical reason. I want to begin
my exploration of how different positions on this matter connect with
different approaches to thinking about and within politics by making
(what else?) a distinction. It can be said to emerge from the divergent
positions various thinkers have asserted in reaction to another, that
between what has been referred to as the 'right' and the 'good' in moral
and political thought. For those who would take a 'neutralist' approach
to morals and politics (and by this, as will soon become evident, I mean
to include more than just the thinkers behind that Kantian form of liberalism), this distinction is considered essential. As they see it, we can,
by following certain procedures of 'right', articulate various principles
which may then be used to govern our practices in a systematically
unified way, meaning that these principles of right are to be sharply distinguished from the often conflicting and unsystematizable principles
that make up the differing, ultimately metaphysical, notions of the
'good' to which people also subscribe. When applied specifically to politics, the idea is that government, as it goes about its business, ought to
ensure that it does so in a way compatible with these principles of right
as neutrally applied for, as such, they are said to constitute a just political framework within which all citizens can pursue their various conceptions of the good.

There are, however, an increasing number of moral and political
philosophers who reject this approach as unfeasible. To them, the
kinds of principles that the neutralist wishes to capture in a conception
of right cannot be sharply distinguished from those used to express
notions of the good, because principles in politics, like those in ethics,
tend to be essentially *incommensurable* with each other. As I will show,
what those who make this assertion consider its ultimate significance
to be certainly varies, but they all nevertheless consider it as ruling out
the kind of right-over-good framework for politics advocated by the
neutralist.

This difference between neutralists and non-neutralists in political
philosophy can be said to mirror, somewhat, one which Larry Siedentop has described between two kinds of liberal political thought by connecting them to the different approaches taken by political thinkers in
England and France as these countries commenced their struggles to
come to terms with modernity.[1] While it would be a mistake to affirm
any direct genealogical connection between these two and the contemporary approaches to political philosophy that I am contrasting here, I
do not think it would be an exaggeration to recognize a parallel, if only
in spirit. For the contemporary neutralist shares with Siedentop's early-
modern English liberal the ambition to attain something like the kind

of objectivity as regards political matters that has been achieved in the natural sciences. Those who reject the neutralist approach to politics, however, do so because, like the French thinkers Siedentop discusses, they recognize an important difference between the methods appropriate to the study of the natural world on the one hand, and those approaches relevant to understanding the purposeful activities of human beings—activities which include politics—on the other. To them, political thought constitutes an inquiry that is necessarily less precise than the neutralist assumes possible, one in which the disengaged stance wielded to such great effect by the natural scientist is considered, if anything, an impediment to reaching an understanding of a given socio-political context, that is, of the norms, *mœurs*, or practices of a people.

The differences between those for whom a strong natural science—human science methodological distinction is significant for political thought and those for whom it is not will constitute the main theme of the rest of this chapter. In it, I will develop the contrast between them by connecting their approaches to diverging ones within the philosophy of science. Their differences here, I will show, are tied to a disagreement over how language and so interpretation should be conceived, for to many neutralists (thinkers such as John Rawls, whose work will serve as my main example) the same kind of interpretation is applicable both to the natural sciences as broadly conceived and to politics. To those who reject neutralism, however, interpretation as so understood must be spurned and, along with this, the whole monistic project of constructing neutral, systematic theories for politics. After introducing these thinkers by emphasizing their differences with neutralists, I will then conclude the chapter by pointing out that they themselves are divided, the division here being that between pluralists and patriots. The stage should thus be set for the argument between them.

Chapter 2 consists of an in-depth examination of the conceptions of politics advocated by pluralists. As I will show, there are two rivals here as well, and as I consider one of these to be stronger, I am going to argue for it by bringing out what seem to me to be the shortcomings of the other. In particular, I am going to focus on Michael Walzer's work on distributive justice and show how his acceptance of the fundamentals of pluralism tells against the political theory he advances, one which shares something of the neatness of those systematic political theories of neutralism. The rest of the chapter will consist of an exploration of what seems to me to be the conception of politics that properly derives from pluralist fundamentals.

Chapter 3 examines the conceptions of practical reason upheld by pluralists and contrasts what I take to be the strongest of these with the 'hermeneutical' conception that, as I will later show, is assumed by the patriot. Where, to the pluralist, there are but two options in moral and political philosophy, pluralism or monism,[2] to the hermeneuticist we should recognize, and indeed endorse, a third. At base, my argument here will aim to demonstrate that pluralists, by virtue of their atomistic approach to moral and political concepts, are led to support a relatively zero-sum notion of practical reasoning, one which makes the aim of finding a *balanced compromise* the only conceivable option for those who would respond to a conflict between incommensurable values reasonably. Hermeneutical practical reason, however, by virtue of its much more holistic conceptualizations, makes room for *reconciliation* or *integration* as well as for compromise as a possible response to moral and political conflict.

Chapter 4 demonstrates how a patriotic politics which relies on the hermeneutical conception of practical reason is significantly different from that of pluralism. For one thing, it spurns the essentially a priori pessimism regarding politics that emerges from pluralist assertions of the inescapability of compromise in the face of conflict. For another, it offers hope for a politics that strives for real understanding between conflicting groups or ways of life, even though they may support norms which are significantly remote and even seemingly incompatible with each other. The result is a patriotic society, one that is neither a unity nor a plurality, neither melting-pot nor mosaic, but something in-between these two. If understanding between different ways of life is to be possible, however, it will have to be demonstrated that the ethics they express are distinct but not in an *independent* sense, that is, that they are not as conceptually *separate* from each other as the pluralist assumes.

Chapter 5 takes up this challenge. The ostensibly separate ways of life posited as examples here are those of classical republicanism on the one hand—the 'political liberty' at the heart of its conception of governance having been considered by many, since the dawn of the modern age, as fit only for the Ancients—and the pluralist version of 'modern democratic' governance on the other. By advancing an immanent critique of both classical republicanism and pluralist democracy, I hope to show how both of these conceptions, far from being distinct from each other in a separate or independent sense, actually *entail* each other, and that appreciating this means recognizing that each needs to be reformed. If I can show this, then it means that the goal of integration or reconciliation, one central to the patriot, becomes at least a potential response to conflicts between their supporters. The chapter concludes with a brief account of the patriotic conception of law-making, one which attempts to weave together the norms invoked by both classical republicanism and modern democracy.

As many have pointed out, there are three major modes of justification in politics today, namely, governance, welfare, and recognition. As it is the ambition of this work to present a whole alternative conception of politics, I feel it necessary to have something to say on a topic within each of these three areas. So where the previous chapter on governance ends up with a focus on the law-maker, Chapter 6 is about welfare, in particular, about the market economy and the question of the proper conception of the corporation and its activities in modern society. Pluralists, I point out, are sympathetic to what business ethicists often refer to as the 'stakeholding' or 'managerialist' model of the corporation, in which good corporate governance involves recognizing that a corporation has responsibilities to a plurality of stakeholders both within the corporation and throughout society— shareholders' demands for profits constituting but one of these. And, in standard pluralist fashion, when the interests of these various stakeholders clash, corporate managers are called upon to engage in the balancing act of making the trade-offs and concessions appropriate to the circumstances. After criticizing this conception, I advance what I consider to be the superior, patriotic alternative.

In Chapter 7, on recognition, I explore what it means to respect individuals in politics, to recognize them as equal in dignity. Pluralists, I show, do this by asserting that individuals bear certain rights and that these impose duties on others. But there are problems here, problems that stem both from their understanding of rights, as well as from their too-quick reliance upon them. The aim of this chapter, then, is to show how and why this is so.

In the final, concluding chapter, I turn to the matter of the contributions both neutralist and pluralist political thought have made to the growing legitimation crises that many have claimed are taking place in the polities of the West today. Pluralists, I will argue, are less guilty of contributing to these than neutralists. And yet their conceptual atomism, and the notion of practical reason that it supports, still encourages a politics which distorts what it is meant to fulfil, which is why I will be aiming throughout this book to escort the reader from what seem to me to be the very real limitations of pluralism on the one hand, and towards the substantial advantages offered by patriotism on the other. I turn first, however, to one of their common enemies.

II

At base, the critique of neutralism to be presented here can be said to consist of a rejection of the kinds of objectivity that neutralists consider a fitting aim for political thought. There exists, it seems to me, somewhat of an intra-mural debate between neutralists over which of two broad notions of objectivity can be said to be realized by the political thinker. As I will show, however, for many of those who would reject neutrality in politics it makes sense to speak of a third.

I want to begin by examining two of the central tenets of the neutralist's approach: first, the assertion of the priority of the right over the good and, second, the extent to which it is considered appropriate for 'intuition' to play a role in practical reasoning. That these positions assume parallels with the methods of natural science comes out particularly clearly in John Rawls's neutralism, and so I will then turn to a consideration of the affinities between his work and one of the latest and most sophisticated conceptions of natural science, that which is known as 'post-empiricism'. Rawls shares with a number of post-empiricists what has been referred to as the 'radical translation' conception of interpretation, one which, as I will show, considers itself relevant to both natural science and politics by virtue of its understanding of language. I will, however, try and articulate an opposing position, first from within the philosophy of science, and then as it extends to the issue of language, my aim being to demonstrate how this alternative underlies the approaches of those political thinkers who reject neutrality. To them, language should be conceived of as, at base, 'expressive' rather than 'representative', a claim which leads them to argue that we should reject the kinds of objectivity sought for by neutralists, at least when it comes to human affairs. One result of this rejection, I will argue, is that expressivists are led to support a conception of political philosophy which has no place for the construction of systematic theories.

III

The idea that there should be a priority of the right over the good has not been without controversy in the literature, but I think it can be described in a way acceptable to all those who might describe their approach as neutralist. The right consists of a procedure, said to be grounded in reason, which calls upon persons to follow a principle, or a unified, in a systematically coherent sense, set of principles, that is designed to frame or regulate their activities. To some neutralists the right is strictly consequentialist, to others it is purely formal, while to others still it involves some mixture of the two. Regardless of these differences, however, all those who affirm its priority will agree that it entails conceiving of the moral or political ideal as something which, as Henry Sidgwick once put it, is *imperative* rather than, as with an ethics or politics which gives priority to the good, *attractive*.[3] The right is thus something which is said to be obligatory or binding upon persons, whatever their wants or desires.

Utilitarianism constituted one of the major forms of neutralism in the twentieth century. It began as a doctrine which affirmed a strictly consequentialist version of the right, in which it is said to encompass a procedure whose aim is discoverable as true in nature, namely, that all sentient beings should have their natural desire to maximize their happiness or utility respected.[4] Conceived of strictly consequentially, however, it fails, as Rawls and others have complained, to give due respect to the 'distinctiveness' of persons.[5] For example, it could be said to endorse such moves as the doubling of the population in order to increase overall utility even though this would mean dramatically reducing each individual's welfare; or it might call for the oppression of a minority if this can be shown to bring happiness to the majority and so greater happiness overall. That is why, to Rawls and his followers, the 'right' ought to be conceived of as a procedure which imposes formal rather than consequentialist requirements. Fulfilling the right, they claim, should not consist of trying to bring about any particular state of affairs, rather, the aim should be to avoid violating certain formal principles while one strives to realize one's own conception of the good. For this reason, the argument goes, utilitarianism should be rejected. As Will Kymlicka has pointed out, however, the most natural and compelling version of utilitarianism is not strictly consequentialist, in which it is understood as calling for nothing but the maximization of total utility throughout society.[6] Kymlicka thus recognizes (although he does not support) an alternative interpretation of utilitarianism, one which claims to give each person's interests equal weight. The central aim here is still the maximization of utility, although now this is understood in a more indirect way, since it is considered achieved as a by-product of a decision procedure that aims for what is said to be the 'fair' aggregation of people's preferences, meaning that utility maximizing must take place within a framework that gives equal consideration to persons. As Kymlicka has pointed out, this is the approach taken by such recent major utilitarians as J. C. Harsanyi, John Griffin, and Peter Singer.

Many neutralists, however, have nevertheless—at least when it comes to politics—turned to a strictly formalist approach. The publication of Rawls's *A Theory of Justice*, combined with the works of such theorists as Bruce Ackerman, Ronald Dworkin, and Jürgen Habermas has led to an eclipsing of utilitarian political thought by a more Kantian-inspired version of neutralism.[7] In the case of Rawls's complex and multifaceted work, many have accepted certain facets of Michael Sandel's well-known interpretation of it, in which Rawls's notion of 'reflective equilibrium' is downplayed and the device of the 'original position' is stressed.[8] As Sandel has explained, Rawls makes use of the latter conception to capture something of the representative spirit of Kant's procedural ethics without relying on his a priori metaphysics. Those who step behind the hypothetical 'veil of ignorance' and enter into the original position are said to be truly representative persons in that they can deliberate 'rationally', which is understood here as requiring them to disengage from any knowledge of their personal values or abilities. With this done, the argument goes, one can formulate a 'thin theory of the good' by identifying certain basic 'primary goods' that are needed by all reasonably valued ways of life[9] and then combining them within a theory that can provide systematic guidance for their just distribution, this constituting Rawls's conception of the right.

Rawls himself, however, has come to stress different aspects of his theory. In his later work, the original position is no longer given as significant a role within the ambit of reflective equilibrium, as is evident from his decision to emphasize the 'reasonable' over the 'rational',[10] by which he means the kind of deliberation involved in the decision to enter the original position rather than that which goes on from within. Moreover, Rawls now considers his use of reflective equilibrium to be a case of '*political* constructivism', emphasizing that, amongst its provisional fixed points, only those considered convictions located within the 'overlapping consensus' of the public political culture of a constitutional democracy should be taken into account, these having been separated from those 'comprehensive' conceptions that are relevant only to morality, which is said to be a purely private matter.[11] One result of this is a conception of right that is meant to apply only to politics, ethics being left as a domain concerned with the good.[12] Another is that Rawls's theory loses the absolutely foundationalist status that it was said to achieve when it was strongly associated with the idea of the original position and this, as I will explain below, means that he no longer—if he ever did—claims the kind of objectivity for it that many other neutralists claim for theirs.

Others have responded to *A Theory of Justice* in another way, affirming a more overtly contractarian brand of neutralism and so placing a much greater emphasis than Rawls did on rational choice and game theory. The idea here is to determine what rules or constraints rational individuals would consent to impose upon themselves so as to promote their long-term interests. To thinkers such as James Buchanan, Robert Nozick, and David Gauthier, the right consists of following whatever principles would emerge from such a procedure, the understanding of what exactly it entails being obviously quite different from either the utilitarian or Kantian approaches.[13]

A fourth and final version of contemporary neutralism can be found in the works of many Marxist theorists. Marx himself, of course, rejected the notion that some conception of right could be used as a legitimate means of mediating conflicts between persons. To him 'justice' and all those other 'bourgeois' concepts, such as 'freedom', 'equality', 'fraternity', and so on, are but 'goddesses' of 'a modern mythology',[14] masks designed to suit existing property relations. The point, as he saw it, was to overcome that circumstance which provides the basis of conflict, namely, material scarcity, and to do so by bringing about communism. To those Marxists who consider this hope for material abundance unrealistic, however, a conception of right, and so justice, should indeed have a place, its first demand being that we respond to the injustices deriving from the wage–labour relation (its exploitation and alienation) by socializing the means of production. The aim for thinkers such as John Roemer and G. A. Cohen is to strive, as much as possible, to fulfil the central Marxist distributive principle: from each according to ability to each according to need.[15]

Regardless of how these various conceptions of right have been formulated, the point I want to emphasize here is that both their development and their use are considered by neutralists to meet certain standards of objectivity. Before I turn to an examination of what exactly these standards are, I want to show how it is that, for the neutralist, their achievement is understood to require the use of concepts which are considered to be 'thin' rather than 'thick', terms which have been introduced to us as carrying certain philosophical meanings by Gilbert Ryle.[16] Ryle asks us to consider two boys rapidly contracting the eyelids of their right eyes. Although the two movements are, taken in one way, identical, taken in another they can be said to express very different meanings, in which we recognize that the first boy is simply suffering from an involuntary twitch, while the second is in fact winking conspiratorially. Two more boys are then brought forward, each performing the same action—rapidly contracting the eyelids of their right eyes—

although the meanings here are also different. For the third boy is doing what he is doing as a parody of the second boy, while the fourth is actually rehearsing a parody of that second boy. All of these descriptive terms, 'twitching', 'winking conspiratorially', 'parodying', and 'rehearsing' may be understood as *thick* descriptions of these acts, in that they are characterizations which depend upon certain *contextual* factors for their differences in meaning. Even the first description is thick in that it is appropriate only in certain contexts, say in a laboratory or a doctor's office. And as the first boy can only do what he is doing if there is a problem with the muscles in his eyelid, the second must be involved in some secret plan with others, the third must have a particular sense of humour, and the fourth will probably be found standing in front of a mirror. Despite these differences due to context, however, all the boys' actions might be said to hold the *thin* description, 'rapidly contracting the eyelid of his right eye', in common.

Now if we turn from descriptions of such actions to articulations of precepts or maxims about what it means to live a good life, it is easy to see why Kantian neutralists such as Rawls consider it necessary to make use of a thin theory of the good as a basis for the development and application of their principles of right. For it seems clear that there is no way that general and systematic principles can be formulated on the basis of the kinds of thick, context-dependent articulations of the good found in everyday discourse, in which principles for living are expressed with such terms as 'honourable', 'cool', 'charitable', and so on. In this form, as all neutralists would assert, such precepts will often be both incommensurable and contradictory and, as such, irreconcilable, which to these thinkers is synonymous with saying that they are unsystematizable. Hence Rawls's statements that:

Mill argued correctly that so long as one remains at the level of common sense precepts, no reconciliation of these maxims of justice is possible . . . [They are] contrary injunctions taken by themselves . . . It is essential to keep in mind the subordinate place of common sense norms . . . None of these precepts can be plausibly raised to a first principle.[17]

And they are 'contrary injunctions taken by themselves' specifically because of their context-dependent nature. For,

each has presumably arisen in answer to a relevant feature connected with certain particular institutions, this feature being but one among many and these institutions of a special kind. Adopting one of them as a first principle is sure to lead to the neglect of other things that should be taken into account. And if all or many precepts are treated as first principles, there is no gain in systematic clarity.[18]

Thus does Rawls turn to primary goods as the bases of his thin theory of the good, since they are said to be relied upon by every reasonable way of life, however articulated. Thus just as the thin description above—'rapidly contracting the eyelid of his right eye'—is held to be neutral to the various and differing thick descriptions, Rawls conceives of his conception of right, one based on his thin theory of the good, as neutral to all reasonable ways of life. As he writes,

I do not interpret this concept of right as providing an analysis of the meaning of the term 'right' as normally used in moral contexts. It is not meant as an analysis of the concept of right in the traditional sense. Rather, the broader notion of rightness as fairness is to be understood as a replacement for existing conceptions . . . Thus if the theory of justice as fairness, or more generally of rightness as fairness, fits our considered judgments in reflective equilibrium, and if it enables us to say all that on due examination we want to say, then it provides a way of eliminating customary phrases in favour of other expressions.[19]

To Rawls that conception of right is best represented by his famous two principles of justice, for which he claims superiority over everyday maxims specifically because of the systematic way in which they are related.

It should be clear, then, that a systematic conception of the right is understood as being made possible only by a disengagement from context, this disengagement being the principal feature of the move from thick to thin description. It is a move, we may say, that consists of stepping back from particularity so as to achieve a perspective which, as Rawls puts it, 'enables us to envision our objective from afar'.[20] That objective is but the conception of the right, one which is understood to be disengaged from those contexts that constitute the domains of the thickly articulated conceptions of the good. And so it is, we may say, by virtue of a *decontextualizing* move that a neutralist such as Rawls considers himself able to reason in such a way that he can, at the very least, achieve what I want to call a *disengaged* objectivity. I say 'at the very least' because other neutralists, and perhaps even the Rawls of *A Theory of Justice*, can be said to make an even stronger claim than this, one entailing an *absolute* objectivity in which the conception of right is conceived as having a universally foundational status, the disengaged move undertaken by the theorist being said to enable him or her to achieve a kind of 'view from nowhere'. Regardless of which of the two kinds of objectivity is affirmed, however, the point I want to make here is simply that while any particular good is always asserted by particular persons in particular times and places, the right, it is claimed, is impersonal and so uniformly regulative of the actions of all who follow it. Just as a thin description of certain activities may be said to be equally true to all of the context-dependent thick descriptions of it, Rawls and the other neutralists conceive of their systematic principles of right as neutral towards persons' conceptions of the good.[21]

The attainment of a conception of the right that is both systematically coherent as well as neutral to citizens' various and conflicting conceptions of the good is considered essential by neutralists since only a right that can claim these qualities may then be applied in a neutral manner. Just as the rules of, say, baseball must be related systematically if an umpire is to be able to apply them neutrally, the application of the rules of right, it is claimed, relies on their having, as much as possible, a systematic relation to each other if that right's (disengaged or absolutely) objective status is to be upheld.[22] Because the rules in a sport's rulebook are completely free of conflict or contradiction, as well as being articulated in a highly precise way, events in the game can be governed by their application in an almost mechanical fashion, thus ensuring that given rulings will be sheltered from an unacceptable degree of controversy. Without such a rulebook referees would have no choice but to pick and choose from amongst the various rules, and perhaps even bend some of them, in order to make any given ruling; in such a case, one could no longer say that the neutral rules have been neutrally applied. In the same way, a systematic account of right is said to make neutral political judgement possible, this being why the right may, in Rawls's words, be 'recognized as a final court of appeal for ordering the conflicting claims of moral persons'.[23] If not for that right, it is asserted, one would have only one's intuition to rely upon in responding to the conflicts between different conceptions of the good.

And with intuitionism, the claim goes, comes a necessary surrendering of precision. That is because when faced with a conflicting jumble of thick precepts and principles, the intuitionist is said to be without a clear method for making decisions.[24] Rather than accept this vague and, to the neutralist, ultimately irrational approach,[25] we are urged to strive for, as Rawls puts it, 'a kind of moral geometry with all the rigor which this name connotes'.[26] The right is but the product of that 'geometry', its use being said 'to make the appeal to intuition more limited in scope, more sharply focused'.[27] And so, while no neutralist would claim that intuition can ever be exorcized completely from political thought,[28] that the application of principles of justice in the real world could ever be as straightforward as deductive logic,[29] the point is nevertheless that, by virtue of a systematic conception of right, 'the reliance on intuition is of a different nature', for it allows us to substitute 'for an ethical judgement a judgement of rational prudence. Often it is quite clear how we should decide.'[30] Thus does Rawls recommend his approach to us because of the degree of precision his conception of right is said to provide: 'It has always been recognized that ethical principles are vague. Nevertheless they are not all equally imprecise, and the two principles of justice have an advantage in the greater clarity of their demands and in what needs to be done to satisfy them.'[31] And when it comes to applying the first part of the second of these, the 'difference principle', which asserts that inequalities in the distribution of goods are permissible only if they improve the conditions of the worst off, the identification of primary goods associated with his thin theory of the good is, because of its precision, said to come in particularly handy: 'The clearest basis for interpersonal comparisons is in terms of primary goods, things that every rational person is presumed to want whatever else he wants. The more we ascend to the higher aims and aspects of the person and try to assess their worth to us, the more tenuous the procedure becomes.'[32] Thus is the difference principle said to have the merit of being 'a relatively precise conception', one which makes 'relatively sharp demands', such that 'it is fairly straightforward to ascertain what things will advance the interests of the least favoured'.[33]

Despite the considerable scope regarding questions of distributive justice to which Rawls's two principles are meant to apply, Rawls nevertheless accepts that there are a number of issues that they do not— nor can they be expected to—cover. These, he recommends, should be dealt with by a politics of what is becoming increasingly known as 'deliberative' or, for those more attracted to Habermas's account, 'discursive' democracy.[34] This approach is often conceived in contrast to those economic accounts of democracy, in which citizens are envisioned as encountering each other as purely self-interested agents. Instead of taking an instrumental stance to each other, the idea here is that political actors should engage in a kind of dialogue which is conceived as rational in that, although not instrumentally driven, it still consists in citizens detaching themselves from their particular interests or perspectives and striving to arrive at a position which represents the interests common to them all. It should be clear that, even here, in the encounters of everyday politics, reason is understood as entailing disengagement, as obliging 'each participant in a practical discourse to transfer his subjective desires into generalizable desires', such that their communication is 'removed from contexts of experience and action'.[35] Though many of those attracted to this conception of democracy disagree over its proper scope, as well as over how the notion of dialogue advocated is to be modelled (i.e. whether it should mirror the conception of fairness represented by Rawls's original position, or be based on

Habermas's conception of discourse[36]), they all share the aim of making room for a dialogue whose participants can achieve a systematically unified 'rational consensus', as David Miller has put it, one conceived of as 'an informed collective judgement based on premises that all can assent to'.[37] Democracy as so construed is thus meant to produce positions that, like the theories of justice that establish the frameworks within which it is supposed to take place, are neutral to citizens' conflicting and particular conceptions of the good.

IV

Neutrality and precision: to neutralists, these are the chief merits of a thin and systematic set of principles of right, in contrast to those vaguer and conflict-ridden thick maxims of the good. Now whether these qualities are actually present in their various conceptions of right, indeed whether they should even be conceived of as merits at all, are matters that I plan to deal with below. At this point I want only to bring out the affinities that neutralists assert between their methods and those of the natural sciences. Let us begin with a statement of Buchanan's: 'The wholly detached role of the social ecologist is important and praiseworthy, and perhaps there should be more rather than less analysis without commitment, analysis that accepts the morality of the scientist and shuns that of the social reformer.'[38] Similar allusions to parallels with the natural sciences can be found scattered throughout neutralist works.[39] Let us, then, make a foray into the philosophy of science and explore what these assertions of methodological affinity might mean. In particular, I want to examine the similarities between Rawls's reflective equilibrium approach and the 'radical translation' conception of interpretation that has its origins in the philosophy of science.

Norman Daniels has perhaps done the most to highlight the connection between Rawls's reflective equilibrium and Willard Quine's radical translation conception of scientific research.[40] Quine, along with such thinkers as Karl Popper, has been recognized as a pioneer of 'post-empiricism', an approach which can be understood as emerging from the rejection of a fundamental tenet of empiricist (or positivist) science: the inductive method taken as absolutely foundational. The problem, first raised by Hume, is that the method rests on an assumption which cannot itself be established by empirical observation, namely, the law of causality. Just because a particular causal regularity has been observed numerous times in the past, there is no guarantee that it will continue to occur in the future; indeed, we cannot even say that there is a *probability* that it will do so. And yet the whole validity of the inductive approach to fashioning laws in empiricist science rests on this assumption.[41]

Quine and Popper have led the rejection of the 'metaphysical realism' associated with this absolutely foundationalist conception of inductive method. Induction, they have claimed, cannot be affirmed as if it was an absolutely grounded premise. But the inability to claim justification on the basis of some Archimedean point should not, they have argued, lead the natural scientist to surrender his or her discipline to scepticism. For, following somewhat in the spirit of Kant's famous response to Hume, they claim that there is nothing wrong with scientists acknowledging that they bring certain background assumptions to bear in their research, as the practical reality is that such assumptions have always been integral to the scientist's ability to make determinations of relevance and significance regarding data and so to judge competing hypotheses properly. As Popper has presented the point, he once began a lecture by instructing his students to do the following:

'Take pencil and paper; carefully observe, and write down what you have observed!' They asked, of course, *what* I wanted them to observe. Clearly the instruction, 'Observe!' is absurd ... Observation is always selective ... it presupposes a descriptive language, with property words; it presupposes similarity and classification, which in its turn presupposes interests, points of view, and problems.[42]

The argument is thus that there never was any place in science for the claim that research can take place from within a stance of absolute objectivity, as if, by virtue of the assertion that their methods rest upon some absolute foundation, scientists could approach phenomena from some view from nowhere. But this does not mean that they cannot claim to achieve something like the disengaged objectivity that, as I have described, is the central ambition of the Rawlsian neutralist,[43] a stance which, while not wholly free of intuition,[44] is nevertheless still considered neutral, as well as being highly precise. Neutrality and precision are, it is claimed, in no way put beyond our reach by the fact that there seems to be no such thing as a 'pure' observation in scientific research, one in which data could be described as 'brute' or utterly free of any connection with the background assumptions brought to bear by the researcher. That is why, as Popper puts it, we must appreciate that observations 'are always *interpretations* of the facts observed; that they are *interpretations in the light of theories*'.[45]

It is important to appreciate what this 'theory-laden' conception of the scientist's background says about how scientists interpret during research. First, what, in the broadest sense, is meant by the term 'theory' here? Hubert Dreyfus has offered a partial definition which, it seems to me, both the neutralist and the radical translation philosopher of science could accept: theory involves 'the systematic interrelation of distinguishable elements'.[46] For both the neutralist's conception of right, as I have shown, and the natural scientist's theory, as should be quite obvious, need to be as systematic as possible in that they cannot be said to consist of parts which contradict each other. And the notion that a theory combines 'elements' (as opposed, say, to 'features') carries with it the idea that the parts of a theory can be conceived of as *independent* from each other, which is to say that they can be *separated*. It is only when theorized that these elements are made part of a conceptual system and so connected in a way which, I would suggest, is best described as 'interlocked' rather than 'integrated'. The difference between these two notions becomes clear when we look at what Quine has to say about how a theoretical system develops.

As Quine has described this, when a researcher, theoretical system in hand (as well as partially in the background), confronts an observation which cannot be immediately reconciled with the current schema, he or she adjusts a part or parts of that theory in order that an account of the data in question may be connected up with it. Any given change should not be seen as affecting all parts of the system, however, for the new hypothesis needs to be connected, at minimum, with only a single part of it, and so it is often only this part that needs to be changed to accommodate the new data. More often than not, Quine has explained, it is those parts of the system closest to its 'borders' that receive the new elements, as these tend to be more directly empirically based, and so are more flexible, unlike the others which are more fundamental. And what kind of parts might be found at or near the borders? Not only those relevant to the natural sciences, but also those of the human sciences and humanities as well. As Quine writes,

A recalcitrant experience can, I have urged, be accommodated by any of various alternative reevaluations in various alternative quarters of the total system . . . Total science, mathematical and natural and human, is similarly but more extremely underdetermined by experience. The edge of the system must be kept squared with experience; the rest, with all its elaborate myths or fictions, has as its objective the simplicity of laws. Ontological questions, under this view, are on a par with questions of natural science.[47]

And so, though in any given addition to the system some part of the whole remains fixed, this is so only provisionally, since no part can ever be affirmed as permanent, as was the case with the induction principle in empiricism, for that would be to grant it an absolutely foundational status.

Moreover, in the case of an especially radical new discovery, it may be that the part of the current theory that is to be reconciled with it might have to change to such an extent that other parts, located more deeply in the theory but connected to this part, will also have to alter somewhat if all the various systematic connections are to be maintained. But in no case do we have to speak of a new discovery being so radical that including it within the theory necessitates that we significantly alter *every* part of that theory. One way of putting this is to say that, for the radical translator, there is a sense in which any new hypothesis must be broadly *commensurable* with those constitutive of the theory, though not, of course, in a certain strict sense of this term, which would require that everything be reduced to a single unit of measure. Rather, the requirement is simply that the interlocking of all parts is done in a non-contradictory way such that the systematic coherence—which is a kind of unity—of the whole theory can be maintained. Had the parts of that whole been integrated rather than interlocked with each other, however, then we would be dealing with what we might refer to as an 'organic' rather than 'systematic' whole, one in which a change to any one part should be understood as transforming the whole in such a way that *every* part of it would be, to some extent, affected. The significance of this 'organic—systematic' distinction will, I hope, become clear below; for now I just want to point out that, when it comes to the radical translation conception of the interpretive process, while the kinds of adjustments to a researcher's theory made necessary by the need to incorporate a significantly new insight do not always take place without tumult, the assumption is that, for any given change, at least one part of the prevailing system will have been held firm. Otherwise, the radical translator might say, we would be faced with an unacceptable break of continuity and, rather than having successfully translated some foreign element and absorbed it into our developing theory, we would have to admit to having abandoned that theory altogether for an incomparable, because incommensurable, other. To the radical translator, then, the development of a theory is, we may say, more of an *incremental* rather than fully comprehensive and so *transformational* process.

All of these elements of theory-development in natural science are retained by Rawls in his conception of reflective equilibrium. After all, as he himself puts it, 'a theory of justice is subject to the same rules of method as other theories'.[48] One of the ramifications of this for him is that, just as absolute foundationalism is rejected by post-empiricists in natural science, so too must it be abandoned by the political theorist: the universalism assumed by utilitarian, contractualist, Marxist, and many other Kantian political theories must go. That is because political theorists, like scientific researchers, cannot ever lay claim to any sort of absolute objectivity as they must accept that they always bring a particular background of assumptions to bear when theorizing. But this background, though largely implicit, does not necessitate an unacceptable degree of intuition for, as with the radical translator, it should be considered as theory-laden and so systematic. As Daniels has written, 'apparently "intuitive" judgements about how "interesting", "important," and "relevant" puzzles or facts are, are really guided by underlying theory'.[49] Moreover, the theorist aiming for reflective equilibrium should not be understood as merely trying to reflect what is already there, for 'wide' (as opposed to 'narrow') reflective equilibrium does not merely systematize some determinate set of judgements, it also permits extensive '*theory-based* revisions'[50] of them. And yet these revisions, like those of the scientist who would incorporate a new insight into his or her overall theory, are done, as I have explained, against a background parts of which having been granted the status of 'provisional fixed points'[51] for the purpose of assessment, in which we, as Daniels has described, 'detach [or disengage] ourselves from some of our values while assessing them in light of our other beliefs'.[52]

The later Rawls's turn to '*political* constructivism', as I have mentioned, retains all the fundamentals of the reflective equilibrium approach except that now the theory is understood to apply only to those overlapping normative principles said to be found in the domain of a democracy's public, political culture, and not to those of the various discordant comprehensive moral doctrines of the good. The idea that these two groups of principles, political and moral, are separable is another assumption in line with the radical translator's conception of meaning, in that each is understood to consist of interlocked but independently distinct parts, of 'elements' or 'components' rather than 'features'. This is why it is assumed that those parts relevant to the political conception that is the right can be undistortively 'unlocked' from the private, comprehensive conceptions of the good, and why, as Rawls puts it, the right should be recognized as a 'free-standing' conception, a 'module' which 'fits into and can be supported by various reasonable comprehensive doctrines that endure in the society regulated by it'.[53] And so, it is because persons' moral-political conceptions as a whole are seen as consisting of independently conceivable parts that are interlocked rather than integrated with each other that they may be divided, without distortion, into separate moral and political sections, with the parts of the latter, as we have seen, then thinned or decontextualized so as to enable the formulation of a systematic conception of right.

Otherwise put, then, Rawls's reflective equilibrium approach consists of nothing but a radical translation of the customarily represented thick political principles affirmed by the various, but reasonable, comprehensive doctrines found in a democratic society, a translation which provides the basis for the independently distinct, thin, and systematic conception of right. Moreover, just like the move to the single thin description of the various boys 'rapidly contracting their right eyelids', Rawls's conception of right is meant to accord with *all* reasonable citizens' politics. The fact that these conceptions can be reformulated from thick to thin forms shows that what one aims to 'get at' when aiming for reflective equilibrium, just as in radical translation, is *what* people are *representing* with their language, that is, the content, the 'truth-conditions', as some would put it, of the meanings in question, truth here being understood in a way which supposes that form, the matter of *how* these meanings are represented, is ultimately extraneous. Only under such an assumption may Rawls claim that the reformulation of certain thick maxims into thin forms can be achieved without distorting their essential meaning, a position which accords perfectly with Quine's doctrine of the 'indeterminacy of translation', according to which *any* systematic translation which does this is as good as any other as long as the requirement of giving a representational account of all the data in question is met.[54] The doctrine, as Donald Davidson, who has been strongly influenced by Quine, affirms it is said to be 'no more mysterious than the fact that temperature can be measured in Centigrade or Fahrenheit'.[55]

Now if the meanings we are trying to capture when thinking about politics are really capable of being rendered in this fashion, that is, if thinking about matters such as justice can really be considered an, at base, representational, theory-laden endeavour, then the use of radical translation to reformulate the thick and conflicting ideals underlying certain politically relevant practices into a thin and systematic conception of right would certainly make sense. Consider the following game: it is played on a grid with nine squares in which two players take turns, the first marking Os and the second Xs, until one succeeds in making a straight line of three marks. Now this would not be a depiction of noughts and crosses or tic-tac-toe as we know it—for in that game X customarily goes first—and yet it still essentially captures the same game. It is because society, for Rawls, is made up of institutions that are, ultimately, rule-based in just this systematically coherent way, that he considers it appropriate to approach them with the reflective equilibrium method. As he writes, an institution, which for him includes 'games and rituals, trials and parliaments, markets and systems of property', consists of 'a public system of rules which defines offices and positions with their rights and duties, powers and immunities, and the like ... [In an institution] various kinds of general norms are organized into a [systematically] coherent scheme'.[56] It is by virtue of this assumption that Rawls can compare his whole project of developing a theory of justice with the concept of grammaticality in Noam Chomsky's linguistics, for systematic rules can always, in principle, be made explicit and so highly precise, though this may be a 'highly intricate task' which 'may eventually require fairly sophisticated mathematics as well'.[57]

It would take me too far afield to present direct arguments here as to why, as I believe is the case, this conception of institutions in society is fundamentally flawed. I want, however, to use the rest of this chapter to present a rough outline of a path of thought which connects certain alternative positions taken within the philosophies of science and language to an approach to social and political thought which is in important ways superior to that of neutralists such as Rawls. To begin, let us return to natural science and raise the following question: is the disengaged kind of objectivity aimed for during research always available to the scientist? In varying ways, Michael Polanyi, Thomas Kuhn, Imre Lakatos, and others have come to argue that there are occasions when such 'normal science', as Kuhn has referred to it, is no longer possible. As Kuhn has argued, scientists sometimes find themselves facing seemingly inexplicable phenomena of such fundamentality that a 'paradigm crisis' ensues in which there is a need for what he calls 'revolutionary science'. Here researchers, dissatisfied with the ability of the current theoretical system to account for a given phenomenon, choose from amongst various competing new alternatives. This, for example, is what is said to have happened with the shifts that took place from pre-modern Aristotelian science to Newtonian physics, and then in the twentieth-century to general relativity and quantum mechanics (these two, of course, having yet to be reconciled). For Kuhn, then, it is essential to appreciate that one paradigm is, significantly, qualitatively different from another.[58]

In what sense 'qualitatively different'? To those who follow Popper and Quine, if a new paradigm is such that it cannot be connected with the current scheme without changes being made to *every* part of that scheme then, as I have shown, the two are understood to be essentially irreconcilable with each other because they are in every sense incommensurable. That is, if paradigm shifts really do necessitate such comprehensive transformations then the move between, say, the Aristotelian and Newtonian paradigms could not, the claim goes, be considered 'rational', for the relations between paradigms would be just like those between the thick everyday maxims that, as in one of my citations of Rawls above, are unsystematizable, there being no way, given the form they are in, to bring them together in a non-contradictory manner. Progress in science, or at least progress as the term is usually understood, would become a chimera, since reason could not be said to govern the comparison of paradigms. Now while there are those, such as Mary Hesse and Richard Rorty, who indeed uphold such a position regarding the comparison of paradigms,[59] others would stick with Quine and Popper and argue that it seems so incongruous with our experience that we might even say that one simply cannot make sense of the notion of paradigms as differing in this way.[60]

Kuhn, Polanyi, and Lakatos, however, have taken a third route. As I interpret them, recognizing the incommensurability of paradigms does not, despite the claims of the radical translator, have to entail rational incomparability. Kuhn, for example, has asserted that it does indeed make sense to speak of progress in the case of paradigm shifts such as the move from the Aristotelian to the Newtonian conceptual schemes, the changes in our understanding of the notion of physical causation being a particularly significant example here.[61] This, however, is said to have entailed the use of a kind of interpretation—Kuhn refers to it as a scientist's 'disciplinary matrix', Polanyi as his or her 'personal judgement'[62] —which is considered to be qualitatively different from the disengaged, theoretical sort employed during normal science. It is one that may be said to share something of the spirit of Aristotle's notion of practical wisdom or *phronesis*, a notion of judgement which aims for a kind of objectivity that, we might say, is *engaged* with rather than *disengaged* from the context at hand, one which, as Bernard Crick once wrote of objectivity, 'is not to be confused with neutrality'.[63] To be engaged with a context is to rely upon an affective kind of perception, one in which the divisions assumed by 'cognitivist' conceptions of science, those between reason and emotion, mind and body, and so on, are rejected. Cold, disembodied reasoning certainly has its place, but it is one that, in this conception, should be limited to the normal modes of natural science.

Of course, if incommensurable paradigms are considered comparable, then this must be because a significantly different understanding of the nature of language is being assumed here. For scientists do what they do with language. But if language must be considered theory-laden throughout for reasoning to be coherent, then it certainly cannot be understood as consisting of fundamentally incommensurable parts as this would fly in the face of the unity of a system. Perhaps, then, language is not, at base, theory-laden after all. This, it seems to me, is the position of those who argue that language is fundamentally *expressive* rather than, as with the radical translator, *representative*. That is, though it is accepted that there are indeed times when we use language as but a tool with which to systematically represent meaning, the expressivist philosopher of language claims that, at base, language must be understood as *manifesting* meaning by expressing it in a certain way, namely, through an embodiment. Another way of putting this is to say that, when we conceive of language as expressive, *what* is expressed is consubstantial with *how* it is expressed.

The notion of consubstantiality rests upon (what should be) an important distinction in the philosophy of language, that between the 'sign' and the 'symbol'. A sign refers to the relation between a 'signifier', what is used to represent an idea, and a 'signified', the idea being represented. Thus the allegory, or story which suggests other stories, might be said to be made up of signs that are equivalent in meaning to other signs. For example, one source of the power of Homer's *Odyssey* for pre-moderns consisted in the allegorical resonances between the notion that Odysseus ought to return home and punish those who had beset his household just as a lion, as king of the jungle, should slaughter whatever animals dared to take up shelter in his den during his absence. Such an allegorical relation between stories is based on the assumption that their meanings are fundamentally commensurable, that stories can be translated into each other in much the same sense as that advocated by the radical translator.[64] The ultimate commensurability of meaning is key to radical translation because its representative-based conception of language assumes that it is the principles of the sign that are most fundamental. With the sign, at least in modern linguistics, the signifier and the signified are recognized as having an ultimately arbitrary relationship to each other, it being possible that another signifier could equally well represent the meaning of the signified and so fulfil its truth-conditions.[65] And this, of course, is but another way of recognizing Quine's doctrine of the indeterminacy of translation.

But where the meaning of allegory may thus be said to be finite and complete, and so in that sense 'dead', that of the symbol is considered to be infinite, inexhaustible, and so 'alive'.[66] To the German Romantics of the late eighteenth century, symbolic meaning was best understood in contrast to the allegory, as the symbol was affirmed as incompatible with the notion that the meaning of a story, or indeed of any work of art, could be carried unchanged by terms other than its own. That is because the notion of consubstantiality entails that there is an extent to which the symbol and the symbolized are fused, form and content interpenetrating each other. This means that *how* an idea's meaning is expressed in language must be considered to be an essential part of that idea. A rose by any other name, we might say, would not smell as sweet. Language is thus no longer conceived of as ultimately a tool which we use to represent a separate thing, the idea, for, to the heirs of Romantic expressivism, philosophers such as Isaiah Berlin and Charles Taylor, 'language' and 'ideas' are 'but alternative ways of saying the same thing'.[67]

Symbols, expressivists are fond of pointing out, are thus more like a soul's body than a body's clothes. Now if that fusion between symbol and symbolized were total, then the meaning being expressed would have to be considered completely autonomous, i.e. internal to the symbol, and so would be to no extent dependent on the context in which the symbol is located. Whether symbolic meaning can ever be expressed in this way will be a central issue of this book. At this juncture, however, I wish only to point out that there are many expressivists who acknowledge that a great deal (if not all) of symbolic meaning is expressed by symbols in which the symbol and symbolized are not completely fused. In such cases, the meaning expressed is also dependent on those meanings around it, and so on the context. Whether someone's tears are of joy or sadness, for example, can only be understood by getting a grasp of that person's situation. This is why, to the expressivist, something significant can be lost in the move from thick to thin description, a move which, as I emphasized above, is essentially about decontextualization. And more than this, to the extent that context is relevant to understanding, we must also acknowledge that the meaning expressed by a symbol is incommensurable with others, for other symbols must always, to some extent, exist in a different context. But if the symbol that is the facial expression must be related to those meanings that constitute the situation of the person doing the expressing, then we must acknowledge that any interpretation of that meaning necessitates a comparison of incommensurables.

These differences regarding the nature of language connect with an important difference over science. To the radical translator, as I have shown, since language is at base theory-laden, all science, both human and natural, is to a greater or lesser extent a variation of what Kuhn would call normal science. But, to the expressivist, while it makes sense to speak of periods of normal science in the natural sciences, these, and the often highly mathematical methods on which they rely, are for the most part considered unavailable to practitioners of the human sciences or humanities. In the natural sciences, because it is *objects* in the world that are being studied, their nature is indeed often best captured by thin, precise, and systematic formulas, with research done in a disengaged manner on a theory-laden bed. After all, the laws of nature are not relative to context; drop something from what has been taken as the standard height relative to sea level and, whether you are in Montreal or the darkest African jungle, it will fall at an acceleration of $9.8 \, \text{m/sec}^2$. Natural science, it is clear, is at its most successful when it is able to operate 'normally', against a theoretical background of disengaged objectivity, one that is achieved from within a framework established by the engaged objectivity aimed for during revolutionary science.[68] But, unlike objects, *persons* often—only 'often' because they also, of course, sometimes fall down—interact with the world and each other in a symbolically meaningful way, which is to say that they act *purposively*, their activities expressing or making manifest the meanings that matter to them. Now while there may be some situations in which these activities can be said to be framed by systematically coherent rules, as with say, sports or games,[69] for the expressivist most social practices and institutions simply do not exhibit the systematic kind of coherence that Rawls claims for them. That is why, according to the expressivist, we should accept some version of Giambattista Vico's *verum/factum* distinction, one which, as Wilhelm Dilthey and the other members of the German Historical School later defended it, asserts that there must be two fundamentally different kinds of approaches to knowledge, each appropriate to a different subject-matter. The distinction, the spirit of which seems to me implicit in this chapter's epigraph from Aristotle, calls on us to accept that when one is trying to come up with an account of objects in the natural world it is the highly precise, disengaged interpretations available in normal science that will be most appropriate, but when one wishes to understand the practices of human beings, only that kind of interpretation which aims for engaged objectivity will do. Because here it is the symbol-ridden activities of ways of life that one is striving to comprehend, and to approach these with a disengaged stance will only distort. The study of human practices, in this conception, can simply never become 'normal' because these practices are considered, in the main, as meaningful in an essentially context-dependent way.[70] If normal natural science is all about seeing reality in the 'cold light of reason', then the interpretation of human practices requires the engagement of a different kind of rationality, one based on what we might refer to as our 'warm reason'.

V

And so there is a connection between positions within the philosophy of language and positions regarding the uniformity of interpretive approaches. To those who see language as, at base, an instrument of representation, there is no reason to affirm a strong distinction between the methods of natural science on the one hand and the approaches appropriate to the human sciences and the humanities on the other. These thinkers may also recognize the existence of distinct paradigms within science, although, if they support the radical translation approach, different paradigms must ultimately be commensurable, while, if they follow Rorty and Hesse, they may not.

When it comes to politics, those who follow Rawls in taking the radical translation/reflective equilibrium approach assume that though, left as they are, the thick moral and political precepts of everyday discourse are indeed incommensurable and so irreconcilable with each other, they can nevertheless be reduced without distortion to thin forms and then reconciled by interlocking them within a neutral and systematically unified conception of right. To those, however, who follow Rorty and Hesse and so maintain that there is a basic uniformity to all interpretation regardless of subject-matter while at the same time recognizing the incommensurability of paradigms, it makes sense to take a postmodernist approach to modern politics that we might refer to here as an 'anti-neutralist neutralism', one which, as the name implies, does not shy away from, and indeed often even trumpets, the paradoxes which it considers integral to its attempt to distinguish sharply between the right and the good on the one hand, while appreciating the impossibility of establishing a systematically unified conception of right on the other.[71] Anti-neutralist neutralists are a disparate lot, unified, it seems to me, only by their characteristically neo-Nietzschean take on the notion of unity,[72] one which leads them to spurn any attempt at overcoming incommensurability through the production of a systematic theory of justice.

It is my contention, however, following expressivists in the philosophy of language, that political neutrality of any sort, including the anti-neutralist's, must be rejected. For following the strong methodological distinction expressivists affirm between the natural sciences and the human sciences and humanities entails that, when it comes to politics, we must reject any attempt to construct a conception of right that is to have priority over the good.[73] This is not because we ought to object to the aims of systematic unity and theory *per se*, rather it is because the disengaged reasoning behind them is appropriate only when it comes to those 'normal' modes of natural science. Political 'theory', which has been defined uncontroversially enough as 'systematic reflection on the nature and purposes of government',[74] should thus be abandoned, since the social practices of human beings, being at base symbolic and not semiotic in meaning, are considered properly apprehensible only in an engaged manner and so are never systematizable.[75] What is needed instead is a practical, rather than theoretical, political philosophy.[76] Indeed, those who would construct theories for politics are not, I would claim, articulating truths about any real society (though, it is worth pointing out, they have yet to reach a consensus amongst themselves as to whether their theories should be advanced as in any sense 'true'[77]), rather they should be interpreted as putting forward imaginary pictures of (sometimes quite beautiful) timeless[78] utopias. The use of this ocular metaphor here seems to me particularly appropriate when we recall that the word 'theory' has come down to us from the Greek *theoria* which translates as a 'viewing/contemplation'. Indeed, the back-and-forth manœuvres of the political theorist of wide reflective equilibrium might even be considered analogous to the photographer's task of preparing her subject and making the adjustments necessary to get it into focus. Presumably, once this is done—the photo taken, the equilibrium reached—so too will be the discipline of political theory. 'Good work everyone', the department Chair will finally be able to announce 'Now we can all go home.'

This rather unlikely scenario is utterly ruled out by expressivists, for it is neither vision nor (in the case of the postmodern, anti-neutralist neutralists) a blinking or vision-blindness dynamic[79] that could be said to provide the dominating metaphors for the kind of interpretation they consider essential to moral and political thought. Moreover, though interpretation, for many expressivists, can entail the comparing of incommensurables, this does not mean that it must be considered an essentially intuitionist endeavour, one which aims for the 'direct insight' that intuition is said to provide. Rather, interpretation here is conceived of as exhibiting a fundamentally *dialogical* nature, with the result that aural rather than ocular metaphors become appropriate. Instead of aiming for a final picture capturing justice theoretically, the expressivist project consists of a never-ending struggle to give the best possible account of what is being interpreted at a given time. To the expressivist, then, it is *logos*, 'reason/speech' from the Greek, rather than *theoria* that should characterize our thinking about human affairs. Now theorists, of course, also consider their projects as requiring *logos*, but, for them, this word does not carry the quintessentially expressivist meaning given to it when it is recognized that, as I pointed out above, language and ideas, and so speech and reason, are understood to be essentially the same thing. For to the ancient theorist reason is only *modelled* on speech, while, to the modern, the latter is considered but a *tool* used by the former.

And so where the neutralist aims for the formulation of a thin, neutral, and precise theory of right that is then neutrally applied to prac-tice, expressivists reject neutrality in human affairs because they con-sider the practices people engage in as fundamentally unsystematizable. In the event of a dispute, then, it is assumed that there can be no theory, and so no neutral umpire, to turn to for guidance, and this means that we have no choice but to do the interpreting for ourselves. Often this entails turning to that kind of judgement which is called for when one has to compare incommensurables, one which, Berlin has written, con-sists in our engaging our 'moral sensitiveness',[80] a capacity which, like Kuhn's 'disciplinary matrix' and Polanyi's 'personal judgement', neces-sitates the taking of an engaged rather than disengaged stance towards the subject-matter.[81] This is but that warm reason that I referred to above, a type of thinking whose aim is still to produce an interpretation that is as coherent as possible, though the kind of highly precise, sys-tematic coherence involved in the attempt to uphold a theory's unity is assumed to be always out of reach.

One result of all this is that those thinkers who embrace an expres-sivist conception of language and so interpretation should be described as affirming, if anything, a priority of the good rather than of the right. Moreover, since those who would reject systematic theorizing accept that they can never claim the status of neutral umpires *vis-à-vis* the moral or political conflicts in their societies, there will also be a recog-nition that philosophers must accept that they must remain participants, interpreters like everyone else, if they are to achieve the engaged rather than disengaged objectivity essential to both good practical reasoning and moral and political philosophizing. Rather than struggling to come up with some precise procedure that is systematically representative of the norms of all, or all those within a given society, the assumption, once again, is that moral and political thought should aim instead to produce the best possible substantive account or expression of the context at hand.

The question thus arises: what of those who nevertheless try to construct systematic rulebooks for morals or politics? One motive that, it seems to me, lies behind such projects involves the wish,

conscious or not, to abandon the freedom integral to the very notion of
engaged, warm reason. That is because while neutralists may point
out that there is much more judgement involved in the neutral application of principles of justice than of the rules of a game or sport, and
that, moreover, there may even be certain extreme occasions (such as
times of war) in which their theories should actually be suspended
(though they have yet, to my knowledge, to provide an account of how
such situations should be determined), it is still clear that their central
aim is to reduce, as much as possible, the need to make decisions without
guidance from a systematic set of rules. They consider this necessary, as
I have pointed out, in order to reduce the scope of intuition and so, as
they see it, irrationality in our lives. But much of what they call 'intuition', it seems to me, is but that 'moral sensitivity' that Berlin has
written of, and this is in fact a kind of, albeit engaged, reason. It is often
said that we relinquish our freedom as human beings and become
animals when we follow our bodily desires too much, allowing them to
overwhelm our judgement. The systematic political theorist, it seems to
me, would lead us to the opposite extreme, in which we abandon judgement and rely on a product of disengaged reason, the result being that
we can be likened, not to animals, but to robots, machines. More
than this, the neutralist's disengaged approach, in demanding that we,
to whatever degree, detach ourselves from and look down upon our
social world so as to construct or apply a conception of right may even
be interpreted as involving an aspiration for a kind of imprisonment.
After all, as Alexander Solzhenitsyn has shown, there is a kind of
comfort to be had from prison-life, one associated with the fact that, not
having to judge for oneself about what is to be done, one is at least not
subject to the weight of responsibility.[82] In a similar way, disengagement
lets us shift the burden of responsibility to the theory. 'We get to feel
small / from high up above,'[83] sing the Tragically Hip. In offering a
formula for justice, a *method*, which is literally 'a way that one follows',
neutralists can thus be said to offer us an escape from all of the
difficulties, all the struggling and questioning of self, that is integral to
real practical judgement. But this is an offer that we should not, and at
any rate cannot, accept.

VI

And so, for many of those who affirm an, at base, expressivist conception of meaning, practical reason can involve the comparing of incom-

mensurables. But how, exactly, should we conceive of this? As I interpret the matter, there are two diverging positions on the answer to this
question, and it is this division, and its implications for politics, that constitutes the central issue of this book. For many of those expressivists
identifiable as 'pluralists' give one answer, in which the dialogical
process of practical reason is modelled on that adversarial kind of talk
which takes place when a person enters into *negotiations* with others (or
even presides over those between parts of his or her self). To 'hermeneutical' expressivists, however, negotiation is certainly a valid mode of dialogue and so of practical reason, but it is to be relied upon only *after*
the primary mode, that of *conversation*, has been unsuccessful. In asserting a role for conversation, the hermeneuticist can be said to assume
that even the profoundest conflicts between incommensurables can, in
the best case, be overcome by their *reconciliation* while, for pluralists,
to be faced with such conflicts necessitates the making of trade-offs or
concessions and so to some extent *compromising* the values involved.
It is because of their differences on this matter that, as I will argue, those
who find themselves sympathetic to hermeneutics ought to reject the
pluralist conception of politics and turn instead to what I call a 'patriotic' politics.

Talk of conversation and reconciliation may lead one to equate the
hermeneutical conception of interpretation and so of practical reason
with that of radical translation, but this would be a mistake. The differences between the two approaches can be brought to the fore by contrasting their understandings of the background brought to bear by an
interpreter during interpretation, a difference captured well by Dreyfus
when he distinguishes between the *theoretical holism* of Quine and his
followers, which assumes a cognitivist understanding of science, and the
practical holism that emerges from the philosophy of Martin Heidegger, it also being evident in the later works of Ludwig Wittgenstein.[84]
Rather than as something theory-laden, hermeneuticists interpret the
background in question as ultimately made up of a somewhat messy,
and certainly disunited, conglomeration of *practices*, it being asserted
that, as Wittgenstein once declared, it 'is our *acting*, which lies at the
bottom of the language game'.[85] Now even if these practices can be said
to involve the following of rules, these are certainly not thought to be
systematically ordered, and so any neutral application of them is
deemed impossible. Instead, what is emphasized is the *skill* that is
involved in following them, skills being conceived of as never fully articulable capacities. In consequence, rather than cognitive *beliefs*,
whether implicit or explicit, the background is said to be constituted by
habits or *customs* which claim a dynamism, flexibility, and depth that

would be distorted by the standards of explicitness and precision associated with theory. In hermeneutics the background is conceived of as,
at base, a kind of *energia* (activity) rather than an *ergon* (finished work),
to use Aristotle's terminology.

To understand the background in this way is to reject the systema-
tizing, the notion of interlocking parts, which underlies the theoretical
holism of radical translation. In hermeneutics, the whole activity of
framing and confirming hypotheses in natural science takes place not
only on a background of theory-laden assumptions, the basis of 'normal'
science, but also on a deeper background of practices. It is because of
this that the idea of incommensurable paradigms being necessarily irreconcilable with each other is jettisoned. For, as I pointed out, in radical
translation irreconcilability arises from an inability to keep at least one
part of a given paradigm fixed when a new part is to be absorbed. But
if, instead of an interlocking of relatively inert cognitive elements, a paradigm is understood to be, at base, constituted by a more-or-less integrated set of features, of fundamentally dynamic, inherently contextual
practices, then the requirement that any given part remain fixed would
have to be ruled out from the start. Indeed, according to this conception, even the disengaged theorizing of normal natural science cannot
be said to achieve the degree of stability that the radical translator
requires.

In consequence, one major difference between hermeneutics and
radical translation is that, for the former, the background claims the fundamentally dynamic nature associated with practice while, with the
latter, we are confronted instead with the rigidity of theory. While
radical translation theories, unlike their absolutely foundationalist predecessors, can adjust and develop rather than collapse or 'snap' in the
face of necessary change (this having been the fate of many a theory,
such as that of logical positivism, which rested upon a foundation for
which an absolutely objective status was claimed), the kind of change
they undergo here is never, as I have asserted, truly transformational,
never, that is, evolutionary, with all of the organic connotations this term
is meant to invoke. That is why we might say that, in radical translation,
the whole is flexible and so open to adjustment only in the way a sheet
of interlocking chains is flexible: when examined closely, it becomes
clear that its parts are as hard as iron.

Recognizing this should lead us to appreciate the second major difference between hermeneutics and radical translation that I want to
point out, this one being based on the differing conceptions of holism
that the two approaches assume. To the radical translator, to repeat the
point, the parts of the whole are conceived of as interlocked, at times

inert, cognitive elements in which a change to one does not necessarily entail a change to all the others, this being why the separation of the parts of a whole, as when Rawls divides political principles from those representing comprehensive doctrines of the good, is considered viable. Not so with the organic, as opposed to systematic, holism of meaning assumed by hermeneutics. That is because though it is true that, when compared with the highly atomistic philosophies of language defended by such Enlightenment thinkers as Hobbes, Locke, and Condillac, radical translators have taken major steps in the direction of holism (indeed, we can point to two: the first, with Gottlieb Frege, in moving the locus of meaning from the single word to the sentence, and the second from the sentence to the whole conceptual scheme), hermeneuticists have gone significantly further in that they may be said to have taken another step or, perhaps better, a qualitative leap towards greater holism. For the hermeneuticist claims that a conceptual scheme is itself part of a tradition of practices[86] shared in a society with others, a never-unified,[87] and so sometimes turbulent, flowing river whose parts are nevertheless all to some extent integrated, rather than interlocked, with each other. This means not only that nothing meaningful can ever fully exist 'in the head', that is, as representations in the mind of a single subject,[88] but also that, due to the conception's more comprehensive organic holism, a change to any single part of a whole must always be understood to *transform* that whole in such a way that *every* part of it is, to some extent, affected. This, it seems to me, is what Hans-Georg Gadamer, one of Heidegger's students and a leading hermeneuticist in his own right, means when he urges us to 'take transformation seriously'.[89]

Affirming this deeper, organic holism should lead us to be critical of the idea that distinguishing the parts of a conceptual scheme or way of life entails their separation, for those parts are integrated and not simply interlocked with each other, and so their separation, by which we might imagine a solid line being drawn between them, can only distort. Instead of Rawls's invocation of Chomsky's notion of grammaticality, then, the hermeneuticist would have us turn to R. G. Collingwood, for whom the grammarian's separation of the parts of a language can only, in a sense, 'kill' them. As Collingwood writes,

A grammarian is not a kind of scientist studying the actual structure of language; he is a kind of butcher, converting it from organic tissue into marketable and edible joints. Language as it lives and grows no more consists of verbs, nouns, and so forth than animals as they live and grow consist of forehands, gammons, rump-steaks, and other joints . . . Language would not remain language unless it remained expressive.[90]

The later Rawls's move of separating overlapping political principles from divergent comprehensive conceptions of the good is thus, to the hermeneuticist, seriously problematic. Because whether overlapping with other ways of life or not, every principle within a single way of life is still considered to be to some extent integrated with all of the other parts of it, for principles should be construed as to some extent integrated features of a whole rather than as separable components. Take Judaism and Christianity for example. There is much disagreement between the two religions, and yet they also hold a great deal in common. In the case of, say, the commandments in Exodus brought by Moses from God to the Israelites, these were endorsed and added to by Jesus in his Sermon on the Mount,[91] though some were later abrogated by St Paul.[92] Now can we not, says the Rawlsian, point to those commandments that are held in common by the two faiths, separate them out from their different origins as well as the other differences, and thus speak, at least here, of an overlapping consensus? Certainly not, replies the hermeneuticist. For Jews follow those commandments *specifically because* they are understood as coming from God with Moses as their messenger, whereas Christians do so because of Jesus. To drop this part of their meaning would be to compromise them fundamentally. This comes out particularly clearly when we recognize that the interpretation of a commandment by those who would follow it must often rely on adjoining material, material which, having been provided by different messengers and not part of the overlap, the Rawlsian would have discarded. 'Thou shalt not commit adultery,'[93] says Moses. 'But I say unto you,' adds Jesus, 'that whosoever looketh on a woman to lust after her hath committed adultery with her already in his heart.'[94] What it means to follow this 'overlapping' commandment should thus obviously be a very different matter for devotees of the two religions. It is the difference, one might say, between the meaning of the Hebrew Bible and that of the Old Testament.

Now pluralists, though they also support a version of expressivism when it comes to the philosophy of language, do not go all the way with hermeneuticists in their assertion, first, that it is practice 'all the way down' when it comes to meaning and, second, that the meaning of the practices are not just at base symbolic, but also thoroughly holistic. It is for both of these reasons that, as I will argue in the following chapters, pluralists sometimes end up failing to 'put practice first'. That is, when it comes to thinking about politics, there are times when they make the mistake of wrongly distinguishing between thought (when it is conceived of as thought about value-concepts) and practice, and then getting their order backwards. For example, when Michael Walzer raises the question

'What should practical political philosophers do?' the answer he gives, we should recognize, is quintessentially pluralist: 'They have to analyze, criticize, refine, and revise the values and commitments of their fellows, and *then* they have to describe honestly the difficulties that these values and commitments encounter in the contemporary world.'[95]

What pluralists do not do, however, is fail to recognize that, when it comes to conflicts, be they moral or political, there is little place for the procedures of disengagement.[96] They understand that we cannot turn to a systematic conception of right to establish a framework that is to provide the ground-rules for our politics for the simple reason that, as Berlin has put it, 'political philosophy . . . is but ethics applied to society',[97] and ethics is a thoroughly messy—sometimes even dirty— affair, a reality missed by the neutralist for whom, as Bernard Williams has pointed out, 'purity' is a central ideal.[98] There is simply no place for the clean, white coats of the natural scientist in politics, and those who would wear them will only end up 'displacing'[99] the activity rather than truly attending to its realities. Like ethics, politics begins with conflicts over notions of the good, notions which would be seriously distorted if those affirming them were either to take on a disengaged stance or simply subject themselves to the dictates of a political theory formulated by someone who had. Neutrality is not the means to a fair, objective politics, but to an antipolitics.

And yet, though they share enough regarding their conceptions of language, social practices, and practical reason to reject neutralism, there are still significant differences between the pluralist and the hermeneutical approaches. My aim in the following chapters will be to show how these differences translate into diverging conceptions of politics, with the hermeneuticist rejecting pluralism in favour of patriotism. I want to begin by using the next chapter to identify the most compelling form of pluralist politics before subjecting it, in later chapters, to the hermeneutical and then patriotic critiques that I favour.

2

Two Pluralist Polities

The only alternative to force, in the ultimate analysis, is
compromise.

Francis Biddle, 'Necessity of Compromise'

I

Attacks on the legitimacy of politics as an activity, one based on the
recognition of the profound conflicts which may take place between
persons' sometimes incommensurable ethics, have been expressed in
a variety of ways throughout the history of Western thought. In the
ancient world, those who defended politics tended to do so for either
classical democratic or classical republican reasons, while those who
attacked it turned either to theory, as with some of the doctrines evident
in the works of Plato or Aristotle;[1] to *realpolitik*, as articulated most
famously by Plato's character Thrasymachus or the historian Thucydides;[2] or to monarchy, the form of government favoured by those whom
many ancient Greeks referred to as 'barbarians'. In the medieval period,
there was no shortage of intellectual support for these alternatives, the
most significant of which being, thanks to thinkers such as Augustine,
the theoretical in theological form, Augustine having counselled
Christians to look, not towards the 'glory in men's eyes' which constituted one of the central military and political aims of the Romans, but
beyond this world, to the 'City on high, in view of life eternal.'[3] With the
rise of modern politics, however, have come new attacks on its legitimacy, these unique to it. Not that the threats of the past are no longer
with us. For the monarchic has combined with those dark *realpolitik*
philosophies articulated by thinkers such as Joseph de Maistre to give
intellectual support to fascist dictatorships, regimes even more antipolitical than were those attempts at royal absolutism during the early
modern era; while the theoretical has taken on, as with those neutralist
doctrines discussed in the previous chapter, technocratic, legalistic, con-

tractarian, and historical materialist forms. But we moderns have also had to contend with a number of unique and unprecedented threats, threats which can be appreciated by the danger they pose to civil society, a domain whose rise, coeval with that of the state from which it is distinguished, culminated with the beginning of the modern era.[4] Since it is fundamental to the concept of civil society that it is in some sense distinct from the state, the domain should thus be interpreted as an addition to, as well as participating in the transformation of, the two of *polis* and *oikos* (household) that had been recognized by the ancients. Where these latter domains once corresponded quite directly with the distinction between public and private, the rise of civil society has certainly complicated matters for, strictly speaking, civil society is in a sense both public and private, and it has, accordingly, been varyingly described as both. On the one hand, it is public in that it refers to activities which can no longer be said to be intrinsic to homemaking; on the other, it is private in that it is considered to be a domain which is to some extent extra-political or, at least, outside the politics of the state. As such, we ought to situate it somewhere in-between the household and the state. I should add here that civil society is itself constituted by two distinct subdomains: the market economy and what we might, following Habermas, call 'the public sphere',[5] the latter containing all those non-economically oriented practices which are meant to take place outside of either the home or the state.

The threats unique to the 'state—civil society' distinction of modern politics have drawn support from a number of antipolitical ideologies. Beginning with a conception of civil society as distinct from the state in a fully independent and pre-existing sense, they end up by asserting programmes which call for the virtual elimination of that state. There are two main types here.[6] One aims for marginalizing politics by approaching anarchy as closely as possible, the *idée force* being the libertarian conception of society as structured on the basis of a self-regulating economy rather than a common will, the latter tending to constitute the only other option conceivable to those supporting of this approach. The second draws on Rousseau's notion of persons forming a common will independent of all governmental structures and, by dropping the political features of his conception of the 'general will'— those which draw on a certain form of the *virtù* ethic of classical republicanism—pushes towards erasing the 'state—civil society' distinction altogether on behalf of that common will, one which represents the wishes of a collectivity identified alternatively as either a 'nation' or the 'proletariat'.

My aim in this chapter will be to contrast two different pluralist

conceptions of modern politics by emphasizing a particular feature of
the political regimes or polities they assert as ideals, namely, how they
differ as regards their conception of the 'state—civil society' distinction.
I am also going to argue against the first of these polities by criticizing
the notion that it can an established framework that should be considered above politics. To those thinkers who would back it—the 'weak
pluralists' as I will refer to them—pluralism is still compatible with
conceiving of a society as 'unified' in a certain way, namely, around a
certain conception of the ideology of liberalism. As such, pluralism
the moral and political philosophy is understood as actually *entailing*
support for liberalism the political ideology. In rejecting this I hope to
show that the 'strong pluralists' behind the second polity tend to have
a better understanding of pluralism in that they recognize that while, at
least when it comes to the increasingly multicultural (i.e. multi-ethnic,
multi-national, multi-pressure group, etc.) societies of the West, it is
incompatible with the various antipolitical ideologies, it is nevertheless
impartial as regards the political ones, and this includes not only the
politically friendly versions of liberalism, conservatism, and socialism,
but also those advanced by other ideologists, including many greens
and feminists.[7] That is to say, these pluralists recognize (though not
always explicitly) that without invoking specifics regarding a particular country's political culture, pluralism-in-itself must be silent on the
matter of which of those ideologies, or mixtures of ideologies, compatible with it deserve endorsement. By contrasting their approach with
that of its weaker cousin my aim will be to set the stage for the more
fundamental contrast between it, which seems to me to articulate pluralist politics in its most compelling form, and the patriotic alternative
that I wish to advance in its stead.

II

The first type of pluralist polity I want to examine is, as I have said, not
just pluralist but also liberal, and intrinsically so. Why have I chosen to
focus on pluralist liberalism, as opposed to, say, conservative or socialist forms of it? Partly this is because the most sophisticated pluralists
have either always been liberals of some sort or other or have recently
become so. The main reason, however, is that virtually all of those pluralists who have come to argue against the first, intrinsically liberal pluralist polity are themselves also liberals, their critique in its essence
being that liberalism, as with any other ideology, cannot be asserted as

if it were theoretically derivable from pluralism. In consequence, as I will show, their liberalism is different, it being considered a much more disorderly doctrine than is that version defended by the weak pluralists. In turning their backs on it, it seems to me, the strong pluralists reveal a great deal about how pluralist politics should be properly understood.

Robert Dahl, Joseph Raz, and Michael Walzer can be considered the leading weak pluralists and so the chief defenders of the view that pluralism and liberalism can be intrinsically linked theoretically. They do not do this for neutralist reasons, it should be clear, because their 'theories', as they sometimes refer to them, are not considered to be the product of disengaged, systematic thought. The versions of liberalism they support must thus be distinguished from those of neutralist liberalism—not on the basis that they appreciate the reality of sometimes conflicting incommensurable values, for many neutralist liberals, including Rawls, also do this, but because their intrinsically liberal pluralism recognizes that, as John Gray has put it, 'these incommensurabilities enter into liberal principles themselves and undermine the possibility of a comprehensive system of such principles'.[8]

And yet, Dahl, Raz, and Walzer, like the neutralist liberal, all assert that it makes sense to uphold, as an ideal, a fully harmonious scheme which provides a framework for politics, one which is not to be subject to the everyday negotiations that, as all pluralists would claim, make up the basic stuff of that politics. Though they take different routes to supporting this ideal polity, Dahl having developed a pluralist theory of democracy, Raz one of multiculturalism, and Walzer of distributive justice, all three can be said to share in the affirmation that two ideals, equality and what we might call 'the respect for the individual', should, when understood in certain ways, each be granted an uncompromisable status. In their ideal pluralist polity the state must assert an unwavering respect for two basic principles: (i) the fundamental equality of all groups and/or the cultures or ways of life they represent, meaning that none of these are to be granted any sort of special status by the state, and (ii) the equal 'autonomy' of every citizen to choose the way of life they wish to participate in, this providing the basis for a civil society whose integrity is not to be compromised in any way. These two do not encompass the whole of their liberalisms, but they are, I want to claim, necessary, central features of them. Moreover, the pluralist polity which respects them—one which, it should be noted, Raz and Walzer, unlike, it seems, Dahl, consider appropriate only for certain societies[9]—is a polity which, we may say, asserts the state—civil society distinction in a particular way, one that could be represented by the drawing of an even line between the two domains. What it means to draw such a line, and why this is significant will, I hope, become clear below.

Dahl's version of this intrinsically liberal pluralist polity first appeared as the normative ideal underlying his work in American political science.[10] Like all pluralist conceptions of politics, it places great emphasis on the conflicts that take place via the state between the many independent groups or associations found in civil society. In Dahl's case, it is clear that he advocates a certain ideal conception of the ground rules according to which those groups and the state should interact. This has come to the fore as a result of his need to respond to the critique that he and other political science pluralists failed to appreciate the extent to which American politics, rather than treating different groups equally, is instead highly elitist, particularly as regards the degree to which it is dominated by business interests.[11] At first, Dahl responded to this criticism by producing a work which rebuffed it.[12] That is, he continued to interpret American democratic practice as fulfilling the principle that, though groups will never be equal as regards their resources and so their ultimate influence on government, it is still the case that 'all the active and legitimate groups in the population can make themselves heard at some crucial stage in the process of decision'.[13] The claim, then, was that there is a fundamental openness to the process of entry into the competition for government sponsorship, and so that, in this most basic of senses, all civil associations at least enter the democratic arena as equals. More recently, Dahl has come to refer to this aspect of democracy as the 'Principle of Equal Consideration of Interests', a principle which, he has explained, is derived from another, one which he labels 'the idea of Intrinsic Equality'.[14] Intrinsic Equality is, however, said to be 'not robust enough'[15] to justify democratic politics as he wants to conceive of it, and so Dahl introduces a second principle, 'the Presumption of Personal Autonomy', which when combined with the idea of Intrinsic Equality is said 'to provide a sturdy foundation for democratic beliefs'.[16] As for this second principle, Dahl defines it as follows: 'In the absence of a compelling [reason] showing to the contrary everyone would be assumed to be the best judge of his or her own good or interests.'[17] As such, we may say that this principle asserts the full integrity of civil society, in that a state that respects the autonomy of its citizens as so understood is one which would not interfere in any way with their decision to join whatever group in civil society that they wished.

In Dahl's version of the ideal pluralist polity, then, the state is to play only an arbiter, broker, or umpire role as regards those conflicts that take place between civil associations over its attention, these conflicts being considered exhibitive of a vibrant and open competition, one unchecked by government control. The state's main objective should thus be only to facilitate the negotiated compromises that all conflicting groups will have to agree to, since no group should necessarily, i.e. in any relatively fixed or ongoing sense, dominate in its clashes with others. The traces of a free-market analogy here are clearly evident, indeed so much so that some have referred to this as a 'laissez-faire' pluralism, the zone of group conflict being perceived as 'a competitive market-place in which any entrepreneur can gain entry to sell his views'.[18] It is clear, then, that this government-as-broker conception draws on that 'balancing of interests' or countervailing powers model which underlay many of the early arguments for capitalism.[19]

Dahl no longer believes that American politics comes even close to meeting the requirements of these ideals in practice, however. In accepting this, he may be read as following David Truman in recognizing that there exist certain regularized relationships between government and particular groups in civil society.[20] As Grant Jordan has pointed out, Truman's work, and much of the political science pluralism that followed it, was based on the assumption 'that there is *not* open competition and that access is denied to groups not in clientelistic relations with [state] departments or agencies. This, he writes, 'is so obviously a different idea from the pluralism of [early Dahl's] *Who Governs?* that it is remarkable that the distinction was obscured for so long.'[21] In accepting this interpretation of American political practice, then, Dahl has come to accept that the United States, like every other country, is so far from meeting the requirements of what he envisions as the 'perfect democratic process', of having 'a perfect democratic government',[22] that he now feels it necessary to refer to those societies that at least approximate his ideal to some degree as 'polyarchies' rather than 'pluralist democracies'.[23] To him, only a polity that manages to fully meet the requirements of the democratic process deserves to be referred to as a pluralist democracy. As he asserts his ideal:

It seems to me highly reasonable to argue that no interests should be inviolable beyond those integral or essential to the democratic process. A democratic people would not invade this extensive domain except by mistake; and such a people might also choose to create institutional safeguards designed to keep mistakes from occurring. But outside this broad domain a democratic people could freely choose the policies its members feel best; they could decide how best to balance freedom and control, how best to settle conflicts between the interest of some and the interests of others, how best to organize and control their economy, and so on.[24]

To Dahl, then, the ideal polity is a version of what I am referring to as the intrinsically liberal pluralist polity, one which compromises neither on the equality of the ways of life within it, nor on the equal autonomy of individual citizens. These constitute a domain which would be invaded only 'by mistake', one which should simply not be subject to the negotiations of everyday politics.

Raz's ideal multicultural polity is also intended to fully meet these two criteria. First, Raz emphasizes the importance to an individual's well-being of membership in one of the society's plurality of cultural groups, and he does this in a way which leads him to assert the recognition of 'the equal standing of all the stable and viable cultural communities existing in that society'.[25] In Raz's multiculturalism, then, there is to be no talk of minorities and majorities, since 'a political society, a state, consists—if it is multicultural—of diverse communities and belongs to none of them'.[26] Second, as regards the autonomy of the individual and so the integrity of civil society, Raz makes it clear that membership in the various cultural groups is to be an 'unimpeded'[27] matter, for the state must ensure not only that 'there will be a multiplicity of valuable options to choose from', but also 'favourable conditions of choice'.[28]

Walzer has, in his own way, also come to support this intrinsically liberal pluralist polity. As I plan to go into his theory of distributive justice in some detail below, I want here only to show how it supports a polity that is broadly in line with those of Dahl and Raz. Like them, Walzer would also grant a significant role to the associations present in civil society. And, like Raz, he considers these groups so important that he has argued that it is legitimate for a liberal state to actively sustain and encourage their existence, this being one of the tasks of a liberalism of 'modest perfectionism'[29] as they both have described it. To Walzer this is considered necessary if government is to fortify the multiculturalism needed to check the individualism that, he claims, always threatens to deteriorate into an unhealthy, anti-social atomism.[30] And yet, Walzer also advocates that government should never fail to ensure that 'all associations are equal under the law',[31] and so, while the state should not be impartial as regards the development of civil associations in general, no particular association should ever be able to obtain any sort of official favour as this would mean granting it a somewhat governmentally approved status. Like both Dahl and Raz, then, Walzer asserts the basic equality of all groups in the polity. 'Join the association of your choice',[32] he has written, may be a government's only official exhortation to its citizens.

Moreover, for Walzer that choice should also be a fully autonomous one, as membership in the various civil associations should always be a completely voluntary matter. That is why, as he has put it, the 'autonomous person [is] . . . the ideal subject of the theory of justice'.[33] Like those of Dahl and Raz, Walzer's theory, as I have said, is not systematic in nature, although it still affirms a certain scheme of understandings which, because it is said to be based on a society-wide consensus, is ideally not subject to negotiation. And yet, though it is assumed that citizens should be unanimous in their support of the scheme, this is not said to interfere with the recognition of the plurality of ways of life amongst them. 'On the basis of some decades of experience,' he has written of American society, 'one can reasonably argue that ethnic pluralism is entirely compatible with the existence of a unified republic.'[34]

Isaiah Berlin is one pluralist who can be interpreted as having supported an intrinsically liberal pluralist polity, that is, who defended a certain form of liberalism as if it was virtually entailed by pluralism. But if he ever understood liberalism and pluralism in this way before—for it is not perfectly clear that he did—then he certainly ended up rejecting the conception of them as theoretically linked. In his later work, Berlin explicitly asserted that, if one wishes to be a liberal (as he clearly still did), then one must recognize that this is an ideological position distinct from any support for pluralism as a moral and political philosophy. 'Pluralism and liberalism', he came to declare, 'are not the same or even overlapping concepts. There are liberal theories which are not pluralistic. I believe in both liberalism and pluralism, but they are not logically connected.'[35]

There are a number of other such strong pluralists for whom the idea of an intrinsically liberal pluralist polity, however articulated, is just too neat. To them, to be a pluralist in politics is to uphold a much deeper appreciation of the disorderly nature of the conflicts that can and do take place between the groups in civil society and between them and government. Politics, it is said, will always be a *thoroughly* messy, even dirty, affair, meaning that there is no way that *any* aspect of it could be conceived within the framework of anything as unified as a 'theory'—even an unsystematic one—nor can government ever assume the role of being a completely impartial arbitrator or broker *vis-à-vis* the conflicts between groups. As I will be touching on some of the difficulties with pluralist notions of democracy and so Dahl's approach in Chapter 5, and since Raz's approach, as I will assert in the next chapter, assumes an inadequate conception of practical reason, it seems to me appropriate at this point to provide a critique of this intrinsically liberal pluralist polity by concentrating on Walzer's theory alone. The argument, in short, will be that theory fails because, as Samuel Huntington once pointed out, 'no theory exists for ordering values in relation to one another and for resolving on a theoretical level the conflicts that inherently exist among them'.[36] On, then, to Walzer on distributive justice.[37]

III

i

'Just doing my job': whether or not it was because they accepted this by now classic excuse, it is clear that both Plato's Socrates and Robert Bolt's Thomas More held no grudge against their executioners. But what was their attitude to the excuse? When Socrates' jailer hands him the hemlock and explains that, as regards his 'errand', as he refers to it, 'others, as you are aware, and not I, are to blame', Socrates reacts by proclaiming the man 'charming'[38] and we are left wondering whether he means this ironically or not. And when More says to the Headman, 'Friend, be not afraid of your office. You send me to God,'[39] it seems clear that he does not mean that he has come to accept his sentence as just, only that, as he construes it, matters will be set aright for him in the afterlife.

Michael Walzer, however, would have Americans (at least) live in a world in which issues such as these would be far less ambiguous. For in his vision of distributive justice, those who would be the agents of distribution—the executioners in the cases above, the distributors of 'punishment'—need look only to the 'internal'[40] logic of their particular distributive spheres, that is, to the principle(s) inherent to the sphere in which they are fulfilling their duties as if that sphere was separate from all the others. Whether someone should be punished or not is thus a matter that, for Walzer, should be resolvable on the basis of an isolated set of considerations. Citizenship, a society's overall welfare, love, friendship, religion, history, politics—these kinds of things should be utterly irrelevant. As long as those who would be distributors 'just do their jobs' and so do not concern themselves with matters that, ostensibly, lie beyond their particular distributive activities, then justice, Walzer claims, will be served. As long as the judge 'just does his job' then the executioner should similarly be able to 'just' do his own, and the condemned should forgive them for it.

Walzer's theory of distributive justice is, we should be clear, no systematic set of principles of right to be neutrally applied. Rather, it consists of a relatively thick but nevertheless general articulation of the meanings of the various goods that are distributed throughout American society. When Walzer speaks of it as a 'theory', then, we should again be careful to appreciate that he is using the term very differently from the neutralist. For one thing, he is much more cautious about the potential role of theory than many neutralists have been. 'A world that theory could fully grasp and neatly explain', he has written, 'would not, I suspect, be a pleasant place.'[41] For another he has been careful to assert that his own theory is by no means meant to encompass all of the practical reasoning necessary for the proper distribution of goods. This is because it is designed to do no more than set the formal framework and so describe, as clearly though as generally as possible, the critical standard of how the various goods should be distributed. It is still up to those persons involved in the actual distributive practices themselves—politicians and the agents of distribution—to interpret the various distributive principles Walzer sets out for them. To Walzer, then, there is simply no place in politics for the figure of the philosopherking,[42] one who can all-too-often be found lurking in the shadows of neutralist thought.[43]

At the heart of Walzer's theory is the affirmation that goods should be distributed 'autonomously', a principle which he considers to have critical, even radical, purchase, since if the limits it asserts are breached in practice then, allegedly, the shared understandings of the goods being distributed have been violated.[44] The principle emerges from one part of the 'theory of goods' (which is actually a kind of universalist, 'meta-theory'[45]) that Walzer outlines at the beginning of his *Spheres of Justice*. 'When meanings are distinct,' he writes, 'distributions must be autonomous. Every social good or set of goods constitutes, as it were, a distributive sphere within which only certain criteria and arrangements are appropriate.'[46] And since Walzer considers the United States to be a society in which goods are indeed (in an independent or isolable sense) distinct, he concludes that the principle of autonomous distributions is the appropriate one for the country. What we get in *Spheres*, then, is an account of various separate distributive spheres and the goods that constitute them. There are arguments for why medicine and other necessities of a decent life should be distributed according to need, punishment and honours according to desert, higher education and offices according to qualification or talent, jobs and wealth according to free exchange, and so on. Ensuring that distributions are autonomous, Walzer explains, means ensuring that each good is distributed *only* by virtue of the distributive principle(s) constitutive of the sphere appropriate to it, and none other. That is why, for example, a person's income should have no bearing whatsoever on his or her ability to attain political power, as power is a good which ought not be purchased but instead be distributed 'democratically', the only distributive principle suitable to it. By upholding the autonomy of distributions in this way, Walzer argues, Americans can bring about not a strict or 'simple equality' of goods (in which, for example, everyone would have the same amount of power or money), but rather a regime of 'complex equality', one in which the justifiable inequalities that occur within one distributive sphere do not convert into inequalities in others. No other kind of egalitarianism, he claims, can be true to the fact that the United States is a 'differentiated society', one in which 'justice will make for harmony only if it first makes for separation'.[47]

All of this will be well-known to those familiar with Walzer's work. It seems to me, however, that there exists a significant yet oft-neglected dimension of his conception of distributive justice, one which comes to the fore if we attend closely to the responsibilities Walzer assigns to politicians in the distributive process. These can be divided into three distinct activities:

1. While the agents of distribution might be said to be situated 'within' a given distributive sphere, interpreting its principles and so distributing the goods found within it accordingly, it is often the role of the politician to ensure that the appropriate goods to be distributed are located in the appropriate spheres to begin with. It is as regards this role that Dworkin has claimed that Walzer's distributive framework is incoherent. To Dworkin, Walzer's assertion that medical care, for example, should be within the sphere of welfare and so distributed solely on the basis of need reflects a failure to appreciate that there is an ongoing debate over this issue and hence that 'the fact of the disagreement shows that there is no shared social meaning to disagree about'.[48] But Walzer has pointed out that his theory has no difficulty with the existence of a debate such as this, one over the meaning of a good and its appropriate distributive sphere. As he has often explained, the meanings of goods can indeed change over time, and this may of course involve debate.[49] As long as those meanings, whatever they may become, remain independently distinct in nature, then they are going to be perfectly compatible with his distributive framework. The lines between the spheres may suffer temporary incursions during the struggles over evolving meanings, but they will ultimately shift to be redrawn smoothly again, the good at the heart of the controversy ending up exclusively within the sphere deemed appropriate for it.

2. The second imperative consists of ensuring that distributions remain autonomous, that is, that goods are not improperly converted and so allowed to cross over into inappropriate spheres. Fulfilling this

requirement can involve both policing the borders between spheres by upholding 'blocked', i.e. banned, exchanges, as well as, at times, regulating certain activities within a sphere. As an example of the latter, Walzer has pointed to the need that sometimes exists for political interference in the market-place if it is to be ensured that market distributions remain true to the distributive principle of free exchange, one which, he recognizes, is not always able to maintain itself. Hence the justice of, for instance, anti-combines legislation.[50]

3. While the previous two roles can be said to be concerned essentially with ensuring that the integrity of the distributive process as a whole is maintained, that is, that the formal prescriptions outlined by Walzer's theory are upheld, this third one has to do not with *how* goods are to be distributed, but rather with *how much*. This, we might say, is a substantive rather than formal matter, one aimed at answering the question 'How should our society look at the end of the distributive day?' To a point, this can be said to involve identifying the minimum amount of provisions necessary to ensure that various spheres are appropriately maintained. Proper distributions within the sphere of welfare, for example, maintain both the sphere of politics, by meeting the basic needs necessary if persons are to be able to stand to one another as fellow citizens,[51] and the sphere of money, by ensuring that 'desperate', i.e. extortionate, exchanges do not take place in the market.[52] The same kind of supportive relationship can be said to exist between the sphere of education and that of politics, since primary schooling provides persons with the basic abilities for critical thinking necessary for democratic citizenship.[53] But beyond these bare minima, there remains the issue, as Walzer puts it, of 'priority and degree'.[54] How much in total should be spent on, say, health care, to the detriment of how much on education, or on security, and so on?

Little attention, it seems to me, has been given to the fact that the kind of decision-making necessary to answer this sort of question involves a form of practical reasoning which is qualitatively different from that which the politician must engage in order to fulfil the other two roles. With the others, guidance is directly provided by the theory's central distributive principle: keep the goods separated from each other within their appropriate spheres and this will help you determine how they are to be distributed. But when it comes to those questions of *how much*, instead of talking about isolated goods we must recognize that there is a sense in which goods can come into contact—indeed clash—with one another, and so there is a need to deal with these conflicts. As Walzer writes in regards to needed goods, for example, 'Since resources are always scarce, hard choices have to be made. I suspect that these can

only be political choices. They are subject to a certain philosophical elu-
cidation, but the idea of need and the commitment to communal provision do not by themselves yield any clear determination of priorities
or degrees.'[55] But these 'hard choices', though they cannot rely on guidance from the principle of distributive autonomy, do not have to be irrational. It is here that Walzer can be said to give a place in his politics to
what he, like Berlin in the previous chapter, refers to as 'moral sense'[56]
practical reasoning, a type of deliberation which, although undirected
by theory, is still understood to receive guidance from a person's way of
life. I plan to examine this conception of practical reason in the next
chapter; for now I mention it only to speak against many of those critics
who, by focusing on Walzer's separation of goods, have failed to appreciate that his theory does indeed accommodate a recognition that there
is a need to respond to conflicts between them.[57]

   That being said, I want nevertheless to assert here that Walzer is
wrong to assume that this moral sense practical reasoning, however conceived, is limited to providing responses to the substantive as opposed
to formal questions of distributive justice, those which provide the bases
of the third of the politician's roles outlined above. My claim is that the
making of formal distributive decisions—the how rather than how much
of distributive justice—must also rely on some version of this kind of
reasoning, and not simply on the principle of distributive autonomy.
Otherwise put, the boundaries to be found between distributive spheres
simply cannot be as sharp as Walzer would have us believe, for there
are, I will try and show, a number of significant distributive practices in
the United States today which, despite being in violation of Walzer's
central distributive principle, are nevertheless at least arguably just. That
is, although it is often true that distributions in that country should be
autonomous, there are important cases in which they should not, and
deciding between them itself entails making the very same kind of
'hard choices' that Walzer would limit to those substantive distributive
matters of 'how much'. Walzer, however, either fails to recognize these
non-autonomous distributions altogether or, when he does recognize
them, goes no further than simply expressing regret that they cannot
feasibly be stopped. I will suggest, however, that such distributions
could, indeed, be stopped, but that there are good reasons for not doing
so. My claim, then, is that in assuming that distributions must take place
only according to the internal logic of a separated sphere, Walzer fails
to appreciate the extent to which goods can come into conflict with each
other, and so the extent to which the spheres they constitute are not
isolable from each other in meaning. In saying this, I am claiming much

more than that the various spheres at times 'overlap', their activities affecting and/or supporting each other in practice, for my argument is that the very meanings of the goods which constitute them ensure that there will be times when they conflict. If this is indeed the case, then it must be admitted that Walzer's principle of distributive autonomy fails to be uniformly true to all the goods being distributed, and so that it fails to capture fully how those goods are, and should be, interpreted by Americans.

ii

The claim, then, is that Walzer's 'art of separation'[58] distorts. This should become evident if we can find enough cases in which there are justifiable transgressions of the limits of the theoretical framework constituted by his principle of distributive autonomy. There are, it seems to me, cases of such transgressions to be identified in the activities of the various distributive agents and in those of politicians. As regards the former, I want to begin by examining one of the 'constrained' conversions of goods that Walzer allows. Amongst the list of the thirteen blocked uses of money he provides, Walzer accepts that some goods may be purchased, although only after a certain minimum has been provided on the basis of need. Such a constrained conversion of these goods, he asserts, needs to be barred only if it 'distorts the character, or lowers the value, of communal provision'.[59] It seems to me, however, that this is often exactly what these conversions—conversions which he nevertheless seems to support—do. Consider money and education. Walzer expresses some regret that parents may use their resources to provide their children with extra help in their studies by hiring private tutors or sending them to superiorly funded private schools.[60] Such sentiments are certainly in keeping with a concern that distributions be autonomous, as such practices mean not only that education is being distributed by the principles of a foreign sphere, but also that, down the road, the distribution of another good becomes 'corrupted', namely that of offices. For as Walzer makes clear, if offices are to be distributed autonomously, entrance committees to higher educational institutions as well as hiring committees in the public service and other professions must ensure that they give equal consideration to every qualified candidate. And this is the type of equal consideration that goes 'all the way down' so to speak. As he writes,

imagine a child of five able to set long-term goals for himself, to shape a project, to decide, say, that he wants to be a doctor. He should have roughly the same chance as any other child—similarly ambitious, similarly intelligent, similarly sensitive to the needs of others—to get the necessary education and win the desired place.[61]

But allowing parents of different means to spend on their children's education could violate even rough bounds as regards the equal training necessary for equal consideration to be possible. Walzer nevertheless refrains from calling for the complete blocking of these exchanges of money for education. Now surely this cannot be because of his concern with the practical difficulties of enforcing a ban on such exchanges, not in a society where such difficult-to-enforce bans as the prohibitions on prostitution or the sale, purchase, or possession of certain narcotics are nevertheless enforced. Walzer does admit that private schools could be 'abolished, legally banned', but then he complacently points to the existence of tutors for hire.[62] My point here is not to advocate that such exchanges should be banned after all, but rather to point out that this move is the only one compatible with the assertion that distributions be autonomous, and that it is one that Walzer himself seems unwilling to make. Walzer is reluctant to do this, I would claim, because there is at least something to be said for the right to purchase basic education, even though it clearly contradicts the distributive framework asserted by his theory. We must accept, then, that to either support or reject such a conversion is to take a position on a conflict that, as Berlin once pointed out, genuinely exists between certain liberties of parents on the one hand and the principle of equal primary education for all on the other.[63] And to do this is to recognize that the goods involved cannot be assumed to exist as isolated from each other in separate distributive spheres.[64]

Should one, however, choose to prevent this conflict between the distributions of money and education by enacting the necessary bans, there is yet another issue regarding the distribution of education that must be faced, this one related to the sphere of kinship. For what of parents who are knowledgeable enough to tutor their children themselves? Walzer admits that 'short of separating children from their parents, there is no way of preventing this sort of thing'.[65] But should we really want to? Surely the parent who takes time out to help his or her child with their homework is properly expressing familial love! In consequence, unless we are willing to follow Plato or Marx and utterly destroy the family as we know it, it seems that we must accept yet another encounter between two distributive spheres, one that seems intrinsic to the meaning of the goods, in this case kinship and education, that constitute them. And this can only indicate that these goods are not distinct in meaning in the sense Walzer would have us believe, for if they were then it should be a relatively uncontroversial matter to demand the separation of the spheres they constitute. By law, parents should not be allowed to help their children with their homework. But this, of course, would be absurd.

Walzer's refusal to call for the complete separation of the educational sphere from those of kinship and money is not, as one might assert, a result of concerns about practicality or the overly coercive intrusion of the state for, as I have pointed out, many other highly intrusive bans on conversions are already enforced, and with relatively little controversy (Walzer has, at least to my knowledge, never complained about them). My claim, then, is that the reason he cannot bring himself to advocate these bans around education is that he simply does not wish to directly violate the meanings that money and familial love actually have for Americans, even though it is evident that the distribution of these goods clashes with the distributive principles internal to the sphere of education. The fact is that when it comes to the distribution of education, Americans simply cannot limit their considerations to the question of what should be done, as Walzer has put it, 'if we stand *inside* the school'.[66]

The same conclusion about the unviability of separation can be reached if we return to money and examine how its distribution is related to that of another good: health care. As pointed out above, Dworkin rejects Walzer's assertion that a minimum provision of health care should be publicly distributed as a needed good because, for Dworkin, medicine belongs to 'no settled sphere of justice'.[67] However, even if we took Walzer's side in this debate and called for a fully public health-care system, I would argue that a version of Dworkin's objection should still stand. For, again, we must return to Walzer's own requirement not to distort the character or lower the value of communal provision. Now surely allowing a good such as medical care to be bought or sold, even after a minimum has been communally provided, cannot mean that its very meaning has changed, that, beyond the minimum, it is no longer really *needed*. After all, without access to certain treatments, some people will simply die. Consequently, while Walzer is correct to point out that determining the minimal degree of provision of such a good will always be a difficult practical decision, the fact remains that, beyond that provision, he would have this needed good distributed by principles that are, ostensibly, foreign to its nature. If we were to follow the dictates of his own theoretical distributive framework, however, it would seem to make much more sense to argue that if the good cannot be distributed by what, according to the theory, is its appropriate means, then it should not be distributed at all. For why, just because an individual has obtained monies by virtue of market exchanges (which, Walzer has claimed, are greatly the result of luck), should he or she be able to spend these on life-saving treatments while others, due to lack of funds, should be allowed to die? And yet, blocking such a conversion would be a highly controversial matter, for it is simply not as straight-forwardly unjust as Walzer's principle of distributive autonomy would have Americans believe. Perhaps this is because there is a sense in which desert and not just luck plays a significant role in the distribution of money, thus giving money some added weight in its encounter with the distribution of health care. Regardless of why, however, Walzer's own acceptance of this constrained conversion belies the fact that we are dealing with a case in which two goods, each with ostensibly separate distributive principles, have rightly come into contact, and so that, if one is to decide what to do, it will be necessary to go beyond the internal logic of a single sphere and make a judgement which involves taking into account the principles of two such spheres.

So far, I have been referring to cases of arguably just transgressions of the separatism fundamental to Walzer's distributive framework that emerge from the practices involved in distributing the goods, these con-stituting the activities of the agents of distribution. I now want to turn to justifiable transgressions of the framework associated with decision-making of the kind that Walzer considers to be the purview of politi-cians. To begin, take his discussion of the sphere of membership (i.e. citizenship), which he claims consists of two distributive principles: the meaning membership has for the community, and mutual aid for refugees.[68] It could be argued, however, that he also affirms a third route to membership, one implied by his critique of the use of guest workers or metics. Walzer recognizes that societies often turn to individuals who are able to do jobs which present citizens are either unable or unwill-ing to do. The demands of political justice, he argues, require that the newcomers should be given the opportunity to become citizens.[69] But if he is right about this, then he must acknowledge that talent or the will-ingness and ability to work, qualities which he has claimed should be relevant only to the distribution of offices or jobs respectively, are also to play a role in the distribution of membership. Moreover, this cross-ing of distributive boundaries becomes even more stark if we recognize that current American immigration policy includes a business immigra-tion programme which reserves places for investors with the aim of cre-ating jobs and contributing to the economy.[70] Here, then, we have a conversion of money to membership which, unless one construes the meaning of membership so loosely as to make it virtually empty, directly violates the principle that it should be distributed autonomously.

Nevertheless it is far from obvious that such a programme, as long as it is not abused, is necessarily unjust.

Another such transgression of the principle of separation on the part of the state arises from a reform that Walzer has called for as regards a number of the society's institutions: democratization. Many of Walzer's critics have argued that his theory, based as he claims it is on the shared understandings of a citizenry, is inherently conservative and so lacks critical purchase. While I do not share this position, I do think that difficulties nevertheless emerge for Walzer as regards his call for the democratic reform of certain spheres. Walzer has come to advocate democratization due to his recognition that there will be times when a significant concentration of power emerges from within the operations of a particular sphere, and that since power is a good which lays claim to its own independently distinct distributive principle, namely democracy, the eruption of a new and separate sphere, one of demo-cratic government, should be duly recognized. This is most forcefully argued by him when he calls for the democratization of those busi-ness enterprises which have reached a certain size such that owners have attained a degree of coercive power over their workers. Walzer points to the example of Pullman, Illinois, and asserts that the existence of any type of private government is a violation of the fundamentals of citizenship.[71]

But Walzer is wrong to consider the new sphere as isolable. Say a corporation, by virtue of the power it has attained over its workers, is, in accord with Walzer's theory, democratized. The distributions that will take place within this worker's co-operative should not, however, be understood as guided by the isolated principles of two wholly sepa-rated spheres, namely, one of money/commodities on the one hand, and one of political power on the other.[72] Instead, we should conceive of the co-operative as located in a zone in which the two spheres have been somehow combined, in that those participating in the enterprise must alternately attend, not to two separate sets of distributive principles, but rather to a new, hybrid set, one which consists of the principles inherent to the two parent spheres. That is why the operating rules of a co-operative must be very different than either those that attend a state and its citizens or those faced by the participants in a capitalist market economy. For example, if co-operatives are to be at all viable they must be allowed to dismiss members, while municipalities cannot be permitted to eject residents, nor states to revoke anyone's citizenship. This is because it is corporate rather than state power that is being distributed within a co-operative and the rights of a 'citizen' of a business enterprise should differ accordingly. Similarly unique hybrid spheres, each necessitating their own particular distributive patterns, must be recognized in universities, where faculty properly claim a greater than equal share in representation on governing boards than students, and in some religions, where ecclesiastical authorities with undeniable power over their members can be true to their faith only by rejecting calls for even minimal accountability to believers.[73] Democratization, we must thus accept, is about combining rather than separating spheres.

Other difficulties arise for Walzer with the notion of democratization. Nationalization is a form of democratization when either the production or distribution of goods are, instead of being co-operatized, taken over by a democratic state. To Walzer, Americans should consider nationalization when it is recognized that the power which has emerged from within a given sphere affects all citizens, and not just those participating in it. For example, he has argued that one of the reasons for the rise of the welfare state is that it was necessary to take over a great deal of the work done by private charitable agencies because their practices sometimes encouraged patterns of dependency rather than the recognition that citizens who receive needed goods are simply getting their rights fulfilled.[74] But the operation of nationalized enterprises, I would argue, necessarily carries with it a transgression of Walzer's distributive framework. This arises from the fact that, for nationalized spheres such as welfare and education, much of the resources needed are originally located in the market. Hence the state, by means of taxation, must transport these funds to their appropriate spheres. Now when this is done, as Walzer points out, it is not that the good of 'money', which when conceived of in a certain strict sense is held by citizens privately, is being converted into any of these others, for while the necessary funds may have been found circulating in the market, they should at no point be understood as representing private money as they are at all times part of the 'common wealth'[75]—it is thus only proper that they be distributed by principles other than those of the market. The difficulty arises, however, with Walzer's claim that the amount to be taxed and for which needed goods are questions which can only be answered by making those difficult, substantive decisions that he has claimed are of the distinctively political sort,[76] decisions which, though they cannot rely on guidance from his distributive principle of autonomy, must nevertheless also abide by the constraints that the principle sets. But surely there is more to taxation than a simple mechanism of transport, as taxes can never be neutral or non-distortive of market exchanges. Indeed, it is widely recognized by economists that purely 'lump-sum' taxation, in which there is nothing individuals can do to change their liability, is infeasible.[77] Having a significant influence over persons' behaviour in the market due to taxation thus seems inescapable. It is a short step from appreciating this to the recognition on the part of government that taxation has consequences for the overall distribution of wealth in society. To Walzer, however, considerations about the distribution of wealth—if they are to be entertained at all—should be dealt with only from within the bounds of his distributive framework, as when he notes that complex equality minimizes economic inequality by impeding the tyrannical conversions that can contribute to it. But since taxation is a practice which necessarily has a significant impact on the free exchange of money and commodities within the market sphere, then there seems to be no way to avoid contravening his principle of distributive autonomy. Ending the practice is certainly not an option for, as I have pointed out, it is necessary for the very existence of a number of spheres. In consequence, we must recognize that interference with the distributive logic internal to the market sphere seems inevitable here, and this means that politicians must always be prepared to face questions about the distribution of wealth in society, questions which, by their very nature, require answers that violate the bounds of complex equality.[78]

There is one final case of transgression by the politician of Walzer's principle of distributive autonomy that I want to put forward. It arises from those few circumstances in which Walzer himself seems quite willing to suspend his distributive framework altogether. One example of this occurs in the case of affirmative action as a response to the reality of excluded groups. In *Spheres*, Walzer acknowledges that the United States has suffered a long history of racism, but rejects the proposal that Americans should suspend the norm of equal consideration for individual citizens and reserve a certain number of offices for African-Americans. Instead of turning to this 'last resort', he recommends responding to the problem with a programme of public expenditures, democratically agreed upon, which would entail heavy investment in certain depressed areas or industries.[79]

Such a position is certainly compatible with his distributive framework which, as I have pointed out, requires that there be equal consideration as regards the distribution of offices. And yet, in later work, Walzer has come to reverse it.[80] His willingness to do this is significant, because it shows that he considers it appropriate for political decision-makers sometimes to step beyond the bounds laid down by his theory's distributive framework. In so doing, however, Walzer reveals a gap in that framework, one which, it seems, he fails to fully appreciate. For he simply has no means of confronting such substantive political considerations without resorting to the rather awkward move of suspending his principle of distributive autonomy altogether. One of the obstacles to justice, Walzer seems to have discovered, is his own theory of distributive justice.

iii

And so, there are a number of cases in which it appears that exceptions to Walzer's principle of distributive autonomy have to be made, cases which ensure that, at the very least, the lines drawn between his distributive spheres cannot be free of indentations, these representing the trade-offs that, it is assumed, will have to be made when those 'hard choices' are undertaken because conflicting distributive principles have had to be compromised. The fact is that the distributive judgements invoked by persons standing within a given sphere cannot be based solely on an isolable principle, or fully harmonious set of such principles, that has been 'quarantined' from those of other spheres. While avoiding the pitfalls of the monological conception of practical reasoning associated with such notions as Rawls's 'veil of ignorance',[81] Walzer is nevertheless mistaken in his demand that those who would interpret the distributive principles of a particular sphere give *no role at all* to principles foreign to that sphere. It is as if the agents of distribution are all wrapped together in a veil which contains a single, Procrustean hole from which they may spy only one isolated good, or subset of goods. But to demand this is to ensure that their interpretive dialogue cannot but be perverted.

In consequence, if we are to follow what are presumably his own standards for the term, it must be admitted that Walzer's principle of distributive autonomy fails to provide the basis of a 'theory' of distributive justice after all, since all of the issues relating to distributive justice, including the formal ones, seem ultimately to be matters for that untheoretical kind of practical reasoning that consists of engaging one's 'moral sense'. Moreover, if for Walzer it is, as I cited earlier, 'the autonomous person' that constitutes the 'ideal subject of the theory of justice', then his inability to sustain his theory consistently means that he cannot hold this autonomy up as an uncompromisable ideal, at least if it is to have this status by virtue of some sort of theoretical endorsement. Moreover, if, as Walzer argues in *Spheres*, there should be an equality of opportunity for all individuals when it comes to the struggle for recognition (this being, as he puts it, 'the promise of the society of misters'[82]), then the collapse of his theory means that this principle of equality must also lose its sheltered status. The 'society of misters' arose out of, and in reaction to, the society of aristocrats, in which hereditary rank was dominant over equal recognition. The latter society is, of course, now gone, but it would be wrong to assert that it could ever be replaced by one which fully and uncompromisingly respected the equality of opportunity as regards the general competition for recognition. This is because certain social groups will, for various reasons (some of which I will describe below), always manage to achieve a special status, and those born into them will always have the option of benefiting, and/or suffering, accordingly.

Now should Walzer ever come to accept that moral sense is all we have got, indeed all we have ever had when it comes to reasoning about political conflicts, then we would be able to say that he concurs with those strong pluralists for whom it is wrong to assume that a polity, simply by virtue of being pluralistic, must adhere to a liberal political ideology. To them no truly pluralist society can claim a consensus that will ever be wholly free of conflict, meaning that any framework for politics will itself always have to be subject to that politics. As Stephen Macedo has put it,

We must accept the fact that at the end of the political day reasonable people will continue to disagree and moral perspectives will remain divergent. At that point, the most reasonable thing may well be mutually to moderate our claims in the face of the reasonable claims of others, to balance, and split at least some of our differences.[83]

No political philosophy, then, should ever be said, on its own, to entail any particular ideology, for political philosophies, like political ideologies, contain features which will sometimes conflict, and how those conflicts are to be settled, and so the specific form the philosophy or ideology is to take, depends on culturally specific, contextual factors. That is why no philosophy should ever be said to endorse a specific ideology for any sort of purely 'logical' reasons. Those pluralists who recognize this, and who also wish to be liberals, will be those who appreciate that liberal values, like those of any ideology, cannot, even in the most ideal circumstances, ever be articulated within the kind of fixed, harmonious framework that underlies the intrinsically liberal pluralist polity. Thus William Galston: 'Liberalism is a basket of ideals that inevitably come into conflict with one another if a serious effort is made to realize any one of them fully, let alone all of them simultaneously.'[84]

Concomitant with this renunciation of any attempt to assert a set of unified or fully coherent ground rules for politics is a rejection of any project that attempts to shelter particular principles or values from politics by granting them an uncompromisable status. Where, for the liberal of weak pluralism, as I have shown, certain conceptions of equality and the liberty of the individual are, ideally, to be non-negotiable, those pluralists who reject this polity do so because they accept that there will inevitably be clashes, not just between equality, however expressed, and the liberty of the individual,[85] but also between these and all the other values relevant to politics, which is why no scheme should be affirmed which assumes that any value could ever be asserted as necessarily beyond compromise.[86] To the strong pluralist, the weight citizens will choose to grant to the various values they uphold will, as we might expect, vary in different countries, in accord with the different political cultures they contain,[87] and so just as no fixed theoretical framework exists for a single country, no such framework can be said to apply to many countries. For it is not theory, but politics and history, that will always have to rule.

IV

We might say, then, that for strong pluralists there is no place for 'hardliners' of any theoretical sort in politics. To them, the ideal pluralist polity will still recognize the 'state—civil society' distinction, but the line to be drawn between the two domains can, like any line drawn to distinguish human practices, never be free of indentations, as the negotiated compromises they may be said to represent are, in any truly pluralist politics, going to be ubiquitous. That is why, as Berlin has written, 'a sharp division between public and private life, politics and morality, never works well'.[88] Or, as Bernard Williams has recommended, political philosophers 'should look towards an equilibrium— one to be achieved in practice—between private and public'.[89] The rest of this chapter will consist, then, of an examination of the indentations in that line between state and civil society, the aim being to further develop the contrast between the two types of pluralism.

What of the principle of the equality of ways of life? There seems to me to be at least two ways in which, to the strong pluralist, it can be legitimately compromised, with particular groups in civil society being granted some sort of special status by government. One of these can be said to result from the pressure that certain groups have managed to place on the state, as noted in Truman's work above. The other involves government recognizing certain groups as special simply by virtue of their historical place in the cultural identity of the society as a whole, as with, say, the Church of England, or Canada's declaration that French and English are the country's official languages. Now since, with either of these routes to special status, what is involved is a kind of 'capturing' of certain parts of government by groups located within civil society, we might represent the more-or-less permanent, structured relationships that this entails with indentations in the line between the state and civil society that penetrate into the state's domain rather than in the other direction.

Compromising the autonomy of the individual and so the integrity of civil society can also take place in at least two different ways in the strong pluralist's polity. One of these has to do with the relations between government and those more socio-economic civil associations, these being a focus of 'neo-corporatist' political scientists. According to neo-corporatist research, it is often the case that certain relatively fixed relationships can arise between government and groups representing capital and labour. Whether government enters into these as a functional means of improving the general welfare of the citizenry, or to maximize economic equality, or for some other aim, it should be clear that they entail compromising, to some extent, the integrity of civil society. That is because in these situations, the negotiations[90] over public policy that take place between these groups and state agencies can lead to binding agreements in which the leadership of the groups agree to discipline and control their members. It should be clear that, in such cases, pressure has been applied not just on government by the groups in civil society, but also the other way around. Too many pluralist political scientists, however, have failed to appreciate this, their work, as Wyn Grant has written, having assumed 'too passive a role for the state, and in particular [having] emphasised the variety of ways in which 'lobbies' sought to exert influence on different parts of government, to the neglect of the influence that government exerted on supposedly autonomous interests'.[91] This is changing, however, it being increasingly recognized by those political scientists who would identify themselves as pluralist that 'government is capable of allowing *only* those groups with which it sympathizes institutional access to policy arenas.'[92]

Strong pluralists not only recognize such practices but also, to varying extents, endorse them. In strong pluralism, there is no 'in principle' reason that, at times, certain civil associations should not be granted special status by the state, even though this will often be a result not only of the pressure they have managed to exert on the state but also because of determinations that have their origins in the state itself. Though located within civil society, such groups, by virtue of leverage that has been applied on them by the state, might in a certain sense be considered extensions of it. In accepting this, strong pluralists may be

said to legitimize the neo-corporatist recognition of 'the growing inter-
penetration of public and private spheres, which is illustrated in the
difficulty of saying unambiguously whether certain kinds of institutions
are public or private'.[93] Public policy, it is thus asserted, can be the
outcome of an ongoing process of *two-way* negotiations between the
state and civil associations, even though this means that, as Alan Cawson
has pointed out, the principle 'that public policy is an activity reserved
to elected governments and their bureaucratic staff, is thus directly chal-
lenged'.[94] We might say then that, for the strong pluralist, it is legitimate
that there be indentations in the line between the state and civil society
which point in the direction of civil society, and not just the other way
around.

There is a second route to accepting such indentations. This one
entails a willingness to give a greater scope to toleration than the weak
pluralists behind the first polity would accept, in which one accepts that
the polity will have to grant a place to whole ways of life that, in certain
forms, may have little if any respect for the health and integrity of civil
society, indeed for the whole activity of modern politics itself. Certain
religions, or rather particular versions of these, can be said to demand
this, as can, in certain forms, nationalism and classical republicanism.
The common goods constitutive of the vast majority of civil associations
are different from these three in that their expression in practice may
be comfortably limited to the bounds of civil society. According to
certain civil theologies, however, religion has a social and not just a
private role and, as such, cannot be wholly, if at all, separated from the
activities of the state. As for nationalism, though the locus of its expression is, for the most part, properly within civil society, nations, unlike
most ethnic groups, also claim an essentially political aspect, one which
needs to be expressed from within the domain of the state. And as
regards classical republicanism, its intrinsic practices are *all* fundamentally governmental. In consequence, we might designate these ways of
life—unlike those expressed by most other civil associations—as constituted by especially 'public' common goods, using this term to give
some indication of the ineliminable role of the state in their realization.

Religious political thought is a vast subject, religious authorities,
prophets, and theologians having taken widely different positions as
regards the preferred relation between church and state. Suffice to say
here that, in the modern world, there are many for whom religion has
an inherently perfectionist role which cannot be fulfilled if significant
matters are left to a state which is considered in any sense independent.
For others, of course, religions should be able to fulfil their educative
role as fully voluntary associations, as groups comfortably ensconced

within civil society like any other. The spectrum of positions here is, to repeat, vast.

With nationalism one speaks of the self-determination of a nation, of a unique people, associated with a particular territory, who share certain norms in common. Participating in the life of a nation involves cultivating and passing on the heritage of this common way of life, activities which, as I have said, take place mainly from within civil society. But the nation cannot be wholly limited to this domain, for there must be some sort of state recognition of it if the collectivity is to consider itself free, meaning that the state must in some way affirm the nation in its politics. Unofficially, this can involve something as minimal as that vicarious sort of political participation that arises when the members of a nation are assured that those in power, even if dictators, will be natives and never foreigners, this having been the first goal of Third World national liberation movements in their struggles against imperialism. Officially, this could take the form of legislation which declares that the government is guided by the principle that it is predominantly for a certain nation, as with, say, the provincial government of Quebec, or that the state affirms a special recognition of certain nations within the society, as would happen if the Canadian constitution was ever amended to include the recognition that the *Québécois*, as distinct from other French-speaking Canadians, constitute a 'distinct' or 'unique' society in the federation. It is when it comes to cases such as this that it makes sense to speak of nationalism as requiring not only an unequal recognition of certain ways of life on the part of the state, but also a possible compromising of the autonomy of individual citizens. Many Canadians, for example, have expressed fears that the inclusion of such a special recognition clause in the constitution, making it justiciable and on par with the country's Charter of Rights and Freedoms, would neutralize the capacity of those who would turn to the Charter as a means of checking any Quebec government which might wish to compromise the civil liberties of its citizens and thus the integrity of the province's civil society.[95]

Classical republicanism is different, it being a matter of the self-government of a citizenry. At its heart is the uncompromising affirmation of a citizenry's 'common good', which is the name given to that ensemble of civic and heroic norms integral to the life of politics. Classical republican politics claims a fundamentally pre-modern character, for it has little place for the respect of the individual essential to civil society; indeed, to the classical republican, civil society and the practices it contains are considered but threats to the good life.[96] As such, there is no place in the ideology for a notion of the liberty of the individual, or at least one in which it could be asserted that an individual might reasonably choose a life other than that of participating with others in government. For, in classical republicanism, the common good of the *polis* should always trump that of any individual, as Machiavelli makes clear when he writes that:

It is not the well-being of individuals that makes cities great, but the well-being of the community; and it is beyond question that it is only in republics that the common good is looked to properly in that all that promotes it is carried out; and, however much this or that private person may be the loser on this account, there are so many who benefit thereby that the common good can be realized in spite of those few who suffer in consequence.[97]

More often than not, those liberals who are weak pluralists philosophically tend to react to this ideology with scepticism. That is, they can be heard either doubting that the notion of 'political' liberty which lies at its heart still exists as a valid, living ideal in the modern West,[98] or even that it could have ever been anything but a deeply incoherent ideal conceptually.[99] If there are a group of citizens who persist in affirming it, however, then they may of course do so, but only as any other group, that is, from within civil society, which means negotiating with government and against others for governmental attention.[100] For when it comes to the intrinsically liberal pluralist polity, as I have shown, government must answer to the demands of civil society and not the other way around. But the whole notion of lobbying, of putting pressure on government from the outside, is, at least to the classical republican, utterly unacceptable. This is because it assumes that the state may be but an instrument, while to the classical republican participation in government must be conceived of as an intrinsically valuable activity. When Walzer calls for the decentralization of political power in American society, however, he does so only because of his recognition that civil society has an instrumental need for 'control over, or use of, the state apparatus'.[101] The point for classical republicans is quite different: one should not lobby government, using it as a kind of tool for one's separate ends, but actually *be* government, for political liberty is a kind of freedom that, to them, can only be achieved by participating within the governmental realm, and not that of any civil society. That is why classical republicans today could be expected to call for the decentralization of political power so that *all* citizens can participate since, to them, *all* citizens should indeed participate. But to demand this is to demand nothing less than the eradication of civil society and hence the modern conception of politics that goes with it.

Strong pluralists, unlike their weak compatriots, accept that there will be times when those supporting certain religions, conceptions of nationalism, or classical republicanism, will have to be negotiated with. As we might expect, the extent to which these pluralists are willing to make the concessions that this would entail differs. In order to distinguish between them, it should help to differentiate between a willingness to simply grant a place to an association somewhere in the society on the one hand, and the acceptance that that association may legitimately enter into the polity's political process on the other. Thus the members of a community such as the Amish in the United States who are, by their choice, marginal as regards the country's politics (in that they wish to avoid any competition with others for government sponsorship) should be distinguished from those who, like the Protestant fundamentalists in that same country, or certain illiberal Muslim groups in Britain, are not willing to be so ensconced. Macedo is one pluralist who, while rejecting the first, intrinsically liberal pluralist polity on the philosophical level, is nevertheless unwilling, when it comes to his ideological position, to tolerate certain practices of groups such as the Amish. As a result, on this matter at least, his liberalism, though connected with a strong conception of pluralism, nevertheless echoes that of the weak pluralists. This is because although, to Macedo, the equal autonomy of the individual cannot be articulated as an overriding, uncompromisable value in principle, it is nevertheless ranked so highly by American political culture that it has become 'something more than one personal ideal among others'.[102] Thus does he oppose the *Wisconsin* v. *Yoder* decision of the US Supreme Court which allowed Amish children to be kept from school beyond the primary grades, a policy which, he has asserted, means that their later ability to live life as autonomous adults will be limited to an unacceptable extent.[103] Where, for Dahl and Walzer and Raz, this position is derivable directly from the theoretical recognition of the pluralist character of the country,[104] to Macedo pluralism means that no ideology may assert a value as having an absolute and so uncompromisable status, which is why we may say that he interprets American political culture as granting great, though not absolute, weight to autonomy. Galston, however, while also a strong pluralist as well as a liberal, clearly interprets that political culture differently, for to him the decision to exempt Amish children from certain educational requirements should be considered a legitimate case of the accommodation of a minority nation within American society.[105]

When it comes to those groups whose practices are, to some extent, incompatible with modern politics and yet who do not wish to be simply left alone but actually try to press their aims on government, then we might expect a pluralist liberal such as Macedo to be, if anything, even more reluctant—though not, in principle, unwilling—to negotiate with them. In this he would be matched by Anthony Arblaster who, commenting on the question of public funding of religious education in Britain, has accepted what the weak pluralist would not—that funding currently goes to the Church of England, Catholics, and Jews—but then rejects the requests of Muslims for funding because he considers their educational teachings to be so illiberal as to be fundamentally incompatible with modern politics.[106] For similar reasons, while Arblaster and Macedo would, to the extent that they would bring their liberal ideals to bear on other contexts, probably have little difficulty with Canada's Official Bilingualism Act, they might be expected to reject the *Québécois's* demand for special constitutional recognition. That is because, to them, only those groups which are broadly compatible with a polity's always contestable yet nevertheless shared political culture should be invited into the political processes of competition and bargaining. They might thus, at least when it comes to this matter, be said to echo the liberals of weak pluralism for whom there should be strict limits as regards which groups may be legitimately allowed to enter the political process. In a sense, they could be said to concur with Dahl's meaning when he writes that 'a group has to be seen as legitimate in some sense in order to gain entry into the political system'.[107]

But if the *Québécois* are claiming that they need such a constitutional amendment in order to consider themselves fully liberated as a nation, and if they will try to separate from Canada without it then, perhaps, other strong pluralists might assert, they should get it. Berlin, for one, has called on us to appreciate that nationalism, though always potentially dangerous, has claimed a legitimate and important place in modern politics, and that it should be respected in its healthy forms, just as it has to be contended with when chauvinistic.[108] Yael Tamir, who has been strongly influenced by Berlin, has also, reluctantly to be sure, expressed a willingness to make concessions to groups which cannot be incorporated within that somewhat attenuated form of nationalism that she has characterized as 'liberal'.[109] Galston has willingly recognized that, when it comes to the United States, though the country's political culture is, on the whole, strongly supportive of the principles protective of civil society, it also contains traditions, such as Protestant Christianity and classical republicanism,[110] which call for those principles to be compromised. Berlin and Stuart Hampshire would probably concur; as regards classical republicanism's political liberty, at least, both have recognized its intrinsic goodness, and so the possibility of it conflicting, and requiring the compromise of, other values, including that of individual liberty.[111] Of course, none of this is meant to speak against the fact that there is a limit as to how far even strong pluralist liberals are willing to go in making concessions to such groups. As Berlin has forcefully put it:

No matter how pluralistic one is, if one has what is called a liberal or democratic society (the two are not the same—still, they are compatible), then any group whose purpose is to destroy this, can only be tolerated if it is not formidable, not a serious danger. If they do become that, then they must be eliminated, legislated against . . . there is a case for coercion, for censorship.[112]

V

Now this, it seems to me, is pluralist politics at its most inclusive and powerful. Accordingly, it is pluralism in this strong form—that which rejects the model of the intrinsically liberal pluralist polity—which will provide the basis of my contrast with the patriotic politics that, I want to suggest, constitutes a superior alternative. The contrast, as I conceive of it, rests on the following question: granted that pluralist politics can rightfully claim to give a place to all of the ideals and ways of life potentially at play in modern politics, does it nevertheless do so in an undistorting manner? The answer I want to give is no.

To understand why, we might begin by asking another question: why is it that, when it comes to political conflict, pluralists assume that the best that antagonists can do is to *negotiate* with each other? If negotiation really is all we can turn to when it comes to modern politics, then perhaps there is something to Alasdair MacIntyre's claim that, reversing Clausewitz's famous dictum, it is but 'civil war carried on by other means'.[113] The patriot's conception of that politics differs significantly from the pluralist's, however, this being a direct result of how the two differ in their understanding of practical reason and so the interpretation involved in political judgement. It is to this difference that I now wish to turn.

3

Compromising Zero-Sum Morals

But as to this very thing, justice . . .
>   Plato, *The Republic*

The secret rules of engagement
are hard to endorse
when the appearance of conflict
meets the appearance of force.
>   The Tragically Hip, 'Grace, Too'

I

However they may differ otherwise, there are two central principles upon which pluralists of every persuasion can be said to agree, namely, that there is a plurality of sometimes incommensurable values in the world, and that these sometimes conflict. That is why, to pluralists, those who would attempt to reduce such values systematically in order to incorporate them within a neutral theory of morals or politics, whether formalist or consequentialist, will only end up distorting them. For when intrinsic, incommensurable values 'collide', as pluralists often put it, we have no choice but to try to reach the necessary compromises without theoretical guidance. Berlin has put it, a conflict between such values is something which is 'logically insoluble . . . The way out must therefore lie in some logically untidy, flexible, and even ambiguous compromise. Every situation calls for its own specific policy, since out of the crooked timber of humanity, as Kant once remarked, no straight thing was ever made.'[1]

All this being said, pluralists nevertheless differ sharply over the extent to which such decision-making can consist in comparisons which can be described as, if not 'logical', then at least in some sense 'reasonable'. The differences here result from the further and diverging significances they ascribe to the recognition that values are sometimes and to some extent incommensurable. I think it makes sense to distinguish between three different pluralist conceptions of practical reason here, these three at times cutting across the twofold division of pluralists *vis-à-vis* their ideal polities as discussed in Chapter 2. According to the first approach, one advocated by thinkers such as Dahl, Raz, and John Gray, whom we might refer to as 'agonistic pluralists', the claim that two or more values are to any extent incommensurable is considered synonymous with asserting that they are rationally incomparable. They maintain this because their conception of practical reason is limited to the essentially instrumentalist terms dominant in economics, in which to claim that two items are incommensurable is to assert that they cannot be reduced to a common standard and that, as such, they are rationally incomparable.[2] Commensurability as conceived here, it should be clear, requires that the value of items be expressed with real numbers, this implying both the principle of identity (that items retain the same value regardless of their context) and transitivity (i.e. if $a > b$ and $b > c$, then $a > c$).[3]

Many pluralists do not accept the limitations of this agonistic conception of practical reason, however. To them, to say that two or more values are incommensurable is to say that, though they are indeed irreducible, there will nevertheless be cases in which they can be rationally compared, and so that reasonable compromises can be reached between them when they conflict. This can be done, the claim goes, by relying upon a version of that 'moral sense' kind of practical reasoning which, in the spirit of Aristotle's *phronesis*, is something of 'a not fully articulable sense rather than a kind of science'.[4] That is, unlike the kinds of weighings undertaken during economic cost–benefit analyses, the presence of a degree of incommensurability is said to require a kind of judgement which necessitates neither the same degree of precision nor of explicitness that economic calculations do. With moral sense practical reasoning one strives for an engagement with the context at hand, the aim being to be sensitive to all of that context's particularities, and this means that there is no place for either transitivity or the principle of identity. Accordingly, as Berlin and Williams have written, it makes sense to 'accept that a value which has more weight in one set of circumstances may have less in another ... It is consistent with this, moreover, that the answer in any particular case [of value conflict] could be the subject of discussion and potential agreement by reasonable people.'[5] And yet, for Aristotle, if one is to engage in practical reason one must be able to rely on the matter in question having, as a background, a set of practices that are organized in a certain way, such that they constitute a whole way of life. The matter is similar for those pluralists who would turn to moral sense for, to them, when there is a collision between values, then if one is to reason about that conflict those values may be only *to some extent* incommensurable, which is to say that, despite their irreducible differences, they are nevertheless comparable as long as this can be done against the background of a shared way of life. Only 'wholly' (in the sense of 'fully') incommensurable values, values which do not share such a background to any extent, are thus considered rationally incomparable. The claim, then, is that when irreducible values that are only to some extent incommensurable clash then although, as Berlin writes, 'clear-cut solutions cannot, in principle, be found', this does not mean that we cannot still reason about the conflict. The reason is that, as he goes on,

to decide rationally in such situations is to decide in the light of *general ideals, the over-all pattern of life* pursued by a man or a group or a society . . . If we wish to live in the light of reason, we must follow rules or principles; for that is what being rational is. When these rules or principles conflict in concrete cases, to be rational is to follow the course of conduct which least obstructs *the general pattern of life in which we believe*. The right policy cannot be arrived at in a mechanical or deductive fashion: there are no hard-and-fast rules to guide us; conditions are often unclear, and principles incapable of being fully analyzed or articulated. [6]

Michael Stocker has offered a metaphor which seems to me to aptly capture how we might conceive of this notion of reasonably balancing values that are irreducible to a common standard. Stocker envisions not a single beam balance, which works well for those trade-offs guided by instrumental reason, but a single pan balance hung by a string in the middle, one which allows for a variety of elements each of which may tip the balance pan in a different direction.[7] Note that the fact that we are still 'balancing' values 'against' each other means that reasoning about conflicting values is still assumed to entail a relatively zero-sum dynamic, in which giving weight to one value in a conflict, and so tilting the pan in its direction, necessitates detracting, to some extent, from another. Compromise is thus considered to be inescapable, and compromise, as Joseph Schumpeter once aptly put it, can only 'maim and degrade'[8] the values in question. In consequence, though there will be cases of value conflict in which one needs to make especially tough decisions, decisions in which the stakes are high and the outcomes non-recompensable, these do not necessarily have to be construed as irrational. Otherwise put, there will be times when it can be justifiable to commit an injustice. Torturing a prisoner may be a wrong, these non-agonistic pluralists would point out, but it is ultimately the reasonable thing to do if it will lead to information that can be used to save many innocent lives.[9] Though the perpetrator of such an act might be appropriately described as having 'dirty hands', this does not mean that he or she has necessarily acted irrationally.

These non-agonistic pluralists disagree over at least one important matter, however, one which can be said to subdivide them, with Berlin, Hampshire, and Walzer forming a second group that I will be referring to from now on simply as 'pluralists', one differing from those 'Aristotelian pluralists', as we might call them, which includes such thinkers as Stocker and Martha Nussbaum.[10] The issue between them is not a new one: to what extent can we say that all human beings share a way of life in common? One of the lessons that pluralists, as distinct from Aristotelian pluralists, have drawn from Machiavelli's writings is that there exist cultures or ways of life in the world that are fundamentally incompatible with each other, and so that there are certain values which simply cannot be said to be present to any significant extent within the same way of life. On the model of a Venn diagram, we might represent a set of values constituting a way of life by drawing a circle around them; the extent to which different ways of life uphold similar values, and so may thus be said to, potentially at least, belong to the same society, may thus be determined by surveying the size of the region in which the circles overlap. Now while pluralists may be said to recognize a minimal overlap of all ways of life—the values here constituting what has been referred to as the 'minimal moral code', that set of prohibitions, varyingly expressed in all the world's cultures, which speak against such fundamentally base acts as murder, torture, and gross cruelty[11]—they also want us to acknowledge the existence of ways of life that do not, and sometimes cannot, overlap very much if at all. Underlying Machiavelli's writings, for example, are said to be two valid yet totally incompatible ways of life, that of the heroism and civicism of classical republicanism on the one hand, and that of Christianity on the other. As Berlin has described these two:

One is the morality of the pagan world: its values are courage, vigour, fortitude in adversity, public achievement, order, discipline, happiness, strength, justice, above all assertion of one's proper claims and the knowledge and power needed to secure their satisfaction . . . Against this moral universe (moral or ethical no less in Croce's than in the traditional sense, that is, embodying ultimate human ends however these are conceived) stands in the first and foremost place, Christian morality. The ideals of Christianity are charity, mercy, sacrifice, love of God, forgiveness of enemies, contempt for the goods of this world, faith in the life hereafter, belief in the salvation of the individual soul as being of incomparable value—higher than, indeed wholly incommensurable with, any social or political or other terrestrial goal, any economic or military or aesthetic consideration.[12]

As I have pointed out, when Berlin says, as he does here, that the values of Christianity are 'wholly' incommensurable with those of classical republicanism, then he is claiming that they cannot, to any extent, be said to be compared against a common background. For the two ways of life are understood to be fundamentally incompatible. As a result, when it comes to a conflict between them, the claim is that one's moral sense will be powerless to provide guidance. In consequence, pluralists assert that to be confronted by such a conflict means that one will have no option but to make something of an agonistic *radical choice* between them. These all-or-nothing, often inescapably permanent affairs are said to involve decisions which are significantly underdetermined by reason, decisions in which, as Hampshire once put it, persons simply have to 'plump'[13] for one culture or way of life over the other.

Moreover, when the members of different ways of life clash, and do so over values which may not be said to exist in any overlap between them, then, as Hampshire in particular has emphasized,[14] they should try to negotiate the conflict rather than turn to force, this being one of the imperatives of the minimal moral code. The decision to negotiate and so to be willing to compromise is, for the pluralist, thus conceived of as an emphatically *ethical* imperative, and should not be interpreted, as it often is, as being but the result of parties recognizing that it is in their instrumental interests to do so. That is because to agree to negotiate only for instrumental reasons is to have been compelled by a form of force[15] rather than by any notion of 'fairness'. Regardless, the kind of negotiation involved here is still considered different from that which consists of persons negotiating over values that they to some extent share. As a result, it makes sense to construe pluralists as distinguishing between two kinds of multicultural politics, each constituted by the different kinds of negotiation engaged in in response to political conflict. When it comes to conflicts between ways of life over values that they share, we may speak of the negotiations involved as leading to the same kinds of compromises that must be reached when a single person is facing a moral conflict, in which what is necessitated could, following Hampshire, be referred to as the making of *trade-offs* of the values involved.[16] When negotiations take place between persons over values that they cannot be said to share, however, pluralists can be heard referring to the necessity of making compromises in the sense of making *concessions* rather than trade-offs. Persons involved in negotiating concessions can still be understood as responding to such conflicts reasonably, but they will be guided in their decision-making by their respective moral sensitivities, these relying on their separate ways of life rather than on any shared norms as a background. And whether conflicts take place on the global stage, or domestically (as pluralists— Walzer, in some cases, excepted—would claim is particularly prevalent within the multicultural societies of the West), the kind of fairness invoked is considered to be essentially the same. As Hampshire has written,

When natural enemies sit down to negotiate, whether they are individuals or governments, we find them calling on a quasi-legal fairness as a respected requirement in their arguments as, for example, in negotiations between the United States and the Soviet Union. In international negotiation, and in negotiation between hostile political groups more generally, procedural fairness, particularly fairness in balancing concession against concession, is the only respected restraint upon the unmoralised manœuvres of realpolitik.[17]

It is, however, just this Machiavellian-derived notion that there exists a plurality of whole ways of life, some of which are fundamentally incompatible with each other, that is rejected by the Aristotelian pluralist. While Aristotelian pluralists would agree with 'pluralists' that one may rely on a *phronesis*-like notion of practical reason when faced with conflicting irreducibles, they do not accept the idea that persons might sometimes find themselves facing agonistic radical choices between wholly incompatible ways of life. The reason is that, to them, in keeping with Aristotle's analogy of ethics as a kind of universal medicine, there exists but one set of values for all, a single universal list. In this conception, different societies are distinguished not by virtue of the very different ways of life they might contain, but rather because they are said to provide 'competing answers to questions about the justice and courage (and so on) with which all societies are (being human) concerned, and in response to which they all try to find what is good'.[18] The account of politics that follows from this is one based on 'good human functioning',[19] one which, according to Nussbaum, is still vague and flexible enough not to impair a sensitivity to concrete contexts and local conditions, for it is still expected that different persons, in different contexts, will need to aim for the unique complex of balances appropriate to their specific situations in order to function well. We are presented, then, with a universal list of values that is far from minimal, since it is meant to be relevant to all on the basis of human nature. As a result, for the Aristotelian pluralist, negotiation in politics can be understood as limited to the making of trade-offs, there being no need for concessions of the sort identified above.

I have chosen to refer to Nussbaum and Stocker as Aristotelian pluralists and not simply Aristotelians, and to their notion of practical reason as a version of 'moral sense' rather than as *phronesis* proper, because I read them as parting with Aristotle over a number of fundamentals, some of which they acknowledge and some of which they do not. At base, the difference can be said to arise from their rejection of a significant part of what has been called Aristotle's doctrine of 'the unity of the virtues'. As I understand it, the doctrine makes two fundamental assertions: (i) that there is a universal set list of virtues or goods, and (ii) that happiness or *eudaemonia* is a supreme, architectonic good, one which orders or ranks all the others, and does so in a way intrinsic to the function or *ergon* of all human beings.[20] What Aristotelian pluralists reject is (ii), for they would historicize Aristotle's naturalistic conception of the ranking. To Aristotle, the best answer to the question of what *eudaemonia* consists in is contemplation, the life of the philosopher,[21] while the life of participating in politics is said to constitute the second best.[22] Below these on the ranking will be found all the other intrinsic goods, these all also being instrumental to those of *eudaemonia*,[23] and finally, yet another rank lower, those strictly instrumental goods, these constituting the responsibilities of women and slaves, which are also to be used specifically for *eudaemonia*.[24] When someone faces a moral or political conflict, then, Aristotle's claim is that they should always aim to deal with it in a way that fulfils, as much as possible, this universally valid ranking of goods.[25] 'For', writes Aristotle, 'we cannot deliberate about ends but about the means by which ends can be attained.'[26]

But it is just this assertion that pluralists of all stripes, including the Aristotelian, reject, for to them there can be no single, fixed ranking natural to all human beings. In so doing, they can be said to give emphasis to one side of a tension that many have remarked upon in Aristotle's writings on ethics and politics.[27] On the one hand, knowledge about the good life is said to derive from an argument about the *ergon* essential to human nature, what MacIntyre has called Aristotle's 'metaphysical biology';[28] on the other, such knowledge is understood to come from *endoxa*, the interpretation of the traditions of a particular society.[29] Now since, as all types of pluralists, including the Aristotelian, recognize, different societies will properly affirm different rankings, we cannot speak of a single ranking that is best by virtue of the basic needs essential to all human beings, for there is no fixed natural architectonic good to which all other goods or values point. The particular ranking that Aristotle affirms is, it is asserted, ethnocentric rather than universal, as it is nothing more than a description of the life of the Athenian philosopher or aristocrat of his day. Rather than being derived from any doctrine of what is natural to man, then, the pluralist argument is that ranking should be taken to be a matter of decision-making in context for each and every one of us.

There is another fundamental feature of Aristotle's ethics and politics which Aristotelian pluralists, along with the other kinds of pluralists, reject (though the Aristotelians, unlike the others, make the error of claiming that it is not actually present in Aristotle's conception[30]). As a monistic philosopher, one who conceives of his philosophy as reflecting a unity, Aristotle asserts that there cannot exist moral or political conflicts in which persons will *necessarily* have to compromise and so get dirty hands. While Aristotle certainly admits that there may be times when persons feel unable to get out of a moral conflict without compromising one or more of the goods involved, for him this will be only due either to an error of interpretation on their part or to flawed political arrangements—it cannot, that is, be necessitated by the nature of the moral reality itself. Though criticizing Plato for his too-tight monism, Aristotle thus nevertheless held onto his teacher's assumption of ultimate unity, according to which, as MacIntyre has described, 'there exists a cosmic order which dictates the place of each virtue in a total harmonious scheme of human life. Truth in the moral sphere consists in the conformity of moral judgment to the order of this scheme.'[31] To pluralists of whatever stripe, however, our moral universe is just not put together in this way. And yet monism, many of them rightly point out, had a virtually hegemonic hold on philosophy right until Nietzsche in the nineteenth century, surviving even the 'disenchantment' of the cosmos that accompanied the rise of modernity. In rejecting it, pluralists of all kinds claim that we must accept the existence of moral and political conflicts in which there will be no way out without some loss, without some compromise.

Of the three groups of pluralists identified here, it seems to me that it is the second, the 'pluralists', that are advocating the most realistic position. In the case of the Aristotelian pluralists, they seem to me unable to avoid—despite their own wariness of the pitfall—a highly distorting reductivism. For though Nussbaum trumpets her account's vagueness, it is obviously not vague enough to avoid some rather blatant ethnocentricities. To point to just one: according to her, following Aristotle's lead means that 'the lawgiver is to take no thought for [religion] in the design of institutions, beyond, apparently some supporting of specifically civic festivals'.[32] The claim, then, is that justice for everyone on earth requires that religion remain a strictly private matter. With a single universal assertion, Nussbaum has thus called for the disestablishment of churches such as those in Britain and Russia, ruled out a Jewish Israel, and rejected any and all forms of an Islamic state. Now while she is, of course, perfectly entitled to such positions, the appreciation that they are derived from an assertion of a long-dead ancient

Greek, rather than from arguments that take local conditions and histories as their starting-point, cannot but disconcert. The danger of following Aristotle too closely, it should be clear, is that one will fail to
appreciate that the wide variety of ways of life in the world are more
than elaborations on a certain basic, philosophically derivable human
biology, for ways of life are also, as Hampshire has aptly put it, 'defiances
of biological constraints'.[33]

As for the agonistic pluralists, they seem to me simply wrong in not
accepting that, as I tried to show in Chapter 1, there are indeed times
when we rationally compare incommensurables. Even Charles Larmore,
no friend to neo-Aristotelianism and so unwilling to avail himself of
a *phronesis*-like account, feels unable to reject this reality. As he has
written,

I suspect that many will regard these remarks about how incommensurable
values may still be comparable as just so much assertion. If not by appeal to a
common denominator of value, then how, they will ask, are the values weighed
against one another? I admit that I have no fully satisfactory answer to this
question. Nonetheless, an inability to solve this problem is not, I believe, as
damaging as it might seem. Sometimes we can legitimately claim to know something without knowing how we know it.[34]

And so, by virtue of their greater realism, it is to those pluralists of the
second group that I will be granting most of the attention in the rest of
this chapter.

In particular, I plan to contrast their approach with what I consider
to be a superior alternative: hermeneutics. I want to begin by pointing
to the example of Charles Taylor. For it is, it seems to me, by virtue of
his following Heidegger, Wittgenstein, and Gadamer[35] in affirming a
hermeneutical conception of interpretation and so practical reason that
Taylor considers himself to be someone who *uncompromisingly* sub-
scribes to both Christianity and republican self-government, someone
who is both a Catholic of 'an orthodox theology',[36] and 'a strong partisan of citizen self-rule'.[37] This can only be possible, I want to claim,
because he interprets these two ways of life as somehow *reconciled* with
each other in meaning, rather than as separate and incompatible ethics
between which one can only make a radical choice for one over the
other. Hermeneutics, as I pointed out in Chapter 1, is also a philosophy
which distinguishes itself from those of monism, although rather than a
'plurality of values' it asserts what we might refer to as a 'diversity of
goods'—'diversity' instead of 'plurality' so as to point to the greater
holism that hermeneutics assumes, and 'goods' rather than 'values'
because the former is free of the mentalistic connotations sometimes

associated with the latter, these being, as I will show, unacceptable to the hermeneuticist's more comprehensive rejection of cognitivism. Throughout the rest of this work, then, I will use the term 'goods' rather than 'values' to refer, in the widest possible way, to whatever hermeneuticists recognize as normatively 'mattering' to human beings, whether these are ends, the formal imperatives we respect while reaching for ends, or virtues, which are capacities or dispositions to do good. I will also continue to use 'goods' to refer, as in Chapter 2, to those items, whether considered of intrinsic or only instrumental worth, that are of concern in distributive justice.

Terminology aside, hermeneutics, it should be clear, shares with pluralism the fundamental idea that many goods or values are irreducible and so, like pluralism, it is incompatible with any theoretical attempt to reconcile them systematically. In hermeneutics, however, the assertion of some degree of incommensurability, and so of the absence of transitivity or identity, is, as I will demonstrate, more radical than in pluralism. Hermeneuticists go further than the recognition that, as in Berlin and Williams's statement above, a value may have a different 'weight' in different circumstances for, to the hermeneuticist, a good can also have—indeed *will* have, and to an extent far more comprehensive than the pluralist is willing to accept—a significantly different *meaning*. This is because, unlike with the pluralist's values, hermeneuticists do not assume that a good can be said to lay claim to anything like an isolable 'shell' or 'skeleton', or any kind of essence of meaning which remains fixed regardless of the context it is in. As a result of this, I will show, what Walzer has dismissively referred to as hermeneuticists' 'high-falutin Germanic accounts of phronesis'[38] entail that it is not only sometimes possible to reconcile rather than trade off the conflicting irreducible goods affirmed by a single person or shared by a number of persons, but also that reconciliations rather than concessions may sometimes be enacted when it comes to conflicts between especially remote and even seemingly incompatible ways of life. Unlike with the Aristotelian pluralist, then, hermeneuticists still maintain a relatively strong distinction between ways of life. It is just that they are unwilling to go as far as the other kinds of pluralists would in conceiving of them as independent or separable.

It will be my aim in the rest of this chapter to compare these two approaches to practical reason, the pluralism which accepts the paradox of 'justifiable injustice' as the final word, and hermeneutics, which does not. For the most part, the discussion will deal with those moral conflicts faced by a single individual, though I will also have things to say about conflicts between persons over their shared values or goods as well as over those which they cannot, at least at first, be said to share in any significant sense. I want to begin, however, with a comparison of the differing assumptions held regarding the meaning of concepts, the differences here marking divergent conceptions of the expressivist philosophy of language that both approaches uphold. Pluralism, I will then try and show, runs into an important difficulty regarding how it portrays an agent's perception of his or her ethical situation and so how we actually begin to reason about moral or political conflicts. After discussing this matter, I will then turn to a more in-depth comparison of the two approaches' conceptions of practical reason. This will entail showing how they differ in their understandings, first, of how one reasons through conflicts and, second, of what the results of such reasoning are or can be. At various points in the discussion, I will also be referring to how the two differ over certain related issues, such as the matters of free will and responsibility. I will not be travelling very far down the divergent paths they take regarding these questions, however, for my aim here is only to establish their distinct positions on the subject of practical reason, positions which can be summed up by referring to the different metaphors that they could be said to rely upon to express them: the complex, balancing *scales* of pluralism on the one hand, and the hermeneutical conception of language as a transforming *hologram* on the other. This should then prepare us for the argument of the next chapter, in which I aim to show how assuming a hermeneutical, rather than pluralist, conception of practical reason lends support to a patriotic, rather than pluralist, conception of politics.

II

Why is it that pluralists are so attracted to the metaphor of balancing scales for practical reason? The possibility which I want to explore here focuses on their assertion that values may be conceived as independently distinct from each other, as separate, self-contained, object-like things which can 'clash' or 'collide', this all contributing to the sense that they need to be balanced 'against' each other when they conflict. To Aristotle, as I pointed out, all virtues or goods are holistically integrated in a unity of meaning as they are either an intrinsic part of *eudaemonia* or nevertheless still 'point' to it in being instrumental to it, whether or not they are also intrinsic in their own right. In dropping Aristotle's architectonics, pluralists also drop his assumption that normative concepts are inherently connected in meaning, replacing it with the assertion that they may be conceived as independently distinct or separable from each other. To pluralists, many values should be understood as existing in two dimensions of meaning, one thick, in which they are present as combined in various ways with others in the context of practices, and another thin, in which they are understood to exist as pure, isolated, mentalistic entities, 'in the head' rather than as parts of any specific context. While pluralists of all stripes acknowledge that values may originally come down to us as constitutive of norms or practices,[39] and so as present in the former, thick dimension, they also assert that at least some of these may be conceptualized thinly and separately and that, when they are, they lay claim to a universalistic quality—universal, that is, not in the sense that they are necessarily present in every way of life but, as I will show below, because anyone with enough imagination is said to be able, regardless of the context they themselves are in, to reconstruct and understand them. Values, then, are said to occupy two realms. As Walzer has summed this up, 'This dualism is, I think, an internal feature of every morality. Philosophers most often describe it in terms of a (thin) set of universal principles adapted (thickly) to these or those historical circumstances.'[40]

The point I want to emphasize here is that, whether we are speaking of the thick or the thin dimensions, values for pluralists are considered to be expressible as independently distinct, separate, and so isolated from each other. This is clearly an atomistic claim and, in making it, pluralists may be said to follow many other modern thinkers in importing the technique from the modern natural sciences.[41] As a method, atomism is far from complicated. In the attempt to discover the true nature of a given entity, it directs the researcher to resolve it, that is, to separate it out into its component parts, and then put it back together. Thus someone who truly knew how, say, a car worked, would be able to open the hood and account for the way in which the various parts of the motor interact with each other to make it run: turning the key in the ignition fires the spark plugs, the spark plugs ignite the fuel in the pistons, the movement of the pistons turns a crank, and so on. Each part of the motor is thus seen as independently distinct in the sense that it is separable from the others, and the car as a whole is considered to be nothing greater than the sum of its parts.[42] Now though many a methodological individualist has approached the study of society with this procedure, pluralists, along indeed with many neutralists (utilitarians and contractarians excepted), would reject the asocial individualism that it entails; in this they may be said to follow Aristotle in recognizing that those basic capacities constitutive of human being depend upon society for their emergence and development. And yet, when it comes to pluralist conceptualizations of the values of these essentially social human beings, atomism does indeed play a role. Even here, however, it cannot be said to be ubiquitous, for pluralists would not go so far as to claim that moral concepts can be reduced to simple, indissoluble parts, for they conceive of them as complex, and so, even when distinguished independently, as still in need of sometimes highly sophisticated interpretation. Nevertheless, atomism can be said to have claimed a significant place in their thought, one which, as the hermeneuticist would complain, is a result of their failure to sufficiently guard the methodological border between the natural sciences on the one hand and the human sciences and humanities on the other, a border which, as I pointed out in Chapter 1, both pluralists and hermeneuticists want to patrol.

To further bring out the differences between pluralism and hermeneutics on this matter it might be useful to borrow an idea from Edmund Husserl about two different kinds of parts. For Husserl, 'pieces' are potentially independent parts of a whole (like flowers, which can be separated from a bouquet), while 'moments' are considered to be utterly dependent (like the colours of an object).[43] Say we constructed a spectrum of symbolic meaning covering different positions as to what it could mean to refer to parts of a whole as *distinct* from each other, a plurality of atomized 'pieces' on one end, and an organically holistic unity of 'moments' on the other. Aristotle's conception of goods or virtues, then, would be located right at the holistic end, while the pluralist's idea that values can be conceived of as independent of each other would place them close to—though not at—the atomistic end. They should not be placed right at that end because this would be where simple, indissoluble concepts, rather than the pluralist's complex values, would be located. As such, pluralists can be said to concur with W. B. Gallie, for whom normative concepts are 'essentially contestable'. To Gallie, amongst the attributes of any such concept is that it is something appraisive, as well as being 'of an internally complex character, for all that it is worth is attributed to it as a whole'.[44] It is because of this complexity that, for both Gallie and the pluralist, the meaning of a concept will always be a matter of legitimate debate. Gallie, however, is somewhat ambiguous about whether the outcomes of such debates are to be understood relativistically or not. This is certainly not the pluralist's position; Berlin's famous 'Two Concepts of Liberty'[45] lecture, for example, is predicated on the notion that one can indeed be more or less right, though perhaps never absolutely so, about the meaning of such concepts.

Nevertheless, the point I want to make here is that pluralists share with Gallie the notion that there is, in principle, a set number of elements that make up each concept, that is, that concepts are independently distinct in that they should not be said to share the elements that make them up with other concepts, this being what is behind the description of them as being 'internally' complex. So though the lines drawn to distinguish between concepts can perhaps never be made fully explicit or precise, they are nevertheless presumed to be solid or unbroken. And when it comes to expressing these independently distinct values in a thin manner, the claim is that we may receive assistance not only from the philosopher,[46] but also from the historian, anthropologist, and other students of the human sciences. According to Berlin, however, perhaps the purest and most genuine expression of moral concepts can be found in the speeches given by the leaders of oppressed groups. Such 'noble eloquence', he has written, arises from the leaders of these groups when,

for a brief instant their utterance has a universal quality . . . The formal possession of power is unfavourable to that truly disinterested eloquence—disinterested partly at least because fulfilment is remote, because principles shine forth most clearly in the darkness and void, because the inner vision is still free from the confusions and obscurities, the compromises and blurred outlines of the external world inevitably forced upon it by the beginnings of practical action.[47]

One of Berlin's own forays into this 'darkness and void' of thin moral concepts takes the form of an essay on 'equality', in which he has written:

The criterion of equality has plainly been influenced by something other than the mere desire for equality as such, namely desire for liberty or the full development of human resources, or the belief that men deserve to be as rich or as powerful or as famous as they can make themselves—beliefs which *are not connected with the desire for equality at all* . . . Many policies and views of life, themselves not particularly wedded to the ideal of equality, have been surreptitiously smuggled in under its cover, sometimes . . . with a certain measure of disingenrousness or hypocrisy. To *isolate the pure ore of egalitarianism* from these alloys which the admixture of other attitudes and ideals has at various times generated is a task for the historian of ideas. [48]

Walzer has also written of the expression of values in such a 'minimalist', as he puts it, way, that is, as both thin or disengaged from any context and distinct in a highly atomistic and so independent sense. As he puts it, minimalist meaning is that which 'is liberated from its embeddedness and appears independently'.[49] And, for Williams, it sometimes makes sense to speak of a value as existing in two forms, as either a thin and isolable 'primitive idea or universal set of conditions', or as thick 'cultural elaborations' of these.[50]

Pluralists also claim that values may be expressed in an independently distinct way in a thick context. Hampshire, for example, has written of certain clearly demarcated contexts in which 'absolute' moral claims, those which are said to never lapse, should be fulfilled, the meanings of these being completely self-contained:

A moral claim, which may be a duty or a right or an obligation, is absolute when it is not conditional upon, or subordinate to, any further moral claim or purpose. A course of action is absolutely forbidden, or absolutely enjoined, when the prohibition or requirement is *not conditional upon the presence of any features not mentioned in the prohibition or injunction*. The prohibition or injunction *contains its own sense*, and *explains itself.*[51]

Indeed, for Hampshire, the very 'individuality of any active thing depends upon its power to resist the *invasion* and dominance of the active things around it'.[52] To him this means that, if collectivities constituted by commonly held values, such as ethnic groups or nations, are to maintain their distinctiveness, then this entails maintaining their independence, their separateness from others. Otherwise put, if they are to 'preserve their individual character and their distinctive qualities', then they must do so 'against the *encroachment* and absorption of other self-assertive things in their environment'.[53]

For Walzer, as we saw in the previous chapter, 'the best account of distributive justice is an account of its parts',[54] the claim being that these parts are, particularly in the United States, independently distinct from each other in meaning. It is because the principles constitutive of the different distributive spheres are considered distinct in this way that Walzer claims that Americans should look only to the 'internal' logic of one of these spheres when making a judgement about how a good in that sphere should be distributed. The meaning of the relevant distributive principle, or set of such principles, is seen as isolated and so separated from those meanings internal to other spheres.

Finally, even among different variants of a single value, as when we speak of the different types of, say, liberty, pluralists claim that we can speak of solid lines constituting the borders between these concepts. Thus when John Gray, in a discussion of Berlin on liberty, writes that 'the boundary between the concept of liberty and other, cognate, concepts is a shifting and variable one which can never be definitively specified',[55] we can suppose that, though the question of where to draw the line is understood to be a complex and so debatable one, the assumption is still that, in principle, there is an unbroken line to draw. In sum, then, we may say that, when it comes to the meanings of values in pluralism, these may be expressed in an independently distinct way, all pluralists sharing in Berlin's sentiments when he proclaims that, hammering the point home, 'everything is what it is: liberty is liberty, not equality or fairness or justice or culture, or human happiness or a quiet conscience'.[56]

I now want to turn, in the spirit of Kant's corrective to Hume, or Herder's to Condillac, towards a more holistic position, in particular, towards the holism of hermeneutics. As regards the meaning of normative concepts, it may be located at the end of a journey which might be said to begin with the significant step towards holism initiated by William Connolly and completed by, among others, Michael Freeden, to which is added a second, final step, also in the holistic direction, so as to reach the hermeneutical position on conceptual meaning. In terms of the 'parts of a whole' spectrum outlined above, we could consider this position as located somewhere near though, due to the hermeneuticist's rejection of monism, not at its holistic end.

Connolly's move emerges from his assertion that an essentially contestable concept is not simply one that, as Gallie has claimed, consists of a set number of elements that are weighed differently by different contestants. To Connolly, these elements are themselves concepts which are not only open to contestation in the same way, but may also be added to or removed as part of the general contest. That this all entails a move towards greater holism is clear when he states, further, that the parts of a concept 'make reference' to 'new', i.e. exterior, concepts,[57] doing so without any talk of a distinction between thick and thin. This is also supported by his statements that 'To make the concept of [say] politics intelligible we must display its complex connections with a host of other concepts to which it is related; clarification of the concept of politics thereby involves the elaboration of the broader conceptual system within which it is implicated',[58] and that, in general,

Concepts, as vehicles for thought and action, have complex rules governing their use, which are never fully stated. Since a particular concept receives its full meaning only in relation to the entire conceptual system in which it is embedded, a change in one of its dimensions is likely to produce unnoted implications for its ability to perform its several conventional functions . . . Concept revision is more analogous to a heart transplant than to a watch repair.[59]

And yet, in other ways, Connolly fails to complete this step to greater holism of meaning. This emerges from a number of passing remarks made throughout his book which seem to contradict those above, as when he describes concepts as being complex in an 'internal'[60] sense, or when, in his discussion of the concept of power, he speaks of the 'limits' accepted by all parties to the contestations of the concept.[61] Furthermore, when differentiating 'power' from 'authority', he asks what a relationship of 'pure' authority between people would be, since 'many actual relationships are different mixes of the pure types we seek to isolate'.[62] The real tension, however, can be said to arise from the principal project of his book, in which the three central chapters are dedicated to providing an analysis of three concepts: 'interests', 'power', and 'freedom'. Now if, as Connolly has himself stated, making a concept intelligible entails displaying its connections with the other concepts to which it is related, then this should lead us to claim that any isolated analysis of a single concept will be a necessarily distortive, or at the very least empty, endeavour. And this is indeed what emerges when we recognize that the individual formulae Connolly provides for each of the three concepts are themselves directly and explicitly connected to each other. Let us examine the hearts of his analyses of the three concepts. First, 'interests':

Policy x is more in A's real interest than policy y if A, were he to experience the *results* of both x and y, would *choose* x as the result he would rather have for himself.[63]

And 'power':

Our exploration of the forms of exercise of power over others supports, then, two related conclusions. First, such an exercise involves the limiting or impairing of the recipient's choice in some respect, and second, before such effects are manifestations of some person's or collectivity's *power* over the recipient(s) there must be some reason to hold the bidder *responsible* for the limitation . . . [And so,] briefly stated, A exercises power over B when he is responsible for some x that increases the costs, risks, or difficulties to B in promoting B's desires or in recognizing or promoting B's interests or obligations. A has power over B as *potential*, then, when he could, but does not, limit B in the ways specified; A *exercises* that power when the constraint x is so introduced or maintained.[64]

And 'freedom':

X is free with respect to z if (or to the extent that) he is unconstrained from conceiving or choosing z and if (to the extent that), were he to *choose* z, he would not be constrained from doing or becoming z. X acts freely in doing z when (or to the extent that) he acts without constraint upon his unconstrained and reflective *choice* with respect to z.[65]

Presented back to back like this, the direct and explicit connections between the three concepts are evident: the concept 'constraint' is present in the descriptions of both the concepts 'freedom' and 'power'; the concept 'interest' is present within the description of the concept 'power';[66] and the concept 'choice' is present in all three.[67] This is not to mention the many indirect and implicit connections between these and other concepts, some of which Connolly himself discusses.[68] Presumably, then, the person who wishes to make use of any one of these formulae in practice will be unable to avoid consulting not just the other two, but numerous others—indeed, those representing *all* of the major normative concepts—putting them all together to make an enormous and unwieldy scheme riddled with variables. If it was difficult to imagine someone benefiting from the application of just one of these formulae in a real case, recognizing its inadequacy without the others makes the scenario even more strained. What, then, should the appreciation of all these connections point to? It is that concepts cannot claim any coherent meaning in isolation, and that, beyond what we can find in a good dictionary (which, moreover, is much more evocative of the use of a concept in a context with others, and so, as I will argue, much more revealing than any formula), the analysis of a concept outside of the context of its place in an actual argument, ideology, or philosophy, is of little worth.

Michael Freeden's paper, 'Political Concepts and Ideological Morphology',[69] is subtler and more thoroughgoing in this step towards greater conceptual holism than Connolly's. To begin with, Freeden follows Connolly in asserting that there is more contestable and contested about a concept than Gallie lets on, that contesting a single concept does not mean arguing only about the relative weighings of the clearly describable components that make it up, but also about what Freeden calls the 'intension' of a concept, that is, about the proper range of components to be included in the concept as well as over the ambiguity of those components.[70] Freeden goes on, moreover, to explain that the main political concepts contain both ineliminable components and quasi-contingent ones, and that a concept is never its ineliminable component alone. When it comes to the quasi-contingent components, he strongly emphasizes that they may be shared with other concepts, that 'political concepts overlap and reinforce each other'.[71] Thus does Freeden wholeheartedly reject the notion that one can speak of a concept as being 'internally' complex, since a concept can never be said to have meaning in isolation, as most of the components that make it up are 'externalized' or 'available to be drawn into its skeletal structure', this being constituted by the ineliminable component.[72] In consequence, as he states, 'the analysis of a (political) concept is inadequate in so far as all its components or properties are treated as internal to it, as independent, self-supporting, and sharply demarcated from other concepts'.[73] And this means that, on the whole, 'ideologies', which consist of concepts, 'constitute semantic fields in that each component interacts with all the others and is changed when any one of the other components alters'.[74]

From the perspective of this more holistic position, it makes sense to understand the terms of a language as being defined *contrastingly*, and so as exhibiting a relation to each other that is perhaps best captured by Wilhelm von Humboldt's metaphor of language as a web, for when we touch any single part of a web the whole always resonates.[75] This greater holism should, it seems to me, actually lead us to shy away from Freeden's description of parts as 'elements' or 'components', terms which smack too much of self-containedness or analytical distinctions in favour of 'aspects' or, even better, 'features', if we are to more strongly express the notion that the parts of a language, and the parts of those parts, are *integrated* rather than *interlocked* with each other (the latter, as I wrote in Chapter 1, characterizing how parts are related within a systematic as opposed to organic whole). I favour 'features' because the term invokes the notion of the parts of a face, and physiognomy seems to me to be one of the clearest examples of holistic expressivism. A face is expressive of meaning in that it makes certain feelings or dispositions manifest through the particular arrangement of its features in a particular context, and if we are to account for how it does so it is clear that we cannot break those features down into independent parts and show the whole to be nothing more than a function of those parts.[76] Taken in isolation, we should understand a part not as expressive of some 'pure' or 'absolute' meaning, but rather of no substantive meaning at all.[77]

I wrote above of a second step towards holism. I am not going to argue for it here so much as describe it, my hope being that its plausibility will receive support from the work it does in some of the arguments that I will advance later in the chapter. This step can be said to have been taken by those for whom, and I would include Humbolt as well as Herder here, even the 'web' metaphor should be insufficiently holistic, for it involves the recognition that language exhibits something of the nature of a holographic synecdoche, that is, that a language, as Taylor has put it, 'is present as a whole in any one of its parts'.[78] In one form or another, this 'holographic holism', as I want to call it, can be said to claim an intellectual history longer even than that of atomism's.[79] In contrast to Freeden's schema, then, adherents to some version of this 'all in every part'[80] conception would be led to claim that there is a sense in which *all* parts of a concept, *including* Freeden's ineliminable one, lay claim to an external dimension. Accepting this characterization means an even further blurring, and in an admittedly paradoxical fashion, of the borders between his ineliminable component and those other parts both within and without a concept. Under such a conception, if we want to continue to conceive of making distinctions as involving the drawing of lines, then these will, at all times, have to be dotted rather than solid.

All this being said, while the hermeneuticist's holographic holism can be understood as sharing Plato and Aristotle's assumption that, when it comes to goods, 'the presence of each requires the presence of all',[81] it nevertheless, unlike Plato and Aristotle's doctrines, does not go so far as to affirm the unity of those goods, and so it cannot be placed directly at the holistic end of the spectrum of meaning outlined above, this being the home of those philosophies which assert that the parts of a whole can be *fully* integrated and so united. 'When a Work has Unity,' as Blake has written, 'it is as much in a Part as in the Whole.'[82] With Aristotle, as I have pointed out, all those goods not directly a part of *eudaemonia* still 'point' to it, and in a way which is said to reflect a perfectly harmonious ordering, with the result that being true to that order means being successful at finding a way out of any moral conflict without compromise. But the guarantee that this is always, in principle, a possibility is something that hermeneuticists, like pluralists, simply cannot accept.

And yet, the two approaches' conceptions of practical reason and its possibilities are not the same. This, as I will show, is a direct result of the hermeneuticist's rejection of the pluralist notion that one can conceive of values separately. To the hermeneuticist, goods, as distinct from the pluralists' values, are, even when we are only thinking about them, *always* a part of practice, and so are always more or less thick, for thinking, indeed thought itself, is considered to be but a kind of practice. Moreover, for the hermeneuticist, the parts of a practice can never, without distortion, be conceived of as fully independent of each other. Thus where, for both pluralists and hermeneuticists, it makes sense to conceive of a tradition of practices with that classic metaphor of a river, it is for pluralists alone that a tradition's standards—its values—are considered expressible, not as relative to its practices, but as self-contained and isolable universals. Rather than constituting an integral part of the river, the values of pluralism are more like self-enclosed objects, in a certain sense 'things' that float along in the water.[83]

To the hermeneuticist, however, a good should never be conceived of as a thing in this self-contained sense. Outside of context, disconnected from the practices in which it is integrated in a certain relation with others, the isolated expression of a good, one to which a *ceteris paribus* ('all other things being equal') clause has been applied, cannot but be a distortion. For when we apply that clause, it is as if we take the good out of historical time, freezing the river of tradition of which it is an intrinsic part and then prying it out of the ice, doing so, we may say, in such a way that certain essential parts of it are left behind. In hermeneutics, as a consequence, to fulfil a good 'uncompromisingly' can never entail being true to it in isolation, for it can only be fulfilled completely when it is realized as more or less thickly integrated with the whole, and so the other goods, of which it is an intrinsic, practical part.[84]

III

Having thus contrasted pluralism and hermeneutics as regards their respective conceptions of the meaning of normative concepts, I want to turn now to the matter of practical reason. The pluralist conceives of it, I want to show, in a relatively linear way, in which it is said to involve something like making rough use of vectors to sail to our destination. But there are problems with this conception of our trip, to the extent that the pluralist may not even be able to account for how we leave the harbour. To depart, I would claim, we need a hermeneutical conception of the voyage, one which, by virtue of its thoroughly holistic and, as I will show, diachronic notion of development, conceives of it as progressing through something more like a spiral.

Though I want to begin this section with a brief account of the pluralist's conception of practical reason, I plan to leave a more in-depth exploration, and the contrast with the hermeneuticist's approach, for the next section. My main objective here will be to bring out how the two differ as regards the question of how we are confronted by moral conflicts in the first place, for this, of course, must happen *before* we may start to reason about them. To begin with, let us note that, when we speak of practical conflicts that we might respond to reasonably, agents must perceive that these involve things, however conceived, that 'matter' to them, these being the values or goods that constitute at least some of the parts of what we might refer to as their 'identities'. Taylor has summed up the notion of a person's identity in a way that, it seems to me, would be acceptable to both the pluralist and the hermeneuticist:

To define my identity is to define what I must be in contact with in order to function fully as a human agent, and specifically to be able to judge and discriminate and recognize what is really of worth or importance, both in general and for me. To say that something is part of my identity is to say that without it I should be at a loss in making those discriminations which are characteristically human. I shouldn't know where I stood, I should lose the sense of what constituted beauty, what nobility, what truly worthwhile fulfilment, and so on. It helps constitute the horizon within which these discriminations have meaning for me.[85]

It is when the parts of a person's identity come into conflict that he or she may then turn to practical reason as a way of responding to that conflict. Now depending on the conflict's nature, it makes sense to say that either one of two kinds of practical reason will be applicable, or some mixture of the two. In those cases in which all the values or goods involved can be fully reduced or commensurated, what is required is only that instrumental kind of reasoning which may be used either to find a systematic means of eliminating the conflict altogether, or to calculate the most appropriate compromise in an economic cost–benefit sense. In the case of the former, in which we may speak of the complete elimination of a conflict by instrumental means, I am referring to the goal of making the items in conflict compossible. Say I realize after waking up one morning that, due to a scheduling error, I have two important commitments to attend to that day: I must finish and submit a piece of academic work, but this is also the day that a close friend of mine needs help moving into a new apartment. The problem is that the flat my friend is moving from is on the edge of town and the bus ride there and back would itself take up half the day. Combine this with the time needed to actually help him move, and there would be little opportunity to finish my paper. It seems, then, that I am facing a moral conflict between my commitment to my studies on the one hand, and my loyalty to a friend on the other. A little instrumental reasoning, however, and I realize that, by borrowing my neighbour's car, I am able to shorten the commute enough to give me ample time to finish the paper as well as help my friend. Conflict eliminated.

Say, however, that there is no neighbour with a car. Because the values or goods involved in this conflict, scholarship and friendship, are irreducible, we cannot use instrumental reason to help us determine what to do. The pluralist, however, may still talk of balancing the conflicting values against each other, although this will be understood as guided by their conception of that moral sense, *phronesis*-like version of practical reason rather than by any instrumental calculations. Part of the reasoning here involves taking in as much of the detail as possible about the context. What is really necessary to do a good job on the paper?

How important is it that I do well? Does my friend have others to help him? How good a friend is he anyway? Answers to these and similar questions should help me determine which, if any, of the morning buses across town I should take: the earlier the bus, the more time will be devoted to my friend and the less to my education, and vice versa. So just as with cost–benefit analyses, pluralist moral sense judgements still assume that a kind of zero-sum dynamic exists between the conflicting values, in which weighing them against each other necessitates that, as I pointed out before, the agent will be unable to escape neglecting either one or both of them to some degree, the compromising this entails constituting what Williams has termed the 'moral remainder'[86] of the decision.

It is important to note the universality of this form of reasoning about conflicting irreducibles for pluralists: weighing values against each other is always a zero-sum issue in form, regardless of how significant the matter is in substance. If one cannot find an instrumentally rational route to making the conflicting incommensurable values compossible, then, whether one settles for a balance between them that is more-or-less equal, or one in which only an all-or-nothing decision seems appropriate, the zero-sum relation assumed to be present ensures that some moral loss will be inescapable. It is for this reason that pluralists often refer to the inevitability of compromise when it comes to reasoning about moral or political conflicts, as with Williams's statement that 'we cannot conceive of a situation in which it was true both that all value-conflict had been eliminated, and that there had been no loss of value on the way'.[87]

Now it is often true that it is when we determine that we need to make all-or-nothing choices that moral conflicts seem most difficult. Say there was only one bus to my friend's flat and it left first thing in the morning. If I am on that bus, then this means I have given up altogether on submitting the work (aware, as I was, of the professor's stern announcement at the beginning of term: 'There will be no extensions!'); missing it, however, means that my friend will simply have to do without me. Of course, whether I consider this conflict particularly significant is still a function of how important what is being remaindered is to me. The need to greatly compromise a not-so-important value does not make for a very significant conflict. It is thus because the stakes are often very high and the conflicts tend to pose acute dilemmas in politics that we can understand why pluralists tend to speak of dirty hands and tragedy as regards that realm.

This whole understanding, however, is intimately linked with the assumption that, when it comes to conceptual meaning, values may be separated from each other in the way I outlined above. But if we reject this, and adopt the holographic conception of goods underlying hermeneutics instead, then the perception of how they conflict, and so of how that conflict may be deliberated over is, I believe, both more subtle and truer to the phenomena. To demonstrate this, I want to take up another case of moral conflict, one which embodies a dilemma that, at first, seems to require an all-or-nothing choice between two incommensurables, and yet one which, as I will later show, demonstrates the possibility of overcoming at least some genuine moral conflicts without compromise.

Let us say that someone has just been awarded a terrific new job as a travelling salesman, one which he has been hoping for for a long time. The problem is that, when he begins work, he will be out of the house for days at a stretch, and this means that he will not be able to care for his cherished guppy, Darius. It seems, then, that Darius will either have to be given away, or be prepared for a swim in the sewer system. Luckily, though, our new salesman has both a relative and a friend each of whom have come to feel a deep love for the fish. The problem, however, is that they each live in separate cities, far away from each other, and so sharing is not a viable option as the veterinarian has recommended that Darius not be moved too much since the shock could kill him. What we have here, then, is a dilemma between the obligations generated by two values, family and friendship: who should get the guppy? Both the friend and the relative might be expected to be very upset upon learning that they lost out on the opportunity to care for Darius. Now let us say that while our new salesman is thinking about this matter the phone suddenly rings: a woman from the local charity at which he volunteers is calling to explain that one of the other volunteers has resigned and that, as a result, they are desperate for even more help on Wednesdays. And as today is Tuesday, they need to know as soon as possible if our new salesman would be able to come in tomorrow. His response is that he was already aware they were understaffed, but that he was pretty sure he would not be able to do more than the six hours a week he promised when he first volunteered, though he would think about it and call them back. He is unable to deal with the question right now, he politely explains, because of a personal problem he is attending to at the moment. The caller thanks him, says she is looking forward to hearing from him, and wishes him a good day.

Now the question I want to ask here is this: how is it that our salesman came to the decision that the issue concerning Darius merited priority? To be clear, the introduction of the charity issue is not just a matter of adding another value (generosity) to the conflict surrounding Darius, but about another conflict altogether, one with its own subset of values: should our salesman spend more time with the charity, or should he continue with the current amount he gives to leisure and other pursuits, which are also important values of his? These values, the pluralist might be expected to point out, seem to conflict with each other without any bearing on the question of what should be done with Darius. Perhaps, then, our salesman should try to conceptualize the two conflicts separately in order to deal with them perspicuously. But how, exactly, did he come to decide that the values involved in the conflict based on the charity were subalternate?

As with any moral conflict, we should expect the pluralist to respond that such a 'conflict between conflicts of values' will be dealt with, first, with an instrumental attempt to make the two compossible. If one can put one conflict off and deal with it later, without any affect to the values involved, then this would of course be the sensible route to take. But say circumstances are such that this is not an option, that dealing with one of the two conflicts at a later time necessitates detracting from some or all of the values in question. In such a case, it seems reasonable to suppose that the pluralist will conceive of this as itself a matter of engaging one's moral sense so as to compare the irreducible values, and this means weighing the two irreducible subsets as a whole against each other, one subset from each conflict, in order to determine which is the most important, and so which merits attention first.

Faced with the phone call, then, it is evident that our salesman took the issue regarding Darius as far more important than the one based on the charity. Perhaps the difference in significance between the two was so great that it did not take much time at all to determine this (after all, he was already putting in six hours a week); indeed, perhaps the proper course was so obvious that he was able to do the necessary reasoning tacitly, without any conscious reflection. According to Hampshire, most of our perceptions and judgements are of this tacit sort, a result, as he puts it, of 'compressed' and 'pre-conscious inference'.[88]

However, we should also accept that this matter of whether Darius or the charity should be granted priority was not the only one potentially confronting our salesman at that time. That is because, being a person who affirms a plurality of values, we should expect that he could have been faced with many sets of conflicts between them at any one time. Indeed, following another observation of Hampshire's, we should recognize that there would have been a potentially *infinite* amount. Hampshire has written of what he has dubbed the 'inexhaustibility of description' of a context: 'Any situation which confronts me, and which is not a situation in a game, has an inexhaustible set of discriminable features over and above those which I explicitly notice at the time because they are of immediate interest to me.'[89] This reality, which essentially refers to the question of what context one is in, includes the matter of which moral conflict should be of immediate interest to a person. For to ask about one's context is to enquire not just about matters relating to the room one is standing in, or the city or country in which one lives, or about one's relationship with others, and so on, but also about which, if any, moral or political issue(s) one ought to confront at that particular moment. Regarding our salesman, then, we should recognize that he did not really have to wait for the phone call to confront the conflict surrounding the charity as he was already well aware that they (or some other charity) had need of more volunteering, and he was until then only resting on the decision which he had made at the beginning of the year when he decided to contribute six hours a week. He could, however, even without the prompting of the phone call, always have decided that it was necessary to return to that decision and rethink the matter. Indeed, there were many other moral or political matters to which he could have directed his attention. Has he been calling his mother often enough? What about his position on abortion? And so on. There truly seems to be an infinite number of possibilities here.

But this then means that Hampshire's statement regarding the 'inexhaustibility of description' of a context can be said to beg the question. For how does a person come to those features, or those conflicts, which 'are of immediate interest'? Pluralists claim that *when* there is a conflict in concrete cases, one may engage in practical reasoning to try and balance the conflicting values. But, as I pointed out, one has first to determine *which* conflict is to get priority, and, for the pluralist at least, this will itself be a matter which entails reflection; such judgements may be of a tacit 'compressed' and 'pre-conscious' sort, but they will be judgements nevertheless. And yet—and here is the essential point— since there will be an infinite amount of these separate conflicts, it seems that one will need to make an infinite number of such judgements in order to determine which conflict merits priority. Now even if we understand the thought process this involves as largely tacit and condensed, it would still be impossible to complete it, for it requires comparing an infinite number of elements. The pluralist, then, is unable to legitimate a person's claim to be right to have given priority to one conflict over all the others since, within pluralism, that person can never actually succeed in attending to all of them.

As a result, the pluralist seems to leave us with only one possible account of the route to practical reasoning: that the choice to give priority to a particular conflict over others cannot itself claim a basis in reason, because there will always be other conflicts that one must admit to having ignored simply by fiat. It is as if persons make an ultimately random choice from amongst an infinite chain of conflicts in order to begin reflecting. And who is to say that, once resolved, a conflict may be properly removed from that chain? Indeed, if we accept Sartre's admittedly banal point that many of our past resolutions (say, to begin a diet) are always open to being re-decided (as we are often well aware during each trip to the refrigerator), then we must recognize that, as long as circumstances have not changed too much, one can often return to a previous decision about a moral conflict and rethink the matter.

Hermeneutics, however, offers us a different account, one based on its more holistic conception of the meaning of goods, in which it is claimed that goods are *at all times* to some extent integrated with each other. This means not only that, as I will show, it can be assumed that some past conflicts have been resolved with the full reconciliation of the once opposing incommensurable goods, but also that, though there is indeed a potentially inexhaustible number of descriptions of, as well as conflicts in, a person's context, these are not always present to him or her since the goods underlying them are, in that context, in an integrated enough state for them *not to be distinguishable from each other at all*, even tacitly. It is by virtue of the direction provided by the integrated structure made up of those indistinguishable goods that we can speak of persons acting from within a *pre-reflective* mode of being, what Heidegger has referred to as the state of 'average everydayness' and Dreyfus as 'everyday coping'.[90] Most of the time we go about the world in this way, in which the goods constitutive of our identities are part of a highly integrated, pre-reflective whole which makes up the background, the enabling *pre*judices, as Gadamer would say, necessary for any part of our context to ever show up and be intelligible to us in the first place.[91] During this mode persons can indeed be said to be acting meaningfully, purposefully, expressing their goods and so engaged with their context,[92] although this might be better described as fulfilling their 'good' (singular), the whole of the integrated goods that constitute their identities. Though this activity can still claim the status of being meaningful, it is not the direct result of practical reasoning, even of the tacit, condensed sort described by Hampshire, for whom actions always follow, and are distinct from, thought, this being, it seems to me, why he chooses to refer to the human agent in general as a 'reflective subject'.[93] Instead of this, the hermeneuticist would conceive of human agency as the activity of what might be called an *engaged self*, 'engaged' rather than 'reflective' so as to make room for pre-reflective agency, and 'self' rather than 'subject' to emphasize that a person's identity expresses his goods in a consistently thick—and never thin—manner. The key here is to recognize that pre-reflective agency is, in a strong sense, the expression of a *skill* which, as I pointed out in Chapter 1, cannot be accounted for as something made up of concepts, rules, beliefs, or any sort of representations in the mind. For rather than a kind of thought separate from practice, skilful behaviour is an activity.[94]

It is, moreover, because this hermeneutical conception of the background whole should never be understood as having attained a state of perfection or unity that it makes sense to speak of moral conflicts showing up to us in the first place. Indeed, if a person could ever claim an identity that had achieved such a unified state, then we should expect that she would never emerge from her pre-reflective mode of agency at all, for it would not make sense to speak of features of her identity as coming forth in conflict and so as in need of reflective evaluation. People emerge from this state only because there are occasions in which they cannot cope with their context pre-reflectively, that is, because the configuration of their integrated goods at a given time is unable to guide them in acting harmoniously with that context, leading parts of it to show up to them as perplexing. Moreover, it is because our goods are to some extent integrated and so *already* stand in a certain meaningful relation to each other that it makes sense to say that we are able to directly, and without reflection, recognize the specific parts, and so the conflict(s), which ought to have the greatest priority for us,[95] this being something we are aware of *before* having to think it out, even tacitly. Indeed, as anyone who has ever struggled to redirect their attention away from a pressing predicament will attest, this pre-reflective focusing on a specific conflict is quite powerful. Despite this, the hermeneutic approach may be said to make (some) room for the predominantly pre-modern ethical notion that persons may be held responsible simply for what shows up as significant to them, even though this 'showing up' is not a direct result of their practical reasoning.

And so, when we encounter a situation, or any sort of text, that we find confusing or perplexing, we can say that what has happened is that some of our goods—these providing the bases of the distinctions that we find significant—have suddenly appeared to us as in conflict. The hermeneutical claim, then, is that goods emerge from the pre-reflective background and show up on their own as distinct from each other only when they are in conflict. And while fully commensurable goods are subject to an instrumental rationality which may succeed in making them compossible, incommensurable ones can never be so treated, which is why, for Taylor, the practices they constitute can be described as 'incompatible in principle'.[96] Contrast this conception of incommensurability with those of John Kekes or Claude Galipeau, who make explicit the often implicit pluralist notion that values are often present as distinct and incommensurable but not in conflict.[97]

Moreover, in hermeneutics, when certain goods show up to an agent as incommensurable and so in conflict, they never do so in an independently distinct way, such that it would make sense to describe their conflict, as pluralists often do, as involving their 'clashing' or 'colliding'. Rather, conflicting goods show up as distinct but inseparable from each other, and so it is more accurate to say that what shows up to persons confronted by a moral conflict is their hologram of goods *as a whole*, it being in a state of discord such that their attention is drawn to those regions within it where the goods most directly involved in the conflict are most present. And in keeping with this hermeneutical holism, tension in one area will always be felt, in varying ways and degrees, throughout the whole hologram, such that we may say that *every* good, and *every* part of every good embedded within that whole, is to some extent affected.

With this alternative conception of how we come to be confronted by moral conflicts we are led to a different understanding of how reasoning about those conflicts can and should take place. With the hermeneuticist, the primary aim of moral sense practical reasoning is to strive for an engaged objectivity which is best achieved, not by the zero-sum balancing of two or more clashing, independently distinct incommensurables, but rather as the product of a struggle to reinterpret the whole of one's goods in such a way that those most directly involved in the conflict can be reconciled, which is to say integrated more fully with each other and the rest of the whole hologram of which they are always an integral part. Rather than weighing separate values *against* each other, then, the claim is that one should, at least at first, strive to harmonize the regions of discord that the goods occupy within the whole. This, I would claim, constitutes a subtler conception of practical reason than that assumed by the pluralist, one which supports an importantly different understanding of our moral and political predicament. It is to a closer examination of these differences that I now want to turn.

IV

i

To begin with, how we understand what persons do, or at least, should try to do, when reasoning about conflicting incommensurables is different. In pluralism, as I pointed out earlier, one can respond to moral conflicts, whether based on the values affirmed by a single person, or between persons over their shared values, with one's moral sense only if those conflicts take place against the background of a way of life. If one wishes to criticize another way of life, say, as regards how its members choose to balance its values when they conflict, then this is possible only to the extent that that way of life overlaps with one's own, and so shares at least some of the same values.[98] Without that overlap, the pluralist claims, it would be necessary to 'convert'[99] to that way of life, such a conversion being the product, as we have seen, of a radical choice to drop the values of one way of life and take up those of another.

And so, for the pluralist, reasonable criticism of another way of life necessitates sharing, to some extent, in its values. If, however, one only wants to get an understanding of that way of life, in the sense of an uncritical grasp of it, then, according to the pluralist, sharing is not required. As Berlin has written, 'to understand the motives and outlook of others it is not, of course, necessary to share them; insight does not entail approval';[100] or, as he has stated more recently, 'if you tell me that somebody else has a quite different outlook, set of intuitions, I can, unless they are unintelligible, with an effort, grasp how someone might come to have such values although I may have to protect myself from such a culture if it endangers my own.'[101] To pluralists, then, one reaches such an understanding not so much by 'reasoning', as by engaging that faculty which they refer to as the 'imagination', one which, as they conceive of it, involves an empathic yet relatively disinterested form of thought, much like Vico's *entrare*.[102] Thus historians can claim to have understood the ideas of the past only to the extent that they have managed to disinterestedly 're-enact within themselves the states of mind'[103] of the thinkers they are studying. To describe this conception of imagination as 'disinterested', it should be clear, is not to equate it with the neutrality appropriate to the natural sciences, as it is a form of thought that is said to involve, as Berlin has put it, 'an effort of imaginative insight such as novelists usually possess',[104] and so is clearly not meant to be associated with any kind of theoretical reason.

The hermeneuticist, however, would reject this conception of imagination. That is because in hermeneutics, an interpreter is considered never able to bypass his or her self, since it is the goods that constitute one's identity that make up the enabling prejudices, to invoke Gadamer's terms once again, which are essential to all interpretive activity. To the hermeneuticist, then, interpretation always involves what Gadamer has referred to as a 'fusion of horizons', one of these being the identity of the interpreter's self, and the other that of who or what is being interpreted. As Gadamer has explained, it was the pre-Heideggerian, Romantic hermeneuticist who argued that an interpreter should aim to bypass his or her self while trying to imaginatively 'reconstruct' the meaning of the other,[105] and it seems to me that it is within a similar understanding of interpretation that the pluralist's conception of imagination largely works.

To say, moreover, that one must always interpret *through* one's horizon is but another way of claiming that an interpreter's thoughts can never escape his or her context, meaning that Berlin's 'darkness and void', the domain of the pluralist's thin moral concepts in which items are said to claim universalistic meanings, is also inaccessible. No moral meaning can ever be universalist because a horizon uninterpreted, unfused with a specific other in a specific context, lays claim not to a status of meaningfulness, but to what we might refer to instead as 'meaning-potential'.

To the hermeneuticist, then, achieving an understanding can never consist of taking an imaginative leap out of one's self and into another's shoes; rather, the point is always to try to put that self into the other's shoes. When one tries to get beyond the limits of one's own perspective, one should aim not to surmount that perspective, but rather to *transform* it into a wider conception which can include the other;[106] there is to be no bypassing or, in the case of the pluralist's radical choice-based conversions, 'leaving behind' of one's older stance. Transformative change, the claim goes, always accompanies interpretation. Because nothing meaningful exists in the world in a perfect, unified state, when one struggles to interpret something which at first seems perplexing, achieving any degree of understanding will always be accompanied by criticism and so a call for change—be it of one's self, or of the other, or both. In hermeneutics, then, criticism and understanding necessarily entail each other, this being a corollary of the hermeneutical principle that interpretation always aims for giving a better account of the subject-matter, that is, for greater truth. This 'truth' is not, of course, that dualist, correspondence conception assumed by the radical translator of Chapter 1, nor is it that notion which sometimes goes by the name of 'the plain truth', the one invoked when, say, someone asks if you did something not particularly admirable and you admit that you did. This latter ideal should be conceived as a single intrinsic good on par with those such as justice, mercy, happiness, and so on, while the 'truth' I'm referring to here is that higher, unabashedly metaphysical conception, the one which is sometimes said to be combined with 'the good' and 'the beautiful' in a unity which, to the hermeneuticist, always lies somewhat beyond the grasp of human beings.

Putting aside, for the moment, the implications of all this for encounters between ways of life over goods that, it seems, they cannot be said to share, I want at this point to go somewhat further into what it means to say that hermeneutical interpretation is transformative. Right off, it should be clear that the fact that goods are understood to *change* in meaning as a result of reasoning about them distinguishes the hermeneutical approach from that of intuitionism, be it of the deontological sort advocated by a thinker such as W. D. Ross, or of the Aristotelian variety as with John McDowell.[107] In intuitionism, deciding what to do involves grappling not so much with what both the hermeneuticist and the pluralist would consider to be a *real* moral conflict, but rather with a prima-facie conflict, one which demands, not a dialogical deliberation, but only a 'seeing' or 'intuiting' of which value or good should get priority. And yet, as I have shown, the hermeneuticist differs from the pluralist in conceiving of the goods that show up during a conflict as being, to some degree, still integrated both with each other and with all of the other of the interpreter's goods. That is why any change to a particular good or goods is always said to have an impact on the whole. The comprehensive renunciation of atomism that this entails also supports a rejection of any sort of incrementalist conception of the development of that whole, the claim being that development, as Taylor has put it, 'cannot be accounted for by the addition or subtraction of elements'.[108] In this, hermeneutical interpretation may be said to take somewhat on board the Saussurean idea of the diachronic relation of linguistic meaning as a way of relating the changes to the meanings of particular goods to a person's whole horizon. For Saussure, while the meaning of a *parole* (a particular speech act) only makes sense within the background of the whole *langue* (the code), it is also the case that any innovative and compelling act of *parole* that does not match with the background can cause that whole to evolve to include it.[109]

The progress through this process is one way of understanding what has been called the 'hermeneutic circle'. The idea is that interpreters, in reflecting on any particular change during practical reason, move at once from the whole as it appears to them, to the conflicting parts of it most directly located in the regions of tension, and then back to the whole again. Since every good may be conceived only against the background of all the others, a moral conflict between particular goods can be interpreted as a kind of invitation to further investigate what they—and, indirectly, all the other goods the agent affirms—mean. The investigation, however, should be described as simultaneously entailing both the *discovery* as well as the *evolution* of the meaning of those goods, since the reconciliation or further integration of conflicting goods involves not only a bringing forth of what had previously remained implicit, but also a rearticulation of, and so a change to, meaning. And since every single good contains within it something of the whole, then changing the meaning of one necessarily means transforming, to some extent, all of the others.

But not just any change will do. In our struggles for engaged objectivity, we aim for an organic—as opposed, as with the radical translation conception of interpretation, to a systematic—coherence of our goods. This is a struggle, then, to make better sense of our overall predicament, one which involves what Taylor has called 'reasoning in transitions', an activity which consists of searching for those 'error-reducing moves' that can provide what may be construed as overall epistemic gain.[110] The rearticulations this entails are far from subjective, however, for as with the criticism or interpretation of any text they must be true to the meaning of that text, that is, they must make sense in a consistent way of everything about the text that shows up to the interpreter. Moreover, since our interpreter shares many of his goods with others, much of what shows up—or ought to show up—to him will do so to them as well, this being why reasoned arguments between them can lead to better understandings of the text or text-analogue for all.

The meaning that shows up during interpretation can do so as more or less organically coherent, that is, with parts that are more or less integrated or in conflict with each other. When the matter is such that there is a particularly acute conflict, then there is need for a kind of dialogue between the interpreter and the text or text-analogue, in which the interpreter must struggle to determine whether the confusion and tension exhibited by the conflict is a result of the standards that constitute his horizon, or those of the text, or to some extent both. If his own, then what is needed is a change or rearticulation of his own standards or identity, one which will be expressed in an interpretation that makes more sense of the previously puzzling issue, this being how one can learn from the act of interpreting. If the problem seems to be more with the text or text-analogue, however, then the interpreter should assert that the tensions or inadequacies are part of its horizon, which, by direct implication, entails a critical recommendation that it be reformed. The call for change, be it of the interpreter or of what is being interpreted, is thus inherent to successful interpretation. With understanding comes progress. Perhaps, then, it makes better sense to refer to a hermeneutical 'spiral' rather than a 'circle'.

Talk of progress in all understanding should lead us to recognize that hermeneutical interpretation is teleological, though in a relatively non-naturalistic sense. Aristotle's teleology was naturalistic in a way which can be understood by focusing on the relation between his doctrine of the unity of the virtues and his statement that 'the whole must of necessity be prior to the part'.[111] As I read it, 'prior' here is meant to carry the notions of being both *before* and *superior*. This is because when Aristotle claims that man is naturally a social animal, he does not only wish to assert that persons are necessarily a part of the whole that is the society which precedes and shapes them, since, as I have pointed out, that society, at least ideally, should also reflect the particular hierarchy of goods that he claims is intrinsic to *eudaemonia*, the architectonic good which orders the whole by ranking all of the others. *Eudaemonia* is thus not only 'the starting-point' but, being 'the source and cause of all good things', it should be 'for its sake [that] all of us do everything else'.[112] There is thus, to Aristotle, no place for an individual to question the particular ranking of goods it asserts, for it is claimed to be natural to man, essential to his very functioning, just as a plant's structure is intrinsic to its potentiality from the moment it comes into being in the form of a seed. As a plant lives and grows, it struggles to maintain its preprogrammed homoeostasis, just as man is said to turn to *phronesis* to deal with specific moral conflicts in a way that should aim to be true, overall, to the ranking of goods natural to him. Homoeostasis, as the term is understood in biology, refers to the tendency of an organism to try to maintain a particular internal stability owing to the co-ordinated response of its parts to any disruptive situation or stimulus. The practical life of the virtuous man, correspondingly, is said to consist of nothing other than the struggle to achieve and maintain the moral and social ranking natural to him. *Phronesis*, then, is but the attempt to engage rational means to discover how to be as true as possible to that fixed and universal ranking when facing particular moral or political conflicts, and so is not meant to bring about any change to that ranking.

Hermeneutics, as I have stated, shares with pluralism a rejection of the doctrine of the unity of the virtues, as well as the naturalistic architectonic good it asserts. Both approaches can thus also be said to reject the notion that such a good, which in a sense encapsulates the whole, is necessarily superior to all others. But pluralists place an even greater distance between themselves and Aristotle than do hermeneuticists since, to them, the whole is not only not superior to the parts, but it is also, we may say, not prior. For, as I described earlier, pluralist practical reason begins, not with a whole, but with independently distinct, clashing parts. It is only *after* being confronted with these that, according to the pluralist, we turn to the background of our whole way of life for guidance on how the conflicting values are to be balanced. Instead of beginning, like Aristotle, with a unified, naturalistically ordered conception of the whole human soul as a model for guidance in practical matters, pluralists thus start with a number of separate, conflicting parts. Hence Hampshire's description of his approach in relation to Aristotle's as a case of 'reversing the tradition', for, to Hampshire, the point is to 'start at the other end of the analogy and proceed in the opposite direction'.[113] For the pluralist, then, it is the parts that are prior. Combine this with the notion that it is their compromising, rather than reconciling through a 'realization' of the whole, that is considered to be the central aim of practical reason, and it is clear that there is no place for any sort of teleological conception of rationality here.

Not so with hermeneutics. In asserting that all parts are always more-or-less integrated with each other in a partially pre-reflective whole, hermeneuticists can be said to share with Aristotle the claim that the whole is prior to the parts, though only in the sense of coming before the parts, not as being superior. For though the interpretive journey begins, as I have shown, with a whole that exhibits regions in tension, the interpreter is led to focus on those regions and the goods they contain and, by rearticulating those goods in an attempt to reconcile them, has an effect which rebounds back on the whole, transforming it. The structure of the whole, then, is in no sense fixed or naturally pre-ordained, for it is part of what we might identify as a 'historicized teleology'. That is why it is a person's never-ending struggle *for* integrity of self, rather than any monistic metaphysical biology, that constitutes the essence of hermeneutic architectonics. In hermeneutics, the truth of one's self is thus not just discovered, but also altered. Moreover, because a person's identity can be considered unique for being partly constituted by his or her own self-understandings, hermeneutics has room for liberties which Aristotle, because of his comprehensive essentialism, simply could not recognize. Thus where, with Aristotle, whether we are speaking of an individual's personal governance or that of a whole *polis*, 'there is no choice if we are to live successful lives',[114] the hermeneuticist, like the pluralist, is able to concur with Coleridge when he proclaims: 'What the plant is by an act not its own and unconsciously, that must thou *make* thyself to become.'[115]

To summarize, when a moral conflict first shows up to an agent as perplexing, to the hermeneuticist this is understood to be because the agent's ability to discriminate between its features in a coherent way seems limited, this being why, at first, she seems unable to make sense of it. But by rearticulating the goods that are the bases of those discriminations, by making those parts of her holographic horizon finer, richer, more powerful, the claim is that she is capable of reinterpreting the meaning of her situation. The standards of interpretation, which are nothing but the conflicting goods to which she is struggling to be true, are features of the meaning of that conflict, and so are inherently contextual. They are not external and self-contained 'criteria' which are 'applied' during an interpretation, both because they only come forth in that context and because, when they do come forth, it is always as more-or-less integrated features, rather than separate or separable elements, of the whole. With pluralism, however, values, even when present in a thick context, may often be understood as laying claim to an independently distinct meaning, as when they are expressed as isolated 'absolutes' or when they appear—absolute or not—as in conflict with others.

The transformation of one's whole identity as a result of the interpretive struggle for greater coherence and articulateness can consist of either a more or a less radical endeavour. As regards those cases of less radical change, one might say that the agent, focusing on those goods which have most directly 'shown up' as incommensurable in a given context, simply comes to a superior understanding of how they relate to each other or, otherwise put, what they 'say' about each other. This makes sense as a goal because the whole hologram of goods is understood to be, to an extent, present in every part, and so there is a sense in which each good *already* contains 'information' about its relation to all the others, including those with which it is in conflict. We might thus describe such less radical cases as entailing more of the discovery than the evolution of their meanings, though always some of the latter since the discovery of the further meaning a good has for one necessarily entails that its meaning has also changed.

In the example of the conflict between the requirements of friendship and academics, hermeneutics makes room for the conception that a decision to give more time to one rather than the other does not necessarily have to be interpreted as the result of a compromise between the two goods; rather, it can be said to emit from a better understanding of what *both* goods would, or should, *fully* support. Say it turned out that the right thing for you to do was to finish your paper and this meant that you would not be able to help your friend. In this case it could be right to say that, if your friend knew of and properly understood your situation, then he too would, because he is your friend, call upon you to make that choice. Finishing the paper rather than helping him move would thus become *his* wish as well. Indeed a true friend, one who appreciated the importance that that particular piece of work should have for you, might even strenuously object if you yourself decided to make the other choice. Say you misjudged the situation, skipped the paper and went to help him move. A friend that knew you well could claim that, as regards this matter, he knew you better than you knew yourself, and so could rightly become upset that you took the decision you did. As your friend, your scholarly pursuits matter to him as well, since they express a good that, as friends, the both of you significantly share. It really is as if the good that is your academics is present *within* the good that is your friendship with him. Because one of the goods involved in this particular conflict means doing good to your friend, and because truly fulfilling it means doing what should make that friend happy, then we can appreciate how a proper understanding of the matter might lead you to do the paper as a means of being true to the friendship just as much as to your academic obligations. And if it turned out that your friend was not happy with your choice, then it might even make sense, on the supposition both that doing your paper was indeed the right thing for you to do and that your friend is not a particularly unperceptive individual, for you to question the quality of your friendship. In short, to the hermeneuticist, friendship is a good that can actually call for the fulfilment of other goods if it itself is to be fulfilled. Socrates was also surely aware of this, as is clear from his reply to his friends when, on the day he is to take the hemlock, they ask if there is anything they can do for him and he says: 'only, as I have always told you, take care of yourselves; that is a service which you may be ever rendering to me and mine and to all of us'.[116]

It is important to appreciate just how different this conception is from that available to us in pluralism. To Hampshire, 'one may have a moral obligation to assist one's partner in a joint enterprise when he calls on one in difficulties; but this obligation may lapse, or cease to exist, if he later makes it clear that he no longer wishes to incur such an obligation on his side'.[117] At first blush, it might seem that Hampshire also has room for the interpretation that the conflict may be overcome by virtue of the friend coming to appreciate the significance of your academic obligations and so dropping his request for assistance. But in pluralism this is understood as involving the virtual *removal* of the obligation expressing the value of friendship from the conflict, not its maintenance and *reinterpretation*, which is essential to the hermeneutical reading. To the hermeneuticist, a conflict such as this is best overcome not by virtue of an obligation lapsing or ceasing to exist, but as a result of it retaining its full (or even greater) power to make demands on us, though being understood in a way different from how it was when the conflict first emerged.

In consequence, we might describe the hermeneutical understanding of the moral sense practical reasoning that goes on in these less radical cases of conflicting incommensurables as involving the attempt to reason out how one or more of the goods involved in a conflict could be reinterpreted so as to make them more 'magnanimous' regarding each other, even synergistic. This is considered possible because, as the hermeneuticist assumes, a conflicting good's 'opponent' can be found within it. Such an approach would make little sense in pluralism because its assumption that conflicting values are meaningfully separate from each other necessitates that, unless one of them lapses, there will be no way out without compromising, as opposed to realizing, one or more of those values. There is simply no place in pluralism for the notion that the right decision might be arrived at through a reinterpretation that ascertains the appropriate integrative relationship between the once-conflicting goods. In hermeneutics, however, the 'external' relations between conflicting incommensurables may be understood as fully 'internal' to each, it being this particular feature that one should, at least at first, aim to bring forth during practical reasoning. Since all parts contain the whole, and so the other parts, within them, one can search *within* a particular good for the call of the good that it is in conflict with. Two goods which initially seem to be in conflict may, upon reflection, be able to be reintegrated, a result of achieving a deeper understanding of what they really should have meant for the agent all along.

The particular conflict that I have considered here can, it should be noted, be read in two ways. If our protagonist arrives at the decision to skip the moving without consulting his friend, then we have a case of a personal moral conflict in which the practical reasoning engaged in might be understood as consisting of him having a kind of 'dialogue' with himself in order to determine what to do. However, if the friend is consulted, and the two struggle with the conflict together, then we have a moral conflict faced by two persons over goods that they both share. To the pluralist, as I have explained, the dialogue in the first situation, just like that which is said to take place during the negotiations in the second, should aim to determine the appropriate trade-off of the values in question. With hermeneutics, however, one should aim, first, for the reconciliation of the conflicting goods, and this requires a kind of dialogue which is best described as involving *conversation* rather than *negotiation*, the former being without the adversarial quality of the latter.[118] Thus while hermeneuticists can join pluralists in recommending that we respect the *audi alteram partem* ('hear the other side') maxim when it comes to moral and political conflicts, the two approaches nevertheless assert different understandings of what it demands. To the hermeneuticist, following the principle means that one should first try to hear the other side in the sense of really *listening* to it, and so of being open to transforming oneself through what one may learn, this being essential if a reconciliation is to take place. Truly listening is always necessary if one is to respond to a conflict with a conversation, though we must recognize that this is something which is often very difficult to do. For one thing, when a conflict involves goods that a person considers particularly significant, it will seem to them that they have potentially a great deal to lose, and this makes achieving the kind of openness that conversation requires especially challenging. For another, as is particularly the case in politics, it is often necessary that a decision be reached under pressing conditions, and yet achieving an understanding often takes time. In consequence, nothing I have said here should lead the reader to think that I have any illusions about the possibilities of conflicting parties ever being able to devote themselves totally to hearing as listening and so ever fully succeeding in treating their opponents as partners in a conversation rather than as adversaries. After all, if just one party does not wish to converse, then this is enough to ensure that conversation will be impossible. This is because, just as it requires all involved in a conflict to jointly take the step from force to negotiation, the same is true of the move from negotiation to conversation. The depressing reality is that it takes only one to carry everyone in the other direction.

Nor have I wished to assert that an escape from a profound moral or political conflict with the total reconciliation of the conflicting goods, one completely untainted by compromise, will ever be anything but the rarest and most extraordinary of achievements. My claim has only been that such an escape, even when it is only partial, is utterly ruled out if we follow the pluralist's interpretation of what it means to 'hear the other side' since, to pluralists, that maxim is but 'the principle of adversary argument'.[119] There is, it should be clear, little room for what I would describe as real listening here. The result: a zero-sum form of practical reasoning that makes compromise inevitable. With hermeneutics, however, giving at least some place to conversation makes way for the possibility that moral or political conflicts can conclude with decisions which may be described as varying mixtures of reconciliations and compromises of the goods in question, rather than as limited to the 'maiming and degrading' effects that necessarily accompany the latter.

The hermeneutical approach of transforming the whole in order to meet the goal of reconciliation can also consist of a much more radical

endeavour, in which we might say that there is more evolution than discovery of meaning involved in the reconciliation of the conflicting
goods. Take the conflict regarding Darius. This one seems intractable
and—at this point in our salesman's life—perhaps it is. But say we
change the example somewhat, and conceive of the agent, not as a salesman, but as a citizen of early classical Rome, one struggling to make a
decision about who should get, not his pet, but his slave. Despite—or
perhaps because of—his thinking long and hard about the matter, he
feels irrecusably struck by the sense that, whoever he chooses, his friend
or his relative, there will be a sense of loss associated with his failure to
meet the needs of the other. As with the case of Darius, there seems no
way out without compromise.

But let us say that our agent does not limit himself to the question
of how these two goods in particular play out in this context, but
begins instead to ask much wider questions, questions about the very
parameters of that context itself. Say he recalls a recent discussion he
had had with one of those Stoics, the one who argued so strenuously
against the practice of having metics or guest workers in Rome without
allowing them to become full citizens. Although our Roman
had rejected this strange proposition at the time, some of the claims
made did, inexplicably, resonate. Delving into the matter further now,
the Stoic's arguments for why metics should be allowed to become
full citizens begin to make more sense, and actually lead our Roman to
a clearer understanding of the meaning of human respect. Suddenly,
it dawns on him not only that the Stoic is right about metics, but
that this has significance for slavery as well, namely, that the practice
is simply unjust (this, of course, would have been the Stoic's next
step as well). And, as a direct result of this, the original dilemma
vanishes.

Now while pluralists, as I have explained, certainly have room for the
notion that persons may undergo significant moral conversions, be it as
the result of making a radical choice, or due to changes brought about
by a reasoning process,[120] there is still an important difference with
hermeneutics. That is because, to the pluralist, though our Roman might
change to the extent that the original conflict between his obligations
to friend and relative is no longer felt, this is not as a result of the goods
expressed by those obligations having been fulfilled. Rather, what
has happened is that, by deciding to free his slave, *both* the friend and
the relative have ended up neglected. Releasing the slave may be the
right thing to do, but it does not, for the pluralist, mean escape from
moral loss.

In hermeneutics, however, because a change to a part of one's hologram of goods always has an impact on all the others, it can be argued that the development regarding our Roman's new understanding of human respect has so affected his whole identity that not only do the goods of the original conflict no longer conflict with each other, but they should also not be construed as conflicting with the decision to free the slave. What has happened is that, from his new horizon, the thought of keeping the slave has simply become out of the question, indeed so much so that it no longer makes any sense to speak of there being obligations that exist for him on the basis of what he could do with a slave. The original conflict has thus been overcome, the transformation of his whole identity being so fundamental that it has caused those goods associated with it to 'disappear' into his pre-reflective background. As regards this particular context, then, they essentially no longer pose a problem for him. There is no reason to bemoan the difficulties associated with his lack of a slave because owning a slave has, to him, become simply inconceivable.

That the slave should be free is, of course, quite obvious to us today. It would, however, have been a great leap for the vast majority of citizens in early classical Rome. The Roman's dilemma regarding his slave would have been very real for him, its overcoming requiring a truly radical reinterpretation of a number of goods that he considered fundamental, even if, at first, they seemed irrelevant to the dilemma at hand. But if we recognize the integrated, holographic relation between the meanings of all our goods then the choice to search wide, throughout the vast reaches of one's whole identity, and the benefits of accepting such fundamental, radical changes to it, can make a great deal of sense.

The possibility of such radical reinterpretations should, once again, not lead one to think that, in hermeneutics, moral conflicts are always open to such satisfying resolutions. For we must remember the requirement that a rearticulation make greater sense of an agent's whole predicament, and so that it must ultimately be in harmony with the narrative, the 'quest' as MacIntyre would put it, that constitutes the meaning of his life. Any new interpretation must truly appear to the agent as providing an epistemic gain—one could not come to a new position on slavery simply because it was a convenient way to dissipate the dilemma. If the Roman did not really consider this move to be more reasonable, did not truly hear its call, then it simply could not become a viable option and he would be stuck with the dilemma as before. Analogously, we might imagine our salesman encountering a radical proponent of animal rights, one who objected to even the domestication of animals. Only if this position was truly considered compelling could our salesman consider the idea of 'freeing' Darius. If not, his dilemma would persist, and his choice between relative and friend would remain a compromising one.

One more point. For Gadamer, as I read him, while the change to an interpreter's identity sometimes necessary for making a successful interpretation can be more or less radical as a matter of degree, depending on the extent to which the goods involved in the moral conflict need to be reinterpreted, there is no sense in which the decision-making involved in the more radical reinterpretations is qualitatively different from that of the less radical ones. The point for him is always to assume a stance of 'self-forgetfulness'[121] or openness during interpretation if understanding, the discovery and evolution of meaning, is to be achieved. Taylor, however, can be interpreted as arguing that, at least when it comes to the responses made necessary by some of our most profound moral and political conflicts, the process of change required should be considered qualitatively different from the others, and to such an extent that it makes sense to understand the kind of originality of perception involved as consisting in something more than just a new 'interpretation', however radical, of the situation. One way of describing the difference here is to say that Taylor wants to grant a place to inspirations that claim a transcendent source, while Gadamer remains relatively anthropocentric. For Taylor, the less radical interpretations are those which take place comparatively comfortably within a certain architectonic structure of goods, that is, in a way that does not fundamentally challenge the foundations of that structure. While Gadamer can, of course, also be said to recognize that an identity is constituted by goods which are integrated into a certain relation with each other, the structure of that identity always remains somewhat more fluid and flexible for him than in Taylor's conception; changes in identity, even those that might be described as involving substantial moral conversions, are thus always more effusive, more flowing and continuous. As a result, Gadamer has been described as rejecting altogether the possibility of radical crisis, and so of being in no sense a 'prophet of extremity'.[122] For Taylor, however, the more radical changes may at times be understood as resulting in something like a shift between mindsets or, more accurately, between 'self-sets'. As he has written of these qualitatively different re-evaluations,

A re-evaluation of this kind, once embarked on, is of a peculiar sort. It is unlike a less than radical evaluation which is carried on within the terms of some fundamental evaluation, when I ask myself whether it would be honest to take advantage of this income-tax loophole, or smuggle something through customs. These latter can be carried on in a language which is out of dispute. In answering the questions just mentioned the term 'honest' is taken as beyond challenge. But in radical re-evaluations by definition the most basic terms, those in which other evaluations are carried on, are precisely what is in question. It is just because all formulations are potentially under suspicion of distorting their objects that we have to see them all as revisable, that we are forced back, as it were, to the inarticulate limit from which they originate.[123]

Such radical re-evaluations can thus be said to question the very foundations of the self's structure, to entail a change which is focused on its architectonic good or 'hypergood', a term Taylor uses to capture a similar idea.[124] They are thus revolutionary, in that they require a direct challenge to the heart of the edifice that is the self at that time, one which can lead the agent to break out of this structure by virtue of an inverting kind of 'transvaluation', to use Nietzsche's term, of the previous ranking of goods so as to establish a radically new structure.[125]

Such a transvaluation, many have noted, has had a central place in the foundation of modernity, in that it lies at the heart of the reversal of the hierarchy of goods affirmed by pre-moderns such as Aristotle. 'Life, and the good life' was how Aristotle described the goods of his ethics, those of 'life' (which Taylor invokes and reinterprets under his term 'the affirmation of ordinary life'[126]) being the subordinate, purely instrumental goods of work and the family, production and reproduction, and those of the 'good life' being constitutive of the higher vocations of philosophy or the honour ethic as expressed in politics. With modernity, however, has come an inversion of this ranking, the whole structure having thus been turned upside-down to such an extent that it is even possible today to speak of the 'obsolescence' of honour.[127] It is only because of a change as fundamental as this that a person today might intelligibly face a dilemma over who should get their pet but not, of course, over who should get their slave.

For Taylor, the kind of radical change that brought this about should be, at least at times, understood as involving something more than the usual interpretive reintegration of these goods into some new relation. As I (sometimes) read him, it is as if the Western identity, facing a series of deep and severe dilemmas, became torn in a way that opened it up to an inspiration, one which helped it to break out of the limits of its previous structure. The kind of change of meaning that this might be said to involve should be distinguished from that described in the less-radical cases above, such that it makes sense to speak of two kinds of change here, corresponding somewhat analogously to two of the kinds of mutation that are recognized in genetics. In genetics, one form of mutation is said to result from the *recombination* of genes as part of the production of progeny through sexual reproduction; another is *radiation-induced*, as when what is called 'base substitution', the replacement of one base pair of DNA by another during replication, is caused by ultraviolet light.[128] Gadamer, who, it seems, does not wish to go beyond hermeneutics is, I would claim, limited to something like the immanent bounds of the first, recombinatory kind of mutation. With Taylor, however, room is made for a version of the second, with the result that he might be said to recognize a distinction between *interpretation*, which, as has been shown, entails some combination of the discovery and evolution of meaning, and a more imaginative, more fundamentally original kind of *creation*, in which we might speak of evolution with little to no discovery.[129] To adopt a notion of creation of this sort, it seems to me, is to move somewhat beyond the dialogue and so the aural metaphors associated with interpretation, whether hermeneutical or pluralist, and recognize the possibility of a not-fully-rational or, perhaps, supra-rational means of responding to our situation, including our moral conflicts. We are moving beyond reason here because creation is, to some extent, beyond language, beyond *logos*. Within such a conception we might say that, when it comes to those difficult and rare moments of inspiration, it is as if some kind of light is able to enter in through the tear in the self and bathe its goods, or those constituting the work or action being created, with a new force, an energy which assists in their mutation into a radically new whole. 'There is a crack in everything,' sings Leonard Cohen, 'that's how the light gets in.'[130] With interpretation, however, the degree of newness or originality is usually more limited, as the interpreter must always strive to maintain a fidelity to what is being interpreted, to 'make sense' of it, to mediate its meaning into our lives, it being either an interpretation itself or a product of creation. This is not to say that interpretation may not also be understood as claiming a connection with the transcendent, though, if so, it must nevertheless be said to do so in a more indirect way than with creation, one that might be summed up with a paraphrase of a line of Simone Weil's: in progressing forward, we also progress up. Taylor, it seems to me, hints at a similar understanding when he writes:

If one of the fundamental uses of language is to articulate or make manifest the background of distinctions of worth we define ourselves by, how should we understand *what* is being manifested here? Is what we are articulating ultimately to be understood as our human response to our condition? Or is our articulation striving rather to be faithful to something beyond us, not explicable simply in terms of human response?[131]

In making room for creative transcendence, as well, however, for what Taylor has referred to as 'epiphanic' creativity as conceived of by the post-Romantic,[132] I am not claiming that it is possible for those who would create to achieve some kind of total purificatory *askesis*, a stance which not even the theistic mystic would entertain, nor that it could be viable to, in any sense, transcend humanity altogether;[133] rather, I am aiming to give a place to something in-between these two and anthropocentrism. And so, if we read the difference between Gadamer and Taylor, both believing Christians, along these lines, then (to take a rather extreme case) where, for Gadamer, Jesus' Sermon on the Mount can never be anything more than an *interpretation* of Christianity, for Taylor his speech may have involved something more. That being said, when it comes to interpreting those words, such interpretations should never be considered even a nominally closed matter, which is why we simply cannot follow the pluralist in summing up the ideals of Christianity in pure and 'uncompromised' forms, as if they could exist as fixed, universal, and isolable meanings.

Before I end this discussion on the matter of how we might respond to conflicts between incommensurable goods, I want to say something about the ramifications what I have said so far about hermeneutical interpretation should have for our responses to conflicts between ways of life over goods which, at the beginning of the conflict, cannot be described as shared, or at least in any significant sense. Though rejecting the pluralist's conception of imagination as a means of understanding remote cultures or ways of life, the hermeneuticist is not locked into ethnocentrism, the reason being that, as I showed above, the struggle to understand an other will demand change and, as such, learning and development. Moreover, the assumption that there exist ways of life which are permanently incompatible with each other is also rejected. For as all goods must always remain part of a context, and contexts change in history, then the pluralist notion that values can have meanings which, in the thin dimension at least, are to some extent fixed or permanent is also abandoned. Moreover, if the goods of every valid way of life are, to some extent, all integrated with the minimal universal few, then this must mean that the goods which, up to a certain point in time, have been exclusive to a way of life very different from one's own are, at least in principle, integratable with one's own as well, for those goods are also to some extent meaningfully connected with the same universal few. In the struggle to understand an especially foreign way of life, then, it should be helpful to focus on those practices most closely related to the minimal moral code, their loci being tied to our corporeal natures and so events such as those of the universal trinity of 'birth, and copulation, and death', as T. S. Eliot once put in.[134]

None of this means that the hermeneuticist has to abandon the recognition that there exist ways of life which are especially remote from each other. Indeed, the very fact that there are often fundamental failures of understanding between the members of different ways of life should be enough to support the notion that radical differences between them do indeed exist. Moreover, the inability to understand another way of life— whether it is one with which one can claim to share many goods, or only very few—is no reason to fail to make a presumption of respect regard- ing it,[135] just as, say, a lover of music for whom modern or alternative rock is appreciated exclusively has no reason to denigrate the classical music which he has never understood, or vice versa. It is this presump- tion that leads the hermeneuticist, like the pluralist, to support the notion that, in the case of a conflict with a way of life that one has not been able to understand, one should indeed be willing to negotiate, to make the necessary concessions. But for the hermeneuticist such nego- tiations should not only be conceived differently than with the pluralist (as I shall demonstrate in Chapter 4), but they should also be enter- tained only *after* a real attempt at conversation has failed.

For the possibility of achieving a real understanding with another should never be ruled out a priori. When there is success at such an endeavour, we should recognize, this will always be accompanied by greater sharing. In hermeneutics, there can be no comprehension without some sympathy of purpose, no way to understand even the remotest way of life without, to some extent, making the goods under- lying it at least partly one's own. The pluralist idea that one can come to know a good and yet refuse altogether to answer its call is thus rejected. In consequence, hermeneutics can be said to position itself somewhere in-between the, on the one hand, Stoic–Augustinian notion that human beings lay claim to a developed will and so the power to give or withhold assent, to radically choose, even as between good and evil and that, on the other, Socratic–Platonic 'to know the good is to do the good' conception. To speak of persons being confronted by a good in hermeneutics is to say that they cannot but recognize it as laying claim to a place on their personal rankings, though where exactly that place will be is still, to some extent, a matter of choice. To the hermeneuticist, then, we might say that goods do not only, as with the pluralist's values, *justify* specific ways of life, this being a notion which allows that an inter- preter may always choose to completely disregard those goods with which he has come into contact, for goods may also be said to actually make a *call* on those who are confronted by them, and such a call may never go completely unheeded.[136]

And yet, since persons always come from more-or-less unique con- texts, that is, since they always bring unique horizons to bear, how they respond to that call and so understand the goods that they have come to share with others will always be to some extent different. That is why there is never a danger of understanding leading to uniformity. Greater sharing, yes, but uniformity, not at all.

ii

On, now, to an examination of the product, as distinct from the process, of practical reasoning about conflicting incommensurables. Hermeneutics, I want to argue, offers us the possibility of resolutions of greater quality than pluralism. As I have shown, in hermeneutics a moral conflict between incommensurables can admit of two possibilities. On the best case scenario, the agent is able to reconcile or more fully integrate the conflicting goods, causing them to fade into her pre-reflective background, thus completely eliminating the conflict without moral loss. While this may be the case with those goods in that particular context, this is not to say that we should understand the agent as ever achieving a transformation of the whole of her goods into some kind of final unity. Though error may be reduced, it cannot be completely eliminated; though the agent may come to understand her hologram of goods as having a more integrated structure than before, it would be wrong to ever speak of it as being totally unified such that she will never again have to face a genuine moral conflict. Indeed, because of the connection of all goods in the whole, reconciling those involved in one particular conflict can easily lead to new conflicts coming forth from regions where, until that point in time, there had seemed to be no difficulties. None of this, however, detracts from the hermeneutical idea that it is sometimes possible, no matter how acute the dilemma, to reconcile the goods involved and so to overcome that conflict with little or no moral loss or remainder. This stands not only for those conflicts faced by a single person or by a number of persons over their shared goods, but also for those involving goods which, at least at the beginning of the conflict, the participants cannot, in any significant sense, be said to share.

I think we can interpret Wittgenstein as claiming something like this as regards the possible outcomes of moral conflicts. When asked about the case of a man who is confronting a choice between either leaving his wife or abandoning his work on cancer research—though he feels deeply committed to both—Wittgenstein is reported as saying:

Here we may say that we have all the materials of a tragedy; and we could only say: 'Well, God help you.' Whatever he finally does, the way things then turn out may affect his attitude. He may say, 'Well, thank God I left her: it was better all around.' Or maybe, 'Thank God I stuck to her.' Or he may not be able to say 'thank God' at all, but just the opposite. I want to say that this is the solution of an ethical problem.[137]

This has been interpreted along pluralist lines, in which it is claimed that Wittgenstein is asserting that the situation is necessarily exhibitive of dirty hands, that it consists of 'a tragic choice faced by the agent, in which there is no guilt-free way out'.[138] But this seems to me to miss the significance of how Wittgenstein puts the second possible outcome, the one summed up with the 'Thank God I stuck to her.' For it is without the 'it was better all around' qualification that accompanies the first outcome, a qualification which, as I read it, points to the presence of a degree of moral loss or compromise. One might object that avoidance of compromise in the second outcome is due to the man having found an instrumental means of making the two goods compossible, but this is ruled out when we recognize that the decision is understood to be one which 'may affect his attitude', for substantial changes to a person's identity are rarely the outcome of instrumental reasoning, such reasoning being more reductive than transformative. The second outcome, then, should be read as pointing to the possibility that, for Wittgenstein, the man may be able to find a way to reconcile the conflicting goods without compromise.

And yet, the first scenario, as well as the third (in which the agent 'may not be able to say "thank God" at all, but just the opposite') points to the other possible outcome of a moral conflict recognized by the hermeneuticist, that in which the agent has been unable to find a way to reconcile the goods without compromise. If he must choose, however, then we are left with an outcome that is closer to that which the pluralist claims is the inevitable result of all conflicts between incommensurables, in which the best thing the agent can think of doing still seems to some extent morally deficient. That being said, there are still important differences between the pluralist and hermeneutic conceptions of this outcome. For where the pluralist would identify the agent's feelings towards the moral remainder as simply those of the guilt associated with a certain kind of regret, that constitutive of dirty hands, the hermeneuticist's greater holism lends support to a significantly different characterization. It is because of its holographic holism that hermeneutics, as I have pointed out, strives to drop notions such as 'criteria' as they invoke a conception of goods as isolable standards. This holism, moreover, also supports the idea that, in cases of conflict where the goods are not able to be integrated, what the pluralist would identify as an independently distinct moral remainder is, instead, a much more hazy phenomenon. To the pluralist, the moral loss embodied in the remainder of a moral dilemma should be just as isolable and clearly identifiable as the extent of moral loss associated with a more straightforwardly immoral act, as when a person does something out of, say, greed or spite.[139] Thus, the pluralist claims, while it may make sense for the agent who does wrong from within a moral dilemma to claim mitigating circumstances, and so properly accept less reproof for his or her actions, the immorality of the justifiable but dirty act is not conceptually different from that associated with an act that is simply bad,[140] hence the unqualified ascription of guilt.[141] For, to the pluralist, the moral remainder = wrongdoing = guilt.

This is all too unsubtle for hermeneutics. To the hermeneuticist, the pluralist's 'moral remainder' is a far too clearly demarcated entity, since the tension arising out of a moral conflict is understood to resound throughout the whole of an agent's hologram of goods and this, we should recognize, will interfere with his or her moral perception. To face up to a moral dilemma of great significance, the hermeneuticist claims, is to put the whole of your self radically in question, this being a time when 'you say your name like you're no longer convinced'.[142] The agent, then, should have about as much difficulty being clear about the contours of a potential moral remainder as he would about the goodness of fulfilling whatever good(s) he thinks he can fulfil.[143] In consequence, when the act is performed, 'guilt' should be considered far too blunt a description of his state of responsibility, for he is in what we might call a state of 'moral discomposure', and so will have great difficulty in discriminating clearly between the moral significances of his actions. Moreover, depending on the extent of that difficulty, we should accept that there will be ramifications for the ascription of responsibility, namely that, in the more muffled cases, we might describe his hands as more 'messy' than 'dirty'. Because if a person's whole self remains highly discordant, if, that is, he must decide despite being unable to find a way to 'pull himself together', then it makes no sense to claim that he is able to isolate one part of his action and understand it as something clearly good while another part, that expressive of the good(s) he is compromising, may be identified as unambiguously bad. Because the agent is acting from within a state of confusion and perplexity about his context as a whole, he will have a rather hazy feeling that he is/might be doing something wrong. Since responsibility is meant to accrue to an agent who is, or should be, largely clear about the meaning of his actions, then we should not speak of responsibility, or at least full responsibility, here. What someone should (and, indeed, normally does) feel in such circumstances is, we must recognize, something significantly different from straight guilt.

Moreover, the pluralist's demand that we pit one part of our selves *against* another rather than attempt to integrate or reconcile them not only does nothing to overcome this confusion and perplexity, but it can actually entrench and even exacerbate the discordance, perhaps to the point of bringing about a distressingly divided, fragmented self. For not only can we assume that, to the pluralist, the longer a person lives the more often he or she will find it necessary to compromise values, and so the dirtier and more fragmented they will become, but it also makes sense to regard the cumulative effects of these compromises as ultimately threatening to their very sanity. Senior citizens may or may not be persons who are particularly wise, but they will, at least in the pluralist perspective, almost certainly be those who, as veterans of many moral conflicts, are particularly dirty and even, perhaps, a bit unbalanced. That is why, according to Hampshire, when people grow older 'they will normally perceive that they are going lop-sided to the grave'.[144] With this, Hampshire seems to be indicating his recognition of the damaging potential the division of a self into independent, clashing parts can have for a person's mental health. To Walzer, however, 'the self is capable of division and even thrives on it'.[145] Contrast this with R. D. Laing's discussion of the problems of a 'schizoid' self in his classic, *The Divided Self*,[146] as well as those more recent developments in the study of mental health, in which the concept of sanity is becoming increasingly associated with a person's ability to maintain a self that is 'cohesive'[147] or, as I would put it, 'integrated'.[148]

Moreover, just as the assertion of a plurality of independently distinct values and the compromising that it makes inevitable when they conflict may be distortive of the 'dialogue' between the parts of a self,[149] so too can it do damage to the relationships between persons or groups, the parts of a society. This is because if parties who share conflicting values can, at best, negotiate trade-offs between them, then this, in certain cases, can actually make the conflict more acute, not to mention doing damage to the values involved. To show how this can be so, I want to take up a phenomenon that the anthropologist Gregory Bateson has identified with his (somewhat awkward) term 'complementary schismogenesis'. Bateson's notion has been used by the linguist Deborah Tannen in her popular study of the kinds of dialogue that take place between genders in the anglophone world. As she writes:

Complementary schismogenesis commonly sets in when women and men have divergent sensitivities and hypersensitivities. For example, a man who fears losing freedom pulls away at the first sign he interprets as an attempt to 'control' him, but pulling away is just the signal that sets off alarms for the woman who fears losing intimacy. Her attempts to get close will aggravate his fear, and his reaction—pulling further away—will aggravate hers, and so on, in an ever-widening spiral.[150]

In this conflict over shared goods, the man clearly desires greater individual liberty while, for the woman, it is the common good constitutive of their romantic relationship that is in need of greater fulfilment. As Bateson has described it, a conflict of this sort is 'a process which if not restrained can only lead to more and more extreme rivalry and ultimately to hostility and the breakdown of the whole system'.[151] In order to stay together, then, the two might try to negotiate a compromise. But part of what is driving the conflict in the first place is their fear of the motives of the other, and this will not go away even if they successfully hammer out a 'fair deal'. Though they may come up with a scenario they would both describe as 'fair' (he will spend somewhat less time down at the pub with the boys; and she will stop nagging him about spending so much time there), the feelings of concern and resentment that drove the conflict will linger, and will do so even if both parties fully meet their side of the bargain. This is because negotiation, lacking the transformative quality of conversation, leaves the meanings of the items at stake compromised but unaltered in any fundamental sense. The point, then, is not, as Bateson recommends, to 'restrain' the process, but rather to overcome it. And to accomplish this what is required is the greater understanding and sharing that comes from conversation. Engaging in negotiation not only does nothing to overcome the conflicts between parties, but it may even exacerbate them. This is particularly true when, as in the case here, the conflict involves a disagreement about a particular kind of good—the couple's romantic relationship—which the parties hold in common. For common goods require an especially close kind of sharing, one which can only be marred by the emphasis on the independence of conflicting parties that is inherent to negotiation.[152]

V

The hermeneuticist, then, would make room for conversation, and not just negotiation, as a response to moral and political conflict. The kind of reconciliation that is aimed for by this hermeneutical understanding of conversation is, to recall the point made in Chapter 1, very different from those associated with neutralist conceptions of interpretation, for it consists of aiming for an engaged, rather than disengaged, objectivity. Indeed, the difference here is so great that it makes sense to interpret hermeneutics as lending support to a conception of modern politics that is neither neutralist nor pluralist, but what I call patriotic. It is towards a more direct examination of this patriotic politics that I now wish to turn.

4

Towards the Patriotic Polity

We must suffer, suffer into truth.

   Aeschylus, *The Orestia*

If I ever do a book on the Amazon, I hope I am able to bring a certain lightheartedness to the subject, in a way that tells the reader we are going to have fun with this thing.

Jack Handy, Deep Thoughts

I

The differences in approach between the pluralist and the hermeneuticist as regards both the process and the product of practical reason lead, as might be expected, to differences as regards their overall attitudes to moral and political conflicts. Pluralists, as should be quite evident by now, feel quite negative about these things. To them, to face up to a genuine conflict between incommensurables is to recognize that one will not be able to escape without doing some moral wrong. And since politics is a realm which is riddled with such conflicts, many of which are especially significant due to the high stakes involved, pluralists will be found clearly echoing Max Weber's pessimism in their portrayals of it.[1] Thus, for Hampshire, politics is the world of 'experience' which is to be appreciated partly by its contrast with 'innocence';[2] it is a realm unique in its level of 'moral disagreeableness', as Williams has described;[3] while, for Walzer, politicians are persons to be feared, for they are the sort that willingly choose to 'fall' into conflicts, to learn 'how not to be good'.[4] And finally, to Berlin,

No body of men which has tasted power, or is within a short distance of doing so, can avoid a certain degree of that cynicism which, like a chemical reaction, is generated by the sharp contact between the pure ideal, nurtured in the wilderness, and its realization in some unpredicted form which seldom conforms to the hopes or fears of earlier times.[5]

A neutralist inference from all this, one that (to their credit) pluralists will not be found endorsing, entails the claim that reason itself calls upon us to try and avoid or minimize moral conflicts in our lives,[6] and so that there must be something irrational about those who would willingly dirty themselves by entering the political realm.

And what of that realm? At least as regards the increasingly multi-cultural societies of the West, the pluralist assertion that negotiation constitutes the best possible response to a conflict between ways of life is based on the assumption that we must draw solid, not broken, lines between them conceptually, that they are 'separate' or even, as Hampshire has put it, 'natural enemies'.[7] And to those pluralists who would be liberal, what seems feasible is only a 'liberalism of fear', to use the title of a set of lectures once delivered by Williams,[8] a regime in which conflicting groups can stand to each other only as threats to their respective conceptions of the good.

If we reject pluralism, however, it becomes possible—but only this—to be much more optimistic about the potential outcomes of moral and political conflicts. For by accepting that such conflicts may sometimes contribute to the reaching of what is, overall, a better position for all by virtue of the transformation of the meanings of the goods involved, there is reason to conceive of them as great potential sources—not just of compromise—but also of learning, of self-development, growth, progress, wisdom, indeed of truth. There is, one may gather, an importantly different interpretation of the tragic dimension of ethics and politics here. When pluralists refer to tragedy, it is clear that they do so to invoke a sense of unmitigated fall or catastrophe, which they associate with the compromises that one is forced to make in the face of particularly acute moral or political conflicts. My hermeneutical arguments can be read, however, as claiming that we should strive to make room for a ray of hope in tragedy. In so doing, we might find it useful to turn somewhat away from the thoroughly catastrophic conception of it found in the works of Sophocles, Euripides, and Shakespeare, and towards Aeschylus. *Pathei mathos*, 'we must suffer, suffer into truth',[9] is the message of his *Oresteian Trilogy*, one rarely taken up again in tragic drama until Goethe and Schiller. In the third play, the *Eumenides*, we are presented with Hermes, the messenger of the gods or, we may say, of the diversity of goods, including those of the earth, as embodied in the Furies, and those of Olympus, as represented by Apollo. It is Athena, the goddess of wisdom, who brings these two groups together in a moment of exaltation, though what is created is not a perfect, unified harmony, but one which is instead a spur to further struggle. In the same way, the compromises necessitated by negotiation can be considered not, as with the pluralist, as simply catastrophic, but also as progressive, as contributing to the teleological journey towards greater truth that should be a central aim of any society.

And yet, is it right to stress, as Gadamer and Wittgenstein do, the tragic character of this quest, even when we conceive of tragedy along Oresteian lines? For one point of the hermeneutical approach is to make possible a reconciliatory or integrative route to dealing with conflict, one free of compromise. The assumption here, then, is that this pursuit of greater integration, of progress, of truth, can take place within a rich and messy—and not just dirty—world. Moreover, if we are right to interpret the West as having undergone a transvaluation with modernity, with primacy now being given to the previously subordinate 'ordinary life', then this is another reason that we should focus our attention, not only on tragedy, but also on comedy. For the comic, particularly in the form of the New Comedy from Menander on, emphasizes progress even more strongly than does the Oresteian type of tragedy. What frequently happens in New Comedy is that a rather ordinary young man tries to get together with an ordinary young woman but their union is obstructed by others, these blocking characters, 'humours' as Ben Jonson labelled them, being the sort that are dominated by a single, isolated obsession. The story ends when the obstacles are overcome and the two are able to get together. As Northrope Frye has described the genre,

In New Comedy an absurd or obviously unjust situation forms most of the comic action, and a more sensible order of things is reached at the end of a teleological plot. In comic drama there is, as a rule, a final scene in which everyone is assembled on the stage, forming a new society that crystallizes around the united pair.[10]

'The theme of the comic', Frye has thus summed up elsewhere, 'is the integration of society.'[11] The point, then, is not to have the humours compromised, but rather reformed, reconciled. The message should be clear. Politically active groups, even when they represent especially remote ways of life, should be encouraged, not so much to negotiate with each other as 'natural enemies' when they conflict, but rather to try to converse with and learn from each other, to come to understand and, in different ways, more closely share in the goods which animate the diverse ethical horizons they express. Because comedy is meant to speak to and about the ordinary person, perhaps it, and not tragedy, has the most to teach us in this regard. Literature has, after all, witnessed something of a 'death of tragedy',[12] and this surely has some relation to the modern shift in focus from the hero, whose great fall is amongst tragedy's most potent fuels, to the everyday individual, the carrier of equal dignity. Comedy shares in this focus. Moreover, there is no reason to think—for those who are willing to grant the capacity to tragedy—that comedy is incapable of its own kind of connection to the transcendent, of its own epiphanies. The first goal of humour is, after all, precisely to 'crack you up'; nor should we forget that Teresa of Avila, recognized as one of the greatest mystics in the apophatic tradition, has been designated the patron saint of hysteria.

What, then, should all this mean for our attitude to politics? Am I claiming that those who approach it, whether as philosophers, ideologists, or practitioners, should do so with a greater sense of humour? Perhaps. I certainly hope that my 'birth of a salesman' tale *vis-à-vis* Darius of the previous chapter was no barrier to understanding. My message, rather, is more that to make room for laughter in and about the political realm is one not insignificant way of putting a needed crack in the seal of its increasingly hermetic prison of pessimism. Though a cynical attitude is, of course, appropriate in the face of a fundamentally corrupt regime, we should allow for at least the possibility of a better politics, and so reclaim that measure of hope being stolen from us by the propagators of 'dirty hands'. Though there is certainly no reason to assume an undue optimism, there is also no place for the essentially a priori pessimism entailed by the pluralist's response to conflict. For it is not the place of philosophy to tell us whether our moral or political lives will be bitter, sweet, or both. That is why even the realities of politics should not only be feared but, as with any great work of art, should be conceived of as expressions of the richness of meaning to be embraced therein. Politics, for those willing and able to grasp it, can be a source of great potential and growth.

Changing attitudes about politics, moreover, is important not only for those of us who are practitioners or interpreters of the art. For the unrelenting pessimism advocated by pluralists and others can only contribute to the legitimation crisis that many have argued threatens modern polities today. If, at best, citizens can interpret the policies emitting from their governments as nothing more than the products of compromises or piecemeal accommodations, then how can they ever be expected to follow them as authentic expressions of their political sensibilities? Like those who, as with the couple in the previous chapter, would 'negotiate' with a lover, they cannot but feel the resentment that stems from the corruption by compromise of ideals they hold dear, and so they cannot be expected to do anything more than reluctantly fulfil whatever 'deal' is finally reached. In time, moreover, those compromises will come to seem less and less palatable, even as they seem more and more inescapable due to the conception of political conflicts as being based upon a 'clash of absolutes', to borrow a phrase from the title of a well-known pluralist work on the politics of abortion.[13] That some of the antagonists in that particular conflict in the United States have recently turned to violence should thus come as no surprise. We need better articulations of our goods as a whole if these 'moral sources', as Taylor has referred to them, are to empower our agency. For it is only due to the power that emits from the integration of once conflicting goods that citizens can be animated to enthusiastically uphold the laws which express what is shared throughout their societies.

II

To take a hermeneutical approach to interpretation and so practical reason is, as I demonstrated in the previous chapter, to assume a particular conception of what it means for goods and ways of life to be distinct. Language, to the hermeneuticist, is expressive in a different way than it is for the pluralist, it being assumed that the parts of a way of life, its goods, are, at base, practices rather than understandings, activities rather than concepts or self-enclosed, inert, mentalistic entities. Unlike the values of pluralism, a practice can never, without distortion, be isolated from the other practices with which it is always to some extent an integrated part, this being a corollary of the hermeneutical principle that all features of a language contain the whole. Under this more holistic conception of meaning, as I also argued, making good distinctions, be it between the goods within ways of life or between ways of life as a whole, should consist of drawing dotted—and not solid—lines. And this means that, if we accept the pluralist's own assertion that there is a minimal moral code shared by every way of life, then the recognition that some sharing exists between all ways of life says something about the limits of their remoteness. Because if no single part of any way of life is ever entirely separate from the other parts, and if some parts are always directly connected with those of this minimal moral code, then this means that all parts of every way of life are at least indirectly connected.

All of this opens up another conception of how we might deal with conflicts between goods, one which is granted a significant place by those who would take a patriotic approach to politics. To the patriot, when two or more goods conflict, whether they exist as parts of the same or different ways of life, the fact that they are *already* to some extent integrated means that, even at the point of conflict, those affirming them may be said to share much more than the pluralist is willing to admit. And the fact of there being something shared means that it makes sense to at least try to respond to that conflict by attempting their reconciliation. The aim, then, should never only be to *accommodate* a political conflict, to encourage the differing parties to tolerate each other and so negotiate, for it may be possible to *overcome* such a conflict with greater understanding through a conversation-produced reconciliation, thus bringing the whole of a society's parts closer together by strengthening the purposes that all its citizens may be said to share. This goal, as I understand it, entails fulfilling a version of the civic aspects of political liberty, that common good which has come down to us from the classical republican tradition. To the pluralist, however, the kind of talk that might go on between antagonists representing remote ways of life cannot aim for sharing as it cannot go beyond that of 'miscommunication', as Andrew Mason has described.[14] But to the patriot it is just this assumption that leads pluralists to respond to moral and political conflicts one step too late, for it is, in order of preference, 'conversation first, negotiation second, and force third' that constitutes the patriot's central maxim of politics.

And so, if a conflict between parties is to be met with a conversation which strives, as described in the previous chapter, to discover and bring about the evolution of the meaning shared by the conflicting goods, then we get a very different conception of the border between state and civil society than that asserted by the pluralist, one in which heeding, to some extent, the demands of those who would reject this border altogether, be they classical republicans, nationalists, or religious devotees, does not always have to involve making negotiated concessions and so putting indentations in the—as the pluralist would have it—solid line that runs between the two domains. Instead, it can also involve a transformation of the conflicting goods, one which may be said to take place through the already present spaces in that line. Indeed, to the patriot, the pluralist's assumption that the line is unbroken necessarily distorts the expression of political liberty. For we must always go at least part of the way with the classical republican and so conceive of the line between government and civil society as dotted, this being another way of saying that members of civil society should never simply *use* government to achieve their separate ends as they must also understand it as at least partly expressive of who they are, of their very identities. Government should not only be a tool of citizens but also one of their ends itself, one which all in society, in various ways and to varying degrees, share. Moreover, depending on the society, other public common goods should also receive their due, and in a way which also requires rejecting the

conception of the line between state and civil society as solid. As regards
the needs of the nationalist, for example, recognition is inherently about
reaching a kind of understanding, one which can be properly arrived at
only from within a process of conversation and not one of negotiation.[15]
This comes out particularly clearly when we take account of the French
and German words for recognition, *reconnaissance* and *anerkennen*,
each of which have 'knowledge', *connaître* and *erkennen*, as their roots.
The fact is that one either knows and so recognizes or one does not, this
being not the kind of thing that can be given or taken away like some
bargaining chip in a negotiating session, a point all-too-often forgotten
by both those demanding, and those offering, recognition.[16]

Of course, nationalists and classical republicans, as well as certain religious believers, have been known to go much further than this. With
nationalism little need be said on the matter, not when we look back
upon a century that has witnessed so many unspeakable horrors committed in the name of its chauvinistic forms. As for the few, if any, classical republicans around today, they can be said to interpret support for
a free civil society as but the demands of that futile, levelled-down nar-
cissism which, the claim goes, took root with the advent of modernity;
to them, citizens should not value participation in government as one
intrinsic good among many, ranked by each individual their own way,
but as *the* privileged locus of the good life. Finally, many religions have,
of course, far from an unblemished history. It is clear, then, that if some
of the advocates of certain public common goods were to fully have
their way, the line between government and civil society would have to
be completely erased. This is certainly true of many who have called
themselves patriots, both past and present. With classical republicanism,
government would be expected to fully overrun civil society and the
nation(s), ethnic group(s), and other voluntary associations within it
while, with nationalism, its followers sometimes conceive of it as requiring the virtual swallowing up of the state within the common will of the
nation. Either way, modern politics would have to be expelled. Patriotism as I defend it could never accept this, for it asserts that, whatever
ideology citizens may wish to support, they will have to, at minimum,
maintain a significant respect of the individual, a principle which, given
special prominence in liberalism, allows that ideology to virtually define
itself 'unceasingly by the refusal of a complete reconciliation between
civil society and the state, one which implies the disappearance of one
of the two terms'.[17] Reconciliation of the goods located in the two
domains should always be a central goal, but it is one which, we must
accept, will never be wholly achieved, which is why it ought to be striven
for in a way that never fails to respect the (albeit dotted) line lying
between them. It is the admittedly difficult task of the follower of

patriotism the political philosophy both to give proper expression to such aspirations as those of national self-determination and citizen self-rule, and yet to do so without failing to respect the individual.

Bernard Crick and Charles Taylor are two political philosophers who seem to me to be calling on us to do exactly this. The case of Crick is slightly less clear, as there are times when he sounds like a pluralist, and others when he seems to echo the philosophers of unity. In keeping with pluralist terminology, he writes of 'values' rather than 'goods', and in a way that, at certain times, indicates that he conceives of them as 'things'[18] in the sense of being independently distinct, separable entities which can not only be conceived in a disinterested, 'value-free'[19] way but which are also not subject to that 'inflated premise' that everything is interrelated.[20] On the other extreme, however, Crick seems to concur with a statement of Aristotle's, one in which, as is typical of a monistic philosopher, Aristotle fails to emphasize that political participation must always be understood as expressing an intrinsic and not only instrumental good.[21] But that Crick is, on the whole, a patriot is clear from the room he would make for an essentially positive attitude to politics[22] (this contrasting with the pluralist's all-too-thorough pessimism and the monist's shunning of its inherently conflictual and disordered nature), as well as a number of other positions advanced in his writings. To begin with, Crick clearly has room for those especially public common goods, those whose expression in practice cannot be limited to the bounds of civil society, and in a way that does not assume that they must necessarily provide the bases for negotiations. For he sometimes goes so far as to designate the politics he defends as 'republicanism',[23] and he has also granted a significant place to nationalism, the intention being that both of these be reconciled with each other.[24]

Though there are times when Crick fails to distinguish his understanding of liberty from that version of it to be found within classical republicanism, the politics he defends should nevertheless ultimately be interpreted as modern, as is clear from what he has to say about the liberty of the individual. For Hannah Arendt, individuals are free to the extent that they can participate in the life of government, this being why she is able to turn to the ancient Athenian *polis* as a model for a society which respects liberty.[25] To most of us in the modern age, however, limiting liberty to this conception will be difficult to accept for many a citizen may choose a life which has little to do with governing in common with others and yet will still be considered free. What Arendt is referring to, then, is the classical republican's *political* liberty, one that is limited to the kind of politics that goes on in and around a government. This political liberty, I have asserted, should indeed be recognized as an intrinsic good, though, unlike with the classical republican, it will have to be conceived of as one such good among many if it is a modern conception of politics that we wish to defend. And among those other goods will be the liberty of the individual, that 'liberty of the moderns' that Benjamin Constant referred to in his famous speech.[26] Individual liberty has, of course, been defended along the lines of some very different philosophical strategies, with the result that it has been articulated in a variety of different ways, including that derived from natural law, or as negative liberty, as self-ownership, authenticity, autonomy (in both Kant's sense and in the very different, socially embedded conception advocated by many pluralists as described in Chapter 2), and so on. Crick, in the course of arguing against Berlin's negative conception, has made it clear that, rather than following Arendt in her call for a return to Athens, he would instead turn to what he has referred to as the 'freedom as citizenship' view which had a certain prominence in the seventeenth and eighteenth centuries.[27] This, it seems to me, is a conception of individual and not, as in the sense above, of political liberty, though it is one that, contra Constant, is not assumed to be fundamentally incompatible with granting a place to some version of the latter as an intrinsic and not only instrumental good. Though room must always be made for the recognition that there will be times when the two ideals—one enabling the choices that are integral to life within civil society, and the other tied to the politics both within civil society and around the activities of a state—conflict,[28] the hope is always that they can be reconciled.

Many pluralists, as I pointed out in Chapter 2, also recognize the conflict between them. But they must be distinguished from patriots in their assertion that compromise is an inescapable part of any response to that conflict, a claim which can only distort political liberty. As I read Crick, however, his preference is for integration rather than compromise, for he has written that 'conciliation'[29] may also play a role in responding to a given conflict. To him the dialogues of politics should not be limited to negotiation but ought to include conversation as well since 'politics is a process of discussion, and discussion demands, in the original Greek sense, dialectic'.[30] Thus where, to a pluralist such as Hampshire, the procedural values included within the universal minimal moral code demand only that representatives of different ways of life negotiate with each other when they conflict, Crick would assert that recognizing such a code also requires giving a place to a 'respect for reasoning', this necessitating 'a *willingness* to give reasons (however ill-informed or simple) why one holds a view and to give justifications for one's actions, and to demand them of others'.[31] One, of course, often gives reasons while negotiating as well, but these are not of the *just-ifying* kind, for negotiation is not about trying to convince one's adversaries that one's position is just, that they should come to affirm it as their own, as the aim is only to get them to accept certain compromises to whatever position they came to the table with. Not so with conversation, the direct and central point of which is truth.

Moreover, Crick's conception of integration exhibits two of the characteristics that I consider fundamental to patriotic politics: (i) it is (potentially) progressive; and (ii) it is allied with the notion of there being a public common good, one which speaks to the society as a whole. In keeping with (i), Crick takes the route of treading in-between the pluralist's comprehensive rejection of teleology on the one hand, and Aristotle's naturalistic teleology on the other.[32] For it is clear that he is much more comfortable with talk of purposive progress in politics than is the pluralist. 'Those', he has written, 'who urge us to remember that our only clearly demonstrable task is simply to keep the ship [of state] afloat have a rather curious view of the purpose of ships.'[33]

That Crick's support of some form of teleology is not at odds with the rejection of monism or unity that both pluralists and patriots consider integral to politics comes to the fore when he qualifies the ship metaphor by making clear that he wants to speak not of a single ship, 'but a convoy'.[34] This seems to me to capture the patriotic conception of politics almost perfectly, for it at once does justice to the various distinct groups in civil society, as well as to the common purpose(s) that they all share. Where the pluralist, at least when it comes to the conflicts between those groups, has no place for even their partial integration, and so might be said to support talk of a number of wandering, sometimes colliding, ships, Crick admirably treads the path in-between plurality and unity. The recognition of distinct and sometimes conflicting voluntary associations is shared with the pluralist,[35] but this done in a way which grants a place to the common good of all. 'If this sounds like a version of "pluralism",' he has written of his approach, 'it is—subject only to the function of the state to preserve order at all.'[36] It is this 'order' that, it seems to me, makes all the difference. For Crick is aptly aware that, properly understood, order is a function, not of the fragmented and fragmenting negotiatory politics of pluralism as I have described it, but of the recognition that, in the long run, a polity can sustain itself, can maintain its legitimacy before its citizens, only by, at least on some occasions, successfully reconciling the goods underlying its conflicts.

I have qualified, somewhat, my praise of Crick's use of the classic 'ship of state' metaphor because it seems to me to have the drawback of perpetuating the notion that the state, understood as not just a tool but also as an expression of the intrinsic goods shared by a citizenry, is not so much an integral part of the 'river' of that citizenry's practices but is more like a self-enclosed thing floating along in the water. It is for this reason that I want to suggest an alternative metaphor, one which compares the state, not to a sailing ship, but to a swimming whale. For whales are often able to achieve what in the study of hydrodynamics is called 'laminar flow', this referring to their ability to harmonize with the current in which they swim, enabling them to move without friction or drag. As Gordon Downie, lead singer of The Tragically Hip, has described this, 'the layers of the whale—the skin, the blubber, the underlying connective tissue—have the ability to replicate fluids in motion, almost as if the big whale itself were a giant piece of fluid going through the water'.[37] Analogously, the successful reconciliation of conflicts between groups in a polity might be conceived of as contributing to the state's ability to achieve a similar sort of laminar flow with respect to the practices shared by its citizenry. By virtue of its doing so the state's legitimacy is enhanced, and this, as I have said, contributes to a secure and ordered society overall.

Such a society, we may thus say, is a product of the successful political struggle to be true to the goods shared in common by its members, and that struggle is best engaged in with the integrative processes encouraged by patriotic politics. As Crick puts it: 'This common good is itself the process of practical reconciliation of the interests of the various "sciences", aggregates, or groups which compose a state ... Ideally politics draws all these groups into each other so that they each and together can make a positive contribution towards the general business of government, the maintaining of order.'[38] Politics should thus recognize diversity *and* help us along the path to unity.[39] And so Crick, we may say, grants an important place to the whole as well as to the parts, to the public common good(s) that are shared by all as well as to those goods which constitute the various distinct civil associations. As he himself writes, 'politics is, as it were, an interaction between the mutual dependence of the whole and some sense of independence of the parts'.[40] The line he would draw between the state and civil society is thus dotted rather than solid for, to him, 'freedom depends both on some distinction and on some *interplay* between private and public actions'.[41] Only a patriot, it seems to me, could make such an assertion.

And this, in effect, is also what Charles Taylor does. To Taylor, civil society should be not so much something 'outside political [i.e. the state's] power; rather it penetrates deeply into this power, fragments and decentralizes it. Its components are truly "amphibious"'.[42] Taylor has obviously been influenced here by Hegel's paradigmatic articulation of civil society in his *Philosophy of Right*, in which the domain is portrayed as existing only in *partial* independence from the state,[43] though, in rejecting the syncretic unity of vision Hegel asserts,[44] Taylor ends up supporting a distinction between the two domains that is necessarily stronger than Hegel's.[45] In consequence, as regards the market economy subdomain of civil society, Taylor has always recommended a corporatist (as distinct from neo-corporatist) 'interweaving'[46] of state and economy. As for the public sphere, Taylor's call for the decentralization of political power is one which, unlike that of most pluralists, is made for intrinsic as well as instrumentalist reasons, for he rejects the conception of civil associations as fully independent of or separate from government. This comes out particularly clearly in his discussion of what he has referred to as 'nested public spheres', in which the kinds of debates that go on within certain civil associations are considered able to contribute to the development of their society's political agenda as a whole.[47] To Taylor, though these groups are formally located outside of the institutions of the state, there is nevertheless a sense in which participating in them entails to some extent participating *in*, and not just *on*, that state. That is why, in what could be interpreted as a direct attack on the solid walls of pluralism, he writes that 'The boundary between the [state] system and the public sphere has to be relaxed. Some of the most effective nested public spheres are in fact political parties and advocacy movements which operate in the grey zone between the two. In a modern democratic polity, the boundary between [state] system and public sphere has to be maximally porous.'[48]

Complementing this concern with making proper distinctions is one regarding the failure to give due place to public common goods. To Taylor, Tocqueville was certainly right to consider atomism, in the form of that unhealthy, asocial form of individualism, as a foremost internal threat to modern politics, but today it seems clear that it is the rise of a fragmentary politics, much more than Tocqueville's 'democratic despotism', that engenders apathy when it comes to the needs of a polity's public common good(s). In consequence, while pluralist writings, to be sure, exhibit an antagonism towards atomist individualism—something which, as pointed out earlier, cannot be said of many utilitarian and contractarian neutralist works[49]—their failure to speak against fragmentation ought to be interpreted as a failure to assert the good that is held in common by all citizens. As Taylor puts it, the fear of fragmentation is a fear of

a people less and less capable of forming a common purpose and carrying it out. Fragmentation arises when people come to see themselves more and more atomistically, as less and less bound to their fellow citizens in common projects and allegiances. They may indeed feel linked in some projects with others, but these come to be partial groupings rather than the whole society: a local community, an ethnic minority, the adherents of some religion or ideology, the promoters of some special interest. This fragmentation comes about partly through a weakening of the bonds of sympathy . . . and partly also in a self-feeding way, through the failure of democratic initiative itself. The more fragmented a democratic electorate in this sense, the more will their political energies be transferred to the promotion of partial groupings, and the less possible it will be to mobilize democratic majorities around commonly understood programs. A sense grows that the electorate as a whole is defenceless against the leviathan state; a well-organized and integrated partial grouping may indeed be able to make a dent, but the idea that a majority of the people might frame and carry through a common project comes to seem utopian and naive. And so people give up. This already failing sympathy with others is further weakened by the lack of a common experience of action, and a sense of hopelessness makes it seem a waste of time to try. But that, of course, does make it hopeless, and the vicious circle is joined.[50]

Taylor is clearly calling on us to be true to all the goods at play in modern politics, and to do so in a reconciliatory, and not only compromising, fashion. As a patriot he supports the goal of meeting the demands of public common goods in a way which is actually more true to a respect of the 'state—civil society' distinction than are those approaches which interpret such goods as inherently incompatible with a free politics. As he himself puts it,

Our challenge is actually to combine in some *non-self-stultifying* [i.e. non-compromising] *fashion* a number of ways of operating, which are jointly necessary to a free and prosperous society but which also tend to impede each other: market allocations, state planning, collective provision for the needy, the defence of individuals' rights, and effective democratic initiative and control.[51]

It is clear, then, that underlying Taylor's politics is an integrative ethics, one which recognizes diversity[52] as well as the aspiration to unity. 'Real ethical life', he has written, 'is inescapably led between the one and the many.'[53] This is a statement of a thinker whose hermeneutical credentials are beyond question, one who, I would say, has rarely failed to 'put practice first'.

III

The challenge, for anyone who wants to advocate a patriotic, as opposed to pluralist, conception of politics should be clear. In order to demonstrate the potential viability of conversation as a response to political conflict, it is necessary to show that the various ways of life present in the modern, multicultural polity are not, as the pluralist asserts is the case, conceptually separate from each other. For if, as the patriot claims, further integration is, at least in some cases, going to be a possibility, then this can only be because there is *already* some integration to begin with. One might be tempted to demonstrate that this is so by appealing to pluralism's own affirmation of the overlap between of all ways of life around the universal minimal moral code, but this is insufficient, and for two reasons. First, in keeping with their conception of values as separable, pluralists can claim that two ways of life, though overlapping as regards a certain minimum of values, nevertheless do not have to be described as *sharing* those values, for the ways of life are, after all, still conceivable as separate from each other and so as not being inexorably *integrated* together. Overlapping, they would rightly point out, is not the same as integration. Now in Chapter 3, I made some comments about how this pluralist position might be rejected for meta-ethical reasons, these based on the more holistic conception of the meaning of normative concepts asserted by the hermeneuticist.[54] But I have to accept that, for many, this will, on its own, be inadequate. Arguments will thus have to be made which demonstrate the point by using actual conceptions of real ways of life as examples.

Second, the minimal moral code is just that, minimal, which accounts for why its universality does not fly in the face of the appreciation of plurality or diversity. For it is nothing more than that meagre degree of moral power that is said to lie between conflicting parties, especially when it comes to the global stage. The patriot's affirmation of a civic public common good, however, refers to that which is shared by persons participating in a country's domestic politics, that is, to what is shared within countries rather than between them. This is not to deny that there is a great deal shared by persons across different states. No one today can ignore the increasing globalization of civil society, with the public sphere reaching across state borders by virtue of unprecedented expansions of the media as well as of the rise of the internet's World Wide Web, and the market economy doing the same by virtue of the widening of free trade and the extraordinary growth of many transnational corporations. In tandem with these developments, we have also witnessed the rise of important globally-focused civil associations, organizations such as Greenpeace or Amnesty International. It should be clear, then, that there are groups and practices in the world today which cannot be situated geographically, for those participating within them share goods which have little connection to any specific piece of territory. That is why global governmental institutions will have to be developed and strengthened if the practices located just inside the borders of these globalized parts of civil society are to have something on the other side with which to integrate. For a dotted line with nothing but empty space on either side is the height of irrationality.

Globalization has, despite the proclamations of some, far from eliminated the significance of borders between and (in some cases) within countries, however. After all there are still many practices that are closely shared within states, still many public common goods which speak to some publics and not to others. And yet, any assertion that citizens can, through them, be brought more closely together still needs to show that those living within a country *already* share much more than the pluralist seems willing to allow.

How, then, to do this? A recent statement by Peter Winch gives us a clue. As he has written, in a new preface to his *The Idea of a Social Science and its Relation to Philosophy*, the idea that modes of social life are separate was insufficiently countered by the qualifying remark in the first edition of the book in which he spoke of their 'overlapping character'. As he now states: 'Different aspects of social life do not merely "overlap": they are frequently internally related in such a way that one cannot even be intelligibly conceived as existing in isolation from others.'[55] My challenge, then, is to demonstrate that the goods of ostensibly separate ways of life are actually to some extent integrated, and necessarily so, with each other in practice by showing how this must be the case when they are properly conceptualized. Ways of life conceived of on their own, in isolation, which is how the pluralist assumes they may be, should display evidence of serious incoherence, of conceptual lacunae which can be filled only if we recognize that every good contained within a way of life is to some extent integrated with others both inside and out. And to speak of integrated goods is to assert that they must be related as more than wholly contingent tools for each other's fulfilment, it being, at least in principle, impossible that some other good(s) could just as usefully do the trick. That is, for a good to be integrated with another, the two must claim a necessary and specific relationship, which is to say that they cannot be coherently conceived as existing apart.

One cautionary note before I begin. The arguments I will be making are designed to flow from the pluralist's conception to the patriot's hermeneutical understanding of goods, that is, to show first the insufficiency of a pluralist interpretation, and then how this is compensated for by features of ostensibly separate, even seemingly incompatible, goods or ways of life. This, then, will be a philosophical attempt to bring separate goods together. I do not mean to give the impression, however, that it is characteristic of the patriotic approach to the interpretation of politics. On the contrary, where the patriot begins is with practices, and practices are understood to be expressions of goods that, as I have stated, are considered to be *already* to some extent integrated with each other. Indeed, the kinds of profound and intense political conflicts to be found in Western societies are understood to be possible only because the antagonists *already* share more in regards to the issues in question than the pluralist is willing to admit. Think, for instance, of the vehement antipathies exhibited during the Canadian free trade debate, or in the American struggle over abortion. For the patriot, as I have argued, when conflicts arise, as they inevitably will, between and within practices, the appropriate response should always begin with an attempt to reinterpret those practices in such a way as to bring the aspirations underlying them closer together. The hope is always to overcome the conflict, and to do so in a way which transforms, indeed improves, the society as a whole. My objective here, then, will be to demonstrate that holding such a hope makes sense. This seems to me to be a far from an unambitious aim, moreover, for it consists of nothing less than reclaiming a place in politics for truth.

5

Governance: Towards the Patriotic Lawmaker

I wish you to write a book on the power of the words, and the processes by which the human feelings form affinities with them.

Coleridge, letter to Godwin, Sept. 1800

Don't feel guilty if you get your way and you hear that someone else is losing out. Fight to win your corner and let other people fight theirs.

Polly Bird, *How to Run a Local Campaign*

I

That we should govern ourselves well remains a central mode of justification in modern politics. But what does it mean to do this? In this chapter, I want to explore two of the ways in which political thinkers in the West have answered this question. The first is classical republicanism, the ideology of an essentially pre-modern way of life, its two greatest proponents, Aristotle and Machiavelli, being located, respectively, at the beginning and end of this tradition of thought, though its principles largely reappeared in the last century in the works of Hannah Arendt. The second I will call 'modern democracy', an approach which emerged from those anti-absolutist doctrines of the seventeenth century, the foremost of which being unquestionably that of John Locke. For the classical republican, as I have shown, no boundary of any sort is to be recognized between the domains of civil society and the state since these two are considered one and the same, man being conceived of as a *zoon politikon* or 'social/political animal'. For the modern democrat, on the other hand, it is necessary to guard a solid wall between these two worlds, since the legitimacy of government is taken to be a function of the *consent* of the people, persons being understood here as laying claim to a wholly pre-political identity. Consent is so central to this modern conception that when classical republicans claim to have a place for democracy in their politics, it is in a form wholly unacceptable to the modern democrat.

To begin with classical republicanism, it is worthwhile to note that, despite the immense differences between it and modern democracy, there are thinkers within the tradition of the latter, these being many of the pluralists on whom I am focusing in this work, who accept classical republicanism as a valid way of life independently distinct from others—just the self-interpretation that a classical republican such as Machiavelli (though not Aristotle) would affirm. What these pluralists cannot accept, however, is the means by which one such as Machiavelli asserts this independence. This is because, to the classical republican, politics is an intrinsically good way of life that should be distinguished from others by virtue of the *unity* of the goods which constitute it, this being why the aims and virtues of a republic's citizens are often referred to not just as a collection of goods (plural), but also as 'the common good' (singular). This unity is considered sustained by the central tenet of classical republican politics, namely, that this common good is to be given an uncompromising priority by all. Citizens may, of course, recognize other goods, but all must share in the affirmation of the common good in a way that grants it unchallengeable pre-eminence. In the case of a conflict between its demands and those of goods located outside its unity, the common good must always prevail, somewhat in the same way as certain values are granted an overriding status *vis-à-vis* all the others in the intrinsically liberal pluralist polities of Dahl, Raz, and Walzer as described in Chapter 2. To say, moreover, that the goods of a republic's common good are, as a whole, independently distinct from the others is to assert that, though they may have need of these others, their relationship to them will be wholly instrumental in the sense that there is considered to be no specific, no uniquely meaningful connection between them. According to this conception of instrumentality, citizens of ancient republics, for example, should have conceived of their slaves not as instrumental in Aristotle's sense, in which they are still meaningfully connected to a certain conception of what is intrinsically good, but rather as fully independent conceptually, which is to say that if some other means could be found to fulfil the needs met with the slaves—say robots—then using these would make little difference to the life of the common good. In this conception, then, the common good is in no sense meaningfully *integrated* with any of the instrumental goods on which it relies, since, morally speaking, it has a wholly contingent relationship to them and so may, conceptually at least, be considered separate or independent.[1]

I want to distinguish here between two families of goods within the unity of the classical republican's common good, those of the heroic and the civic, each of which, we might say, having glory and honour as their respective aims. Indeed, different classical republican thinkers can be distinguished by the varying ways in which they choose to affirm these two sets of goods: Aristotle emphasizes civicism, Arendt gives great weight to heroism, and Machiavelli, depending on the situation, stresses both. To all of them, however, the variety of goods constitutive of their visions of the life of politics ensures that it is not just the *obligations* that one follows in a given situation that matter, but also whether one can claim to have the *dispositions* of the good person in following them. Conceptions of the good of this sort ensure that we are dealing with what Williams has called an 'ethic' and not just a 'morality', the latter term being used to refer to those more circumscribed modern ethics of obligatory action, such as Kantian formalism or (albeit somewhat less justifiably so) utilitarianism.[2] As Williams has explained, ethics do not assert the sharp boundary for their goods that moralities do, such that in an ethic we may speak of the intrinsic goods it affirms regarding questions of means, and those which constitute ends, as all to some extent integrated with each other. When it comes to classical republicanism's common good, then, both how one strives to achieve it, and the actual attainment of its proper ends, are considered necessary and intrinsic features of its goodness.

As regards heroism, the aim of the heroic individual is to perform an action of such originality or greatness (the means of this ethic) that it will be remembered, glorified by the community for all of its history (its end). By virtue of such an act the actor is said to become immortal, not, of course, in the sense that he will physically live forever as the Greek deities were said to do, but rather in that his name will never be forgotten.[3] If such an action and its later veneration is to be possible, however, it must take place within 'public space', that is, outside of the privacy of the household. Where, in the Homeric vision, this meant either the battlefield or the lonely odyssey to be recounted later by poets, with the classical republican it referred to the *polis*, that *res publica* or 'public thing' sustained by the laws of a community. In consequence, those classical republicans who stress heroism also recognize its reliance on civicism, on those goods constitutive of the political community. For an individual's words or deeds can only be judged original or great by virtue of their relation to the traditions of a community, glory relying for its very existence on the recognition of others, as is clear from the Greek word *doxa* which means both 'splendour or fame' as well as 'opinion'. Thus is it appreciated that the virtuous hero, the follower of that central Homeric motto, 'always to be the bravest and best and excel over others',[4] could not be who he is without the existence of a hierarchial community that gives great weight to honour. This need for a closely shared background, moreover, led those classical republicans who stress heroism to affirm the ancient Athenian conception of law, in which laws are construed as the walls which enclose and sustain the realm of politics.[5] Laws in this conception are, in a sense, the struts which support the public stage, that space of appearance in which individuals can act out the requisite great words and deeds and have them appreciated by an audience.[6]

There are also, as I pointed out above, classical republicans who accentuate the civic over the heroic facets of the common good. If an action is to be judged excellent, they would emphasize, it must be understood as contributing in some exceptional way to the end that is the common good of the community. Laws for these thinkers do not just perform the function of supporting the stage upon which individuals may act, for the very process of making them is considered to be of significant intrinsic value. In consequence, they turn to the conception of law found in early (by which I mean pre-Gaian) classical Rome[7] rather than that of ancient Athens, as law-making there is granted much more than just a supportive role.[8] To these highly civic classical republicans, legislation, understood as that activity in which equal citizens come together to deliberate and debate, in the sense of having a conversation about the laws, is central. As a result, they give greater emphasis to the idea of equality amongst citizens, though, to be clear, this is not the kind of equality of the individual that we find much later in modern politics, in which the respect of individuals is, in one of its dimensions, asserted without regard for where they are or what they are doing, as it is meant to accrue simply by virtue of their being human. Classical republican equality is different, as it involves an attitudinal kind of respect, one which consists of citizens recognizing that, when and only when they participate in the public, political realm and not in the household, they are among equals. As for what that participation should consist in, it is simply a matter of citizens conversing (the means of this ethic) with the aim of discovering those laws that properly reflect the common good of their community (its end). Getting the law right, then, means that the goods shared in common by the citizenry receive their due regard, and so that the citizens themselves will be 'virtuous', a term which refers to them having, as Montesquieu once famously put it, an 'amour pour la république'.[9] Good laws, it follows, means an honourable political community, since it is one in which the citizenry identifies with those laws and so willingly puts the common good they express ahead of their personal interests.

Regardless of whether it is the goods of heroism or civicism that are stressed, however, all classical republicans may be said to affirm with one voice the imperative that the common good as a whole—one which, to repeat, consists of a unified combination of these two families of goods—must consistently be granted an uncompromising priority over any other goods citizens may hold; anything else, the argument goes, and citizens become 'corrupt' and the republic is lost. One might picture how an 'ideal-type' classical republican would conceive of that unity in practice by looking, in an analogous spirit, at a game popular today amongst those who play football.[10] In the game, a group of players stand in a closed circle and, using only their feet and heads, pass the ball around, always with the aim of keeping it aloft. Each time a player receives the ball, he or she has the option either of attempting to do various tricks with it, or of just passing it on to someone else within the circle. As an analogy to the *polis*, the fit is quite tight. For the circle is but that public space of appearance in which all participants have an equal opportunity to perform an excellent action, its maintenance thus capturing something of the civic ethic, while the performance of stunts with the ball may be seen as a case of heroic striving for glory.

And so, classical republicanism has a place for greatness, for élitism as well as equality, in that all citizens are said to have the equal opportunity to distinguish themselves, to perform glorious acts which will earn them an elevated place in the socio-political hierarchy. That there is a not insignificant degree of individualism affirmed by this vision is something that the vast majority of classical republicans, with the exception of those who turned to dour Sparta as a model, were indeed attuned to. To Spartans, the common good, understood with a highly (though not exclusively) egalitarian civic emphasis, constituted a tightly unified ethical world, there being no place for the diversity practised by, say, the Athenians, amongst whom much more room was made for heroism. The principle that all must give uncompromising priority to the republic's common good is thus not exclusive of a recognition of at least a limited diversity amongst individual citizens. The goods included in that common good might even be described as constituting a spectrum of practices within which one could locate three kinds of activities, activities which, at least to the 'ideal-type' classical republican I am constructing here, all citizens are considered potentially capable of participating in. On one end, where we could place those words or actions that most strongly answer the call of heroism, we get those practices that involve individuals leading others in a *kingly* fashion through glorious endeavours. With the range in the middle, in which the goods of heroism and civicism are more equally significant, we cover those activities by which citizens distinguish themselves in ways which fit comfortably within the *aristocratic* socio-political hierarchy. Finally, with respect to the other, civic pole, we find those practices consisting of citizens recognizing their fellows as equal participants in the shared *democratic* enterprise of the republic.

That citizens are said to be capable of these varied activities has led classical republicans to advocate what has been known as 'mixed government' when it comes to their constitutional thought. The doctrine, first advanced in various ways by, among others, Thucydides, Plato, and Aristotle,[11] received its paradigmatic articulation in the work of the Greek historian Polybius. To Polybius, the best form of government is that in which the *polis*'s constitution embraces all three of the kinds of activities covered in the spectrum above, i.e. those of the monarchical one, the aristocratic few, and the democratic many.[12] For example, monarchical rule might be evident with those who command the republic's military forces, aristocratic with a senates' control over finances, and democratic when it comes to the participation of all citizens in the juries which mete out honours and punishments.[13] Polybius is best known, however, for his claim that a polity, if it is without the suitable presence of all three features in a blended, unified whole, is doomed to an endless developmental cycle, one in which each of the three forms degenerate and dominate in turn. Only the founding of a properly mixed republic, he argues, can enable a citizenry to put a stop to the sequence.[14]

It is important to note, because the point is often overlooked, that this 'mixed government' of classical republican constitutionalism is distinct from what we might refer to as 'balanced government', a vision which came into being only in the seventeenth century and so one which could have a place only in later republican as well as other forms of modern constitutional thought. With mixed government, the unity of the republic claims an organic quality, one in which 'the three kinds of government . . . all [share] in the control' of the governing apparatus as a whole.[15] Each distinct form is considered healthy when its members regard 'nothing as of greater importance'[16] than the common good and so participate in a 'well-blended harmony',[17] one in which each part of the mix has been combined in a 'proportional'[18] (as distinct from 'balanced') way, a result of being true to something like Aristotle's notion of excellence as the striving for the mean.[19] Asserting the organic unity of the whole does not mean that conflicts between the different groups participating in government cannot arise, just that, to recall the discussion in Chapter 3 it is assumed, a way always exists to resolve any ethical conflict with a reconciliation that is truly for everyone's benefit, that is, without any compromising of the goods of a given group of citizens. One may not, of course, succeed in finding that way, but that is said to be due to the limitations of the seeker, and not the fault of the moral reality itself. For Polybius, for example, those emergencies in which the republic faces a foreign enemy seem to so focus the minds of all citizens on the common good that their reaching the perfect solution for any conflicts over what to do and implementing it with the utmost efficiency becomes, at these times, virtually guaranteed.[20] And yet, there will also be occasions when they find themselves unable to achieve such a reconciliation, and this means that some sort of balancing of the goods affirmed by the conflicting parties will be called for. It is during times like these, says the classical republican, that some individuals or groups in the republic are particularly tempted to start down the road to corruption by turning away from the common good. When the republic is a healthy unity, however, the assumption is that other citizens will inevitably step in and check the potentially wayward ones, thus ensuring that, as Machiavelli has put it, 'a bad citizen cannot do much harm in a republic that is not corrupt'.[21] So though some compromising of good, as with all balancing, will be unavoidable, whatever balance is ultimately reached in the process is still understood as contributing, on the whole, to the common good, which is to say that even those suboptimal solutions proffered by differing parties may be considered as bringing progress. All of this means, then, that when classical republicans refer to the balancing that sometimes takes place between conflicting individuals or groups, they do so only with the republic's organic unity as a background, as this is what allows them to interpret the mutual checking between parts productive of that balancing as contributing to a unified republic, one of the 'greatest perfection'.[22] That is why Polybius and Machiavelli, and all other classical republicans who give great attention to a politics of checks and balances, can still fully agree with Aristotle's assertion in *The Politics* that everyone who has a hand in ruling should always aim to rule with an unwavering view towards the 'common advantage'.[23]

Matters are very different with 'balanced government'. In this conception the parts of the polity are at no point the integrated features of an organic unity, for they are understood to be separate from each other, and so are at all times 'factions' whose nature is to consistently aim, not for any common good, but for their own, independent self-interests[24]. In this vision, however, it is not considered unhealthy or corrupt for them to do so, for it is just because all groups are said to have their own self-interests in mind that they are led to check each other, the assumption being that the end-result of all this checking will be an acceptable set of compromises overall, one in which no one group manages to predominate by gaining too much power. With balanced government, then, one begins and ends with checking and balancing, any talk of the whole remaining at all times secondary, it being no organic entity but rather the complex product of the compromised aims of various separate groups. The transformation of the mixed doctrine into this balancing vision culminated, as I have said, in the seventeenth century, the idea of an equilibrium of clashing forces having taken a powerful hold on many of that century's political thinkers due to the great success of and interest in physics and mathematics at the time.[25] In the following century, Montesquieu used the sort of checks and balances notion associated with balanced government (this, once again, being different from the kind of checking and balancing that may take place within the organic unity of mixed government) as a means of describing the mutual restraining between the aristocracy and the monarchy that he considered central to good governance,[26] as well as as a support for his well-known articulation of the very different, functional doctrine of the 'separation of powers'.[27]

To return briefly to Polybius, his image of cyclical recurrence, it is worth mentioning, became one of the sources of the later classical republican conception of 'Fortune', of history as a stream of irrational events.[28] In pre-Augustinian Christianity, eschatology and history, inte-grated as *saeculum*, were, in association with the various cosmological doctrines of correspondences, submerged under a sacred time. Augus-tine, however, broke this connection, separating the sacred and history, and so making way for the conception of history as meaningless, because mutable, Fortune. It was this division that was adopted by later classi-cal republicans such as Machiavelli, though he, of course, rejected the Augustinian conception of how that history should be surmounted;[29] to him it is the image of the *vivere civile*, the life of participation in the public realm of the republic, that constitutes that stable island— the closed circle of the football analogy above—which rises above the swirling, amoral currents of contingent history.[30] And though this embedding of the republic amidst a contingent, profane time is far from Aristotle (for whom the political community was natural to man and so, by virtue of an ontic *logos* cosmology, an integral part of a fixed uni-versal order), the sense that the republic is constituted by a universally identifiable set of goods, those embodied in its common good, remains. Where, for Aristotle, that universality accrues as a result of the common good's place in his naturalistic teleology, with later classical republicans all the republics of history are considered affiliated with each other as those fragile and temporary 'Machiavellian moments', to use J. G. A. Pocock's phrase, in which that rare and precious 'public thing' of political liberty makes its appearance amidst the chaotic contingencies of Fortune.

A universalistic, self-enclosed, unified ethic, one which is described as, in this sense, a kind of 'thing'[31]—that is what classical republicanism purports to be. Predictably, one of my aims in this chapter will be to 'open up' this ethic. But though I plan to speak against its unity, I will not be going as far as a pluralist would, for I do not wish to do this by resolving or separating its goods; rather, I want to put forward a position which conceives of them as only to some extent integrated with each other, which is to say not so tightly that we could consider them as the parts of a unity. In doing so, I hope to show a way towards their realization in practice which is, on the whole, even more effective than that advocated by classical republicans themselves.

First, however, I would like to introduce 'modern democracy', one of the modern alternatives to the classical republican's vision of good governance. This approach, as I pointed out, is based on the central notion of government by consent, that is, of a government as ruling or legislating by virtue of a resolution made by persons who may be said to claim a pre-political status. For the advocates of this view, then, there is a solid line to be drawn between civil society and the state, the activity of politics being understood as purely instrumental to the conceptually separate aims of the citizenry in civil society. This is utterly different from the classical republican's vision in which, as I have shown, no distinction of any sort is to be made between state and civil society—there is a border to be patrolled between the household and the public, governmental realm, but this is not because the household is a distinct realm of the good, rather it is conceived of as a place of exclusively instrumental relations, in which a master may appropriately rely upon force and violence in dealing with his slaves. In his household the citizen is always a ruler, and not one who rules and is ruled in turn as when fulfilling the common good by participating in the public realm.

Advocates of modern democracy can be divided into two groups. The first, which consists of the vast majority of those classical and neo-classical democratic theorists beginning with Locke (who himself drew upon a number of fundamentals that had been established by Hobbes) right through to nineteenth-century thinkers such as Bentham, affirms a vision of democracy that incorporates principles both of instrumental means and intrinsic ends. As an instrumental process, democracy is

construed as that political method whereby persons achieve their self-
determining freedom through the use of the government to which they
have granted consent. As regards its ends, the rationality of the process
is intricately tied to what these thinkers consider to be in the 'public
interest'. Of course, there are great differences as regards what this
public interest is said to consist in, whether we speak of Hobbes's order
and security, Locke's affirmation of various civil and property rights,
or Bentham's utility. What all these thinkers nevertheless share is the
notion that this public interest, being the end of an instrumental good,
is itself a *convergent* good, meaning that, though it exists for all those
served by a government, it does so for them as separate individuals, that
is, as something acknowledged as being 'for me and for you' rather than
'for us' as Taylor would put it.[32] The public interest must therefore
be distinguished from the common good of the classical republican, or
indeed from any common good for that matter, as it is but a general-
ized version of what welfare economists today refer to as a 'public good',
something which is said to fulfil an aggregate of individuals' interests
and nothing more. To the thinkers in this group, the notion of 'the public'
rests upon an atomist or asocial individualist ontology, and so is conceived in tandem with a vision of society as consisting of nothing more
than a collection of separate individuals, there being no hint of the
organicism necessary for it to be considered as in any sense greater than
the sum of its parts, and so no room for anything like the classical republican's common good. But though separate, all persons, or at least all
instrumentally rational persons, are nevertheless still considered to be
one in the sense that their collective will, as communicated through the
democratic process, should be in complete accord with the public interest.[33] It is a necessary but not sufficient condition for a government to
be considered legitimate, then, that it fulfils this will as a means to the
public interest. The result is a conception of democracy that assumes a
systematically interlocking unity of its means and ends.

　　The second group of modern democrats, the pluralists, have come to
the fore in the twentieth century, and can be distinguished by their rejection of the classical and neo-classical theories of democracy for reasons
made famous by Joseph Schumpeter.[34] Schumpeter's conception of
democracy focuses on competitive elections and the élites empowered
by them, while pluralists, as I have pointed out, tend to give greater
emphasis to the ongoing pressures applied on government by the many
and varied groups or associations within civil society. But what both
Schumpeter and pluralist democrats share is the rejection of the classical and neo-classical assertion that democracy encapsulates a unity of
means and ends. To them, democracy can refer to a process only, in that

it may consist of nothing more than the means by which those in civil society impose their will on government, the claim being that there are two fundamental difficulties with the notion of the public interest affirmed by the democratic theories of their predecessors. First, the reality of moral pluralism puts into question the very idea that there could be a public interest shared as a goal by all. Since, the claim goes, persons can be expected to affirm a plurality of incommensurable values that sometimes conflict and, when they do conflict, there is no guarantee that an instrumental solution will be available, the existence of such conflicts, conflicts of 'irreducible differences of ultimate values',[35] means that compromise will be unavoidable. Second, even if there was a public interest which all members of a society could be said to share, this far from guarantees that there will be definitive answers to the questions of how it should be achieved. After all, ' "health",' as Schumpeter writes, 'might be desired by all, yet people would still disagree on vaccination and vasectomy. And so on.'[36]

Interestingly, this difference between pluralist democrats and their classical and neo-classical predecessors parallels, somewhat, two of the Enlightenment-inspired responses to the notion that men are driven by passions. As Albert Hirschman has summarized them,[37] the suspicion of moralizing and religion that arose with the Enlightenment brought with it the view that political thinkers should look at man 'as he really is', by which was meant giving a scientifically neutral account of human nature. This led thinkers such as Hobbes to assert that man was driven by 'passions' or 'interests' rather than 'goods' or 'virtues', and the question arose of how to respond to this reality. One answer was to call upon society or the state to 'harness the passions', to be a civilizing medium, and it is in the related spirit of a rationality of enlightened self-interest that many of the classical and neo-classical democratic theorists worked. Another response was to 'countervail the passions', to play them off against each other in the hope of producing a balanced, beneficial effect overall, it being appreciated that there would necessarily be some compromising along the way. It was this latter vision that provided the basis for the balanced government constitutionalism discussed above, and which found its way into the work of the American founding fathers[38] as well as, through them, the pluralism of twentieth-century American political science.[39] And it is, of course, this countervailing spirit that is behind the balancing or compromising response to moral and political conflict that is so integral to contemporary normative pluralist thought, though pluralists today would reject as reductive the purely interest-driven conception of human agency associated with the Enlightenment. Now, to these pluralists, the inevitability of compromise means that there is no place in the concept of democracy for the idea that rationality itself, however enlightened, calls upon all of us to support any particular public interest. In consequence, the notion of democratic legitimacy is considered applicable only as regards the process of governance, democracy itself being considered a value which can conflict with any and all of the others that citizens might find it reasonable to affirm, including ends such as justice. To (at least some) pluralists, then, a majority may vote to oppress a minority, and, though this may be unjust, it is not necessarily 'undemocratic'. There can be no unity of means and ends in democracy because there is said to be no single end that we can expect all citizens to share; to assume that one exists is to have an unwarranted faith in a 'communistic fiction',[40] one dreamt up by the political economists of classical democratic theory long before Marx.

Rousseau's political thought occupies a unique place *vis-à-vis* classical republicanism and modern democracy, one worth briefly mentioning here. For his 'Jacobin democracy', as it has been called, can be said to combine, albeit somewhat paradoxically, features of both visions. In the dimension of 'means' we find much of the process of modern democracy, Rousseau's 'general will' being a way of articulating the self-determination of a people that lay claim to a pre-political identity, one independent of any political structures. That there is little here held in common with the classical republican's conception of political processes is clear when Rousseau prohibits dialogue between citizens during their deliberations as legislators of the general will,[41] conversation about the meaning of the common good being, as I have shown, integral to the means of classical republican civicism. And yet, for Rousseau, legitimate governance also necessitates meeting a specific end, one which is not any version of the public interest but is instead a highly civic variant of a republic's common good.[42] That is because his public is neither a collection of atomized individuals nor a plurality of separate groups or factions; rather, it is a kind of *soi commun* or 'social self' which lays claim to an organic unity. The paradoxes within this vision are numerous, as should come as no surprise when dealing with a thinker for whom persons, as he famously claimed, can be forced to be free. To mention just one: Rousseau's social self seems to claim, at one and the same time, both a wholly non-political and a wholly political status. On the one hand, government attains legitimacy by virtue of the mechanism of consent which, it is clear, necessitates the existence of an extra-political entity; on the other, it is this very entity that legislates through the general will. This is no contradiction for Rousseau because, to him, 'government' is but the executive branch;[43] matters are very different for those of us who cannot accept this rather strange conception, however. Rousseau thus seems to want to have it both ways: (i) a society in which there is no border of any sort defended between government and civil society; and (ii) a social self that legislates from within a wholly non-political civil society. Moreover, to mention yet another paradox, underlying all of this is a philosophical anthropology which asserts, at one and the same time, that man is both the social/political animal of the classical republican, as well as the participant in a social contract, that mechanism central to those classical democrats for whom asocial individualism was a fundamental starting-point.

All of this has been by way of an introduction to my main aim in this chapter, which is to put forward a conception that reformulates both the common good of the classical republican and the pluralist's vision of modern democracy such that the two can be integrated with each other, and in a way which avoids the paradoxes of Rousseau. I have argued, however, that if integration is to be possible, then there must *already* be some integration, some sharing, to begin with. But if there is one matter on which, as I have pointed out, both my ideal-type classical republican and the pluralist can agree, it is that different ways of life are conceptually *separate* from each other, and so that no integrating dialogue, no real conversation, could ever be possible between, say, the virtuous citizens of a given republic and those of a different loyalty. That is why, when it comes to an encounter between a Machiavelli and a group of Christians, Berlin can write: 'He has nothing to say to them, nothing to argue with them about.'[44] Of course, as I pointed out, the reasons for recognizing this separation are very different for the two approaches. For the classical republican it is by virtue of the unity of those goods constitutive of the republic's common good that this way of life is to be conceived as meaningfully autonomous from those without. This the pluralist cannot accept for, with pluralism, being conceptually separate is a predicate not just of different ways of life as a whole, but also of the values they contain. The pluralist would thus have us shatter the unity of the 'Machiavellian moment' republic; not in such a way that we are barred from collecting its pieces into a group and calling them a 'way of life' in order to distinguish them from others, but this, the claim would go, is far from asserting anything like their intrinsic integration. Correspondingly, when it comes to pluralist democracy, we find a plurality of groups that are each understood to affirm at least partially different, and so separate, ways of life. They may all be present within the civil society of a single modern political regime but, when it comes to conflicts between them, these must be interpreted as driven by the groups' attempts to have government serve their separate goals and interests.

Those who would take a hermeneutical approach, however, reject the assertions of both unity and plurality and advocate instead the voyage in-between these two worlds. In the critique of classical republicanism that I am going to present below, my aim will be to emphasize certain incoherences in its conception of the common good in order to show how its own moral imperatives require a politics that does not partake of unity. There will be much here with which the pluralist can be expected to agree. But in rejecting the unity of the common good I will not be going to the other, pluralist extreme, since my intention is to demonstrate how only the integrative, hermeneutical ethics of the patriot can meet the requirements of good governance for us today. My next move will thus consist of a critique of pluralist democracy, in which I will argue that only by integrating some of the classical republican's intrinsic goods with the pluralist's purely instrumentalist conception can pluralist governance be rescued from its own particular conceptual incoherences. Finally, all of this integrating will, I hope, lend support to the patriotic conception of good governance, and so it is with a more direct and in-depth exploration of it that I plan to close the chapter.

II

Where, for the pluralist, as I have shown, values are those sometimes clashing, independent things which may be said to float down the river of history, the classical republican envisions an island in that river, a unified, stable, self-enclosed 'public thing' that is to be the home of a citizenry's common good. My intention here is to question the conceptual unity of this way of life, and so show that, rather than being constituted by a unified set of goods that are, as the classical republican asserts, separate from those instrumental goods outside of it, it must, in reality, be integrated with them to some extent. This is certainly how the patriot would have it for, as I have argued, the hermeneutics of patriotism encourages us to conceive of goods as, at base, practices, meaning that there is no way they could ever be combined so as to constitute a self-contained, unified world, one which somehow rises above the water-line of history. This is not to say that one may no longer speak of the common good of a whole citizenry, rather, it is just that what citizens share in common is understood differently, as no part of politics, it is claimed, can ever be wholly separated from history. No good, I want to assert, is an island.

I plan to 'open up' classical republicanism's common good by closely examining that facet of it which affirms heroism. To many of the thinkers in the tradition, heroism has long been a source of worry. For one thing, there seems to be a tension between it and the civic aspects of the common good. Socrates and Plato were the first philosophers to attempt to civilize Homeric heroism, to bring the warrior ethic summed up by Polemarchus as the principle of 'doing good to friends and harm to enemies'[45] into the *polis*. But where Aristotle put Plato's particular vision of unity into question, granting greater independence to his aristocratic politicians than Plato did to his guardians, the history of classical republican thought has been repeatedly marked by republican thinkers' own worries that neither Aristotle's alternative, nor any other vision of the republic, has ever fully succeeded in harnessing heroism. The challenge has been clear: how to put social controls on those who exhibit the exceptional characteristics epitomized by the powerful, swift-footed 'lion' Achilles, or the quick-witted, cunning 'fox' Odysseus? It is, to be clear, not that the Homeric hero was ever affirmed as being completely without social obligations, for there are times when even he was expected to concern himself with honour and not just glory. The obligation to exact revenge is a case in point, it being a practice which, despite the disenchantment of the pre-modern cosmic order (acts of revenge having been justified as those designed to realign matters with that order), still somewhat resonates with many of us today, though it is granted little if any recognition in contemporary Western law.[46] And yet, when the hero engages in glory-seeking, the question has inevitably arisen: can his actions be said to be completely in harmony with the needs of society? Aristotle's answer seemed to be no, this, presumably, being one of the reasons why he advocated a *polis* which had no place for the monarchical 'one'. Classical republicans since Polybius, however, have struggled to grant a significant place in their politics to the great individual, though they have also rarely failed to appreciate the risks involved. To return for a moment to my football analogy of the republic, we might recognize that each time a player receives the ball he or she is confronted with a choice: either to pass it along without trying to do anything fancy and so ensure the continuance of the game by maintaining the circle, or, more ambitiously, to strive to keep the ball aloft on their own even though this increases the risk of losing control and having it go out of the circle, destroying the circle's integrity and so suspending the game. For all the while the ball is out of the circle and someone has to run along and fetch it the players can only stand around aimlessly and wait for its return; the fragile republic is, for the time being, no more. And so, these two distinct activities—maintaining the circle and pursuing individual glory within it—can counter as well as complement each other. Correspondingly, many classical republicans have remarked that there seems to be an amorality to the ambition of the glory-seeker, one which could seriously threaten the stability of a civic order.[47]

It is a part of the originality of Machiavelli that he responded differently than those classical republicans before him to this tension between heroism and civicism. To most of the thinkers in the tradition, the consummate republic is considered to be that which succeeds in overcoming the tension and affirming a tightly unified common good, one in which the hero is present but successfully restrained within a strong and stable civic order—Venice being perhaps the best model here. Machiavelli, however, rejected the restriction of heroism entailed by this conception, and turned instead to the less unified, more dynamic Rome for inspiration. Though he, in characteristically ambiguous fashion, continued to refer to the more stable, predominantly civic vision as the basis of the 'perfect'[48] republic, it is clear that his preference was for the greater flexibility and opportunity for glory which he considered possible in discordant and conflict-ridden Rome, that imperialistic, not-yet-perfect republic. But although he is more attracted to the strife-ridden dynamism associated with the checking between conflicting parties described so well by Polybius than to the more stable, highly unified republic, his Rome is still envisioned as upholding a fundamentally mixed—as distinct from balanced—constitution.[49] That is because the conflicts between patrician and plebian within it are still assumed to be progressive in that they, on the whole, are said to contribute to the unity of the common good and so the perfection of the republic.[50] Machiavelli, then, never accepted the presence of self-interested factions in his ideal republic, neither in the way nor in the extent to which they are essential to balanced government.[51] It was just that he had no wish for the process of checking within mixed government to be too successful too soon, in that he was captivated more by the conflict-ridden journey towards the perfectly unified republic—and the support in adaptability that this gave to an imperialistic foreign policy—than by the arrival at its destination. As he saw it, the flexibility of dynamic Rome gave it a strength in the face of the chaos accompanying any military engagement that was simply not available with the rigidity of a tightly unified Sparta or Venice. Machiavelli, we could say, would probably have heartily endorsed the lesson behind that fable of Aesop's, the one which speaks of the greater durability to be had by a pliable twig over a hard-barked tree when it comes to the turbulent, rushing waters of a river in a storm.

In consequence, even though Machiavelli interprets the common good as a less tightly wound set of goods than the classical republicans before him, he still considers it as constituting a more-or-less stable, unified whole, one which is by no means to be understood as making way for any kind of 'divided'[52] republic. Where Aristotle rejected Plato's unity as too tight and offered his own more loosely unified vision as an alternative, Machiavelli can be said to have performed a similar move in relation to Aristotle and his followers. For his republic is still one in which, ultimately, factions are shunned, too much faction being seen as leading inevitably to corruption, the compromising of the common good.

What I want to argue, however, is that the striving for glory is incompatible with even Machiavelli's less tight but still unified conception of the common good. My claim here is based on the following assumption: the activity of heroic glory-seeking—when, that is, it is meant to arise as the outcome of a conflict[53]—simply cannot be consummated without there being some real sense of the conquest of an adversary. This is what is behind Polemarchus' talk about the need to do 'harm to an enemy', and it is also, I would claim, what Pericles was referring to when he boasted that the Athenians had left behind an everlasting reminiscence of their evil—and not just their good—deeds.[54] For doing harm to your enemy means but doing harm to his or her goods, and doing harm to a good, any good, is, of course, an evil (or, at least, something we would describe as 'bad'). That is why there is more to the classical republican's praise of 'virtue' than simply an affirmation of the civic aspects of the common good, that evoked by Montesquieu's talk of the love of the republic. For the virtuous citizen must also be the courageous citizen, the *vir* or man of strength and virility, one capable of participating in the kind of conflicts which produce not just glorified winners, but also disparaged losers. It is because of the real risk that one could end up the loser that the citizen is said to need courage to leave his home and enter public life, for losing means not just having what one cherishes damaged or destroyed, that is, losing one's cause, good reputation, etc., but also being remembered along with the immortal hero as the one who failed, as the infamous, defeated one, the vanquished. It is because this kind of heroism is inextricably linked with such conflicts that classical republicanism's affinity with militarism is so unsurprising, as well as why it is that today, when war is (thankfully) construed in a much less favourable light and heroes are also those who have been able to control or overcome adversaries which are not only gods or other persons but also themselves,[55] or nature,[56] the greatness that comes from defeating others in sports is still immensely valued. In ice hockey, for example,

Wayne Gretzky is known as 'The Great One' not simply because of his
superb talents, but because he has been fortunate enough to have translated those abilities into victories, leading his teams to the defeat of
others in championship matches, as well as replacing others' names with
his own in the record books.[57] Glory of this sort, it should be clear,
depends on a conflict between real adversaries, one in which someone
must lose if there is to be a hero who wins.

My claim, however, is that there is simply not enough room for such
adversaries within the republic unified around an uncompromisable
common good. To demonstrate this, I want to build upon the arguments
advanced in Chapter 3 and draw a contrast between the conception of
political conflict available within a moral/political unity, and that supported by the hermeneutical approach which underlies patriotism. To
be clear, I do not wish to claim that the fact that classical republicans
assume that we are dealing with a united set of goods shared in common
by all of a republic's citizens means that their vision has no room for
any sort of conflicts when it comes to domestic politics. On the contrary
they clearly accept that there may be divergences over questions of how
the common good's civic and heroic facets should be properly combined, or of what it means to fulfil either in a specific instance (examples of the latter including those disagreements about how the law
should be interpreted in order to deal appropriately with a specific
situation, or how a particularly excellent contribution to the community
should be suitably honoured). Moreover, it is worth pointing out, it
is conflicts such as these, conflicts in which the goods in question are
more—rather than less—closely shared, that tend to be the most
bitter and intense. Conflicts between remote groups which have little
understanding of each other tend to be devoid of passion.[58]

And yet, despite—or rather because of—all of this, it is not appropriate to refer to the parties involved in disagreements within a unified
republic as adversaries. For the very fact that, to the classical republican, no citizen should ever advocate a position that supports their personal interests while compromising the common good means that every
position must be advanced in the spirit of the good of all, as no one who
strives to put the *common* good first can at one and the same time wish
to do harm to a fellow citizen. But this then means that there would be
no room for the kind of encounters that might end with victory for some
and the real defeat of others, which is why the participants in the conflict
should at no point be considered adversaries, real enemies rather than
just opponents with a disagreement. Moreover, all of this stands even
when a citizen advances a position in the full knowledge that it is
far from the perfect solution to a particular issue, i.e. that it will be

unavoidably accompanied by some loss or compromise, and that loss may not be his own. For though, as I stated above, affirming a unified ethical vision means assuming that a way always exists to resolve a moral or political conflict without compromise, this does not preclude the possibility—even the probability—that those addressing a given issue may fail to find that way. Someone involved in a particular conflict, then, may acknowledge that he has been unable to come up with a position that 'solves' it altogether without loss, and yet he may still interpret that position as being the best one around, ethically speaking, for *all* concerned. It can thus still be offered, when compared to all the available alternatives, as the one closest to the as yet undiscovered ideal, and so as being in the interests of all concerned, including those persons advancing other positions. Indeed, to the classical republican, this is also how one should interpret the spirit in which one's opponents—not adversaries—are advancing their own particular positions, provided, of course, that one considers them to be disagreeing in good faith (which, to the classical republican, means that one believes that one's opponents honestly believe that their positions best fulfil the common good). But all of this means, then, that when success is interpreted as success for one's opponent as well, even though they may nevertheless fail to appreciate this, there is no place for glory. After all, the sense of satisfaction accompanying this kind of success is not the sort associated with the vanquishing of another, but is instead of a highly paternalistic type, it being more accurate to say that, rather than routing an enemy, one has perhaps thwarted a friend for his own good.

All this means that classical republicans, including Machiavelli, are wrong to assume that the domestic conflicts faced by the citizens of the republic as they conceive of it are possible sources of glory, and so are on par with those conflicts engaged in during military exploits. While military endeavours always have the potential of resulting in glory—indeed, to the classical republican, those defeated, by virtue of their being foreigners, are not considered to share *any* virtue with one's own fellow citizens and so more than meet the requirements necessary to be considered outside the scope of the common good and so as being adversaries rather than friends—matters are very different when it comes to the domestic politics of a republic, all of whose citizens are supposed to be striving to put the common good first. This is because though there may indeed be conflicts within such republics—even, as Machiavelli hoped, a great number of these—the fact that these are not to be driven by factions means that those engaged in them cannot be considered real adversaries. But without adversaries, there can be no glory.

Patriotism, however, despite sharing something of the wariness for wholly self-interested factions, does have room in its conception of domestic politics for the kinds of conflicts that may emit of glory. For one thing, the patriot accepts that there could be more than one set of public common goods when it comes to domestic politics, for example, those of nationalism and civil religion as well as that granted centrality by the classical republican. That being said, this recognition might simply take us no further than Machiavelli's assertion that the goods of the common good ought to be unified in a loose enough manner that they be allowed to conflict, meaning that there is not necessarily any room for adversaries here. Where that room does arise, however, where, that is, it is appreciated that politics is a practice which does not take place within even a loose unity, comes to the fore when we recognize the following patriotic fundamental: individual citizens cannot be expected to grant any particular public common good the same place on their various and idiosyncratic rankings of goods, and certainly not a transcendent, uncompromising place. With this notion of 'ranking' I mean to refer to how someone tends to weigh their goods in response to a conflict in which negotiation and so compromise seems unavoidable. Now where the unity asserted by the classical republican requires that the republic's common good should claim a transcendent place on every citizen's personal rankings and so be wholly uncompromisable, the patriot rejects the assumption that any good, or set of goods, should, or indeed could, ever hold such a privileged position. For one thing, patriotism demands that its ideologies recognize something which those especially civic classical republicans would not: that conversation as a means of responding to political conflict can, and often rightly does, break down. For another, the goods not included amongst a modern society's public common good as a whole cannot be interpreted as always and only instrumental to it, since there will always be citizens (indeed, we are probably speaking of the vast majority here) for whom those goods will have an intrinsic value in their own right. A person may thus still be considered good and reasonable, and not just 'corrupt' or 'self-interested', if he or she refuses to automatically negate their goods when it comes to a conflict between them and the common good.

In rejecting a unified public common good patriots may, of course, be said to concur with pluralists, for whom the rejection of unity is fundamental. But the two conceptions are not the same, the patriot's hermeneutics supporting as an alternative in which all goods are (though to different degrees, and in different ways) conceived of as integrated with each other and so shared by all. The atomism underlying the isolated conceptualizations constituting pluralist values in the thin dimension is, as I have shown, rejected in favour of a much more holistic conception of meaning.

To assert, as the patriot does, that all goods are more or less shared by all citizens will sound rather striking to some, and so needs some explanation. Indeed not even the classical republican would affirm this, since the instrumental goods situated within the republic's private realm are understood to be affirmed only by the members of each particular household. Let us, however, take as an example the common good constitutive of the friendship of two particular persons. Those not included in that friendship, indeed, those who have never even met the two individuals in question, can certainly not be said to, in any direct way, affirm that friendship as a *common* good. And yet, what does it mean when they concur with the assertion, as we may presume they would, that 'it is good that people be friends'? Surely it is that, all other things being equal, friendship is, for them, a good. But saying that this is so when 'all other things are equal' is to distort matters somewhat, for nothing meaningful actually exists in a world where all other things are equal, in which the flow of history around it has somehow been arrested. Even a conceptual ideal-type, and this includes the one I have developed of classical republicanism above, cannot be extricated from the context that gives it its place in history. Readers of this book, for example, must always do so in a particular time and place, and this will also be where whatever they take it to mean will be located.

In keeping with this, when someone says that it is good that there are friendships in the world, then, even if they do so within the context of some highly abstract argument, they must still be referring, in an albeit very general way, to a matter that shares its meaning with actual, context-dependent friendships, that is, to a set of real practices participated in by real people. Rather than advancing some thin, universalistic assertion of friendship, then, it would be better to describe them as making a highly general, but ultimately still thick contextual, reference to a practice whose meaning is actual in the world, the friendship of the two individuals in the example above being but a case of this. So whoever would endorse the statement 'friendships are good' may be said to affirm the particular friendship in question, though albeit to a very minimal degree (that friendship being, understandably, much, much lower on our endorser's particular ranking of goods than it is for those participating directly in it). But just as a man can value motherhood though he knows he will never participate directly in the practice, so may someone be said to share, to some extent, in the good constituting a friendship of which he is not included. What I am saying is that, to extend the argument beyond this example, no expression of a good in the world can be said to capture that good as if it were an independent entity, some kind of universal, Platonic form that is 'out there', disconnected from any context; rather, goods are necessarily expressed in practices which are always 'down here', they being manifestations that are more-or-less shared by persons who are themselves, as Heidegger would put it, 'beings-in-the-world'.

And so, the fact that all goods can be said to be to some extent shared by all means that it is possible that a conflict between very different persons, or groups of persons, can at times still be met with an integrating or reconciling interpretation, one which, by virtue of the way it transforms the whole of their respective conceptions of the good, avoids compromising their differing ethical loyalties. When conflicting parties appreciate this and try to achieve an interpretation that brings about such greater sharing, we may say that they remain partners in a conversation, interlocutors with a common aim rather than enemies.

But matters, as I showed in Chapter 3, do not end there. Because, in the hermeneutical conception, there is no assumption that the whole is a unity, i.e. that perfect solutions are, if not always found, then at least always there waiting to be so, there is room for a different scenario when it comes to genuine moral and political conflicts, one which is closer to that which, as the pluralist would have it, is always necessarily with us. As was evident in the case of the travelling salesman who had to give up his cherished pet, the disunified character of our moral world, the fact that its goods can never be conceived of as *fully* integrated, means that there will be times in which escaping from a moral conflict without some loss, some compromise to the goods at issue, is simply an impossibility. It is this fact of diversity, the fact that, though all citizens may, ultimately, be said to more or less share the same goods, they will nevertheless affirm significantly different rankings of them, that ensures that there will be times when interlocutors cannot but become enemies of a sort, and so true adversaries. For when it comes to those cases in which there is no 'solution' to a conflict of goods, no way out without compromise, or worse (by which I mean to allude to the use of force), different parties will tend to support different positions on how the moral loss should be distributed, on which good(s) should lose out more than others. In such cases, they will find that they have no choice but to either negotiate or fight.

Otherwise put, at times like these, in which an interpretation which all can fully affirm seems unavailable, conversation must come to an end and some form of negotiation or, as a last resort, force will have to be engaged. And in such cases those involved will be aware that someone, indeed possibly everyone, is going to lose something of value. Since the time when one strives for understanding and greater sharing has come and passed, the protagonists must turn to the matter of distributing the moral loss, to the compromising of their goods. Truth being no longer the primary aim, they find that they must strive to emulate the fox and the lion in an attempt to, as much as possible, protect their own conceptions of the good from those who cannot be said to share them in the same way. In such cases, their opponents are also adversaries, for they aim for the compromising of goods that are significantly lower on their own ranking scales than they are on those of their own enemies, this making a contest which will end with a winner and a loser (or even, of course, two losers) inescapable. Moreover, when such a conflict takes place between groups, though these should not be identified as the fully separate, self-interested 'factions' of pluralism, they are not very far from being so, in that the opposing sides can in no way interpret their positions as being for the good of all concerned. The parties are thus truly adversaries, more or less 'strangers' to each other at least as regards the matter in question, and this means that their conflict may be one which can result in glory for the victor. Moreover, that conflict will be experienced by all as less bitter than it would be if the participants were more friends than strangers, an irony which Arendt seems to appreciate when she writes that conflicts which, among other things, meet the 'desire for fame and glory', are those which partake of 'the spirit of fighting without hatred'.[59]

And so, the hermeneutics of patriotism, in assuming that goods are always more or less integrated with each other, though never as parts of a unity, supports a politics which has room for both civic and heroic goods, as well as for all those intrinsic or instrumental goods which are relevant to, but not wholly included among, those held in common by all who share a government. There being no unity of goods, there is no reason to follow the classic republican in sharply distinguishing between those goods publicly shared in common and those which are not. Otherwise put, there is no reason to consider the public common good(s) of patriotic politics as transcendent or uncompromisable *vis-à-vis* the others.

Matters are quite different with the pluralist, however. In separating values conceptually pluralists also separate the ways of life that are constituted by them, with the result that they end up shattering the notion of there being one or more public common goods shared by all citizens, regardless of group membership. To the pluralist, democracy is nothing more than a single, instrumental value, one which can be used by, though is not a source of integration of, the various groups in society. Such a conception of governance, one which makes way for the fragmentation of a citizenry, seems to me to lay claim to its own unique conceptual incoherences. In consequence, it is to this pluralist democracy that I now wish to turn.

III

Pluralists, as I pointed out in Chapter 2, tend to respond to the classical republican's common good in one of two ways. For some, those for whom pluralism actually entails liberalism, classical republican politics is considered wholly untenable in the modern world and so must be utterly rejected. For others, however, those strong pluralists such as Berlin, Hampshire, and Galston, it is considered as valid that some may still wish to advocate the ideology as way of life separate from others, although the pluralist reality of modern politics is said to mean that they will have to fight for it like everyone else.

It should be clear, then, that pluralism, like patriotism, has room in its politics for the kind of adversarial conflicts that can result in heroism and so glory. And yet, what pluralism, unlike patriotism, lacks is the ability to grant an undistorted place to some version of those more civic aspects of the classical republican's common good. That is because the conception of democracy available in pluralism is incompatible with the idea that the parts of a multicultural society must, or even could, share a public common good, and it is exactly this sort of sharing that is necessary if a reconciling, rather than compromising, response to political conflict is to be possible. Unlike the patriot, then, the pluralist goes much further than just rejecting the classical republican's assertion that the common good should be uncompromisable, for recognizing the plurality of ways of life within the societies of the modern West is understood to mean that there simply cannot be an intrinsic value, uncompromisable or not, shared in common across the whole of any one of them. But this claim, I want to argue, reveals an incoherence at the very heart of pluralist democracy.

To pluralists, as described above, democracy is essentially a process, a means by which political power, which is considered a separate value, is distributed and so particular governments constituted. Democracy is thus understood as conceptually independent not just from the power it distributes, but also from all other values in the society. As such, it should be definable by putting forward a list of criteria making up the concept's necessary and sufficient conditions, each individual criterion having one of those *ceteris paribus* clauses attached to it. For Schumpeterians, the concept can be summed up quite simply, it being said to consist of but two basic criteria, contestation and participation, as in the following definition: 'The democratic method is that institutional arrangement for arriving at political decisions in which individuals acquire the power to decide by means of a competitive struggle for the people's vote.'[60] With Dahl, however, democracy is interpreted as being somewhat more complex, his conceptualization being made up of five independently distinct necessary and sufficient conditions.[61] And Walzer, by virtue of the place he gives to the political rights upon which democracy must rely, supports a definition of the concept that is closer to Dahl's than Schumpeter's.[62] Regardless of the level of complexity of the definition, however, it is clear that what all these thinkers share is the notion that democracy is but a procedure, and that it is an instrumental and not intrinsic value, it being that process by which civil society is said to advance its self-determination through conveying its preferences to government. To be clear, civil society here is in no sense taken to be a unified entity, the absence of any necessarily shared values amongst the separate groups within it ensuring that it is far from some Rousseauian *soi commun*. Moreover, this plurality of groups ensures not only that compromise and negotiation, as opposed to any nature-identifying transformation *à la* Rousseau's general will, will characterize the process of self-determination, but also that the relation of civil society to the legislature is essentially instrumental.

But there are problems with this conception of democracy, problems associated with the failure to recognize that the concept needs to be integrated with some of those intrinsic, civic goods that have come down to us from classical republicanism. I am referring, in particular, to all that is entailed within the classical republican's notion that law-making involves the interpretation of those purposes shared by a citizenry *as a whole*. To accept this as an integral part of democracy is to assert that legislating cannot consist simply of the feeding of the demands of a plurality of groups through to some decision-making process, for it must at least to some extent also involve the formulation of a common understanding of the shared aims of the whole citizenry.[63] Under this conception, governance can no longer be considered a purely instrumental process, for it must also be understood as intrinsically valuable, and by every citizen. Without this, I want to argue, the pluralist's conception suffers from a fatal flaw.

The matter has to do with an aspect of what Dahl has referred to as 'the problem of inclusion', that is, the question of how, or whether, a democracy can justifiably discriminate between those who merit the rights of citizenship and so may rightly participate in the polity's democratic process and those who do not. Dahl presents two possible general answers to this question: there is the *categorical principle*, which states that 'every person subject to a government and its laws has an unqualified right to be a member of the demos (i.e., a citizen)', and there is the *contingent principle*, under which 'only persons who are qualified to govern, but all such persons, should be members of the demos (i.e., citizens)'.[64] Dahl begins his discussion of the matter by criticizing Schumpeter for advocating a position that Dahl considers wholly contingent, one which envisions any and all possible answers to the question of who should get the vote as 'inherently particularistic and historical'.[65] This, Dahl argues, is what led Schumpeter to the absurd view that the exclusion of African-Americans from the franchise in the southern United States was democratic, it being derived from Schumpeter's principle that we should 'leave it to every *populus* to define himself'.[66]

To Dahl, this position carries 'historicism and moral relativism to their limits'[67] and so is unacceptable. In its stead, he thinks we should aim to get as close to the categorical principle as possible, but, as he himself admits, this cannot be done without making certain exceptions. For there are at least three matters about which questions that invoke the notion of qualification seem inescapable, namely maturity, mental competence, and residency. As regards the first two, Dahl is well aware that democrats have always excluded children and the mentally incompetent from the franchise,[68] even though it cannot be claimed that the boundaries between childhood and adulthood on the one hand, and sanity and madness on the other, are not open to disagreement. And as regards residency, Dahl is quick to rule out transients[69] even though, later on in the very same work, he recognizes that one facet of the highly controversial 'problem' of the 'unit',[70] as he refers to it, has to do with the domain of persons entitled to exercise control with respect to matters falling within a certain scope of governance. This 'problem'—the question of who is affected as a citizen by a particular policy and who is not, and so of who should be in and who out as regards the democratic process—is one that, Dahl concludes, simply cannot be solved from within democratic theory; the matter of the unit, he writes, must be simply presupposed by the democrat. Dahl does, nevertheless, try to make the matter less vague and open-ended by, in standard pluralist fashion, putting forward a list of criteria for judgement, 'the hidden clause of each [being] the famous 'all other things being equal'.[71] Overall, though, the problem of the unit is, he claims, one more case of a conceptual hole that no definition of democracy seems able to avoid; indeed, as he has written in an earlier work, 'The question is, in fact, an embarrassment to all normative theories of democracy, or would be were it not ignored.'[72]

Let us be clear on the significance of this issue for the pluralist democrat. To the pluralist, concepts, as I described in Chapter 3, are considered independently distinct such that all the elements that make them up are assumed to be internal to their meaning. A concept should thus be definable in a 'thin' manner, that is, universally and in the abstract, in a way disconnected from any particular context, such that it may be conceived of as floating within, though still not as a part of, that 'thick' river of practices that come down to us from tradition. It is only when such separate moral concepts clash that we are said to be confronted by a matter which is necessarily thick and so relative to context. Now, as regards democracy, to go the route of the categorical principle and include every person subject to a given government would be to affirm the self-sufficiency or self-enclosedness of the ideal conceptually, i.e. to see it as distinct in a thin and fully independent sense. But to make room for 'contingent' qualifications is to do the opposite, that is, to leave open parts of the concept's definition to contextual, historically relative factors. And to do this is to admit that right within the heart of the concept are holes which cannot be filled if one limits oneself to the thin dimension of meaning, and so that the concept is not self-enclosed or self-sufficiently coherent after all. Nevertheless, it is difficult (indeed, we might hope, impossible) to find a democrat who would opt wholly for the categorical principle, which is why we get exceptions of the kind included in Dahl's final articulation of the inclusion criteria for his concept of democracy: 'The demos must include all adult members of the association except transients and persons proved to be mentally defective.'[73]

Now how, exactly, are we to fill in these holes, these exceptions to the categorical principle, in the pluralist's concept of democracy? As pluralists must surely recognize, these matters—maturity, residency, and mental competence—are open to debate. The first and third, it might be pointed out, are questions for the social sciences, in particular for psychology, while the second seems wholly political, this, for the pluralist, meaning that it will probably have to be subject to negotiation. But this then means that it is necessary to turn to the thick realm of contingent politics in order to fill in that particular hole in the concept of democracy. As Dahl himself writes,

In the real world, then, answers to the question, what constitutes 'a people' for democratic purposes? are far more likely to come from political action and conflict, which will often be accompanied by violence and coercion, than from reasoned inferences from democratic principles and practices. For as we have seen, in solving this particular problem democratic theory cannot take us very far. Democratic ideas, as I have said, do not yield a definitive answer. They presuppose that one has somehow been supplied, or will be supplied, by history and politics.[74]

'History and politics': to Dahl, it is clear, this means but contingency as an outcome of negotiation and/or force. And by contrasting, as he does, the 'violence and coercion' of this conception of politics with 'reasoned inferences', he seems to place himself squarely in the camp of those 'agonistic' pluralists such as Raz and Gray, for whom there cannot be a role for practical reason when it comes to responding to political conflicts, at least when the values involved are at all incommensurate with each other. But this, then, seems to mean that Dahl's approach cannot really be said to be that far from the irrationalism and moral relativism for which he criticized Schumpeter.

Whether one goes along with agonistic pluralism or not, it should be clear that when pluralists, of whatever stripe, turn to politics, history, or social science to fill in the holes that seem to be present in their concept of democracy, they do not conceive of these as involving that truly conversational form of dialogue available in hermeneutics, in which the central aim is for the reconciliation or integration of conflicting goods. Indeed, it only makes sense to speak of 'holes' in the first place because we are dealing with what is assumed to be a fixed, self-enclosed, universalistic concept, one ostensibly expressible in a completely 'thin' manner by use of a set of necessary and sufficient criteria. As such, the concept is certainly not open to the kinds of comprehensive transformations that, as I have described, are essential to hermeneutical conversation. Through transforming the goods of a conflict one aims to realize them without compromise and so to come up with a decision which benefits all concerned. The echoes of classical republicanism's civicism here should be unmistakable.

In patriotic politics, however, we are indeed presented with the option of further integrating a non-independent concept of democracy with those goods located at the hearts of issues such as maturity, sanity, and residency. As regards maturity, a developmental psychology which was hermeneutical would be one that recognized the unavoidability of taking into account interpretations of the conception of the good shared by a whole citizenry.[75] As for sanity, I have already alluded to what it would mean to interpret it hermeneutically, in which it is understood to consist of the integration, rather than balancing or compromising, of the parts of a fragmented or divided self.[76] Finally, the question of residency should be no different than the other two. When politics is interpreted hermeneutically, the question of who is to be considered an official member of the polity and who is not is understood to be one that concerns the meaning of relevant goods and the *extent* to which they are shared by persons. 'Conversation first, negotiation second, force third' is how, one may hope, the issue will always be confronted. Classical republicans, we may say, go too far in the sharpness of the division they assert between those citizens who share in the supposedly unified common good within a republic, and those foreigners without.[77] For those without, be they 'barbarians' or the citizens of other republics, are considered, most explicitly by Machiavelli, as fit either for conquering and then eliminating or assimilating, or for making contractual pacts, there being no place for that 'middle course' which would consist of the *sharing* of virtue between distinct regimes.[78] It is clear that, to classical republicans, the solid wall raised between republics is higher even than that which is meant to divide the public and private realms within a republic, for the citizen who transgresses the former does so on pain of being branded a traitor. In consequence, the distinction they affirm between domestic and international politics can only be characterized as extreme.[79]

But while the classical republican's 'friend or foe' mentality should be interpreted as being too stark, the pluralist's ubiquitous 'foe or foe' affairs are, if anything, too dark. That is, pluralists may be said to be guilty of advocating the opposite extreme, at least as regards their failure to differentiate significantly between domestic and global politics *vis-à-vis* the multicultural regimes of the West, since, to them, all conflicts between different ways of life, including those found within the same polity, are understood to be conflicts between 'natural enemies'.[80] This, of course, is only consistent with their assertion that to recognize a plurality of ways of life is to appreciate that these are distinct because there are values that cannot be said to be shared at all between them, and so that no public common good can be used to mark one polity as a whole off from another.[81] Conflicts between the ways of life within a polity are thus considered to be little different from those which occur between the ways of life (and the states that represent them) of different polities. And it is because those conflicts are said to take place over independently distinct values that they are considered open only to the compromises that emerge as the products of negotiation, rather than to the reconciliations that are the aim of conversations.

Matters are very different with the patriot. In patriotism distinct polities can be recognized as such by virtue of the extent to which persons do or do not share in a public common good, as well as by the varying extents to which all other kinds of goods are shared. And since these issues involve identifying the tradition(s) shared by people, the patriot's first goal is always, as I alluded to above, that they be discussed and not just negotiated over, the aim of those conversations being the articulation of political borders that are true to the public common goods shared by all those living within them. The result, we may say, is a conception of the regime which takes Machiavelli's lesson of 'strength in flexibility' more to heart than even he did. For while not going as far as the pluralist in forgoing the idea that a polity as a whole may lay claim to any integrity whatsoever, nor does the patriot try and erect a unified island which is somehow braced against the currents of history, one which, as classical republicans themselves never fail to remind us, is going to be particularly fragile. Instead, the patriot defends a more flexible, and so stronger, regime, one conceived of as always striving to flow along with the currents of history.

To conclude, pluralists are not able to opt for the categorical principle as regards the problem of inclusion for a reason only the patriot seems able to explain: the real meaning of democracy must be that it is, at base, a *practice*, and so is, in a historically specific manner, integrated to some extent with other practices, one of those others being, as I have tried to demonstrate here, that of engaging in reconciliatory conversations about shared goods. And this, it must be recognized, is but a version of the civicism that has come down to us from the classical republican tradition.

IV

On, now, to a more direct examination of patriotic governance. In patriotism, governing practices can be conceived of as the result of a (sometimes uneasy) weaving together of features from both the classical republican and modern democratic traditions. Constitutionally, this gives us a conception which can be located somewhere in-between the mixed government of the former, and the balanced government associated with the pluralist version of the latter. What I want to discuss here is what all this should say for two governing practices in particular: elections and policy-making.

i

What, exactly, should happen during an election campaign? For one thing, there should be, and indeed there often seems to be, a real competition between candidates bidding for power. The competition is sometimes modelled on a free-market analogy, candidates being understood as putting forward their platforms as if commodities on offer to some voter-as-consumer.[82] This is not, however, done to downplay the combative nature of such contests, though capitalism has often been portrayed as that *doux-commerce* antithetical to the warrior ethic.[83] For it is often recognized that the leader of a successful election campaign may, like some great military general, come into power 'in a halo of glory'.[84]

The struggle involved in winning an election, then, has an agonistic dimension. Candidates do much more than simply converse with their opponents, than simply disagree with each other during the hustings of all-candidates' debates, for they also engage in contests which require tactics, strategy, and the use of non-intellectual resources, all of these invoking the abilities of the lion and the fox. The battle often engaged in for publicity is a good example of this, in that the matter of how, say, a candidate wins a 'poster war' has a great deal to do with resources, hard work, and timing, and very little to do with the coherence of his or her ideological stance. In consequence, MacIntyre's claim referred to back at the close of Chapter 2—that modern politics is but a kind of civil war carried on by other means—must be accepted as at least partially right, though it loses its critical purchase when we recognize that it must necessarily be so if glory is to receive its due.

As I have demonstrated, pluralist and patriotic ideologies, unlike classical republicanism, have room in their conception of domestic politics for the adversarial dynamics necessary if political conflicts are to admit of glory. And yet, the pluralist conception is missing something crucial for that glory to be given its due: the idea that the recognition of glory is, ideally, something which should take place before the *whole* of the *demos*, and so something which depends upon the existence of a citizenry that is to some extent integrated, one in which *all* of its members can be said to share in the affirmation of a public common good. That is because the appreciation of greatness, the classical republican has taught us, requires a *community* to do the appreciating.

Moreover, just as, ideally, an electoral victory may be understood as bringing glory to the victor before the whole of his or her constituency, so too should we appreciate that the elected is, again in an ideal sense, meant to act not just on behalf of the whole of his or her constituency, but for the whole society as well. Different institutional arrangements have expressed this in different ways. In the Westminster model, for example, there is a sense in which each member of parliament is responsible both to his or her constituents and to all the other members of the society, the latter notion being captured in the figure of the monarch who, as a symbol of all subjects in the realm, passes that symbolism on to the bills which only become law by virtue of his or her official endorsement. Similarly in a republic such as the United States, the federal government is also meant to act on behalf of all citizens, the

separation of its powers constituting only a functional, and not representative, division since, as Garry Willis has pointed out, 'each department of the American government is to speak for the same interest, that
of the people'.[85]

To the patriot, this fully inclusive character of representative scope is
essential if elected individuals are to act as true *representatives* and not
simply as *instruments* of one particular group of citizens against another.
In patriotism, to represent a group of people involves aiming to be true
to their goods as an integrated whole, and this necessitates entering into
conversation with others over the meaning of those goods, an activity
precluded if one is considered but a partisan of some. The partisan is,
when taken in relation to the whole, but an *agent* or *tool* for some of its
goods as against others, one who exhibits the compromising partiality
integral to negotiation and/or force rather than the integrating inclu-
siveness of conversational dialogue. Hence Hannah Pitkin's useful
distinction between an 'agent' and a 'representative':

When we call a man someone's agent we are saying that he is the tool or instrument by which the other acts. He is a corporation's information-receiving tool
(agent, organ), its money-dispensing tool (agent, organ), and so on. When we call
him a representative, on the other hand, we are saying not so much that he is a
part or tool of the corporation as that the entire corporation is present in him.[86]

And so, if a candidate is both to receive the recognition due him or her
as a result of a successful election campaign, as well as to become a true
representative, then the candidate's constituency must be in some sense
characterizable as an organic whole. That is why the elected representative should be elected to, among other things, do good by the
whole of the community he or she is to represent, and it is only by succeeding at this that he or she may rise up the recognitional hierarchy
that the organic character of that community sustains. Aristocratic hier-
archies likewise depended upon an organic social structure, and we may
say that it is this very same structure that the patriot reformulates rather
than abandons, reinterpreting aristocratic élitism in a way compatible
with the recognition of the equal dignity of all integral to modern
society. There is thus a sense in which the elected representative is, for
the patriot, a kind of aristocrat, although one that has, to a significant
extent, earned rather than inherited his or her position, which is why
that representative's very existence does not, as the pre-modern aristocrat did, fly in the face of a respect for the liberty and equality of
individuals.

All of this being said, it must also be recognized that candidates make
a great deal of promises during election campaigns and that, in so doing,
they can indeed be interpreted as offering themselves up as tools of their

specific constituencies. Voters, understandably, want to hear what candidates' plans are should they be elected, and one of the reasons they vote is to give their consent to these, thus granting a 'mandate'. In revealing their plans, then, there is a sense in which candidates are offering an account of their 'fixed' properties ('fixed', of course, to the extent that they keep their promises), and so of how it is that they 'work'. This aspect of an election campaign thus exemplifies of the modern democrat's notion of governance, one which, as I have shown, is based on the inherent connection between the notion of consent and a citizenry's instrumental stance towards its government. We have, then, another reason why the market analogy of elections has some resonance. Because just as a consumer has reason to complain upon discovering that the product just purchased does not seem to do what the salesperson promised it would, so too can the elected politician who fails to keep his or her promises be understood as failing the modern democrat's test of good governance.

And yet, the market analogy also distorts. The reason for this is that, though the authorization carried by the idea of a candidate receiving a mandate is essentially symbolic, it is none the less significant for that. But if we limit ourselves to modern democratic terms, then the idea that a *majority* of the whole has gone one way or another cannot be said to grant added significance to anything. For if we follow those modern democrats who divide the whole of an electorate into individuals or groups,[87] there is no way to support the idea that an extra sense of legitimacy can accrue from the fact that a candidate has succeeded in claiming a majority of the whole as his or her supporters. This is because that whole, being nothing more than the sum of its separable parts, cannot claim a kind of identity in which a half or more of it has any more significance beyond the exact number it represents. If such added meaning is to be recognized, the whole must be able to lay claim to an organic quality, in which it is in some sense greater than the sum of its parts. And for this, one needs the notion that all members of that whole share, to some extent, in a public common good. But the recognition of a society-wide organic holism that this requires is simply not present within modern democratic political thought. In practice, though, many of us do indeed recognize that the ability of a candidate to receive the support of something more than half of the electorate properly leads to talk of him or her as having gained some sort of a 'mandate', and this is considered no empty accomplishment.

Thus, even when we assert that the politician who carries a mandate is a kind of agent or tool of his or her constituency, that constituency must still be understood as being, to some extent, a more-or-less integrated organic whole, a notion which comes down to us from the classical republican, rather than modern democratic, tradition. But there is also another idea that the patriot borrows from the classical republican and then reformulates, one which should lead us to be even less willing to interpret the elected representative as simply a tool of the electorate. It comes to the fore when we examine the elected politician's role as a legislator. To the classical republican, as I have shown, laws are meant to be representative of the conception of the good shared by the whole citizenry, good laws being understood as those which are true to that good, i.e. its identity, this being what allows us to describe them as 'powerful' in the sense that citizens do not just find it useful that others follow them but also actually *want* to follow them themselves.[88]

But this 'power' of the law necessitates that there be a certain kind of connection between the citizenry and its legislators, one which would be utterly severed if the law is interpreted as nothing more than the product of an instrument of that citizenry. This is not, of course, an issue for classical republicanism, for that ideology has no place for representatives in its conception of governance. To the patriot, however, it is important to point out that those elected to make and enforce the laws must also represent the citizenry in a way that no 'tool' could ever do. Partly, this is a result of the fact that the sense of legitimacy which comes from receiving a mandate from the electorate applies not just to the platform that the candidate advanced during the election campaign, but also to the candidate himself. For voters may be said to take into account not just a candidate's promises, but also his character, and in so doing they go much further than simply asking the question of whether that candidate will keep his promises or not. This is because the candidate's character, being his identity—who he is and who he might be expected to become—is something distinct from his platform, just as the meaning or identity of a text is distinguishable from that of its author.[89] During an election campaign, the electorate is presented not just with a proposed set of policies, but also with a person, someone with a particular identity and so a particular capacity for making political decisions, many of which cannot possibly be covered in an election platform. In judging his merits as a person, then, voters ask themselves if they can identify with the candidate, if, that is, he is someone who seems to share in the same goods that matter to them, that power their own lives. But this is something that no tool, no matter how sophisticated, could ever do, for nothing 'matters' to a machine.[90]

So the idea of voters granting a mandate consists of them endorsing not just a political platform, but also the person(s) behind it. That there can be a tension between these two should come as no surprise, just as we should not be shocked if our representative refuses to come down on one side or the other of that classic, but by now rather tired, debate over the proper responsibilities of a representative, i.e. whether a representative should aim to mirror her constituents' wishes or, to take the other extreme, to do what she thinks is right for them regardless of their expressed desires. Because to vote not just for someone's political platform but also because of who she is means that one endorses that person's ability to make decisions concerning matters which will not only reach far beyond anything specified in the platform, but which will also, at times, even contradict it. It is for this reason that we may say that a representative, by virtue of having been elected to make decisions on others' behalf, ought to be recognized as a kind of *authority*. For the election has authorized her to decide on matters which her electors feel unable or (perhaps due to lack of interest or time) unwilling to decide themselves. Their choice, then, is at least partly the result of a determination that the candidate has good judgement and so that it would be good for her to play a direct role in policy-making. In this sense, the candidate becomes an 'author' of the laws and other decrees that will shape the political narrative in which both she and those she represents play roles. By accepting an authority in this way, it should be noted, citizens do not have to be considered as having abdicated their own reason and responsibilities. Rather, the notion of authority here may be understood as resting on an idea that Gadamer captures well (though, as I will explain below, only partially) when he writes that,

the authority of persons is ultimately based not on the subjection and abdication of reason but on an act of acknowledgement and knowledge—the knowledge, namely, that the other is superior to oneself in judgment and insight and that for this reason his judgment takes precedence—i.e., it has priority over one's own. This is connected with the fact that authority cannot actually be bestowed but is earned, and must be earned if someone is to lay claim to it. It rests on acknowledgment and hence on an act of reason itself which, aware of its own limitations, trusts to the better insight of others. Authority in this sense, properly understood, has nothing to do with blind obedience to commands.[91]

Authority, then, as Crick has pointed out, 'depends on the giving of relevant reasons'.[92] It is only when the powers of a legitimate authority are extended into domains in which it has either no mandate or competence that we must begin to speak of 'authoritarianism'.

ii

So, how, then, is the elected representative, our new authority, to decide? A great deal has already been said in this work about practical reason,

about how the hermeneutical approach to interpretation advocated by
the patriot differs from those conceptions associated with pluralism. All
of this feeds into the patriot's conception of policy-making as well, by
which I mean to refer both to how representatives can be said to arrive
at the positions they do regarding legislation and to the decision-making
made necessary by day-to-day political events. And yet, the path
towards greater truth here, to making the right decision, is, I would point
out, not necessarily a fully rational one, in the sense that we might want
to distinguish somewhat between the 'judgement' and the 'insight' that
Gadamer seems to use as synonyms above. Before I go into this matter,
however, I want first to ask the question of what, exactly, this 'truth' that
our representative should be striving for is.

The patriot's answer is nothing other than that it is the meaning of
the public common good(s) shared by the citizenry, one which includes
standards of both means and ends, these resonating with features that
come down to us from both the classical republican and pluralist political traditions. The hope is always to come up with a position that is true
to all of this, that is, to the meaning of all the goods shared by the citizenry as a whole, both as interpreted by the policy-maker as well as by
the public itself, the latter constituting the public's 'will' as communicated in elections, opinion polls, letters to the editor, and the like. More
often than not, the representative should begin by trying to get at all of
this with an interpretation, one which aims to integrate all the conflicting
positions held by the various parties involved. Being an interpretation,
it is not necessary that it be simply a reflection, the product of a 'discovery' of the meaning of the citizenry's common good, for it can also
lay claim to some degree of originality as well since, as I described in
Chapter 3, an interpretation may involve both the evolution as well as
the discovery of meaning. We may say, then, that the patriotic lawmaker,
in contrast to the classical republican, often does not just *follow* his
citizenry's common good, which would be the case if his or her interpretations aimed only to mimetically reflect its meaning, for he or she
may also try to *lead* it in the sense of advocating a position which
requires it to change, to evolve in such a way that it becomes truer to
itself. As such, the politician should be described as striving for an
appropriate 'expression', and not just a 'reflection', of the common good.

That being said, it is often the case that interpretations which are true
to all of the goods in question around a particular issue turn out not to
be at hand. At times like these, it is reasonable to expect that our politician will, at least at first, turn to time. That is, if there seems to be no
way to deal with a particular issue without compromise, then he or she
might be expected to try and delay, to put the issue temporarily aside

in favour of others. Making such a move is particularly appropriate within the patriotic conception because, all parts being more-or-less integrated within an organic whole, dealing with what may seem at first to be a very different issue can in fact lead to a transformation of that whole in a way which affects the original question, perhaps to the point that it becomes no longer as intractable as before. For no issue can ever be truly put 'on hold', ever fully fixed and isolated from the others, which is why one may become open to new, reconciling interpretations as a result of changes made to others with which the given issue's goods are always to some extent integrated.

Now just as both pluralism and patriotism are, as I have asserted, impartial as regards the various political ideologies compatible with them, the same is true regarding these two and the various kinds of political organizations which can act as 'inputs', to borrow a term from structural-functionalist political science, to the policy-making process. But when it comes to the matter of *how* these organizations should go about their business, the two approaches do indeed diverge. For example, to the extent that pressure groups, by which I mean to refer to interest groups as well as new social movements, tend to advocate their positions narrowly, disregarding the goods underlying any of the others with which their stance may conflict,[93] the patriot will shun them. The reason is that by virtue of their self-imposed narrowness of scope these groups articulate their positions as if they were independently distinct matters and, advanced in this form, it becomes particularly difficult to reconcile the good(s) they support with the needs of others with which they may be in conflict. This, combined with the often shrill and the self-righteous tones adopted by many of these groups' spokespersons, virtually ensures that the kind of dialogue that may lead to reconciliation is ruled out, the result being that the compromising of negotiation becomes the policy-maker's best option. Moreover, to frustrate matters even further, the very same pressure groups which make such compromises inescapable will often have none of them, this being why it tends to be left to the politician to impose a settlement amidst wails of protest. For regardless of where the line representing the compromise is ultimately drawn, many pressure groups simply never seem to be satisfied.

Now while pluralism certainly discourages the taking of uncompromising, hard-line stances in politics, there is no reason intrinsic to the approach that speaks against such groups having a narrow focus. Indeed, if anything, we might expect them to be interpreted as making a positive contribution to the negotiating processes underlying pluralist politics in that they help to ensure that the values involved in a given political conflict will be articulated in an independently distinct and so, to the pluralist, especially clear and undistorted way. Not so to the patriot, which is why patriotism may be said to favour instead those political organizations with a wider focus. To the extent that political parties, as distinct from pressure groups, aim to win office, it is often the case, at least in first-past-the-post electoral systems, that they end up developing platforms which cover wide policy ranges. To the extent that they do so, patriots will favour parties over pressure groups. Pluralists, of course, certainly have no reason to exclude political parties from their politics, although it seems to me that their approach encourages us to understand them in a limited way, that is, as but brokers which act as intermediaries between a divided civil society and government. This is because, at least when it comes to those weak pluralists behind the intrinsically liberal pluralist polity of Chapter 2, there is an assumption that politics should take place on top of a basic consensus existing throughout the society, with the result that parties are left with the role of putting forward various combinations of compromised, liberal-compatible values as they strive to achieve their singular goal of achieving and holding onto power.[94] Strong pluralists, however, are, at least in principle, open to a much more ideologically varied party system. To them, it will be considered legitimate that a given political party might be found supporting values that other parties have no place for; in consequence, parties in general will be incompatible with any brokerage model. And yet, regardless of these differences, all pluralists can be said to conceive of party platforms as consisting of a series of value trade-offs, and so as doing nothing more than expressing positions on how the various accommodations required by the politics of the day should be effected.

But all of this, the patriot would complain, ensures that party politics may offer us little beyond what we have with the politics of pressure groups. Because when it comes to the conflicts that constitute most political issues, parties as the pluralist conceives of them can advocate nothing other than particular compromises of the wishes of different social groups and so can only re-enforce the society's 'complementary schismogenesis' dynamic, to recall Gregory Bateson's term. If we limit ourselves to pluralism, then those mainstream parties which put themselves forward, as most in first-past-the-post electoral systems favour doing today, as parties of 'change', can really do so only in a limited sense, for they may differ from each other only as regards how they would compromise certain generally recognized values. A pluralist socialist party, for example, might call for a 'change' in which the trade-off between the values of individual liberty and equality is adjusted so as to give more weight to the latter, while a pluralist conservative might simply call for the reverse. No one, however, seems to have anything to say about how the two values, and all the others at play in the country's politics, may be fundamentally reinterpreted and so transformed. As a result, nothing, in any significant sense, gets done to alter the basic hostilities and dissatisfactions present in the society; indeed, if anything, these, as with any vicious-circle dynamic, are only allowed to get worse.

In patriotic politics, however, there is room for the notion that parties may advance positions that differ in much more substantial ways, which is to say that their platforms could indeed have something to say about how the goods shared by the citizenry as a whole should be transformed and not just compromised. For the point is always to try and rearticulate the goods involved, reintegrating them and so the whole into some new, presumably better relation. Disagreements between parties as to whether or how this should be done, then, are going to be much more meaningful than those available in pluralism. For this reason, we might say that, in patriotism, political ideologies can differ in much more substantial ways. Moreover, when political parties reflect those differences, developing wide-ranging and comprehensively integrated political platforms as opposed to those designed simply to fulfil fragmented 'us-first' pressure group demands, then they can be said to meet what should be considered the central requirement of patriotic policy-making. Of course those platforms, like the ideologies they are meant to express, will never be 'perfect', meaning that they will inevitably have to include proposals for compromise as well as for reconciliation. But the advocating of trade-offs should still never constitute a party's basic purpose, its hope.

I referred above to the representative using other than 'fully rational' means in political decision-making. With this I am, of course, entering onto highly controversial terrain, and I do not wish, nor do I feel able, to go into too much detail on the matter here. It is a question, however, which cannot be avoided, because I think that it is clear that, when voters vote for a candidate because of his or her character, as distinct from their platform, then they cannot always be said to do so solely because of their having concluded that the individual in question has good judgement. For it is here that the candidate's 'charisma' can be said to be a factor, this being a quality which, it seems to me, cannot be fully captured with talk of his identity. The idea is that when voters are attracted to a particular candidate because they find him charismatic, then this is because they see him as laying claim to certain extraordinary qualities, some of which, it is hoped, might help in reaching solutions to some of the most intractable political problems of the day. As Max Weber has pointed out, in the course of a discussion of what he conceives of as a pure, ideal-typical charismatic authority, it is the central mission of the charismatic leader to bring 'well-being' to his followers, for such a leader 'gains and retains [his authority] solely by proving his powers in practice'.[95] Put in terms of the distinction between interpretation and creation I introduced in Chapter 3, we might say that what voters are hoping for when they are attracted to a charismatic individual is that he or she claims a creative capacity which allows them to fashion the necessary radical transformations of the goods involved in certain, seemingly intractable, conflicts, transformations which would allow even the most acute conflicts to be overcome with little or no compromise. Such radical transformations, as I have described, can be understood as creatively, and not just interpretively, original, being enacted by individuals who are sometimes described as 'inspired' or, if this sounds overblown, 'just plain lucky'. Such enactions, it should be clear, are in some sense irrational[96] or, rather, supra-rational. Creative originality, as I have written, does not require a fully asketic overcoming or negating of the self, and so does not have to entail a complete rejection of the dialogical processes of interpretation. But it does seem to involve something like an infusion of an individual's—perhaps fragmented[97]—self with a kind of energy that must be distinguished from that sort of expressive power associated with the notion of a compelling interpretation. This is because the visionary capacity of creative originality is one that, it seems to me, cannot be captured by the strictly aural metaphors appropriate to talk about practical reason. The person of good practical judgement may very well be the individual lucky enough to be graced by such creative inspirations,[98] but these two capacities may also be distinguished.[99] We may say, moreover, that the policy-maker who manages to overcome conflicts by such means can earn a special sort of glory for him- or herself, one which arises not so much from the vanquishing of an adversary (for, in these cases, the conflict is transcended or overcome rather than won for one side over another) but, as with the artist, from achievements of great originality. That such deeds are often described as 'inspired' invokes something of the sacred quality that some associate with this kind of glory, this being complemented by the notion that the actors should be understood as situated, not so much on the margins of society (which seems to me to be the too-conservative assumption underlying Taylor's conception of the epiphanic artist) but rather to some extent *outside* that society, this making them, in a sense, 'beasts or gods' as Aristotle might say.[100] Indeed, by virtue of their having this relation to society, such individuals might even be described as 'strangers' in the elemental sense of the term,[101] since if they are to partake of this sacred kind of glory then they must be able to lay claim to a connection with the transcendent. After all, at least when it comes to the three major monotheistic faiths, the divine is often referred to as 'glorious' but rarely 'honourable', the latter term being reserved for those who are in some sense great, but nevertheless always full members of their societies.

6

Welfare: Towards the
Patriotic Corporation

Papa! what's money?

   Charles Dickens, *Dombey and Son*

[Money] is called a customary thing . . .

   Aristotle, *Nicomachean Ethics*

The least infamous of all businessmen is the one who says: Let us be virtuous in order to earn more money than the fools who are corrupt.

   Charles Baudelaire, 'Mon cœur mis à nu'

I

Imagine that, one day, a corporate manager realizes that she can improve her corporation's competitiveness by having it enter into certain informal and implicit trust agreements in order to limit competition from businesses outside of those agreements. Moreover, that same day she receives a report about a potential competitor who has developed an innovative new product and decides that the thing to do is to buy them out and then hold the product back, thus ensuring that her own firm's profits are not jeopardized. Perhaps in a few years, when the current production line has run its course and the factory will be ready to be re-equipped anyways, her company can bring the new product out on the market. The question I want to begin this chapter with is the following: do our manager's activities on this day make for good business?

One answer, one given perhaps most forcefully by Milton Friedman, working within what is often called the 'neo-classical' *laissez-faire* business philosophy, is yes. In a well-known article, Friedman argues that whatever a firm can do to increase its profits for its shareholders—provided, of course, that it remains within the bounds of the law—it should do.[1] Echoing Adam Smith's famous 'enlightened self-interest' based conception of the 'invisible hand',[2] Friedman argues that if businesses compete by restricting their focus to this aim and this aim alone then all in society will benefit, and to an extent much greater than any alternative approach to business could bring about.

Pluralists, however, can be said to proffer a significantly different answer to our question, one which is best summed up as a qualified no. For when it comes to corporate business practice, pluralism is associated with a conception that anglophone business ethicists tend to refer to as 'managerialism' (in the United States) or 'stakeholding' (in Britain), in which good corporate governance is said to recognize that a corporation has responsibilities to a plurality of stakeholders both within the corporation and throughout society—shareholders' demands for profits constituting but one of these.[3] Customers, suppliers, employees, competitors, the needs of the state, the environment, and various other social interests, all are conceived of as having a valid stake in the activities of the corporation. And, in standard pluralist fashion, when the interests of these various stakeholders clash, corporate managers are called upon to engage in the balancing act of making the trade-offs or concessions appropriate to the circumstances. Moreover, if they do this properly, and so attend, to some extent, to the needs of the corporation's stakeholders, pluralist business philosophers argue that the corporation will, in the long run, actually be more—rather than less—profitable.

The pluralist response to our question is a qualified and not an outright no because, to pluralists, our manager's actions can indeed be justified to an extent, in that they aim to meet the demands of at least one value, that of her firm's (and so its shareholders') profits. It is just that, in this case, other values, those represented by the other stakeholders, are so neglected that, overall, the pluralist can be expected to be highly critical of her activities. For the exclusive pursuit of a single value without regard for others is anathema to pluralism. After all, the pluralist might be expected to point out, what do we mean by the word 'greed' if it is not to refer to behaviour such as that of our manager's?

I want to argue, however, that the answer to our question should indeed be, or at least aim to be, an outright no. This, I will show, would be the patriot's response, and it is one that entails rejecting the pluralist's conception of profit as a single, independently distinct value, one present amidst a plurality of stakeholding others. Because when we appreciate that profit is to some extent integrated with those others and so is conceptually distinct from them only in a non-independent,

inseparable sense, then, I would claim, we are led to a better conception of how it ought to be pursued as well as to a better understanding of both the nature and proper activities of the corporation in
modern society. We are led, in short, to what I want to call 'the patriotic
corporation'.

II

Pluralist business ethics arose in the twentieth century in response to a
perceived growth in the size and impact, both economic and political,
of the modern corporation, one which has been great enough to raise
concerns about a lack of competition as defined in the neo-classical
model. To pluralists, government may have a much more active role in
the economy than is acceptable to the followers of *laissez-faire*. Eco-
nomically, then, pluralists have tended to be Keynesians, at least to the
extent that they have abandoned the notion that markets ought to be
fully self-regulating.[4] And regarding their model of the corporation,
pluralists should be interpreted as having made the same move that they
did against the classical and neo-classical modern democrats of the previous chapter. Because where the neo-classical economist envisions a
kind of island of unified planning in a sea of market relationships,[5] the
pluralist would shatter that island into fragments, emphasizing the plurality of independently distinct stakeholders present both within and
without the firm. As John Kay, for example, asserts: 'The essence of the
firm is a set of relationships among its stakeholders and between itself
and other firms.'[6] In consequence, as I pointed out above, pluralists have
come to conceive of the firm's responsibilities differently. As the Committee for Economic Development (CED) has put it, in a work that
probably constitutes the most succinct expression of pluralist business
ethics, corporations should recognize that they must 'assume broader
responsibilities to society than ever before and to serve a wider range
of human values [than just profit]'.[7] Moreover, according to the CED,
the modern professional manager

regards himself, not as an owner disposing of personal property as he sees fit,
but as a trustee balancing the interests of many diverse participants and constituents in the enterprise, whose interests sometimes conflict with those of
others . . . This interest-balancing involves much the same kind of political leadership and skill as is required in top government posts.[8]

Corporate managers take on these responsibilities, it is said, for three
reasons: (i) the professionalization of business management this century

has meant that managers have developed a wider scope of social awareness; (ii) pressure (not only regulatory or legal) from the state; and (iii) pressure from the corporation's other stakeholders, including the general public. Where early pluralist works stressed the first of these three factors,[9] later statements, such as the CED's, emphasize the latter two, this being a result of their greater appreciation of the competitive realities of contemporary markets and so a scepticism about the assumption that managers have the discretion or leeway assumed by the earlier pluralists. Indeed, the reason these pressures ought to be responded to, it is asserted, is that doing so is considered to be in the long-term, profit-making interests of the firm. To the CED, these are best fulfilled, not by a direct focus on profit, but by attending to the interests of all the corporation's various stakeholders, for 'the pursuit of profit and the pursuit of social objectives can usually be made complementary'.[10]

But there is, depending on how this rather vague statement is interpreted, a dilemma here for the pluralist business philosopher. On the one hand, if doling out some of the corporation's short-term profits to various stakeholders contributes to its long-term profits, then the question arises: is it really right to say that the corporation has forgone some of its profits in order to meet the needs of non-shareholding stakeholders? For hasn't it just sacrificed some of its short-term gain for long-term benefit, that is, hasn't it, for strictly instrumental reasons, simply made an investment? When Michael E. Porter and Claas van der Linde argue, for example, that government regulation in the area of environmental protection can, by stimulating innovation, actually contribute rather than detract from the competitiveness of firms in the long run, they limit themselves to highlighting a strictly instrumental route to, as they put it, 'relaxing the tradeoff between competitiveness and the environment'.[11] This is a case, then, of an instrumental commensuration of what, at first, seemed to be two conflicting incommensurable values. Like our student in Chapter 3, the one lucky enough to be able to borrow his neighbour's car and so help his friend move *and* finish his academic work,[12] we have here a case of corporations taking a reductive route to meeting one of their stakeholder's needs on the one hand, and maintaining—even perhaps improving—their long-term profits on the other.

But then the meeting of the needs of non-shareholding stakeholders cannot be said to have been done because the corporation was in any sense truly *accountable* to them,[13] that is, as if the value represented by the stakeholder was considered intrinsically valuable, valuable 'in-itself', and so not reducible to that of the maximization of profit. And this

would then mean that, when it comes to the ultimate aim of corporations, there is, in the end, little significant difference between the
pluralist and neo-classical approaches. This is because, like the neo-classicist, the pluralist who would emphasize long-term profit-making as a
result of meeting various stakeholder needs considers profit as but a
result of instrumentally efficient activity aimed, ultimately, at profit.[14]
Where the neo-classicist speaks of 'enlightened self-interest' and asserts
that working for oneself is in the best interests of others, the
pluralist as understood here advocates what we might refer to as an
'enlightened other-interest' in which working for others is considered
to be in the best interests of oneself. These pluralists can be said to
reject the neo-classicist's 'enlightened self-interest' only because they
recognize that competition aimed directly at profit can often lead to
unprofitable results. As Kay relates Albert Tucker's infamous game-
theoretical tale of 'The Prisoner's Dilemma':

Two prisoners are arrested and put in separate cells. The sheriff admits he has
no real evidence but presents the following alternatives. If one confesses, he or
she will go free, and the other can expect a ten-year gaol sentence. If both
confess, each will be convicted, but can expect a lighter sentence—seven years
perhaps. If neither confesses, the likely outcome is a short one-year sentence
for each on a trumped up charge.[15]

Whatever each conjectures about the actions of the other (i.e. whether
it is assumed that the other will confess or not), it seems that reasoning
instrumentally in a purely self-interested way will lead each to confess,
with the result that both end up going to prison for seven years. By
acting solely for themselves, then, a less than optimum result ensues for
both. It should be easy to see how such a pattern would only repeat
itself when it comes to competition between firms whose strict instrumental focus remains fixed on nothing but their own respective profits.
For example, as Kay points out, firms that limit themselves to this sort
of behaviour will only frustrate the establishment of joint ventures in
which the transfer of skills and expertise between them can be to their
mutual advantage.[16]
    And so, as should be clear, the pluralist who would conceive of
profit-making as the result of indirect, long-term profit-seeking, of
enlightened other-interest, still shares a fundamental assumption with
the neo-classicist, namely, the unity of the interests of all (i.e. of oneself
and others). That is why we can recognize, as Danely has pointed out,
that nothing in the Keynesian framework entails, or even suggests, that
corporations should, ultimately, act in any other way than to maximize
profit.[17] Hence Kay's own statement that 'the corporate chief executive

correctly points to the profits of the company as a measure of its success'.[18]

But surely this assumption of unity, given both pluralist fundamentals and the reality of business experience, is unwarranted. Should pluralist business philosophers accept this, however, then they might find themselves confronted by the other horn of the dilemma that I have claimed they face. For say they forgo talk about long-term profit maximization through enlightened interest and turn instead to an appreciation of the genuine conflicts that can take place between sometimes incommensurable values, that fundamental that they purport to be so sensitive to. It is such conflicts which lead, at times, to the inescapable need to compromise some or all of the conflicting values. If pluralists truly appreciate this, as we might expect they would, then we could indeed say that for them the corporation should be, to some extent, really accountable to all of its stakeholders and so that it should try to meet their needs even though this will often mean forgoing real profit, in both the short and long term. But there is a problem with taking this route as well. For what, we might ask, of the competitive realities of the market? Did not the earlier pluralist business philosophers assume too much freedom of manœuvre on the part of corporate managers? As Danely has pointed out, there are, at least in the United States, numerous forces at play which encourage managers to maximize profit by allocating resources efficiently, not to mention disciplines against inefficient behaviour. Indeed, as many have argued, managers in that country are so directed toward short-term profits as a way of maintaining the value of a company's stocks that important long-term considerations are often neglected by necessity.[19] Managers may wish to recognize the requirements of values other than profit, but often this has to remain but a wish. After all, if the business environment is so competitive that attending to stakeholders other than shareholders threatens the very survival of the firm, then surely the manager will have to act accordingly. Indeed, with the increasing globalization of the market economy accompanying the expansion of free trade, we might expect this to apply to all corporations, not just those in the United States. It seems, then, that the pluralist who would take this route comes up against the bars of what Weber famously referred to as the 'iron cage' of modern capitalism.[20]

I am not sure if pluralist business philosophers appreciate this dilemma, but they certainly act as if they do. For they end up trying to avoid it by, strangely enough, grasping both its horns and so asserting a paradox. Somehow, the claim goes, corporations, by aiming to act *not* in their own self-interest, whether in the short or long term, maximize their self-interest. Here, for example, is how Kay expresses what others have called 'the profit-seeking paradox':

Look at companies which would be towards the top of everyone's list of the world's most successful corporations. It might include IBM, Volkswagen, and Matsushita; Honda, Glaxo, Hewlett-Packard. Profits and profitability are certainly important to them all. Yet none of these companies is characterized by an exclusive preoccupation with profit maximization. All would acknowledge a wider set of responsibilities . . .[21]

What Kay is saying here, essentially, is that the most profitable corporations are those with wider concerns than just profit. By making this assertion, he certainly avoids impaling himself upon either of the two horns of the dilemma I have outlined. But it is still a paradox, one which, I would claim, is a direct result of pluralist assumptions about values and practical reason. If we turn away from those assumptions, however, I think we can have access to a much better account of what really is, and should be, going on.

III

The problem, essentially, is that pluralists begin with a concept of profit that, as with the neo-classical economist, is equated with money, and so is conceived of as independently distinct. Only then, unlike the neo-classicist, they throw other values into the picture, though they do this in an incrementalist rather than transformational way in that the addition is assumed to not alter the conception of profit at all. Profit as money remains a thin, highly precise, independently distinct value. In leaving it as such, pluralists, as I have argued, have no means of integrating or reconciling it with others when it comes to conflicts in thick contexts.

But even money is not as thin and as isolable in meaning as both neo-classicists and pluralists assume, and this is so even when it is considered a 'purely' instrumental good.[22] This is because just as the disengaged paradigms of 'normal' natural science need to be established upon engaged backgrounds,[23] so must economic units of measure such as money rely upon, and so be to some extent meaningfully connected to, non-economic, social backgrounds if we are to reason, even instrumentally, about them.[24] And, more than this, money should also be understood as expressing much more than can be captured by the figures used to measure it. The concept of a 'price', for example, is much more than just a number, for it is also an expression of the purposes of agents within specific economic contexts and, as such, it cannot be properly understood when detached from those contexts.[25] That, for example, is why the same quantity of money tends to be worth much less to the rich man than to the poor man. To appreciate this dimension of money, moreover, is to recognize that even reasoning instrumentally about how to get it necessitates taking into account its relationships with other goods. For, like any tool, money is meant to do certain things and not others,[26] as is clear from the fact that some things cannot, or should not, be bought. This means that we must understand money as always to some extent integrated into specific relationships with other goods, rather than as being conceptually isolable and so as having an utterly contingent relationship to either the means used to achieve it or the ends for which it is used.

But if we grant that money, when looked at, as sometimes it must be, from the standpoint of the accountant, is considered a highly (though never completely) isolable concept, then we must be careful not to limit our conception of profit and so business success to money as so understood. This, however, is exactly what pluralists do. Not that they are led to accept those asocial individualist economic approaches which fail to recognize that economic agents must also act in a social context. After all pluralists are well aware that while the fictional *homo economicus* can, perhaps, be conceived of as that lone, atomized individual making purely instrumental calculations aimed at maximizing his or her income, any real person who lives in a real society will subscribe to more values than just that one and so a great deal will be missed if they are understood in this limited way. But simply recognizing the non-economically driven elements of a person's identity is not enough. That is because economics is not an isolable element of a divisible self, and the pursuit of wealth can only be properly understood by first recognizing the whole of a more-or-less integrated self and only *then* distinguishing between its parts, one of those parts being constituted by the valuation of profit. Understood in this way and the pursuit of money to the exclusion of all other purposes becomes not just, as with the pluralist, ethically wrong, but also conceptually incoherent.

This is why the pluralist business philosopher is forced to refer to a 'profit-making paradox' when it comes to corporate activity. The pluralist's error is that 'profit' is conceived of as an independently distinct value with the result that maximizing it through instrumentally efficient behaviour is considered an activity which is itself independently distinct from those aimed at meeting the requirements of non-shareholding stakeholders. The patriot, however, would interpret the matter differently. Within patriotism, those corporations that ultimately attain the largest bottom-line earnings tend to do so because they consider the requirements of stakeholders other than their shareholders as expressing, not concerns other than, or beyond, profit, but nothing but that profit itself, it being understood as including much more than simply the bottom-line. They are able to achieve this profit as broadly understood only because the relationships between the firm and its stakeholders (including states) are often shaped—not by negotiation, which is the pluralist's understanding[27]—but by conversation. That is to say, the various goods at stake in stakeholder claims—and this includes the profits desired by shareholders—must be interpreted as to some extent integrated with each other and so, in the best case, open to a non-compromising reconciliation as a means of overcoming conflicts between them. Only with this assumption can one truly enter into a conversation with others, it being one that all interlocutors must share, and must be known by each other to share. Should one party sense that the other is in it, not for the mutual benefit of all, but for their own ends as separate from one's own—this being the assumption underlying the pluralist's conception of negotiation—then reconciliation will simply not be viable, and the parties will be left with but two prospects, these being the two horns of the pluralist's dilemma mentioned above.

Conversation, then, is what good corporate business is all about. That is why corporations should aim to compete not, with the neo-classicist, strictly to make money, nor, with the pluralist, to make money as well as to contribute to a number of other independently conceived social needs, but rather to be 'successful' which, in this reading, consists of contributing profitably to a whole constituted by the integration of all of these aims. And that whole, moreover, is but the goods shared *in common* by all of the corporation's stakeholders, including its shareholders. The corporation should thus be understood as a kind of community, one embedded within the larger community that is the political society. When this happens, we get a very different conception of business practice than that advanced by the pluralist, one that has been well-articulated by Hubert Dreyfus, Fernando Flores, and Charles Spinosa when they write:

We compete [in business] because we enjoy the on-going exercise of our skills in a context where those skills make sense as components of a meaningful way of life. That is, we compete to make things and ourselves more worthy. We compete to make the qualities of the products we care about or the qualities of ourselves that we care about stand out. In short, we compete to develop identities within communities. In saying this we are saying, as well, that we do not normally compete to make money . . . Business owners do not normally work for money either. They work for the enjoyment of their competitive skills in the context of a life where competing skillfully makes sense. The money they earn supports this way of life. The same is true of their businesses. One might think that they view their businesses as nothing more than machines to produce profits [as narrowly, i.e. independently, conceived], since they do closely monitor their accounts to keep tabs on those profits. But this way of thinking replaces the point of the machine's activity with a diagnostic test of how well it is performing.[28]

But pluralists, by fragmenting the corporation into independent, separate parts, are barred from conceiving of those parts as relating to each other conversationally and so from conceiving of the corporation as a community. The result: a misinterpretation of successful business practice, one which leads to recommendations regarding that practice that, in neglecting conversation, are, in fact, counterproductive.

The pluralists' fragmenting of the corporation leads to another difficulty, this one centred around the question of ownership. Kay, for example, follows A. M. Honoré's assertion that there are eleven criteria within the 'full' concept of ownership: there are rights to possession; to use; to management; to gain income from; to alienate, consume, waste, or destroy; to a secure sense that one will remain the owner as long as one chooses; to transmit the item to one's successors after death; to an unlimited term of ownership while one lives; and to 'residual control' (i.e. one's rights to an item return when the period it had been leased to another ends); just as there are duties not use the item in a harmful way; and to expect that one's rights to the property can be taken away for reasons of liability.[29] This, of course, is standard pluralism, that is, the definition of a concept with a closed set of criteria such that a solid line can be drawn around it conceptually, it being understood universalistically and as independently distinct from other concepts.[30] Applying this understanding of ownership, Kay is led to point out that, when it comes to corporations such as British Telecom (BT), shareholders simply do not meet the test of ownership. 'Does a BT shareholder have a right of possession?' he asks, 'Not at all: if he goes to a telephone exchange, or the BT head office, he will be turned away at the door. Does she have a right of use? Only the same rights to use its services—no more, no less—as any other BT customer. And the right to manage—somewhat tenuously.'[31] In fact, Kay asserts, only two of Honoré's eleven criteria are unequivocally satisfied by the relationship between BT and its shareholders; three are partly met; and six are not fulfilled at all. He goes on to claim that a better case could be made for the claim that BT was owned by its directors, as they have rights of possession and management, as well as the ability to decide on the disposal of its assets. What they do not have, however, are personal rights to income and capital.[32]

But Kay, as we might expect, wants to go further than this. Since, to him, we must understand a corporation as made up of the parts represented by *all* of its stakeholders and the routinized and negotiated relationships between them, he argues that it makes little sense to speak of 'ownership' regarding a structure of relationships. His conclusion: 'No one owns or could own BT.'[33]

This conclusion does not seem to worry Kay, though it should—and this not just because there is an air of absurdity about it. Before I explain why, however, we might remark upon how predictable it is given his pluralist assumptions. In rejecting the neo-classicist's unified 'island of planning' model of the corporation, the pluralist, as I have shown, turns to a conception of it as a set of relationships between separate, independently conceivable parts. But now, there being nothing there with any integrity to it, it is easy to see how there is nothing there to own. To the hermeneuticist, however, as I have described, we should take a position that lies in-between unity and plurality. Yes there are a number of distinct stakeholders present, but they are not distinct in an independent, separable sense for there is always some integration between them, some degree of integrity to the whole. This is what allows them to, at least at times, relate on the basis of conversations and not just negotiations. And just as the conceptual borders between the criteria of ownership asserted by Honoré need to be reinterpreted as permeable, so too ought we to say that all of these groups share, to varying extents and in varying ways, in the ownership of the corporation.

Recognizing this shared ownership, moreover, allows us to speak of shared responsibility. Because if no one owns a corporation, then who is to be held responsible for its actions? But, as should be obvious, managers, shareholders, workers, even customers, *all* share, in their own ways, responsibility for a corporation's activities. Moreover it does indeed make sense to speak of the impact of a single corporation's actions. After all, Nestlé did have an effect on infant mortality rates in Africa due to its baby-formula campaign in the 1970s and 1980s; tobacco companies are responsible for the deaths of millions of smokers (a responsibility that has, of course, been increasingly passed on to their customers since proper warning labels have been affixed to their products); and The Body Shop has spared many animals from suffering by refusing to sell cosmetics tested on them. We certainly gain a great deal of sophistication in our understanding of the corporation by rejecting the neo-classicist's unified, shareholder-centred conception, but this should lead us to nuanced and richer, and so stronger, conceptions of ownership and responsibility, not to an opposite extreme where these notions are made problematic.

IV

Because I have chosen, in this work, to limit the discussion to the level of philosophy, little more can be said here on this matter of the responsibilities of corporations. There have been excellent works which take what I consider to be patriotic approaches to the economy, though they make the mistake (paralleling that of the weak pluralists described in Chapter 2) of advancing a particular ideology as if it could be 'logically' derived from the assertion of patriotic, and so philosophical, fundamentals.[34] That is an error that I do not wish to repeat. In consequence, I will go no further here than asserting that, regarding corporate law, it should be central to any statement of principles on corporate governance that, as James Boyd White has put it, 'The business corporation should always endeavour to act as a responsible citizen in its economic and other activities.'[35] This way of putting the matter, it seems to me, admirably emphasizes the *whole* of a corporation's responsibilities by avoiding the pluralist notion that profit-making is something independently distinct from the corporation's other, more socially sensitive activities, and so avoiding, or at least not entrenching, the antagonisms that attend it. This is what allows us to steer clear of a profit-making paradox, because the reality is that corporations, by aiming for nothing other than maximizing their profits, often can and do find non-instrumental ways of reconciling the demands of all their stakeholders, including their shareholders. We fail to appreciate this, to repeat the point, only when we limit our concept of profit or business success to that of money, a limitation which bars relationships between stakeholders based on conversation. Corporate law should always strive to encourage and facilitate those conversations, particularly since, as I pointed out in Chapter 3, it takes all parties together to mount each step on the 'force, negotiation, conversation' ladder, and just one to take everyone down. That is why we ought to reject the pluralist's assumption that the hunt for profit as a value conceptually separate from all others is one amongst a plurality of valid business ends, and it is also why a qualified no is an inadequate answer to the question posed at the beginning of this chapter. Because if it takes just one to 'corrupt' all the rest, then we should strive to ensure that there is as little room as possible for that one to do so.

One way of doing this is to ensure that governments, both within countries and globally, enact laws which require that finance serves productive enterprise and not speculation or hostile corporate takeovers.[36] Legislation such as this is important not only because it protects the business environment necessary for conversation to thrive, but also for the role it can play when we appreciate that conversation will, in many cases, simply not be a viable option. For while the pluralist is mistaken in neglecting the role for conversation in business, there is nevertheless a great deal of truth to the recognition that, just as in any other ethical context, conflicts between the needs of stakeholders will indeed often require negotiated solutions, and not only because of the ignorance of those involved but also as a result of the nature of the context itself. And here, perhaps, due to the competitive realities of today's marketplace, corporations will indeed tend to favour their shareholders over other stakeholders, if only to guarantee their very survival. Not that competition between firms is bad for business; on the contrary, not only is it an important engine for the production of wealth, but it also provides another peaceful context for the hunt for glory, an intrinsic good which, we can say, maintains yet another integrating bridge between the domains of state-oriented politics and business.[37] But competition can be structured in unhealthy, unproductive ways, which is why it is the responsibility of government to enforce legislation which ensures that stakeholders other than shareholders, be they representatives of labour, of consumers, of the environment, and so on, do not always end up with the short end of the stick when it comes to enacting the trade-offs or concessions that are, in the end, often inescapable. In a perfect world, perhaps, conversation in business would make such laws unnecessary. But this is not a perfect world.

7

Recognition: Towards a Patriotic Respect for the Individual

It is uncultured people who insist most on their rights, while noble minds look on other aspects of the thing.

Hegel, *The Philosophy of Right*

What is the liberty of the press? Who can give it any definition which would not leave the utmost latitude for evasion? I hold it to be impracticable; and from this I infer, that its security, whatever fine declarations may be inserted in any constitution respecting it, must altogether depend on public opinion, and on the general spirit of the people and of the government. And here, after all . . . must we seek for the only solid basis of all our rights.

Alexander Hamilton, *Federalist*, 84

I

The third major mode of justification in politics today is that of recognition. Often, it is demanded that persons be recognized by governments and others in a certain way. One form of recognition is that of cultural difference, as when women or the members of particular groups, such as ethnic minorities or nations, call upon the state to recognize their unique ways of being in the polity.[1] Another is exhibited in the inherently hierarchical honouring, and even glorifying, of certain individuals when they are, say, knighted, awarded the Order of Canada, or laid to rest in France's Parthenon. Though such events are often of great political import, they also, surprisingly enough, have tended to escape substantial controversy. Even less controversial is the idea that all individual persons, simply by virtue of being persons, ought to be recognized as laying claim to a kind of equal respect or dignity. And the most popular way of expressing this form of recognition, one encouraged by pluralists as well as by many others, has been in terms of rights.

Rights will constitute the main topic of this chapter. In it I want to argue that what has become the virtual equation of the respect for the individual with rights is actually much more problematic than has been assumed.

The move from natural law to 'natural', and then 'human', personal, or subjective rights is well-known.[2] The move to a partial historicization of those rights, to the recognition that rights lay claim to a thick dimension in which they are ascribed, not to the abstract entity 'man', but to the social and historical entity 'man', is still under way. This move is one in which pluralists have naturally participated. Their talk of a universal minimal moral code, for example, claims an important historical dimension. All the cultures of the world are understood to have come to give a place to the values embodied within it, and it is here that we can find, albeit in a limited form, the respect for the individual. But those values, and so the rights which are meant to express them, are not considered 'absolute' if by that it is meant that, in practice, they are to be uncompromisable. For a relative sensitivity to context and so history is, for the pluralist, meant to apply even to those rights expressive of the respect for the individual, including life, security of the person, freedom from torture, and so on. This is because the rights of individuals are understood to generate duties which can, in certain thick contexts, conflict with each other as well as with duties based on other values, and when this happens, pluralists can be counted on to remind us, compromise will be unavoidable.

This talk of 'rights generating duties' is already to assume a particular approach to rights, one known as the 'interest theory' approach, it being particularly favoured by pluralists.[3] Indeed, one of its most prominent defenders, Joseph Raz, is also, as we have seen, a prominent pluralist. According to Raz, rights are ascribable to those whose well-being (which consists of various interests of theirs) is sufficiently important in itself to justify holding others to be under a duty. Right off, it should be clear that this conception does not require that rights be attributable only to individuals. Many of those who support rights, as well as many critics, have, however, made this assumption.[4] But the idea that a group based around a value that its members hold in common can have rights is increasingly gaining support, and Raz's approach is certainly flexible enough to allow for this.[5] For the time being, however, I want to put this matter aside and focus only on the rights said to be expressive of the respect of individuals.

As Raz has pointed out, the interest approach can be used to defend this sort of respect in that a person can be said to have an interest in being respected.[6] Their interest here thus expresses certain intrinsic or 'ultimate'[7] values—here the liberty and equality of the individual—and that interest becomes the basis for rights. As Raz points out, however, interests can also express values which are only of an instrumental nature, as when we speak of the rights of journalists to protect their sources, these being justified by the journalist's interest in being able to collect information.[8]

While being based on interests, which are themselves based upon values that are either intrinsic or instrumental, rights are also said to be dynamic in that they are understood to generate different duties in different contexts.[9] Jeremy Waldron, in a discussion of the interest approach, has provided a particularly illuminating case of this:

The right not to be tortured, for example, clearly generates a duty not to torture. But, in various circumstances, that simple duty will be backed up by others: a duty to instruct people about the wrongness of torture; a duty to be vigilant about the danger of, and temptation to, torture; a duty to ameliorate situations in which torture might be thought likely to occur; and so on. Once it is discovered that people have been tortured, the right generates remedial duties such as the duty to rescue people from torture, the duty on government officials to find out who is doing and authorizing the torture, remove them from office, and bring them to justice, the duty to set up safeguards to prevent recurrence of the abuses, and so on. If these duties in turn are not carried out, then the right generates further duties of enforcement and enquiry with regard to *them*. And so on.[10]

Waldron goes on to point out that, with all these duties created by rights, it is reasonable to assume that there will be conflicts, both 'intra-right', between the many duties created by a single right, and 'inter-right', between different rights and the duties based on them.[11] And these conflicts, as we might expect, are said to be of the kind that will often require trade-offs, balancing, and so compromise.[12]

Though he does not use the terminology, it is clear that Raz's interest approach assumes the 'thin' and 'thick' distinction standard to pluralism. The distinction parallels one that he asserts between a right's 'general' and its 'specific' forms, the former existing in isolation in the thin, decontextualized dimension, the latter being an application of the former in particular contexts. It is in its application that a right, and the duties that it generates, are said to be able to come into conflict with other rights and duties, and so to be potentially overridden by them, this being why, as Raz states, 'a general right is . . . only a prima facie ground for the existence of a particular right in circumstances to which it applies'.[13] For Raz, then, a general right is something that always exists, it being something that can be overridden or 'defeated'[14] only when it is in its specific form, when it may conflict with others. For example, in the case of a conflict between the right of free expression and the

protection of persons' reputation or the need to suppress criticism of
the authorities in times of emergency, Raz writes that 'if in these circumstances the reasons against free expression override those in favour
of free expression, then while it is true that one has a right to free
expression [i.e. the right, in general, still exists], one does not have a right
to libel or to criticise the government in an emergency'.[15] Similarly, Raz
claims that 'one may know of the existence of a right [in general] and
of the reasons for it without knowing who is bound by duties based on
it or what precisely are these duties', and that 'the implications of a right
. . . and the duties it grounds, depend upon additional premises and
these cannot in principle be wholly determined in advance'.[16] It should
be clear, then, that Raz understands a 'general' right to be a thin, isolated, practice-free concept, the 'implications' of which come to the fore
only in practice, when that right is expressed in a thick context and the
specific duties it generates become evident. Under this schema, then, it
is still appropriate to describe a right as 'absolute' but only when the
term is assumed to have the meaning pluralists tend to give it, which is
to say that though the right is not necessarily uncompromisable in practice it may nevertheless be articulated independently, as a moral imperative which 'contains its own sense' or 'explains itself', to recall
Hampshire's wording.[17]

II

But there is a problem with expressing the respect for the individual
with rights as so understood. I want to begin identifying it by referring
to the fact that, as many have pointed out, there is something inappropriate about the assertion of rights in the context of families, or friendships. That is because, in such cases, rights talk is considered a sign that
the relationship has broken down, the persons employing it having
asserted themselves, not as participants in a common enterprise, but as
individuals separate from it. As John Hardwig has pointed out, 'a large
part of the pain that comes from realizing that your loved one or friend
has begun scrupulously respecting your rights . . . comes from the
awareness that he or she is treating you as a separate being'.[18] Now
Hardwig assumes that rights go with an atomist conception of individualism, but we need not go that far to appreciate the separating and
adversarial qualities of asserting one's individuality in terms of them.
Thus Waldron: 'To stand on one's right is to distance oneself from those
to whom the claim is made; it is to announce, so to speak, an opening

of hostilities; and it is to acknowledge that other warmer bonds of kinship, affection, and intimacy can no longer hold.'[19] And so the rights of the individual, we may say, have no place within a value or good that is meant to be held in common with others.

But what about the respect for the individual, the principle which these rights are meant to express? I want to say that such a respect does indeed have a place, that the good of the equal liberty of the individual can and should be understood as integrated with those of common goods. Think, for example, of those voluntary associations in civil society, which are common goods and yet which, being voluntary, ought to be considered as fully reconciled with the freedom of the individuals that choose to join them. Or think of the following statement: 'When I'm in this marriage, friendship, community, etc., I feel more authentic, more true to myself.' Here, it should be clear, the speaker is assuming that his individuality and so, to some extent, his respectability, is reconciled with the given common good, that it is present *within* it. This is to say much more than that his interests as an individual are conceptually independent but simply not in conflict with the value underlying the common enterprise; rather, the assumption is that they and the common good are all highly integrated, actually dependent upon each other such that, without the marriage, friendship, or community, the speaker would feel less authentic, less true to himself as an individual. Such a conception, it should be clear, assumes the viability of a holographic holism when it comes to the meanings of the goods involved, one which, as I have shown, must be contrasted with the conceptual atomism underlying pluralism.

Understanding matters in this way should leads us to conclude that it is not the assertion of respect for the individual *per se* that is the problem when it comes to common goods, it is only doing so in terms of rights. For the adversarial quality of rights injects a distance between the rights-holder and others, one which serves to undermine those things which they share in common. Invoking rights, we might say, is like pouring corrosive acid on a common good. After all, from the moment one enters into negotiations with a friend, one should not be surprised if the dialogue leads to the end of the friendship.

Not that there cannot be ongoing conflicts between one's obligations to a common good and those to one's individuality. 'I'm not sure if I can act respectably in this relationship' or 'I'm not sure if I can be authentic in this friendship' are certainly conceivable concerns to raise, and doing so in these ways allows for a conversational, rather than negotiational, response to the conflict, the interests of the individual being expressed in a way that the duty to fulfil them does not, right from the start, compromise the common good. It is only the reference to rights that does this.

Why do pluralists miss this step, the assertion of one's individualism within a conflict in a non-adversarial way? In the case of Raz and his followers, it seems to me, it is because they simply have the matter backwards. Because when it comes to conceptualizing the respect of the individual, Raz begins, not with the goods of individualism as they exist in a thick and pre-reflective practice, integrated with others, *before* any conflict may arise between them and those others, but with thin, isolated, universalistic concepts that are understood to exist outside of the context of any practice, in some (as I have been claiming) non-existent, mentalistic realm of practice-free thought. Only *then* does he go from values in this form to the interests of the individual that stem from them, and *then* to certain general rights 'generated' by those interests, and *then* to specific rights and duties 'generated' by those general rights. As a result when a conflict arises the duties necessary for fulfilling certain values in practice are conceived, not as part of a more or less integrated mesh but, being at the end of a conceptual train that begins with thin, separate concepts, as but the independently distinct fragments expressive of them. And because those duties are understood as capable of having unbroken conceptual lines drawn around them, they are open—not to the transformations conducive to their reconciliation with others—but only to the zero-sum, adversarial relations productive, at best, of compromise.

If we begin from the other, practical end, however, we can acknowledge the reality that our conflicts tend to show up first as conflicts of thick, more-or-less integrated duties, and these are open to being dealt with conversationally, reconciliation thus being a viable aim. It is only when these conversations break down that we need to turn to rights talk and the negotiations that (hopefully) attend it. Moreover when we come at rights from this direction, we can appreciate why even rights ought not to be conceived as distinct from each other in a wholly independent sense, the lines we should be drawing around them being dotted rather than solid (although the spaces in those lines might be said to be smaller than the more integrated, and so less inherently adversarial, duties associated with them). This means that even the rights of the individual that I have been focusing on here should be understood as intrinsically connected to, and so as conceptually entailing, other rights, those connections existing in the spaces of the lines drawn around them. And arguments have indeed been advanced in support of this idea.

For example, individual rights can be understood as justifying the rights of nations to some kind of political expression, and this without necessarily passing through the aspiration to self-rule. This argument begins with the assumption that, because persons are cultural beings, meeting the conditions necessary for them to have identities is indispensable to their being full human subjects. Now since a crucial pole of many persons' identification today is their language/culture and hence their linguistic community, then this means that that community's availability as a viable pole of identification is indispensable to their identities and so to their being full human individuals. In consequence, they have a right to demand that others respect the conditions of their linguistic community fulfilling this role, conditions which can entail (i) the maintenance of the health and expressive power of their language, this giving support to certain language rights; (ii) the support of endeavours which assist their community in making achievements in certain crucial fields such as artistic creation, technological innovation, economic productivity, and political self-rule itself, so that the language or culture of the community can continue to command its members' allegiance; and (iii) some degree of political recognition of their nation's difference, both globally and, in the case of multi-national states, domestically. The rights that emerge from these three, we should be clear, are the rights of a nation, not of the individuals within it, but they are entailed by the latter.[20]

A similar kind of argument can be made to bring to the fore the inherent conceptual connections between the negative rights of individuals and their social or welfare rights. For example, once we abandon the premises of an atomist individualism, the right to life can be understood as entailing much more than that a person must be free from being attacked by others. Because if the very conditions of a fully human life depend on society, that very same right to life requires much more than the non-interference of others for it will also, at times, demand the active assistance of the society's members. Being fully human involves laying claim to certain specifically human capacities. These capacities, however, do not only command the respect expressed by negative individual rights, for our valuation of them also calls forth a commitment to foster their development. And it is this that demands, at the very least, a respect for certain social and welfare rights, these requiring the provision of minimum income and health care, as well as basic education and employment if the required development is to take place.[21]

So certain rights of individuals, rather than standing as independently distinct, can be shown to entail other rights. Not so from Raz's perspective. As pointed out above, his interest approach certainly *allows* for the possibility of such other rights but, as these are derived from separately conceived interests, it does not *necessitate* them, for the conceptual atomism he assumes prevents him from referring to any inherent conceptual connections between them. Thus when Raz writes that 'states, corporations and groups *may* be right[s]-holders', or 'whether certain groups, such as families or nations, are artificial or natural persons is important for determining the conditions under which they *may* have rights. But we need not settle such matters here',[22] it is clear that, to him, the rights of the individual is a matter that can be fully comprehended in isolation from questions concerning other kinds of rights. As he is a pluralist, this should come as no surprise.

III

i

So what, then, is the appropriate role for rights, properly understood, in politics? For reasons that will become clear below, I want to begin answering this question by distinguishing between domestic and global politics. Regarding the former, the patriot, for whom politics at its best begins with a struggle to be true to a polity's civic public common good of the heart of republicanism in modern politics, will consider the assertion of rights, with their inherently adversarial character, as at the very least an impediment to the conversational process essential to fulfilling this good. For, as I have shown, conversation requires that interlocutors really listen to each other, and this entails being open to making the often difficult transformations of self that are required if a, to some extent, reconciliatory rather than compromising solution is to be found for the conflict at hand.

In consequence, the patriot will have difficulty with a constitutionally enshrined schedule of rights. To be clear, the problem here goes far beyond the notion of the justiciability of such a document, in which the rights, the defence of which being the special responsibility of the judiciary, are granted something of a 'trumping' status when it comes to conflicts between the goods they express and those not included on the list. To say a little something about this matter, recall that the idea that a constitution should, or could, defend certain goods in a way that constitutes a closed set of uncompromisable ground rules for politics, rules which are not themselves to be subject to that politics, has already been criticized in this work. It is, after all, central to many neutralist political theorists, with their prioritizing of the right over the good, or to those weak pluralists of Chapter 2, for whom pluralism in-itself is considered to uncompromisingly endorse a respect for the individual and the equal regard of cultures. But constitutions, I have argued, are based on politics, not the other way around. Constitutional law, in other words, is but a form of politics.

Developments in American constitutionalism, the country claiming the longest history with a justiciable schedule of rights, are particularly revealing in this regard. As T. Alexander Aleinikoff has argued, constitutionalism in the USA, in the twentieth century, entered the 'Age of Balancing'. By this he means that constitutional questions have come to be analysed in terms of competing interests and the compromising balances that, it is assumed, need to be struck between them.[23] But the interests considered in US Supreme Court deliberations have not been only those of the rights enumerated in the constitution and its amendments, as they have often included other interests, such as those of the states, as well. Now Aleinikoff is by no means happy about this development, but arguments such as those I advanced against Walzer in Chapter 2 should lead us to see how futile is any attempt to advance a set of principles as if they could form a self-contained unity, one which may then be asserted as uncompromisable in the face of external values conflicting with it. This, as I have shown, is the central message of the strong pluralists in that chapter, and it is one of which we should take heed.

This does not mean, however, that the very idea of a justiciable constitution must be ruled out in principle. What *is* unacceptable is only certain justifications for it, those which assume that judges' rulings are able to take place from within a realm of decision-making that is somehow neutral, somehow sheltered from the conflicts which constitute the stuff of everyday politics. But even the American Bill of Rights ought to be understood as, albeit implicitly, assuming the 'non-trumping' status of the rights listed within it.[24] It can thus be interpreted as recognizing that no theory-based, qualitative distinction can be asserted between the deliberats engaged in by a court and that of a legislature. But this is just what Aleinikoff fears. As he writes,

Balancing opinions gives one the eerie sense that constitutional law as a distinct form of discourse is slipping away. The balancing drum beats the rhythm of reasonableness, and we march to it because the cadence seems so familiar, so sensible. But our eyes are no longer focused on the Constitution. If each constitutional provision, every constitutional value, is understood simply as an invitation for a discussion of good social policy, it means little to talk of constitutional 'theory' . . . Ultimately, the notion of constitutional supremacy hangs in the balance. For under a regime of balancing, a constitutional judgment no longer looks like a trump.[25]

Aleinikoff nevertheless admits that there is a case to be made for a 'balancing' constitutionalism, which (in the terms of this work) means that those who would do so in the name of strong pluralism may still claim that the Court does not simply replicate the job of a legislature. That is because the judges on the bench, judging from within a different context than legislators, can be expected to balance the conflicting values in different, and perhaps preferable, ways. Aleinikoff points to two areas in which we might expect a Supreme Court to weigh matters differently than a legislature: (i) rights and interests explicitly referred to in the constitution might be expected to be a deeper concern for a judge, given his or her 'job description', than a politician; and (ii) the interests of unpopular or under-represented groups could be expected to be given somewhat more weight than they would be by the politician who, unlike the judge, is concerned with getting (re-)elected.[26]

There is an aspect of (i) which, as the reader should by now be able to predict, is problematic to the patriot. Because by articulating the goods involved in the conflicts in the adversarial terms of rights, a compromising, rather than reconciling, approach to political conflicts is encouraged, this being, to perhaps belabour the point, inherent to the pluralist's 'balancing' approach to practical reason. More than this, however, the goods are also distorted by being separated from each other conceptually and this, we might say, 'disempowers' them to an extent, detracting from their ability to motivate citizens to follow them. By approaching cases with a schedule of rights, judges end up reducing the situations they embody to the more fragmented, antagonistic terms of those rights, both distorting the goods involved as well as ensuring a practical reasoning of poorer quality, the possibility of finding a reconciliatory solution to the conflict being ruled out from the start. The answer to all this should be clear: states should remove schedules of rights from their constitutions.

I realize that this suggestion will not fall on many sympathetic ears. The trend this century has been in exactly the opposite direction, with many countries adopting constitutions with schedules of rights only in the past few decades.[27] But, to be clear, I in no way wish to object to constitutional references to the goods those rights are meant to express. Indeed, if anything, judges, as well as politicians and all other citizens, should be able to turn for inspiration to a document which provides a thick, profound, perhaps even poetic articulation of the ideals of their country. Is this not exactly Alexander Hamilton's point in *The Federalist*, 84, when he writes:

'We, the people of the United States, to secure the blessings of liberty to ourselves and our posterity, do *ordain* and *establish* this Constitution for the United

States of America.' Here is a better recognition of popular rights, than volumes of those aphorisms which make the principal figure in several of our State bills of rights, and which would sound much better in a treatise of ethics than in a constitution of government.[28]

There really is an emptiness, one derivative of a failure to put practice first, associated with the projects of those who would provide us with lists of thinly conceived, independent virtues or values,[29] and the same can be said of the lists of rights based upon them. For goods only show up to us on their own when they are in conflict, which is to say in a thick context, and so as more-or-less integrated in specific relationships with others. If they, and the rights connected to them, are to be articulated, then they should be done so together.

But this says nothing about whether a given constitution should be justiciable or not, this being a matter, not for political philosophy, but for the greater sensitivity to a country's specific political culture associated with arguments made at the level of political ideology. The philosopher should only point to the various dynamics encouraged by different institutional arrangements. The one relevant here is what I want to call 'the civic balance'. With this I really do mean to refer to a relatively zero-sum relationship: the more decision-making power is concentrated in a wise élite, the better, overall, will be the quality of those decisions in terms of content, though, in form, the policies based on those decisions will be both less representative of the majority of citizens (as they will differ from the positions held by that majority) and less the result of the participation of a larger number of citizens in their making. This should be a concern because, if we make what should be the rather banal assumptions that some people are wiser, that is, better interpreters, than others, and that the best of these will be fewer in number, we can say that giving decision-making power to such an élite can be expected to result in policies which, if they stray too far ahead of the views of the majority, make that polity susceptible to a legitimation crisis. For no matter how 'enlightened' their 'dictators', the citizens of a modern polity can always be expected to demand that its laws both reflect their interpretation of the good and are to some extent the product of their participation. The maintenance of this civic balance, then, must remain an ongoing concern of policy-makers and, more fundamentally, of those who are concerned with the distribution of power in society. The aim must always be to prevent, on one extreme, policies which too closely reflect the will of the (sometimes poorly thinking) majority—policies which, among other things, can cause undue harm to those unpopular or under-represented groups referred to in (ii) above—and, on the other, a legitimation crisis, with all the difficulties it creates for both conversation *and* negotiation in politics, not to mention the associated dangers of demagoguery, this being a standing temptation for citizens who feel alienated from the institutions governing them. And one of the first victims of demagoguery, the previous century has surely shown us, is respect for the individual.

Now assuming (and I realize that this can be quite an assumption) that it can be ensured that members of a supreme court are politically wiser than politicians and the citizens they represent, then this, combined with the fact that, wiser or not, the justices will be deliberating in a context different from the more representative-oriented elected parts of the state, allows us to conceive of the judiciary as possibly fulfilling the role of one of the two scales of the civic balance, in that judges might be expected to produce decisions superior in content to those of elected politicians.[30] But the legislature could, albeit to a lesser extent, also be considered able to play that role, for legislators, as I have pointed out,[31] do not simply echo the will of their constituents.[32] The question of how and the extent to which this 'content' side of the civic balance requires some form of institutional backing, say with a justiciable constitution, is, again, one for the ideologist and social critic, not the political philosopher, for it requires a judgement about the state of a given country's political culture, about the extent to which it is 'balanced' in the sense I have outlined.

Conversation, I have acknowledged, often breaks down in politics (as elsewhere), and when it does so the hope is that the conflicting parties will turn to negotiation. And when one is negotiating, there may indeed be a place for expressing the goods involved in terms of rights (though even here they should not be conceived of as distinct in a fully independent sense, and so utterly disconnected from the evolving *telos* that is the common good of the polity). But just as rights talk, as pointed out above, is greatly at odds with the aims of those more private common goods such as families and friendships, this applies to the more public common good(s) of communities and whole polities as well. That is why the invocation of rights should be understood as drawing on a document to which the polity is a signatory, but which is external to it, rather than an explicit part of its own constitution. For this is a way of encouraging its citizens to turn to rights talk only when the aim of being true to the good(s) they hold in common has had to be abandoned.

ii

I want to turn now to global politics. There are, and have always been, political regimes which are not only antipolitical, but which also regularly fail to meet even the much less stringent demands of the minimal moral code. Those in charge, we must recognize, simply do not recognize the goods contained in that code, and no amount of conversation aimed at getting them to do so can be expected to succeed. For, as only the most naïve will fail to appreciate, they are simply not listening.

Now if one believes, as I do, that some version of the minimal moral code is intrinsic to all of the world's cultures, then this means that there is justification for powers external to the regime in question to turn to negotiation and/or force to encourage compliance with the code. And here the blunt language of rights does indeed make sense as a means of articulating the reasons for doing so. After all, there is no need to be concerned with further empowering the goods those rights express through integrating articulations of them, for those goods are not being recognized in the first place. The problem, however, is that the various global-oriented declarations on rights, from the French Declaration of the Rights of Man to the UN Universal Declaration of Human Rights, suffer from a fundamental inadequacy: the rights listed are not ranked.

This is a problem for the following reason. Wu Jianmin, chief delegate of China to the 1998 session of the UN Commission on Human Rights, recently made the following statement: 'May I remind you that China has endorsed the universality of human rights at the policy-making World Human Rights Conference in Vienna of 1993. There may be different priorities and viewpoints about the application of collective and individual human rights, but the international community is marked by diversity of opinions.'[33] Now China has been in clear violation of the minimal moral code; it tortures political dissidents, and has committed numerous other fundamental abuses. It is able to do so under the banner of human rights, however, because those rights are articulated without the assertion of any particular priorities amongst them.

While pluralists could object to one of the reasons for this, they must, and do, have nothing to say about the other. That is, if the assumption is that rights need not be ranked because they fit together in some kind of perfect, systematic unity and so are not expected to conflict as incommensurables, then the pluralist will certainly be among the first to object, and rightly so. But where pluralists, as we have seen, are silent is on the inherent conceptual connections between rights, for to them rights are articulable in a thin, independently distinct manner. For this reason, a universal list of rights in no particular order must, to them, be unobjectionable. But recognizing, as the patriot does, that even rights are in reality concepts which are to some extent integrated with each other opens the door to articulating them, even at a very general level, as related in a prioritized manner.

Of course, this is a move that we do not want to make too hastily, particularly when it comes to documents that are meant for global application. Because different countries, with their affinities to different political ideologies and mixtures of these, can be expected to rank rights differently when they conflict. And yet, though the minimal moral code captures only that bare minimum of (negative) rights associated with respect for the individual, and though it asserts these in a highly limited manner (meaning not only that they cannot be considered uncompromisable in any circumstances, but also that they can be expected to speak against only the most basic abuses to respect for the individual), the very point of the code should be that it is inherent to the meaning of *all* rights that those of the code ought to be granted a rough priority over all the others. This is what should be reflected in any global declaration on human rights, a move that I would argue is endorsed by the patriot but upon which the pluralist can only be silent.

I should admit that I feel incapable at this time of going into more detail on precisely which rights should be granted priority, as well has how this should be expressed, but the basic point I am trying to make should be clear. If rights are going to be a useful tool in the confrontation with oppressive regimes, then they are going to have to be ranked, and in a way that only the hermeneutics of patriotism can allow.

8

Conclusion: Aim Higher

Who cops all the cops is all I ask of you.
The Tragically Hip, 'Trickle Down'

I

Why call it a 'patriotic' politics? One reason is that, by invoking the republican tradition of political liberty, we are reminded that politics should always strive to be true to the goods shared in common by all of a polity's citizens. And if it is to do this, I have been arguing, a place needs to be granted to the reconciling kind of dialogue that is conversation as a means of responding to the conflicts on which politics is based. In neglecting this, and so leaving us with but a politics of negotiation and compromise, pluralists end up so distorting this political liberty that they can almost be said to deny it.

There is at least one other reason for 'patriotism'. For as well as saying something about where (at least some of) a person's loyalties should lie, the term also invokes a particular sense of *how* these should be affirmed. As the *OED* defines the term, there seems to be a certain 'zealousness' about the patriot. To the neutralist, of course, this is considered a somewhat vulgar quality, it being a sign of the failure to achieve disengagement. To the pluralist, alternatively, it could be said to indicate a failure on the part of a political actor to temper his or her commitments, this being considered essential if there is going to be a willingness to compromise. But should we be forgoing our political passions so quickly? For is it not the case that neutralists, in adopting the stance which, I have claimed, is appropriate only in the natural sciences, tend to take on the scientist's cool reserve as well, and this is an attitude which, I would claim, actually 'unplugs' them from the moral sources, the goods that are the essential lifeblood of whatever ideology they happen to support. Neutralist ideologies thus tend to undercut their motivations for following them, with the result that what Rawls has referred to as the 'strength'[1] of their followers' sense of justice gets sapped. I say 'tend to' do this because Marxists, for some reason, often constitute an exception in this regard. But this is certainly not the case with the neutralist liberal. Indeed, neutralist liberals will often themselves be heard admitting that their doctrines—in contrast to what, to them, are those more 'irrational' creeds—are relatively uninspiring. As for pluralist politics, the politics of fear and negotiation, it seems to me to fare only a little better on this front. For its central message of the plurality of values points to a political arena constituted by divided, qualified loyalties,[2] one in which the willingness to compromise those values, and so to moderate one's attachment to them, is considered perhaps the central political virtue.

That they conceive of their politics as more discouraging than motivating does not seem to worry either the neutralist or the pluralist. In taking a different tack, the patriot can be said to reflect a different understanding of the nature of political thought and its relation to practice. To the neutralist, as I have shown, practical reason in politics maintains an intimate connection with theoretical reason by virtue of its reliance on a thin and systematic theory of justice for guidance. The pluralist, however, brings to politics not a thin and systematic theory, but a plurality of independently distinct, thin normative concepts, concepts which are to be given their appropriate place in relation to each other only when grasped in a thick and context-dependent way by political practitioners. To the patriot, however, because goods must always be conceived as more-or-less integrated with each other, it never makes sense for the moral or political philosopher to try and escape the domain of the thick. The point of normative thought is, as a consequence, understood to consist of striving for articulations that are true to *all* of the goods present in our practices. A political practice which appears confused, contradictory, and so in certain respects unjust, is considered to require a rearticulation such that those parts of it which are in tension, in conflict, may be more fully integrated or reconciled with each other, the whole practice thus being transformed into something more coherent and clairvoyant to its participants. The point of reforming a practice should always be to make it better fulfil the goods it expresses, a goal which, when achieved, will show itself as such because the practice will appear as more legitimate, the power of the goods underlying it having been augmented. To the patriot, then, an ideology should not only try to answer the question of *what* is to be done, for it should also affect persons' dispositions by motivating, indeed energizing, those who would follow it. Ideologists, by interpreting the world, can help change it. And since this is meant to be true just as much of the more abstract but qualitatively similar kind of thought practised by the political philosopher, philosophy, it seems to me, should be considered a friend—and not an enemy—of rhetoric.[3]

The political thinker should thus not be indifferent to his or her ability to persuade citizens not just to act in a certain way, but also simply to act. Many have written of the inadequate response of Western democratic regimes to the first news of Nazi atrocities,[4] or of the widespread violation of basic human rights taking place in various places around the world today. Surely this must say something about the failure of our politics to adequately express its goods—some of which take their place in the universal minimal moral code—and so to adequately inspire our citizens to realize them. Since apathy, as we all know, can kill, or at least allow killing to take place, this matter ought to be a major priority for any political thinker today. The question of how citizens can be motivated to stand up for their ideals should not remain neglected.

All of this applies just as much to domestic politics as it does to global concerns. That is because it seems to me that the most direct threat to the political regimes of the north Atlantic West today is not, at least in the short term, fascism, nor that chauvinistic form of nationalism, but rather the kind of legitimation crisis which can open the door to a demagoguery which, all-too-often, clears the way for these ideologies. And the neglect or distortions of our goods by those political practices which find support in neutralist and pluralist thought have, I would claim, only contributed to an increasing disaffection on the part of the citizenry. The growing legitimation crisis of which this is a symptom has been much remarked upon.[5] Vast numbers of citizens in the West have come to conceive of their society's institutions as pointless and unworthy of their allegiance, with the result, I want to claim, that two sorts of behaviour get encouraged. The first consists of citizens developing strong feelings of apathy regarding state politics, this itself being a complex function of two developments. On the one hand, there is the inability to hear the call of the political liberty that has come down to us from the classical republican tradition, political participation having lost its intrinsically valuable status. On the other, the increasing concentration of political power in institutions such as the bureaucracy and the judiciary, a development that has received at least implicit support from both many neutralist political theorists as well as from the leaders of those narrowly focused pressure groups encouraged by pluralism, only entrenches the sense of alienation from government. The necessary impersonality and invasiveness of dealings with bureaucracies contributes to this in one way, while the notion that the judiciary, when backed by a justiciable charter of rights, is there as a means of protecting one's rights *against* the state does so in another.

One might be tempted here to take up Tocqueville's theme of the connection between political apathy, social atomism, and the sense of alienation from government, these being said to contribute to what he called a 'democratic despotism' in which citizens, fully engrossed in their private concerns, welcome a 'benevolently' intrusive state.[6] But although apathy may characterize many citizens in the West today, this is far from true of them all, their behaviour here constituting the second reaction to the decline in the legitimacy of political institutions in the West that I want to point out, one particularly evident in the United States. For many citizens in that country have been known to make vociferous demands for a greater say in political decision-making and so to call for the decentralization of political power. They rarely do this, however, because of any wish to participate in the larger life of political liberty. Rather, they are often driven by a sceptical distrust of politics and politicians, of 'those guys in Washington', one which, as William Connolly has pointed out,[7] has translated into the increasing intransigence these citizens display *vis-à-vis* the political conflicts in which they involve themselves. For, as I pointed out in Chapter 5, to many pressure groups and their members, compromise has become a dirty word.

In consequence, Tocqueville's concerns notwithstanding, we must acknowledge the rise of a significant minority of citizens, or rather minorit*ies* (plural), who are anything but apathetic, citizens who can be found directing their not insubstantial energies and resources towards a vigorous, 'us-first' pressure group politics. But this politics, by virtue of its ever more grasping, indeed virtually unsatisfiable, temper, threatens to establish—not a version of democratic despotism—but what we might refer to instead as a kind of 'tyranny of the pluralities'. And the first victims of this new form of tyranny, ironically enough, are those who hold political power. Because politicians, facing a society consisting of a cynical and apathetic majority, find themselves quaking before those pressure groups which, with their ability to either provide or withhold significant amounts of funding and electoral support (many of the majority not bothering to vote), have been able to obtain an inordinate influence over policy-making when compared to the majority.

But the members of that majority are also victims since, ensconced as they are within their homes or deep within civil society, there is a sense in which they are often beyond the very reach of the law, the reach, that is, of its 'power' as distinct from its 'force'. To speak of a law's power, as

I have explained, is to refer to its moral legitimacy as considered by the citizens living under it, while its force, in contrast, is a function of the effectiveness of the police. The distinction can help us understand events such as those surrounding the abortion issue in the United States today. Abortion, as is well known, was made legal under certain circumstances in the country as a result of the US Supreme Court's *Roe* v. *Wade* ruling, but this 'legality', I would claim, tends today to refer more to the responsibilities of the police in enforcing it than to the idea that it should be considered legitimate by the citizenry. This seems to me to be a result of the fact that there is today far too much emphasis on the notion of the law as but a tool separate from citizens who use it, this being encouraged by the purely instrumental conception of the state found in the works of neutralists and many pluralists. This conception, I would assert, has contributed to the law's disempowerment, to a kind of facile disrespect for it amongst the citizenry. What has happened is that the decline in the legitimacy of government has, understandably enough, been reflected in a lack of respect for the decisions that emerge from it. That is why, having lost the *Roe* v. *Wade* legal battle, the American pro-life lobby has had little compunction in adopting such tactics as picketing the homes of doctors who perform abortions. This, and other 'legal'— used here in the narrow, strictly technical sense—measures taken by some in the movement, have meant that there are now fewer doctors willing to practice abortions, and fewer medical students willing to do the training to learn how to perform them, with the overall result being a significant reduction in access to abortions throughout the country.[8] A law which stands over and above, rather than being integrated with, the practices of civil society is, one might expect, powerless against such tactics. It is a symptom of the general malaise surrounding those institutions which make and uphold the laws that it has become almost inconceivable for a pressure group to accept that it has lost 'a fair fight' as regards some policy battle and so that it should, in consequence, go along with the policy's 'spirit'. Regardless of one's position on abortion or any other such issue, developments such as these should lead us to ask whether the kinds of victories available on the political terrain offered to us by the neutralist and most pluralists, one which rests upon the notion that the state is but an instrument, are not in some important sense empty.

And so, combined, these two developments—the growth in political apathy amongst the majority of citizens and the tyranny of the pluralities—point to increasingly unhealthy political cultures, in which governments are finding it increasingly difficult to cope with the evergreater pressures to which they are subjected. And their failure to do so, of course, only erodes their legitimacy further. That 'ungovernabil-ity' has become an increasingly popular term in political science circles should thus come as no surprise.

Pluralists have been aware of these developments, though not, I would claim, of their causes. Talk of 'overload' as well as of the ungovernability of the system, a result of the increasing 'indivisibility' of the conflicts being engendered, has begun to appear in their writings.[9] And yet their response does not, indeed, as I have argued, *cannot* consist in a call for a progressive transformation of the whole polity, for a break-ing out of its deteriorating complementary schismogenesis dynamics. Instead, we are offered only 'promises of disharmony', to invoke the subtitle of Huntington's book.[10] And with these come demands either that someone come up with more imaginative routes to compromise solutions,[11] or that those citizens involved in the conflicts accept that they will simply have to be more 'reasonable' or 'civil'[12] with each other, by which is meant that they should accept the inevitable and, damn it, start compromising after all. But the simple imperatives 'Negotiate! Compromise!' are—especially, ironically enough, when one limits oneself to pluralism—not particularly compelling. Because conceived of as a formal value *separate* from the others, some of which are ends, the pluralist conception of justice as negotiation remains, as Hampshire has admitted, a wholly 'negative virtue'.[13] The idea is that we are to engage in negotiation not because it is in any way consistent with a positive goal that we are all striving to achieve, or because it should be in any sense *attractive* to us, but only because it is a formal *obligation* that we ought to respect while we each separately reach for the ends that really do attract us. But by being interpreted in this way, shorn of any form of teleology, a great deal of the power of the notion of justice to motivate us is lost.

What is needed instead, I want to claim, is a conception of justice which gives us a *positive* reason to fulfil it, even when it turns out that this often means engaging in negotiations and so accepting compromise. Justice should, as much as possible, be conceived of as an intrinsic end, one which is integrated with all the other goods that a person and, pre-sumably, his political opponents, affirm. This, it should be evident by now, is how the patriot conceives of the matter, for patriotism strives for a politics that takes place within the context of the common good of political liberty, one that all citizens, regardless of their differing mem-berships in partial groupings, can be said to share. This is why, to the patriot, even negotiation can be conceived of as a matter involving goods that are distinguished by dotted, and not solid, lines. For all goods are, to some extent, connected, if only through the political liberty which should constitute the shared background to any political debate. This good is indeed an intrinsic end, one whose needs the pluralist's emphasis on separate interests utterly fails to meet. We can say, moreover, that it is because of this neglect that pluralists are finding it increasingly necessary to repeat their calls for compromise. The irony here is that only in a politics that pays due attention to the goods shared in common by a whole citizenry can some version of pressure group politics be made to work.

Common goods, of whatever sort, tend to be fragile in a way that those goods which can be fulfilled more individualistically are not. That is because they rely, for their very existence, on some sort of acknowledgement of their commonly shared status by all who would fulfil them. Friendship, for example, needs all who would participate in it to affirm it, unlike romantic love which, alas, can sometimes exist unrequited.[14] Those who would take a purely instrumental stance towards their government, however, have no place for the notion, handed down to us from the classical republican tradition, that the law can be an expression of something analogous to a friendship between citizens, one based on the public common good(s) which they all share. Sharing in such a good does not in itself demand a return to the small, city-state version of the *polis*, Aristotle's requirement that all citizens be within the reach of a herald's call being more than met today by advances in modern media and telecommunications.[15] The purely instrumentalist stance to politics, however, would destroy this fragile bond between citizens, making the law not an expression of what is shared but of something which is used, or feared, or both. In instrumental politics citizens *use* the law-making process and what it produces as tools with which to get what they want. And increasingly, as might be predicted, what they want is to be protected from each other. For there seems to be a fear present between citizens that is only encouraged by the wholly adversarial politics advocated by the pluralist.

Pluralists have, at least, offered us three differing reasons for why those involved in this politics should not turn to violence. First, for those attracted to agonistic pluralism, differences over the relative weights to be assigned to the values involved in political conflicts should be interpreted as based on rationally incomparable positions, meaning that each should be conceived as 'morally as respectable'[16] as the others. But while this rather facile moral relativism might be acceptable to the odd philosophy undergraduate, it will appear quite bizarre to those who have ever been involved in a real political arena. Second, there is the moral imperative to negotiate asserted by those pluralists who argue that it is a value to be found amongst those expressed by the universal minimal moral code. But this, as pointed out above, is a rather weak formal requirement, especially when it is interpreted as demanding that one be willing to compromise some of one's most cherished ends. Moreover, just as, as discussed in Chapter 3, the cumulative dirtiness admitted by the pluralist to be the result of the experience of many moral conflicts can lead to an unbalanced, divided self, one whose very mental health is threatened, so too can a politics which fails to go beyond the making of trade-offs lead to a legitimation crisis as regards the whole polity. As for those who refuse to make the concessions required of them, some pluralists have spoken explicitly of a third reason that they should nevertheless do so: force. Here, for example, is what Charles Lindblom has to say about why we should accept our laws:

If one asks, then, why people outvoted in a democratic election do not mount an insurrection but instead accept their defeat without disturbance to social stability or the continuation of democracy, one finds an answer in the many external controls exercised over them . . . Whatever their internalized norms, many people will not turn in defeat to insurrection, sabotage, terrorism, or street violence because they fear, among many external influences that bear on them, the law, the possibility of their own deaths in resulting violence, or their social isolation from their friends.[17]

In this conception, one obeys the law because one fears imprisonment; no appeal is made to the notion that citizens, of their own volition, should be expected to *want* to do so. What is forgotten here is that the weaker the sense of the law's legitimacy amongst the citizenry, the greater the strain on law enforcement and the legal system as a whole. Such a dynamic, surely, cannot continue forever. Because without a strong sense of devotion amongst citizens to their political institutions and governments' policies, then they—the citizens as well as the institutions—cannot really be said to be secure. This, if anything, is surely the lesson to be drawn from the fall of the Weimar Republic. That is why it is always a grave error to measure the security of our rights solely on the basis of how well they are currently being enforced, and why the patriot would raise instead the question of what happens when they are not. How do the residents of a municipality react when their police force goes on strike? Or what is the level of civility when a natural disaster strikes and public services are disabled? Only the answers to these sorts of questions can tell us anything about the health of a political culture, the real 'strength' of a polity. 'Who cops all the cops?' We all do. But we will forget this if we follow the neutralist or pluralist in failing to appreciate the necessary place of political liberty in any politics, ancient or modern.

II

There has been a great deal of criticism of pluralism in this work. And yet, despite all of the disapproving things I have had to say about it, it still seems to me a richer, indeed 'truer' philosophy than is that underlying those neutralist approaches which are only now beginning to lose their grip on the mainstream of Anglo-American moral and political thought. Pluralism appears to be where most thinkers today are now headed and, to the extent that this involves a rejection of neutralism, this is certainly for the good. Its greatest virtue is that, despite its propensity to distort through atomistic conceptualizations, it at least does not lead us to read any particular goods out of the story of who we are. As a result, it cannot be said to participate in the kind of self-mutilation that seems to me symptomatic of so many other moral and political philosophies.

In Chapter 1, I wrote of how neutralists are led by their disengaged rationality to distort many of the goods that we affirm in ethics and politics. Here I want to point to a move that many of them, though they are not alone in this, have made which has resulted in the rejection of certain valid goods outright. This is done not as a result of any methodologically induced error, but because of the (often understandable) temptation to reject a good which has been heeded to such a fanatical extent that great harm has been the result. That there have indeed been goods behind some unquestionably destructive practices may certainly say something against that particular expression of the good in question, but it should not, nevertheless, invalidate the good altogether. Taylor, for one, has pointed to this error.[18] The classic case here is probably glory, a good which, located at the heart of the ancient warrior ethic, drove those who wished to fulfil it to commit terrible devastations. But does that mean that glory should, or even could, be rejected altogether? A form of it, as I have at least hinted in Chapter 5, can be fulfilled in sports just as well (indeed better, by virtue of its complementing other goods) than in war. And it also, as I have tried to show, plays an important role in the adversarial aspects of politics. Other examples of this error have been committed by some of those (mainly Anglo-American) feminists who have pointed to the harm done to many girls and women as a result of eating disorders in order to back up their attempts to invalidate beauty as an intrinsic good; as well as by Nietzsche who, due to his concerns about the guilt-inducing, levelling down effects of certain strands of Christianity, advanced an interpretation of some of its highest ideals as but forces of *ressentiment* which should be overcome rather than respected. And many have, of course, trotted out the case of Nazism in support of arguments for the rejection of any and all forms of nationalism. The lesson here should be clear: too much of a good thing is indeed bad, but the good remains. Our aim, then, should always be to reinterpret an exaggerated good such that it can be reconciled with, rather than suppress or destroy, the others we hold dear.

Pluralists, like patriots, are encouraged by the inclusive spirit of their respective interpretive approaches to avoid errors such as the above. Subscribing to no unified philosophical system, they do not feel beholden to any Procrustean grids which can lead to the ruling out of certain goods altogether. And yet, and this has certainly been the central critique of pluralism advanced in this work, though pluralists aim to give a place to all goods, they nevertheless fail to do so without distortion. I want to conclude here by trying to make this point in a somewhat different way than has been attempted so far.

It has been pointed out, by more than one historian of ideas, that the goods which make a call on us in the West today can be grouped together as members of one of two 'teams', each sharing something of the spirit of the two major epochs that followed the advent of modernity: the Enlightenment and Romanticism. The most successful political ideologies of the twentieth century, Marxism and liberalism, both owe their appeal to the wide-ranging sympathies they display towards the goods found on both sides of this intramural divide. Marxism claims to lead to their unity, while the liberalism of the neutralist keeps them sharply separated in systematically divided domains of public and private. The result has been that both of these ideologies have found it necessary to reject some of our most important goods outright. Not so with the ideologies of pluralism and patriotism.

But these two nevertheless subscribe to significantly different aims. For my patriotic claim has been that we ought to set our political ambitions much higher than the 'damage control'[19] recommended to us by the pluralist, that we have a responsibility to strive for the mending and transforming or, in the Hebrew, *tikkun* of our world. The primary aim of any political ideology that would speak to a citizenry in the West should thus be to reach for the reconciliation, and not just compromising, of those politically relevant goods that have come down to us from the Enlightenment and Romanticism, to strive, we might say, for a wedding of Echo and Narcissus. Isaiah Berlin, however, will have none of it: 'As for us,' he has declared, 'we inherit both these traditions . . . and oscillate between them, and try vainly to combine them, or ignore their incompatibility.'[20] Reconciliation, integration, the vehicle of any journey towards unity, is abandoned.

Or is it? It seems to me that, despite its adherents' own failure to acknowledge it, the pluralist conception of 'moral sense' or warm prac-· tical reasoning embodies its own particular integration—and not compromise—of ideals that have come down to us from both the Enlightenment and Romanticism. On the one hand, pluralist moral sense is, as I have shown, meant to deal with the clash of incommensurable values, values which, in typically Enlightenment fashion, have been atomized, which is why they need to be dealt with in the zero-sum terms characterizable by balancing, another Enlightenment-charged metaphor. And yet, the kind of objectivity aimed for in this very same conception of practical reason is of an engaged rather than disengaged sort, one which must rely upon an affective perception that strives to be true to the particularities of a context. But such an aim, of course, invokes the spirit of the Romantic rather than that of the *aufkläler*. My claim, then, is that pluralists' own conception of practical reason is itself a product of an integration of ideals that have come down to us from the Enlightenment and Romantic traditions, and this, if nothing else, speaks against their claims about the impossibility of combining them.

All this being said, reconciliation, we must accept, will always remain only a sometimes possibility. That is because there is never any guarantee that it will be viable in all circumstances, this being a corollary of the recognition that we do not live in a unified moral cosmos. And yet, even when it does seem potentially viable, there will be cases in which it should be foregone, or at least the attempt cut short. For there are times when engaging one's political opponent in conversation can, when it fails, actually exacerbate the conflict, so much so that a later turn to negotiation is made even more difficult. This is because the attempt to understand another, to get at the truth of the history that brought the both of you to a given point may, it must be admitted, sometimes engender such powerful feelings that one's ability to make concessions later can then become impaired. But appreciating even this reality should not lead us to give up on conversation in politics altogether, for the gains to be had from answering an opponent as a friend rather than as an enemy are often simply too great to pass up. It is because pluralists have, I think, wrongly encouraged us to do so that I have advanced patriotism as the best political path to reconciliation, to the truths of who we are and should be.

Notes

NOTES TO PREFACE

1. For a good account of these developments, despite its over-emphasis of economic motivations, see Michael Mandel, *The Charter of Rights and the Legalization of Politics in Canada*, 2nd edn. (Toronto: Thompson Educational Publishing, 1992).
2. See Alain G. Gagnon and A. Brian Tanguay, 'Introduction', in Gagnon and Tanguay (eds.), *Canadian Parties in Transition*, 2nd edn. (Scarborough: Nelson, 1996), 4–5.
3. See Rainer Knopff and F. L. Morton, *Charter Politics* (Scarborough: Nelson Canada, 1992), 26–9.
4. I discuss the differences and relations between these two in my 'Political Philosophies and Political Ideologies', [forthcoming].
5. For more on contemporary antipolitics, see Andreas Schedler (ed.), *The End of Politics?: Explorations into Modern Antipolitics* (London: Macmillan, 1997).

NOTES TO CHAPTER 1

1. See Larry Siedentop, 'Two Liberal Traditions', in Alan Ryan (ed.), *The Idea of Freedom: Essays in Honour of Isaiah Berlin* (Oxford: Oxford University Press, 1979).
2. As Gregor McLennan e.g. makes clear in his *Pluralism* (Buckingham: Open University Press, 1995), p. x. Or, as Michael Walzer has written, 'In social, political, and cultural life, I prefer the many to the one.' *On Toleration* (New Haven, Conn.: Yale University Press, 1997), p. xii.
3. See Henry Sidgwick, *The Methods of Ethics*, 7th edn. (London: Macmillan, 1907), 105.
4. 'Nature has placed mankind under the governance of two sovereign masters, *pain* and *pleasure*. It is for them alone to point out what we ought to do, as well as to determine what we shall do.' Jeremy Bentham, *The Principles of Morals and Legislation* (Amhers, Mass.: Prometheus Books, 1988), 1.

5. See John Rawls, *A Theory of Justice* (Cambridge, Mass.: Harvard University Press, 1971), 26–33.

6. See Will Kymlicka, *Liberalism, Community and Culture* (Oxford: Clarendon Press, 1989), 24–33. See also the discussion in Michael Freeden, *Rights* (Milton Keynes: Open University Press, 1991), ch. 6.

7. See e.g. Bruce Ackerman, *Social Justice in the Liberal State* (New Haven, Conn.: Yale University Press, 1980); Ronald Dworkin, *A Matter of Principle* (Cambridge, Mass.: Harvard University Press, 1985); and Jürgen Habermas, *The Theory of Communicative Action*, trans. Thomas McCarthy, 2 vols. (Boston, Mass.: Beacon Press, 1984 and 1987).

8. 'The key [to *A Theory of Justice*] is to see the original position as the fulcrum of reflective equilibrium, in so far as it can be achieved. The original position is the fulcrum of the justificatory process in that *it* is the device through which all justification must pass, the place at which all arguments must arrive and from which they must depart.' Michael Sandel, *Liberalism and the Limits of Justice* (Cambridge: Cambridge University Press, 1982), 47.

9. See e.g. Rawls, *Theory of Justice*, 396 ff.

10. See John Rawls, *Political Liberalism* (New York: Columbia University Press, 1993), 55 ff.

11. See e.g. Rawls's rejection of Kant's moral constructivism, *Political Liberalism*, 99–101.

12. See also Charles Larmore, 'Political Liberalism', in *The Morals of Modernity* (Cambridge: Cambridge University Press, 1996).

13. See James Buchanan, *The Limits of Liberty: Between Anarchy and Leviathan* (Chicago: University of Chicago Press, 1975); Robert Nozick, *Anarchy, State, and Utopia* (New York: Basic Books, 1974); and David Gauthier, *Morals by Agreement* (Oxford: Clarendon Press, 1986).

14. Marx, letter to Friedrich Adolph Sorge, 19 Oct. 1877, in *Karl Marx, Frederick Engels: Collected Works*, xxxxv (London: Lawrence & Wishart, 1991), 283. See also Marx, *Capital: A Critical Analysis of Capitalist Production*, i, ed. Frederick Engels, trans. Samuel Moore and Edward Aveling (Moscow: Foreign Languages Publishing House, 1958), 84–5 n. 2.

15. For a good summary of some of the forms these Marxist notions of justice have recently taken, see Will Kymlicka, *Contemporary Political Philosophy: An Introduction* (Oxford: Clarendon Press, 1990), 169–89.

16. See Gilbert Ryle, 'Thinking and Reflecting' and 'The Thinking of Thoughts: What is "Le Penseur" Doing?' in *Collected Papers*, ii (London: Hutchinson, 1971). These terms have also been taken up in a particularly resonant way by the anthropologist Clifford Geertz in his 'Thick Description: Toward an Interpretive Theory of Culture', in *The Interpretation of Cultures* (New York: Basic Books, 1973).

17. Rawls, *Theory of Justice*, 304, 305, 307.

18. Ibid. 307–8.

19. Ibid. 111.

20. Ibid. 22.
21. See e.g. Rawls, *Political Liberalism*, 191–5; Ronald Dworkin, 'Liberalism', in Stuart Hampshire (ed.), *Public and Private Morality* (Cambridge: Cambridge University Press, 1978), 127; Buchanan, *Limits of Liberty*, 2; and Gauthier, *Morals by Agreement*, 3, 16, 95.
22. I've borrowed this baseball analogy from Stephen Holmes, 'The Permanent Structure of Anti-Liberal Thought', in Nancy Rosenblum (ed.), *Liberalism and the Moral Life* (Cambridge, Mass.: Harvard University Press, 1989), 245.
23. Rawls, *Theory of Justice*, 135.
24. As Rawls says of intuitionist approaches: 'They include no explicit method, no priority rules, for weighing these principles against one another: we are simply to strike a balance by intuition, by what seems to us most nearly right. Or if there are priority rules, these are thought to be more or less trivial and of no substantial assistance in reaching a judgment.' *Theory of Justice*, 34. And as Kymlicka states (*Contemporary Political Philosophy*, 51), 'These intuitionist approaches, whether at the level of specific precepts or general principles, are not only theoretically unsatisfying, but are also quite unhelpful in practical matters. For they give us no guidance when these specific and irreducible precepts conflict. Yet it is precisely when they conflict that we look to political theory for guidance.'
25. 'If we cannot explain how these weights are to be determined by reasonable ethical criteria, the means of rational discussion have come to an end.' Rawls, *Theory of Justice*, 41.
26. Ibid. 121.
27. Ibid. 94.
28. See e.g. Rawls, *Theory of Justice*, 41, 44, 94, 124, 246, 320.
29. With Rawls this comes out in his distinctions between 'pure' and 'quasi-pure' procedural justice (ibid. 201); 'ideal' and 'non-ideal' theory or 'the problems of extension' (ibid. 8–9, 245–6, 364, 391, and Rawls, *Political Liberalism*, 20–1), and 'perfect' and 'imperfect' procedural justice (e.g. Rawls, *Theory of Justice*, 85–6, 221, 353, and *Political Liberalism*, 72–3). Even contractarians recognize that there will always be a need for the kind of judgement exercised by the judiciary.
30. Rawls, *Theory of Justice*, 44.
31. Ibid. 321.
32. Ibid. 174.
33. Ibid. 281, 320. Of course, there have been those who have complained that the difference principle is not precise enough. See e.g. Thomas C. Grey, 'The First Virtue', *Stanford Law Review*, 25/286 (Jan. 1973), 286–327, 320; or Jan F. Narveson, 'Rawls on Equal Distribution of Wealth', *Philosophia*, 7 (1977), 281–92.
34. See Rawls, *Theory of Justice*, esp. s. 36; and Habermas, *Legitimation Crisis*, trans. Thomas McCarthy (London: Heinemann, 1976), part III.
35. Habermas, *Legitimation Crisis*, 109, 107.

36. E.g. Jon Elster and Joshua Cohen recommend that we follow Habermas rather than Rawls on this matter. See Elster, 'The Market and the Forum: Three Varieties of Political Theory', in Elster and Aanund Hylland (eds.), *Foundations of Social Choice Theory* (Cambridge: Cambridge University Press, 1986); and Cohen, 'Deliberation and Democratic Legitimacy', in Alan Hamlin and Philip Pettit (eds.), *The Good Polity: Normative Analysis of the State* (Oxford: Basil Blackwell, 1989).

37. David Miller, *Market, State, and Community: Theoretical Foundations of Market Socialism* (Oxford: Clarendon Press, 1989), 269.

38. Buchanan, *Limits of Liberty*, 2.

39. See e.g. Rawls, *Theory of Justice*, 22 n. 8; Nozick, *Anarchy State, and Utopia*, 277–9; and Jeremy Waldron, 'Theoretical Foundations of Liberalism', in *Liberal Rights: Collected Papers 1981–1991* (Cambridge: Cambridge University Press, 1993), 44. And though the early Marx does not go as far as Engels in declaring socialism itself to be scientific, he does assert that his historical materialist social science will lead us to a complete *unity* of science: 'Natural science will one day incorporate the science of man, just as the science of man will incorporate natural science; there will be a *single* science.' *Economic and Philosophical Manuscripts*, in *Karl Marx: Early Writings*, ed. and trans. Tom B. Bottomore (London: C. A. Watts, 1963), 164. The later Marx even more strongly emphasized the affinities between his socialism and natural science, as did many post-Marxists such as the structuralist Louis Althusser. Habermas should be considered somewhat of an exception in this respect, however, for he explicitly asserts a methodological distinction between what he describes as the 'empirical-critical' discipline that is political theory and the 'empirical-analytic' approach appropriate to the natural sciences. Nevertheless, both the disengaged nature and universality he asserts for the 'ideal speech situation' that undergirds his conception of right allows us to say that the kind of objectivity he wishes to claim for it is on par with that considered attained by successful theories in natural science. See Habermas, *The Theory of Communicative Action*; as well as the appendix to Habermas, *Knowledge and Human Interests*, trans. Jeremy J. Shapiro (London: Heinemann, 1972).

40. See Norman Daniels, 'Wide Reflective Equilibrium and Theory Acceptance in Ethics', *Journal of Philosophy*, 76 (Jan.–Dec. 1979), 256–82, esp. 262, 269–74. Rawls himself has cited Quine in *Theory of Justice*, 111 n. 26, 579 n. 33.

41. See David Hume, *An Inquiry Concerning Human Understanding*, in *On Human Nature and the Understanding*, ed. Antony Flew (London: Collier-Macmillan, 1962).

42. Popper, *Conjectures and Refutations: The Growth of Scientific Knowledge* (London: Routledge & Kegan Paul, 1961), 46. See also Popper, *The Logic of Scientific Discovery* (London: Hutchinson, 1959), 106.

43. Thus Daniels, in the course of highlighting parallels between the

approaches of Rawls and Quine, writes ('Wide Reflective Equilibrium', 279): 'Coherence constraints in wide equilibrium function very much like those in science. If I am right, this suggests that we may be able to piggy-back a claim about objectivity in ethics onto the analogous claim we are assuming can be made for science.'

44. Popper grants a place to intuition in scientific research when he writes: 'My view may be expressed by saying that every discovery contains "an irrational element", or "a creative intuition".' Popper, *Logic of Scientific Discovery*, 32.

45. Ibid. 107 n. *2.

46. Hubert L. Dreyfus, 'Hermeneutics and Holism', *Review of Metaphysics*, 34 (Sept. 1980), 3–23, p. 6. For more of Dreyfus on 'theory', see his 'Why Studies of Human Capacities Modeled on Ideal Natural Science can Never Achieve their Goal', in J. Margolis, M. Krauz, and R. M. Burian (eds.), *Rationality, Relativism and the Human Sciences* (Dordrecht: Martinus Nijhoff, 1986), 11–12.

47. Willard Quine, 'Two Dogmas of Empiricism', in *From a Logical Point of View: 9 Logico-Philosophical Essays*, 2nd edn. (London: Harvard University Press, 1980), 44, 45.

48. Rawls, *Theory of Justice*, 51.

49. Daniels, 'Wide Reflective Equilibrium', 263.

50. Ibid. 266.

51. Rawls, *Political Liberalism*, 8; or see Rawls, *Theory of Justice*, 20.

52. Norman Daniels, 'Introduction', in *Justice and Justification: Reflective Equilibrium in Theory and Practice* (Cambridge: Cambridge University Press, 1996), 8.

53. Rawls, *Political Liberalism*, 12.

54. See e.g. Willard Quine, *Word and Object* (Cambridge, Mass.: MIT Press, 1960), ch. 2; and 'Ontological Relativity', in *Ontological Relativity and Other Essays* (New York: Columbia University Press, 1969).

55. Donald Davidson, 'A Coherence Theory of Truth and Knowledge', in Alan Malachowski (ed.), *Reading Rorty* (Oxford: Basil Blackwell, 1990), 127.

56. Rawls, *Theory of Justice*, 55.

57. Ibid. 47.

58. See Thomas Kuhn, *The Structure of Scientific Revolutions*, 2nd edn. (Chicago: University of Chicago Press, 1970).

59. See e.g. Richard Rorty, 'The Contingency of Language', in *Contingency, Irony, and Solidarity* (Cambridge: Cambridge University Press, 1989); and Mary Hesse, *Revolutions and Reconstructions in the Philosophy of Science* (Bloomington, Ind.: Indiana University Press, 1980).

60. Davidson argues this position in his 'On the Very Idea of a Conceptual Scheme', in *Inquiries into Truth and Interpretation* (Oxford: Clarendon Press, 1984). He has, however, since moved considerably closer to Rorty, as in his 'A Coherence Theory of Truth and Knowledge'.

61. Although Kuhn has been somewhat ambiguous about this at times, he

has made clear statements regarding a role for reason in paradigm shifts. See e.g. Kuhn, 'Reflections on my Critics', in Imre Lakatos and Lan Musgrave (eds.), *Criticism and the Growth of Knowledge* (Cambridge: Cambridge University Press, 1970), 264; and Kuhn, 'Notes on Lakatos', in Roger C. Buck and Richard S. Cohen (eds.), *PSA 1970, in Memory of Rudolf Carnap* (Dordrecht: D. Reidel, 1971), 144. For a good discussion of Kuhn and Lakatos on this matter, see Alasdair MacIntyre, 'Epistemological Crises, Dramatic Narrative and the Philosophy of Science', in Stanely G. Clarke and Evan Simpson (eds.), *Anti-Theory in Ethics and Moral Conservatism* (Albany, NY: SUNY Press, 1989).

62. See Michael Polanyi, *The Tacit Dimension* (New York: Anchor Books, 1966), 77.

63. Bernard Crick, 'On Theory and Practice', in *Political Theory and Practice* (London: Allen Lane, The Penguin Press, 1971), 2.

64. Gerald L. Bruns has also pointed to the parallels between allegory and radical translation: *Hermeneutics Ancient and Modern* (London: Yale University Press, 1992), 83–7.

65. That the sign has an arbitrary nature has been fundamental to much of modern linguistics. See the structuralist Ferdinand de Saussure's *Cours de linguistique générale*, ed. Charles Bully and Albert Sechehay (Paris: Payot, 1987), esp. 100–3.

66. Tzvetan Todorov has explored these contrasts in his *Théories du symbole* (Paris: Seuil, 1977), 235–59.

67. Isaiah Berlin, '"From Hope and Fear Set Free"', in *Concepts and Categories: Philosophical Essays*, ed. Henry Hardy (Oxford: Oxford University Press, 1978), 189. See also Isaiah Berlin, 'Herder and the Enlightenment', in *Vico and Herder* (London: Hogarth Press, 1976), esp. 165–73; Charles Taylor, 'Action as Expression', in Cora Diamond and Jenny Teichman (eds.), *Intention and Intentionality: Essays in Honour of G. E. M. Anscombe* (Brighton: Harvester Press, 1979); Taylor, 'Language and Human Nature', and 'Theories of Meaning', in *Human Agency and Language: Philosophical Papers 1* (Cambridge: Cambridge University Press, 1985); Taylor, 'The Importance of Herder', and 'Heidegger, Language, and Ecology', in *Philosophical Arguments* (London: Harvard University Press, 1995) and Robert B. Brandom, *Making it Explicit: Reasoning, Representing and Discursive Commitment* (London: Harvard University Press, 1994).

68. For, as Iris Murdoch has declared, 'We are men and we are moral agents before we are scientists.' Murdoch, 'The Idea of Perfection', in *The Sovereignty of Good* (New York: Routledge & Kegan Paul, 1970), 34. Appreciating that disengaged objectivity must come from within a world of engaged objectivity does not, however, mean that natural science cannot be said to give an account of nature as it exists 'in-itself', or independent of human purposes. A discussion of this matter would take me too far afield here, but see Hubert L. Dreyfus, 'Heidegger's Hermeneutic Realism', in David R. Hiley, James F. Bohman, and Richard Shusterman

(eds.), *The Interpretive Turn: Philosophy, Science, Culture* (London: Cornell University Press, 1991).

69. Indeed, depending on the extent to which a sport is structured by its rules, statistical science will have a directly proportional relevance. For example, statistics are much more revealing in baseball than in ice hockey.

70. For some representative discussions of how contemporary expressivists have taken up Dilthey's distinction between *Natur* and *Geist*, see e.g. Berlin, 'The Divorce between the Sciences and Humanities', in *Against the Current: Essays in the History of Ideas*, ed. Henry Hardy (Oxford: Oxford University Press, 1981); Taylor, 'Understanding Human Science', *Review of Metaphysics*, 34 (Sept. 1980), 25–38; Stuart Hampshire, *Morality and Conflict* (Oxford: Basil Blackwell, 1983), ch. 3; Bernard Williams, 'Preface', in *Moral Luck: Philosophical Papers 1973–1980* (Cambridge: Cambridge University Press, 1981); and Williams, *Ethics and the Limits of Philosophy* (London: HarperCollins, 1985), ch. 8.

71. For some examples of this approach to politics, also sometimes referred to as 'pragmatic' or 'aesthetic'—one which, it is worth mentioning, tends to take on liberal forms ideologically—see Richard Rorty, 'The Priority of Democracy to Philosophy', in *Objectivity, Relativism and Truth: Philosophical Papers, i* (Cambridge: Cambridge University Press, 1991); William E. Connolly, 'Identity and Difference in Liberalism', in R. Bruce Douglass, Gerald M. Mara, and Henry S. Richardson (eds.), *Liberalism and the Good* (New York: Routledge, 1990); David Cook, 'The Last Days of Liberalism', in Thomas Docherty (ed.), *Postmodernism: A Reader* (Hemel Hempstead: Harvester Wheatsheaf, 1993); and Richard Bellamy, *Liberalism and Modern Society* (Cambridge: Polity Press, 1992), esp. 248–61. Foucault can also be interpreted as having flirted with this brand of liberalism near the end of his life. See 'Polemics, Politics, and Problematizations: An Interview with Michel Foucault', in Paul Rabinow (ed.), *The Foucault Reader* (New York: Pantheon, 1984), 383–6.

72. Here is Nietzsche, writing ironically, on behalf of theoretical philosophers: 'We have no right to *isolated* acts of any kind: we may not make isolated errors or hit upon isolated truths. Rather do our ideas, our values, our yeas and nays, our ifs and buts, grow out of us with the necessity with which a tree bears fruit—related and each with an affinity to each, and evidence of *one* will, *one* health, *one* soil, *one* sun.' Frederick Nietzsche, *On the Genealogy of Morals*, trans. Walter Kaufmann and R. J. Hollingdale (New York: Random House, 1967), 16.

73. See e.g. Berlin, 'Does Political Theory Still Exist?' in *Concepts and Categories*; Bernard Crick, *In Defense of Politics*, 4th edn. (London: Weidenfeld & Nicolson, 1992), ch. 5; Taylor, 'The Nature and Scope of Distributive Justice', in *Philosophy and the Human Sciences: Philosophical Papers 2* (Cambridge: Cambridge University Press, 1985); and Michael Walzer, *Spheres of Justice: A Defense of Pluralism and Equality* (New York: Basic Books, 1983), esp. 284–90.

74. David Miller, 'Political Theory', in Miller *et al.* (eds.), *The Blackwell Encyclopedia of Political Thought* (Oxford: Basil Blackwell, 1987), 383.

75. I say '*should* thus be abandoned' because many expressivists continue to use the word 'theory' to refer to research in the human sciences and humanities, though they would acknowledge that 'the word has different connotations in morals than in science'. Hampshire, *Morality and Conflict*, 17. See also Berlin, 'Political Judgement', in *The Sense of Reality: Studies in Ideas and Their History*, ed. Henry Hardy (London: Chatto & Windus, 1996), 50. That being noted, I should add that Hampshire has also warned of the danger of being 'corrupted' by theory. See Hampshire, *Morality and Conflict*, 116. For a good account of the calls to reject 'theory' in moral and political thought, see Stanely G. Clarke and Evan Simpson, 'Introduction: The Primacy of Moral Practice', in Clarke and Simpson (eds.), *Anti-Theory*.

76. For more on the 'theoretical', 'practical', as well as 'postmodernist' conceptions of philosophy, see my 'Athens and/or Jerusalem? Three Conceptions of Philosophy' (forthcoming).

77. Radical translators, who can be said to subscribe to the correspondence theory of truth, in which truth consists of accurately representing an independent order, can be roughly divided into two camps here, each affirming different degrees of realism. What Quine refers to as his more 'robust realism' emerges from the albeit blurry distinction he advocates between 'analytic' sentences, those said to be meaningful by virtue of their relation to other sentences, and 'synthetic' sentences for which meaning is tied more to experience. See Quine, 'Epistemology Naturalized', in *Ontological Relativity*, 86–90. What makes this distinction somewhat indefinite is that, as I have pointed out, Quine asserts that these two kinds of sentences are themselves connected in a scheme and so there is no place for the positivist's sharp analytic–synthetic dichotomy. Others, however, have tended to reject the possibility of synthetic sentences altogether, a stance which has led Davidson and, in a different way, Rorty, to affirm a much weaker realism. So where Quine would 'accentuate the positive' (as in his 'Let me Accentuate the Positive', in Malachowski (ed.), *Reading Rorty*; and Quine, 'On the Very Idea of a Third Dogma', in *Theories and Things* (Cambridge Mass.: Harvard University Press, 1981), Davidson admits that he shares with Rorty 'a minimalist attitude towards truth' ('Coherence Theory', 135). Rawls, who has limited his focus to the issues relating to justice, has shied away from this debate, designating his political conception as 'reasonable', which, for him, means that it may or may not be 'truthful', the question of truth being, he claims, a metaphysical matter intrinsic only to those non-public, comprehensive doctrines of the good. See Rawls, *Political Liberalism*, 94, 126–9, 209. And, to Daniels, 'wide reflective equilibrium embodies coherence constraints on theory acceptance or justification, not on truth'; in this, 'ethics may be no worse off than science'. Daniels, 'Wide Reflective Equilibrium', 277, 278. As for the view that political liberalism, whether or not

'true', is at the very least 'correct', see Larmore, 'Political Liberalism', 146–51.

78. As Rawls himself has described his aim, a theory of justice should achieve a perspective on society that is *sub specie aeternitatis*, the view from eternity. Rawls, *Theory of Justice*, 587.

79. As seems to me most evident in e.g. Paul de Man's use of these metaphors in 'The Rhetoric of Blindness: Jacques Derrida's Reading of Rousseau', in *Blindness and Insight: Essays in the Rhetoric of Contemporary Criticism*, 2nd edn. (London: Routledge, 1983). See also Emmanuel Lévinas, *Autrement qu'être ou au-delà de l'essence* (The Hague: Martinus Nijhoff, 1974), 37, where he writes of the 'shadows' as well as the 'reflections' of the concepts he uses.

80. Berlin, 'Equality' in *Concepts and Categories*, 97.

81. Of course, one should not go too far in asserting the parallels between this 'moral sensitiveness' and the kind of judgement that goes on in revolutionary natural science. For one thing, moral sensitiveness seems to require a kind of open-mindedness, even humility, towards one's subject-matter, while at least some of the most successful revolutionary scientists have been quite dogmatic when it comes to their hypotheses. For example, Louis Pasteur, partly for political and religious reasons, simply refused to accept the results of experiments which supported the theory of the spontaneous generation of life and so worked against his pioneering of the 'germ' theory of disease. See Gerald L. Geison, *The Private Science of Louis Pasteur* (Princeton: Princeton University Press, 1995), 113–25, 131.

82. 'During his years in prisons and camps he'd lost the habit of planning for the next day, for a year ahead, for supporting his family. The authorities did his thinking for him about everything—it was somehow easier that way.' Solzhenitsyn, *One Day in the Life of Ivan Denisovitch*, trans. Ralph Parker (London: Victor Gallancz, 1963), 51. Here is Margaret Laurence on the same theme: 'When she was a young child she used to believe that everything would be all right once she was grown-up and nobody could tell her what to do. Now she wishes someone *could* tell her what to do.' *The Diviners* (Toronto: MacClelland & Stewart, 1974), 168. Berlin refers to the turn to neutrality as an abandonment of responsibility in his 'Historical Inevitability', in *Four Essays on Liberty* (Oxford: Oxford University Press, 1969), 116.

83. The Tragically Hip, 'Gift Shop', in *Trouble at the Henhouse* (Toronto: MCA Music, 1996).

84. See Dreyfus, 'Hermeneutics and Holism', 3, 7.

85. Wittgenstein, *On Certainty*, ed. G. E. M. Anscombe and G. H. von Wright, trans. Anscombe and Denis Paul (Oxford: Blackwell, 1979), s. 204.

86. Note that I use the term 'tradition' here only as a subset of that larger notion, 'history', and so it would be a mistake to claim, as Terry Eagleton does, that hermeneutics assumes a purely idealist conception of history:

Literary Theory: An Introduction (Oxford: Basil Blackwell, 1983), 73. This is, none the less, a difficult issue, one which Taylor tackles in his *Sources of the Self: The Making of the Modern Identity* (Cambridge, Mass.: Harvard University Press, 1989), ch. 12; as well as in Taylor, 'The Hermeneutics of Conflict', in James Tully (ed.), *Meaning and Context: Quentin Skinner and His Critics* (Cambridge: Polity Press, 1988).

87. That practices in the hermeneutical conception are never considered to be unified seems to me to be the chief distinguishing point between it and that conception of a tradition of practices defended by Michael Oakeshott. See e.g. Oakeshott, *On Human Conduct* (Oxford: Clarendon Press, 1975).

88. It is the assumption that hermeneuticists conceive of meaning in this way, combined with a failure to appreciate their natural science–human science methodological distinction, that leads Stephen Turner awry in his critique of their conception of society. See Turner, *The Social Theory of Practices: Tradition, Tacit Knowledge and Presuppositions* (Cambridge: Polity Press, 1994).

89. Gadamer, *Truth and Method*, 2nd edn., trans. Joel Weinsheimer and Donald G. Marshall (New York: Crossroad, 1989), 111. Richard Bernstein and Joel Weinsheimer are two thinkers who, however, fail to do just this, with the result that they tend to blur the methodological distinction between natural science on the one hand, in which, as I have implied, a version of theoretical holism is appropriate when it comes to normal science, and human science and the humanities on the other. In consequence, they end up failing to distinguish between hermeneutics and radical translation. See Bernstein, *Beyond Objectivism and Relativism: Science, Hermeneutics, and Praxis* (Philadelphia: University of Pennsylvania Press, 1983), esp. part 2; and Weinsheimer, *Gadamer's Hermeneutics: A Reading of Truth and Method* (New Haven, Conn.: Yale University Press, 1985), 1–36.

90. R. G. Collingwood, *The Principles of Art* (London: Oxford University Press, 1938), 257.

91. See Matthew 5: 17; and Luke 16: 17.

92. See Colossians 2: 8, 3: 11.

93. Exodus 20: 14.

94. Matthew 5: 28.

95. Walzer, 'Pluralism and Social Democracy', *Dissent* (Winter 1998), 47; my italics.

96. Nicholas Rescher and Baruch Brody are, however, two thinkers who seem to me to be articulating positions somewhere in-between that of the neutralist on the one hand and that of the pluralist on the other. See Rescher, *Pluralism: Against the Demand for Consensus* (Oxford: Clarendon Press, 1993); and Brody, 'Pluralistic Moral Theory', *Revue Internationale de Philosophie*, 49/193 (Sept. 1995), 323–39. Politically oriented versions of such hybrids have been advanced by Georgia Warnke,

J. Donald Moon, and Mark Kingwell, for whom it makes sense to support
a conception of the priority of right over the good, though their versions
of right not only claim a much less ambitious scope than does, say, that of
Rawls, but they also allow that these will sometimes have to be subject
to negotiation and so the compromises inherent to pluralist politics.
See Warnke, *Justice and Interpretation* (Cambridge: Polity Press, 1992);
Moon, *Constructing Community: Moral Pluralism and Tragic Conflicts*
(Philadalphia: Princeton University Press, 1993); and Kingwell, *A Civil
Tongue: Justice, Dialogue, and the Politics of Pluralism* (Philadelphia:
Pennsylvania State University Press, 1995).

97. Berlin, 'The Pursuit of the Ideal', in *The Crooked Timber of Humanity:
    Chapters in the History of Ideas*, ed. Henry Hardy (London: John Murray,
    1990), 2. See also Berlin, 'Two Concepts of Liberty', in *Four Essays on
    Liberty*, 120.

98. See Williams, *Ethics and the Limits of Philosophy*, ch. 10.

99. See Bonnie Honig, *Political Theory and the Displacement of Politics*
    (London: Cornell University Press, 1993), chs. 2, 5. For a critique of delib-
    erative/discursive democracy along these (though specifically pluralist)
    lines, see Joseph V. Femia, 'Complexity and Deliberative Democracy',
    Inquiry, 39/3–4 (Dec. 1996), 359–97.

NOTES TO CHAPTER 2

1. The most obvious of these being the conception of justice that Plato puts
   in the mouth of Socrates in his *The Republic*, trans. Allan Bloom (New
   York: Basic Books, 1968); as well as Aristotle's declaration that his first
   (though not ultimate) choice for the ideal political regime would be a
   kingship. See Aristotle, *The Politics* 1284^b. The extent to which Plato and
   Aristotle themselves actually supported these antipolitical positions
   has, of course, been a matter of great debate. For Plato's *Laws* in *The
   Dialogues of Plato*, 4th edn., trans. Benjamin Jowett (Oxford: Oxford
   University Press, 1953) and the main thrust of Aristotle's *Politics* advocate
   versions of classical republicanism. Regardless, my point here has only
   been to acknowledge that there have been many who, inspired especially
   by Socrates' vision in *The Republic*, have been led to support antipolitical
   doctrines.

2. See Plato, *The Republic*, 336 b–354; and the infamous 'Melian dialogue' in
   Thucydides, *History of the Peloponnesian Wars*, ed. W. Robert Conner,
   trans. Richard Crawle (London: Everyman, 1993), 5.

3. Augustine, *Concerning the City of God Against the Pagans*, trans. Henry
   Bettenson (Harmondsworth: Penguin, 1972), 5. 16; see also 5. 20.

4. See the concluding discussion in Quentin Skinner, *The Foundations of
   Modern Political Thought, ii. The Age of Reformation* (Cambridge: Cam-

bridge University Press, 1978), 349–58. Note that I am using the term 'state' here in a very wide sense, and so do not mean it to refer to only those conceptions which assume an absolute notion of sovereignty. As such, 'state' can sometimes be taken as synonymous with 'government'—though only sometimes because there are also, of course, governing bodies at work in many of the associations located within civil society.

5. See Jürgen Habermas, *The Structural Transformation of the Public Sphere: An Inquiry into a Category of Bourgeois Society*, trans. Thomas Burger (Cambridge: Polity Press, 1989). See also Charles Taylor, 'Modernity and the Rise of the Public Sphere', in Grethe B. Peterson (ed.), *The Tanner Lectures on Human Values, xiv* (Salt Lake City: University of Utah Press, 1993); and Charles Taylor, 'Liberal Politics and the Public Sphere', in *Philosophical Arguments* (London: Harvard University Press, 1995).

6. See Taylor, 'Invoking Civil Society', in *Philosophical Arguments*, 220–1.

7. For an authoritative study of these five, see Michael Freeden, *Ideologies and Political Theory: A Conceptual Approach* (Oxford: Oxford University Press, 1996).

8. John Gray, 'From Post-Liberalism to Pluralism', in *Enlightenment's Wake: Politics and Culture at the Close of the Modern Age* (London: Routledge, 1995), 133.

9. That Walzer intends his ideal to apply only to federal Canada (excluding Quebec) and the USA is made clear in his 'Comment', in Amy Gutmann (ed.), *Multiculturalism and 'The Politics of Recognition'* (Princeton: Princeton University Press, 1992). Raz's theory, however, is not recommended for these 'immigrant' societies, for he considers their political cultures too individualistic. See Joseph Raz, 'Multiculturalism: A Liberal Perspective', in *Ethics in the Public Domain: Essays in the Morality of Law and Politics* (Oxford: Oxford University Press, 1994), 158.

10. See Dahl, *A Preface to Democratic Theory* (Chicago: University of Chicago Press, 1956).

11. A good short review of the literature constituting American political science pluralism and the critique that it defends an 'elitist' politics can be found in David Nicholls, *Three Varieties of Pluralism* (London: Macmillan Press, 1974), ch. 3.

12. Dahl, *Who Governs? Democracy .and Power in an American City* (New Haven, Conn.: Yale University Press, 1961).

13. Dahl, *Preface to Democratic Theory*, 137; see also 145, 150.

14. Dahl, *Democracy and its Critics* (London: Yale University Press, 1989), 84–7.

15. Ibid. 87.

16. Ibid. 88; see also ch. 7.

17. Ibid. 100.

18. Grant Jordan, 'The Pluralism of Pluralism: An Anti-Theory?', in Jeremy J. Richardson (ed.), *Pressure Groups* (Oxford: Oxford University Press, 1993), 64. Jordan cites William Alton Kelso as coining the term 'laissez-

faire pluralism' in his *American Democratic Theory: Pluralism and its Critics* (Westport, Conn.: Greenwood Press, 1978), 13–19.

19. On the model, see Albert O. Hirschman, *The Passions and the Interests: Political Arguments for Capitalism Before its Triumph* (Princeton: Princeton University Press, 1977), esp. 20–31. Martin J. Smith discusses how this form of pluralism relies on it in his 'Pluralism, Reformed Pluralism and Neopluralism: The Role of Pressure Groups in Policy-Making', *Political Studies*, 38/2 (June 1990), 302–22.

20. Business, for example, is said to partake of such a relationship in David Truman, *The Governmental Process* (New York: A. A. Knopf, 1951), 225.

21. See Jordan, 'Pluralism of Pluralism', 64.

22. Dahl, *Democracy and its Critics*, 109.

23. For a discussion of the 'defects', as Dahl refers to them, of polyarchies, see Dahl, *Dilemmas of Pluralist Democracy: Autonomy vs. Control* (London: Yale University Press, 1982), esp. ch. 3.

24. Ibid. 182.

25. Raz, 'Multiculturalism: A Liberal Perspective', 159.

26. Ibid.

27. Ibid.

28. Joseph Raz, *The Morality of Freedom* (Oxford: Oxford University Press, 1986), 412.

29. Walzer explicitly endorses Raz's argument for this: 'The Communitarian Critique of Liberalism', *Political Theory*, 18/1 (Feb. 1990), 6–23, 23 n. 17.

30. See Walzer, 'Multiculturalism and Individualism', *Dissent*, 41/2 (Spring 1994), 185–91.

31. Walzer, 'The Civil Society Argument', in Chantal Mouffe (ed.), *Dimensions of Radical Democracy: Pluralism, Citizenship, Community* (London: Verso, 1992), 101.

32. Ibid. 105.

33. Walzer, *Spheres of Justice*, 279.

34. Walzer, 'Pluralism in Political Perspective', in Stephan Thernstrom (ed.), *The Politics of Ethnicity* (Cambridge, Mass.: Harvard University Press, 1980), 16. See also ibid. 12.

35. Isaiah Berlin and Ramin Jahanbegloo, *Conversations with Isaiah Berlin* (London: Peter Halban, 1991), 44. See also Berlin and Bernard Williams, 'Pluralism and Liberalism: A Reply', *Political Studies*, 62/2 (June 1994), 306–9, 308–9. There are, to my knowledge, at least two statements in Berlin's earlier writings where he can be read as assuming that pluralism entails liberalism, though they may also be read as making the more limited claim that pluralism is partial to political, as distinct from antipolitical, ideologies. In one ('The Originality of Machiavelli', in *Against the Current*, 79), he writes that accepting pluralism means accepting toleration, while in another ('Two Concepts of Liberty', in *Four Essays on Liberty*, 171), he connects pluralism with 'a measure' of individual liberty, articulated as negative liberty. But neither of these two statements necessarily calls for anything more than that minimal degree of toleration which

is found in the pluralist's conception of the 'universal minimal moral code' (more on this in Ch. 3). For when, in the second statement, Berlin demands that we accept 'a measure' of negative liberty, we are nevertheless left with the question of 'How much is meant by a measure?'. That is, is it enough to defend a liberalism? This being said, he did once describe liberalism as asserting certain individual rights as 'absolute', as well as supporting the idea of an 'inviolable' frontier of non-interference around persons (ibid. 165), characterizations which speak in favour of the notion that the ideology assumes some theoretically endorsed, uncompromisable principles. And yet, this is contradicted by his assertion that negative liberty can sometimes rightly be compromised by the demands of its positive cousin (ibid. 166).

Many have overlooked these tensions in Berlin's work and assumed that he, quite straightforwardly, connected liberalism and pluralism intrinsically. See Bernard Williams,' 'Introduction', to Berlin, *Concepts and Categories*, p. xvii; Williams, 'Conflicts of Values', in *Moral Luck* (Cambridge: Cambridge University Press, 1981), esp. 71; Alasdair MacIntyre, *After Virtue*, 2nd edn. (Notre Dame, Ind.: University of Notre Dame Press, 1984), 109; Robert Kocis, *A Critical Appraisal of Sir Isaiah Berlin's Political Philosophy* (Lampeter: Edwin Mellen Press, 1989), 1–2; John Gray, 'Berlin's Agonistic Liberalism', in *Post-Liberalism: Studies in Political Thought* (London: Routledge, 1992); Gray, 'What is Dead and what is Living in Liberalism?', in ibid. 323; Claude J. Galipeau, *Isaiah Berlin's Liberalism* (Oxford: Clarendon Press, 1994), esp. 120; and Gray, *Isaiah Berlin* (London: HarperCollins, 1995).

36. Samuel Huntington, *American Politics: The Promise of Disharmony* (Cambridge, Mass.: Belknap Press, 1981), 15.

37. The following section was presented under the title 'Walzer's Two Kinds of Practical Reason to the Ethics and Practical Reason Conference held under the auspices of the Dept. of Moral Philosophy, University of St Andrews, Scotland, on 25 Mar. 1995. I am grateful to all those participants who offered advice and suggestions.

38. Plato, *Phaedo*, in *The Dialogues of Plato*, i. 116c–d.

39. Robert Bolt, *A Man for All Seasons: A Play of Sir Thomas More* (Oxford: Heinemann Educational Books, 1960), 99.

40. Walzer, *Spheres of Justice*, p. xv.

41. Walzer, 'Civil Society Argument', 89.

42. See Walzer, *Spheres of Justice*, 284–90.

43. See Walzer, 'A Critique of Philosophical Conversation', *The Philosophical Forum*, 21/1–2 (Fall–Winter 1989–90), 182–96.

44. See Walzer, *Spheres of Justice*, 10; and Walzer, *Thick and Thin: Moral Argument at Home and Abroad* (Notre Dame, Ind.: University of Notre Dame Press, 1994), 39.

45. As William Galston refers to it in his *Liberal Purposes: Goods, Virtues, and Diversity in the Liberal State* (New York: Cambridge University Press, 1991), 46.

46. Walzer, *Spheres of Justice*, 10.

47. Ibid. 319. See also Walzer, *Thick and Thin*, 32–5.

48. Ronald Dworkin, 'What Justice isn't', in *A Matter of Principle* (Cambridge, Mass.: Harvard University Press, 1985), 217. J. Donald Moon also makes this point in his *Constructing Community: Moral Pluralism and Tragic Conflicts* (Princeton: Princeton University Press, 1993), 18–19.

49. See Walzer, *Spheres of Justice*, 319; Walzer and Dworkin, 'Spheres of Justice: An Exchange', *The New York Review of Books* (21 July 1983), 44; and Walzer, *Thick and Thin*, 27–8.

50. See Walzer, *Spheres of Justice*, 114.

51. See Walzer, 'Justice Here and Now', in Frank S. Lucash (ed.), *Justice and Equality Here and Now* (Ithaca, NY: Cornell University Press, 1986), 143.

52. See Walzer, *Spheres of Justice*, 121.

53. Ibid. 215.

54. Ibid. 67.

55. Ibid. 66.

56. See Walzer, *The Company of Critics: Social Criticism and Political Commitment in the Twentieth Century* (London: Peter Halban, 1989), 229.

57. See e.g. Joshua Cohen, 'Review of *Spheres of Justice*', *The Journal of Philosophy*, 83/8 (Aug. 1986), 457–66; and Brian Barry, 'Social Criticism and Political Philosophy', *Philosophy and Public Affairs*, 19/4 (Fall 1990), 360–72, esp. 369–70.

58. The expression is from Walzer, 'Liberalism and the Art of Separation', *Political Theory*, 12/3 (Aug. 1984), 315–30.

59. Walzer, *Spheres of Justice*, 102.

60. Ibid. 213.

61. Ibid. 144.

62. Ibid. 213. The argument that the abolition of private schools follows directly from the affirmation of equality of opportunity has been succinctly put by MacIntyre in his *After Virtue*, 7.

63. See Berlin, 'Introduction', in *Four Essays on Liberty*, p. liv.

64. One of the reasons for accepting the conversion of money into basic education is because one believes that, when it comes to the distribution of money, Walzer is wrong to assert that, due to the great deal of luck involved in the market-place, it should be recognized as a matter of 'free exchange' rather than of desert. See Walzer, *Spheres of Justice*, 108. Desert would certainly be the principle invoked by the average parent if asked why they should be able to purchase education for their children ('Look, I *earned* this money, so I should be able to spend it on my child as I wish!'), and it seems counter-intuitive (at least to me) to rule out such an account completely. Indeed, as David Miller has pointed out, empirical studies confirm that the principle of reward for contribution certainly has a strong hold on Americans: 'Distributive Justice: What the People Think', *Ethics*, 102/3 (Apr. 1992), 555–93, 564. Perhaps, then, it makes better sense to interpret the distribution of money as the result of some combination of

desert and free exchange. Such a move would not necessarily rule out a market populated by workers' co-operatives (an idea with which Walzer is sympathetic) as is clear from Miller's work on market socialism. Miller advocates granting a place to desert in his *Market, State, and Community*, ch. 6.

65. Walzer, *Spheres of Justice*, 213.
66. Ibid. 215; italics mine.
67. Dworkin, 'What Justice isn't', 218.
68. Walzer, *Spheres of Justice*, 51.
69. Ibid. 59–60. The 1990 US Immigration Act has set aside about 120,000 places every year for such immigrants. See Charles Gordon and Stanley Mailman, *Immigration Law and Procedure* (New York: Matthew Bender, 1993), ch. 1, 24.
70. Approximately 10,000 places are set aside every year for immigrants who commit to investing at least $1 million in active enterprises which will 'create at least 10 jobs and benefit the U.S. economy'. Ibid.
71. See Walzer, *Spheres of Justice*, 295–303.
72. Michael Howard raises questions to this effect in his 'Walzer's Socialism', *Social Theory and Practice*, 12/1 (Spring 1986), 103–13, 109–10.
73. Walzer has come to accept the necessity of such qualifications, though he has failed to admit that they contradict his theoretical framework. See Walzer, *Thick and Thin*, 58.
74. See Walzer, 'Socializing the Welfare State', in Amy Gutmann (ed.), *Democracy and the Welfare State* (Princeton: Princeton University Press, 1988), 16.
75. Walzer, *Spheres of Justice*, 120.
76. Ibid. 66.
77. See Anthony B. Atkinson and Joseph E. Stiglitz, *Lectures on Public Economics* (London: McGraw-Hill, 1980), 356–8.
78. Moreover, entertaining such considerations will certainly be necessary if one considers that, following Miller, the end-results of complex equality may still not be equal enough. See Miller's discussion of 'the equality of status' in his 'Equality', in G. M. K. Hunt (ed.), *Philosophy and Politics* (Cambridge: Cambridge University Press, 1990), 95–8; as well as in Miller, 'Complex Equality', in Miller and Walzer (eds.), *Pluralism, Justice, and Equality* (Oxford: Oxford University Press, 1995), 214. And Taylor has pointed to Walzer's need to entertain principles of an 'intra-framework sense'—principles which, in reaching across Walzer's spheres, necessarily transcend any art of separation—if incomes policies are to be enacted. See Taylor, 'The Nature and Scope of Distributive Justice', in *Philosophy and the Human Sciences*, 300 n. 9.
79. See Walzer, *Spheres of Justice*, 152–3.
80. See Walzer, 'Justice Here and Now', 145; and Walzer, 'Exclusion, Injustice, and the Democratic State', *Dissent*, 40/1 (Winter 1993), 56–64. More recently, in reply to a paper by Amy Gutmann, Walzer has described his

support of affirmative action as a *temporary* exception to the principle of distributive autonomy. See Gutmann, 'Justice Across the Spheres', in Miller and Walzer (eds.), *Pluralism, Justice and Equality*, 104–11; and Walzer, 'Response', ibid. 283. Walzer's apparent acceptance of draft exemptions for college students seems to be a parallel example of such a 'breach [of] the liberal wall', as he himself refers to it. Walzer, 'Liberalism and the Art of Separation', 316 n. 2.

81. 'We can view the choice in the original position from the standpoint of one person selected at random.' Rawls, *Theory of Justice*, 139.

82. Walzer, *Spheres of Justice*, 256.

83. Stephen Macedo, *Liberal Virtues: Citizenship, Virtue, and Community in Liberal Constitutionalism* (Oxford: Clarendon Press, 1990), 71.

84. Galston, *Liberal Purposes*, 95.

85. As is implied by Huntington's statement on American political culture that 'Americans generally give liberty precedence over equality, but different groups assign different weights to each.' Huntington, *American Politics*, 17.

86. Thus, for Huntington, again on the USA: 'Though every American may have his own view of the proper balance among these conflicting values, few Americans would unhesitatingly give absolute priority to one value over another.' Ibid. 16.

87. E.g. the USA is said to grant more weight to individualistic values than does Canada. See ibid. 45.

88. Berlin, 'The Decline of Utopian Ideas in the West', in *The Crooked Timber of Humanity*, 32. See also Berlin, 'Two Concepts of Liberty', 124.

89. Williams, 'Conflicts of Values', 82.

90. That neo-corporatists interpret such relations as limited to the kind of dialogue structured by 'negotiation' or 'bargaining', as distinct from conversation, which aims for reconciliation rather than compromise (more on these distinctions in Ch. 3), is clear from their repeated use the two terms. See e.g. Wyn Grant, 'Introduction', in Grant (ed.), *The Political Economy of Corporatism* (London: Macmillan, 1985), 3, 21; and Alan Cawson, *Corporatism and Political Theory* (Oxford: Basil Blackwell, 1986), 12, 14–15, 19–21, 25, 35–8, 41, 67, 73, 146. This is one of the differences between 'neo-corporatism' and that older conception, 'corporatism', the former having shed the latter's organicism, a result of the greater distance it has placed between itself and Catholic social thought. For a short (if somewhat cynical) intellectual history of neo-corporatism, see Andrew Cox, 'Neo-Corporatism versus the Corporate State', in Cox and Noel O'Sullivan (eds.), *The Corporate State Tradition in Western Europe* (Aldershot: Edward Elgar, 1988), esp. 27–39; or see the discussion of its American variant, sometimes referred to as the 'Administered Society', in Robert N. Bellah *et al.*, *Habits of the Heart: Individualism and Commitment in American Life* (London: University of California Press, 1985), 267–9. As for classical corporatism, see Otto Newman, *The Challenge of Corporatism* (London: Macmillan, 1981), 1–30; and Peter J. Williamson,

Varieties of Corporatism (Cambridge: Cambridge University Press, 1985), part II.

91. Grant, *Political Economy*, 1.
92. Lars Christiansen and Keith Dowding, 'Pluralism or State Autonomy? The Case of Amnesty International (British Section): The Insider/Outsider Group', *Political Studies*, 52/1 (Mar. 1994), 15–24, 16. And Charles E. Lindblom, in the course of emphasizing (and criticizing the extent of) the special status of business, has also affirmed the *two-way* dynamics of its relationship with government: *Politics and Markets: The World's Political-Economic Systems* (New York: Basic Books, 1977), chs. 10, 13.
93. Cawson, *Corporatism*, 18; see also p. 35.
94. Ibid. 69.
95. I am thinking, e.g., of the Quebec government's infamous 'sign law' of the late 1980s, which banned the use of languages other than French on commercial signs anywhere in the province. The law was later struck down by a decision of the Supreme Court of Canada which cited its failure to meet the freedom of speech provision in the Charter. In response, the Quebec government invoked the 'notwithstanding' clause of s. 22 of the constitution, thus keeping the law in force. It has since amended the more offensive parts of it, however.
96. See e.g. Hannah Arendt, *The Human Condition: A Study of the Central Dilemmas Facing Modern Man* (Garden City: Doubleday Anchor edn., 1958), ch. 2.
97. Machiavelli, *The Discourses*, ed. Bernard Crick, trans. Leslie J. Walker (Harmondsworth: Penguin Books, 1970), 275.
98. See e.g. Walzer, 'The Communitarian Critique of Liberalism', 19–20.
99. See Dahl, *Democracy and its Critics*, chs. 20–1.
100. See e.g. Walzer, 'The Civil Society Argument', 91–2, 97–107. As Walzer has stated elsewhere, modern society is 'a complex and differentiated' place in which 'separation and division make for the primacy of the private realm'. Walzer, 'Citizenship', in Terence Ball, James Farr, and Russell L. Hanson (eds.), *Political Innovation and Conceptual Change* (Cambridge: Cambridge University Press, 1989), 218.
101. Walzer, 'Civil Society Argument', 103. See also Walzer, 'The Good Life', *New Statesman and Society* (6 Oct. 1989), 31; and Walzer, 'Communitarian Critique of Liberalism', 20. And, in a statement which properly applies only to weak pluralists, Louise Marcil-Lacoste asserts that pluralism 'leads to a ban on going beyond the instrumentality of politics'. 'The Paradoxes of Pluralism', in Mouffe (ed.), *Dimensions of Radical Democracy*, 35.
102. Macedo, *Liberal Virtues*, 204.
103. Ibid. 268.
104. Dahl's position *vis-à-vis* the Amish can be easily derived from his declaration that: 'To reject the democratic creed is in effect to refuse to be an American. As a nation we have taken great pains to ensure that few citizens will ever want to do anything so rash, so preposterous—in fact, so wholly un-American. In New Haven, as in many other parts of the United

States, vast social energies have been poured into the process of "Americanization", teaching citizens what is expected in the way of words, beliefs, and behaviour if they are to earn acceptance as Americans.' Dahl, *Who Governs?*, 317. As for the other two, see Walzer, *Spheres of Justice*, 215; and Raz, *Morality of Freedom*, 423–4.

105. See Galston, *Liberal Purposes*, 295.

106. Anthony Arblaster, 'The Proper Limits of Pluralism', in Ian Hampsher-Monk (ed.), *Defending Politics: Bernard Crick and Pluralism* (London: British Academic Press, 1993), 108. John Gray once affirmed virtually the same position, i.e. when he backed the first, intrinsically liberal pluralist polity: 'Toleration: A Post-Liberal Perspective', in *Enlightenment's Wake*, 24. Gray sums up his reasons for supporting this polity in 'Agonistic Liberalism', ibid.; although he has come to argue against it and for a version of the second one in 'After the New Liberalism', and 'From Post-Liberalism to Pluralism', both ibid.

107. Dahl, 'Rethinking *Who Governs?*: New Haven, Revisited', in Robert J. Waste (ed.), *Community Power: Directions for Future Research* (Beverley Hills, Calif.: Sage, 1986), 182. See also Dahl, *Preface to Democratic Theory*, 132–3.

108. See e.g. Ian Berlin, 'The Life and Opinions of Moses Hess', 232–51, and 'Nationalism: Past Neglect and Present Power', both in *Against the Current*. See also Hampshire, 'Nationalism', in Edna and Avishai Margalit (eds.), *Isaiah Berlin: A Celebration* (London: Hogarth Press, 1991).

109. See point 4 in Tamir, *Liberal Nationalism* (Princeton: Princeton University Press, 1993), 138.

110. See Galston, *Liberal Purposes*, 15–16.

111. See e.g. Berlin, 'Introduction', in *Four Essays on Liberty*, pp. xlix, lviii; and Hampshire, *Innocence and Experience* (London: Allen Lane, The Penguin Press, 1989), 162–8.

112. Berlin, correspondence with the author, 19 Mar. 1996.

113. MacIntyre, *After Virtue*, 253.

NOTES TO CHAPTER 3

1. Isaiah Berlin, 'Political Ideas in the Twentieth Century', in *Four Essays on Liberty* (Oxford: Oxford University Press, 1969), 39. See also Berlin, 'Historical Inevitability', ibid. 92.

2. See Joseph Raz, *The Morality of Freedom* (Oxford: Oxford University Press, 1986), esp. chs. 12, 13; John Gray, 'What is Dead and what is Living in Liberalism?' in *Post-Liberalism* (London: Routledge, 1992), esp. 287–98; and John Gray, *Isaiah Berlin* (London: HarperCollins, 1995), esp. 15, 49–62. Dahl has not made use of the term 'incommensurable' in his work, but his willingness to accept some of the conclusions of social choice theory indi-

cates that he also assumes a strictly instrumentalist notion of practical reason. See Dahl, *Democracy and its Critics* (London: Yale University Press, 1989), 154.

3. In mathematics, unlike in economics, one does not deal only with real numbers, and so 'commensurability' could be said to carry a different sense, one which implies the principle of identity but not necessarily transitivity; that is, items might be described as commensurable/mathematically comparable without being transitive. If this sounds strange, think of the following example: consider a consistently ordered circle, in which, for *a* and *b* on the circle, take any diameter of the circle intersecting it at *a* or *b*; say *a*. Now define *a* < *b* if *b* is on the right of the diameter oriented with *a* on top. I owe this example to Olivier Collin.

4. Charles Taylor, *Sources of the Self* (Cambridge, Mass.: Harvard University Press, 1989), 125. For more on Aristotelian practical reason, see Ronald Beiner, *Political Judgement* (London: Methuen, 1983), 72–97.

5. Isaiah Berlin and Bernard Williams, 'Pluralism and Liberalism: A Reply', *Political Studies*, 62/2 (1994) 306–9, 307. See also Michael Walzer, 'Introduction', to Isaiah Berlin, *The Hedgehog and the Fox: An Essay on Tolstoy's View of History* (New York: Simon & Schuster, 1986); and Michael Walzer, 'Are there Limits to Liberalism?', *New York Review of Books* (19 Oct. 1995), 29. That Berlin is drawn to something like Aristotelian *phronesis* for his conception of practical reason has been noted by Galipeau but missed by Gray, for whom Berlin's pluralism is agonistic like his own. See Claude J. Galipeau, *Isaiah Berlin's Liberalism* (Oxford: Clarendon Press, 1994), 66; and Gray, *Isaiah Berlin*.

6. Isaiah Berlin, 'Introduction', in *Four Essays on Liberty*, pp. l, lv; my italics. More recently, Berlin has described this moral sense practical reasoning as 'dictated by the forms of life of the society to which one belongs': 'The Pursuit of the Ideal', in *The Crooked Timber of Humanity*, ed. Henry Hardy (London: John Murray, 1990), 18.

7. See Michael Stocker, *Plural and Conflicting Values* (Oxford: Clarendon Press, 1990), 148–9.

8. Joseph Schumpeter, *Capitalism, Socialism and Democracy*, 6th edn. (London: Unwin Paperbacks, 1987), 251.

9. See Berlin, 'Introduction', in *Four Essays on Liberty*, pp. lx–lxi; or Michael Walzer, 'Political Action: The Problem of Dirty Hands', *Philosophy and Public Affairs*, 2/2 (1973), 160–80, 166–8.

10. Bernard Williams cannot be situated within either of these two non-agonistic pluralist camps as he argues that we are not yet ready to decide the issue which I am claiming distinguishes them. See Williams, 'Saint-Just's Illusion', in *Making Sense of Humanity: And Other Philosophical Papers 1982–1993* (Cambridge: Cambridge University Press, 1995).

11. See e.g. Stuart Hampshire, *Morality and Conflict* (Oxford: Basil Blackwell, 1983), 142–3; Michael Walzer, *Interpretation and Social Criticism* (Cambridge, Mass.: Harvard University Press, 1987), 23–5; Isaiah Berlin,

'Rationality of Value Judgements', in Carl J. Friedrich (ed.), *Nomos VII: Rational Decision* (New York: Atherton Press, 1964); Berlin, 'Introduction', in *Four Essays on Liberty*, p. xxxii; Berlin, 'Pursuit of the Ideal', 18; and Isaiah Berlin and Ramin Jahanbegloo, *Conversations with Isaiah Berlin* (London: Peter Halban, 1992), 37–9.

12. Isaiah Berlin, 'The Originality of Machiavelli', in *Against the Current*, ed. Henry Hardy (Oxford: Oxford University Press, 1981), 45. See also Berlin, 'Pursuit of the Ideal', 7–8; and Stuart Hampshire, *Innocence and Experience* (London: Allen Lane, The Penguin Press, 1989), 162–8. Walzer is somewhat less sure that, according to Machiavelli, a decisive choice needs to be made between these two ways of life *as a whole*, as opposed to simply a recognition that Christian virtues may be maintained though they will have to be seriously compromised in practice. See Walzer, 'Political Action: The Problem of Dirty Hands', 175–7.

13. Hampshire, *Morality and Conflict*, 152. As Gray has rightly pointed out, pluralist radical choices are not Sartrean in that they are not said to be done *ex nihilo*: 'for the self that transforms itself through the choices it makes is itself unchosen, since it is always a deposit of the choices made by others, now and in generations that have gone before'. Gray, *Isaiah Berlin*, 73. For Sartre's advice to the existentialist to 'just choose', see Sartre, *L'Existentialisme est un humanisme* (Paris: Gallimard, 1996).

14. See Hampshire, *Innocence and Experience*; as well as Walzer's positive review of the book in 'The Minimalist', *The New Republic* (22 Jan. 1990), 39–41.

15. Walter Benjamin has referred to making compromises for this reason in his 'Critique of Violence', in *One Way Street and Other Writings*, trans. Edmund Jephcott and Kingsley Shorter (London: NLB, 1979), 143.

16. See Hampshire, *Morality and Conflict*, 118.

17. Hampshire, *Innocence and Experience*, 74.

18. Nussbaum, 'Non-Relative Virtues: An Aristotelian Approach', in Nussbaum and Amartya Sen (eds.), *The Quality of Life* (Oxford: Clarendon Press, 1993), 249.

19. Nussbaum, 'Aristotelian Social Democracy', in Douglass, Mara, and Richardson (eds.), *Liberalism and the Good* (New York: Routledge, 1990), 205.

20. See Aristotle, *Nicomachean Ethics*, trans. Martin Ostwald (New York: Bobbs-Merrill, 1962), bk. 1.

21. See *Nicomachean Ethics*, 1095^b14–1196^a5, 1141^a18–$^b3$, 1143^b33–1144^a6, 1145^a6–11, 1178^b8–32.

22. See *Nicomachean Ethics*, 10. 8–9. It should be clear that, in articulating Aristotle's notion of *eudaemonia* in this way, I am trying to avoid taking a position here on whether he is claiming that one should lead a philosophical life *instead of* a political one, or whether the two should somehow be combined.

23. See e.g. *Nicomachean Ethics*, 1097^b1–5.

24. For this, combine *Nicomachean Ethics*, 1097^b2–5 with 1099^a32–1099^b2. See

also Aristotle, *The Politics*, 1. 13. Note how, for Aristotle, even instrument-al goods do not have the wholly contingent relationship to ends that they do in most modern conceptions of economics, as they cannot be conceived separately from *eudaemonia*. This is why, to emphasize this inseparability, we might follow David Wiggins's suggestion and speak not of 'means' in Aristotle's ethics, but of 'toward the ends'. See Wiggins, 'Deliberation and Practical Reason', in Amélie Oksenberg Rorty (ed.), *Essays on Aristotle's Ethics* (London: University of California Press, 1980), 223–4.

25. I am aware that this 'non-inclusivist' reading of Aristotle, in which *eudae-monia* is not interpreted as including *all* intrinsic goods, is not uncontro-versial. I find support for it in Richard Kraut, *Aristotle on the Human Good* (Princeton: Princeton University Press, 1989); as well as in Hampshire, *Innocence and Experience*, 23–36; and in Raymond Plant, *Modern Politi-cal Thought* (Oxford: Basil Blackwell, 1991), esp. 27.

26. Aristotle, *Nicomachean Ethics*, 1112^b33–4. See also Aristotle, *Rhetoric*, trans. W. R. Roberts, in *The Works of Aristotle*, xi, ed. W. D. Ross (Oxford: Clarendon Press, 1924), 1362^a17–10.

27. See e.g. Plant, *Modern Political Thought*, 37.

28. MacIntyre, *After Virtue*, 2nd edn. (Notre Dame, Ind: University of Notre Dame Press, 1984), 162. See Aristotle, *Nicomachean Ethics*, 1097^b–1098^a.

29. See *Nicomachean Ethics*, 1098^b–1099^a.

30. Nussbaum and Stocker have been criticized for this most pointedly by MacIntyre: see his *Whose Justice? Which Rationality?* (London: Duckworth, 1988), esp. 187; and 'A Partial Response to my Critics', in John Horton and Susan Mendus (eds.), *After MacIntyre: Critical Perspec-tives on the Work of Alaisdair MacIntyre* (Notre Dame, Ind.: University of Notre Dame Press, 1994), 301–2.

31. MacIntyre, *After Virtue*, 142. See also MacIntyre's discussion of Aquinas's Aristotelianism in MacIntyre, 'Moral Dilemmas', *Philosophy and Phe-nomenological Research*, 50 (supp., Fall 1990), 367–82, 379–82.

32. Nussbaum, 'Aristotelian Social Democracy', 235–6.

33. Hampshire, *Innocence and Experience*, 138. John R. Wallach criticizes Nussbaum on similar grounds: 'Insofar as her Aristotelian humanism would be politically determinate, it appears to authorize a new class of world-philosophers, who would advise leaders and legislators about how to make the world more functional for human beings . . . Insofar as her essentialist philosophy could be applied more pluralistically, it tends to elide the hard edges and actual dimensions of practical, political life.' Wallach, 'Contemporary Aristotelianism', *Political Theory*, 20/4 (Nov. 1992), 613–41, 629.

34. Charles Larmore, 'Pluralism and Reasonable Disagreement', in *The Morals of Modernity* (Cambridge: Cambridge University Press, 1996), 162.

35. Many have read Wittgenstein as quite different from these other two, but see Charles Taylor, 'Lichtung or Lebensform: Parallels between Heideg-ger and Wittgenstein', in *Philosophical Arguments* (London: Harvard Uni-versity Press, 1995).

36. Charles Taylor, 'Balancing the Humours: An Interview with Charles Taylor', *The Idler* (Nov.–Dec. 1989), 24. See also Taylor, *Sources of the Self*, 241; and Taylor, 'The Rushdie Controversy', *Public Culture*, 2/1 (Fall 1989) 118–22, 121.

37. Taylor, 'Irreducibly Social Goods', in *Philosophical Arguments*, 142.

38. Walzer, 'Flight from Philosophy', *Times Literary Supplement* (2 Feb. 1989), 43.

39. 'How do you reach these norms? . . . One just finds that one's form of life presupposes certain concepts, categories and belief.' Berlin and Jahenbegloo, *Conversations with Isaiah Berlin*, 113. See also Walzer, *Thick and Thin*, 4.

40. Ibid.

41. As a technique, i.e. as the analytic method, atomism has had a long history. Emerging first with the pre-Socratic Atomists, Leucippus and Democritus, it later received attention in Europe through Robert Grosseteste's commentaries on Aristotle in the 13th cent. See James McEvoy, *The Philosophy of Robert Grosseteste* (Oxford: Clarendon Press, 1982), 330–1. From Francis Bacon, who was strongly influenced by Grosseteste, it was then taken up by Galileo and, by the time of his death, had achieved a strong hold on the experimental natural sciences. See Thomas Kuhn, 'Mathematical versus Experimental Traditions in the Development of Physical Science', in John Rajchman and Cornel West (eds.), *Post-Analytic Philosophy* (New York: Columbia University Press, 1985), 175. Galileo became one of the sources of its entrance into the human sciences, and modern philosophy in general, as a result of Hobbes's visit to him in 1636. For it was at their meeting that Galileo introduced Hobbes to the 'resolutive-compositive method', which the Englishman then passed on to Descartes and the other philosophers in Marin Mersenne's group in Paris. See Scott Gordon, *The History and Philosophy of Social Science* (London: Routledge, 1991), 71–4; C. B. Macpherson, *The Political Theory of Possessive Individualism* (Oxford: Oxford University Press, 1962), 30–1, 101; or, for an alternative to this standard view, Donald W. Hanson, 'The Meaning of "Demonstration" in Hobbes's Science', *History of Political Thought*, 11/4 (Winter 1990), 587–626. In 20th-cent. philosophy, atomism has, of course, been fundamental to logical positivism. See e.g. Bertrand Russell, *The Philosophy of Logical Atomism*, ed. David Pears (La Salle, Ill.: Open Court, 1985).

42. This would, of course, be in contrast to a structuralist approach, in which one would look not so much at the interactions between the car's parts, but try instead to identify correlations between the more holistic phenomena underlying its operations. What, for example, are the different rates of speed reached when one pushes the gas pedal down to a certain extent? Or what mileage is achieved when one uses motor oil of a certain viscosity? Or how do the various feedback mechanisms work?

43. See Edmund Husserl, 'On the Theory of Wholes and Parts', in *Logical Investigations*, ii. trans. J. N. Findlay (London: Routledge & Kegan Paul, 1970), 436–7.
44. W. B. Gallie, 'Essentially Contested Concepts', *Proceedings of the Aristotelian Society*, 56 (1956), 167–98, 171–2.
45. In Berlin, *Four Essays on Liberty*.
46. See Isaiah Berlin, 'An Introduction to Philosophy', in Bryan Magee (ed. and interviewer), *Men of Ideas* (London: BBC, 1979), 33.
47. Berlin, 'Political Ideas in the Twentieth Century', 10, 11. See also Michael Walzer, *Thick and Thin* (Notre Dame, Ind.: University of Notre Dame Press, 1994), 1–3.
48. Berlin, 'Equality', in *Concepts and Categories*, ed. Henry Hardy (Oxford: Oxford University Press, 1980), 94–5, 100; my italics.
49. Walzer, *Thick and Thin*, 3.
50. Williams, 'Saint-Just's Illusion', 137.
51. Hampshire, *Morality and Conflict*, 115; my italics. See also ibid. 93.
52. Hampshire, 'Justice is Conflict: The Soul and the City', in Grethe B. Peterson (ed.), *The Tanner Lectures on Human Values,* xix (Salt Lake City: University of Utah Press, 1998), 166; my italics.
53. Ibid.; my italics.
54. Walzer, *Spheres of Justice* (New York: Basic Books, 1983), 312.
55. John Gray, 'On Negative and Positive Liberty', in *Liberalisms: Essays in Political Philosophy* (London: Routledge, 1989), 50–1.
56. Berlin, 'Two Concepts of Liberty', 125.
57. William E. Connolly, *The Terms of Political Discourse*, 3rd edn. (Oxford: Martin Robinson, 1993), 14; see also pp. 10–14, 22–3.
58. Ibid. 14.
59. Ibid. 78 n. 9.
60. Ibid. 13.
61. Ibid. 98.
62. Ibid. 110.
63. Ibid. 64.
64. Ibid. 96–7, 102–3.
65. Ibid. 157.
66. Connolly himself points out the connection when he states that 'adversaries might agree that the concept of interests is crucially tied to the concept of power'. Ibid. 127.
67. Connolly also mentions that the concept 'autonomy' (as choice) plays a role in 'interests' (ibid. 46) and 'freedom' (ibid. 157).
68. Ibid. 191–7.
69. *Journal of Political Philosophy*, 2/2 (1994), 140–64.
70. Ibid. 143–4.
71. Ibid. 151.
72. Ibid. 155.
73. Ibid.

74. Ibid. 158. Freeden cites Giovanni Sartori in this regard. See Sartori, 'Guidelines for Concept Analysis', in Sartori (ed.), *Social Science Concepts: A Systematic Analyses* (Beverly Hills, Calif.: Sage, 1984), esp. 52. Hannah Pitkin's similar view on the matter can be found in her discussion of what she calls 'language regions'. See her *Wittgenstein and Justice: On the Significance of Ludwig Wittgenstein for Social and Political Theory* (London: University of California Press, 1972), esp. 140–9.

75. See Wilhem von Humboldt, *On Language*, trans. Peter Heath (Cambridge: Cambridge University Press, 1988), 31.

76. See Charles Taylor, 'Language and Human Nature', in *Human Agency and Language* (Cambridge: Cambridge University Press, 1985), 221.

77. Hence Herder: 'The tear which moistens this lustreless and extinguished, this solace-starved eye—how moving is it not in the total picture of a face of sorrow. Take it by itself and it is a cold drop of water.' Johann Gottfried Herder, 'Essay on the Origin of Language', trans. Alexander Gode, in Jean-Jacques Rousseau and Herder, *On the Origin of Language* (London: University of Chicago Press, 1966), 90.

78. Taylor, 'Language and Human Nature', 231. Hans-Georg Gadamer refers to this conception in his *Truth and Method*, 2nd edn., trans. Joel Weinsheimer and Donald G. Marshall (New York: Crossroad, 1989), 11, 29, 63, 68–70, 77, 415–16.

79. Something like it first appeared, to my knowledge, in the context of those 'man as microcosmos' assertions of ancient Babylonian literature and the Jewish Midrash, as Henry Malter points out in his classic 'Personifications of Soul and Body', *Jewish Quarterly Review*, NS 2/4 (Apr. 1912), 453–79, 453. It was also given great prominence in Neoplatonic thought and in some of the writings that followed it (e.g. the works of Proclus, Augustine, and Bonaventure), as well as in the Jewish Kabbalah (see Gershom G. Scholem, *Major Trends in Jewish Mysticism*, 3rd edn. (New York: Schocken, 1954), esp. 269; and Rabbi Hayyim de Volozhyn, *L'Âme de la vie: Nefesh hahahyyim*, trans. Benjamin Gross (Paris: Éditions Verdier, 1986), i. 6). 'Man as microcosmos' also reappeared in some Renaissance doctrines, while in modern times another version of the holographic principle has emerged as central to Hegel's philosophy (see *Hegel's Logic*, trans. W. Wallace (Oxford: Oxford University Press, 1975), 20), as well as playing a major role in Romanticism. Shelley gives a particularly powerful expression of it in his *Hellas*: 'this Whole | Of suns, and worlds, and men, and beasts, and flowers, | With all the silent or tempestuous workings | By which they have been, are, or cease to be, | Is but a vision . . . | All is contained in each. | Dodona's forest to an acorn's cup | Is that which has been, or will be, to that | Which is.' *Shelley's Poetry and Prose*, ed. Donald H. Reiman and Sharon B. Powers (London: W. W. Norton, 1977), 431–2. And as Coleridge has put it, 'every partial representation awakes the total representation of which it had been a part': *Biographia Literaria*, in *The Collected Works of Samuel Taylor Coleridge*, i, ed. James Engell and W. Jackson Bate (Prince-

ton: Princeton University Press, 1983), 103. More recently, the idea has also found its way into modernism: e.g. I think it is implicit in one of Rilke's most famous poems, the 'Archaic Torso of Apollo', in *The Selected Poetry of Rainer Maria Rilke*, ed. and trans. Stephen Mitchell (New York: Vintage International, 1982), 61; and many have pointed to its role in James Joyce's *Finnegans Wake* (Harmondsworth: Penguin, 1978). See e.g. Klaus Reichert, 'Fragment and Totality', in Bonnie Kime Scott (ed.), *New Alliances in Joyce Studies* (London: Associated University Presses, 1988), 88; and Dirk Vanderbeke, 'Physics, Rhetoric, and the Language of *Finnegans Wake*', in R. M. Bollettieri Bosinelli *et al.* (eds.), *The Languages of Joyce* (Amsterdam: John Benjamins, 1992), 251–2. Variations on the idea have also turned up in the natural sciences, most obviously in biology, where it has been discovered that the nuclei of plant and animal cells contain chromosomes of DNA-encoded information for the make-up of *every* cell in the *whole* organism, as well as, of course, in holography, the construction of holograms being made possible on its basis, and in theoretical physics. On these latter see e.g. Robert Jacob Collier, 'Holography and Integral Photography', *Physics Today*, 21/7 (July 1968), 55–63; David Bohm, *Wholeness and the Implicate Order* (London: Routledge & Kegan Paul, 1980); and Ken Wilber (ed.), *The Holographic Paradigm and Other Paradoxes* (Boston: New Science Library, 1985).

80. Coleridge, quoted in M. H. Abrams, *The Mirror and the Lamp: Romantic Theory and the Critical Tradition* (Oxford: Oxford University Press, 1953), 174.
81. MacIntyre, *After Virtue*, 142.
82. William Blake, 'On Homer's Poetry', in *Blake's Poetry and Designs*, ed. Mary Lynn Johnson and John E. Grant (London: W. W. Norton, 1979), 428.
83. Walzer has referred to values as 'things' in this way through a citation of Ralph Waldo Emerson: 'Things are in the saddle | And ride mankind.' *Spheres of Justice*, 7. See also Walzer, *Thick and Thin*, p. x; Berlin, 'Two Concepts of Liberty', 125; Nussbaum, 'Non-Relative Virtues', 248; and Williams, 'Saint-Just's Illusion', 137–8. In doing so, however, these pluralists fail to appreciate what Heidegger has referred to as the 'thingness of the thing', i.e. that nothing ethically meaningful can, without distortion, be conceived of in a thin and self-contained way. See Martin Heidegger, 'The Thing', in *Poetry, Language, Thought*, trans. Albert Hofstadter (New York: Harper & Row, 1971). In fact, it would be only somewhat of an exaggeration for me to claim that the whole contrast I am presenting here between pluralism and hermeneutics comes down to diverging interpretations of one of the fragments left behind by the pre-Socratic Heracleitus, in which he refers to what it means for different persons to talk about the same 'thing'. See *The Art and Thought of Heraclitus*, ed. Charles H. Kahn (Cambridge: Cambridge University Press, 1979), fragment 23. For a pluralist reading of the fragment, see Nussbaum, '*Psuchē* in Heraclitus, I', *Phronesis*, 17 (1972), 1–16, 11.

84. For Walzer, however, the reverse is true: 'In moral discourse, thinness and intensity go together, whereas with thickness comes qualification, compromise, complexity, and disagreement.' *Thick and Thin*, 6.

85. Charles Taylor, 'Legitimation Crisis?', in *Philosophy and the Human Sciences* (Cambridge: Cambridge University Press, 1985), 258. For a full account, see Taylor, *Sources of the Self*, part I.

86. See Williams, 'Ethical Consistency', in *Problems of the Self: Philosophical Papers, 1956–1972* (Cambridge: Cambridge University Press, 1981).

87. Williams, 'Conflicts of Values', in *Moral Luck*, 71.

88. Hampshire, *Morality and Conflict*, 15. As he describes this implicit mode of thought in an earlier work: 'The possibility of the inner debate, the making up a mind, is not conceivable without the actuality of public discussion, and, in describing the inner debate, we naturally model it on the public discussion, even if it usually has no such explicitness, and if the distinct steps and stages are normally implicit and not articulated. The explanation follows the m\odel of an argument.' Hampshire, *Thought and Action*, 2nd edn. (London: Chatto & Windus, 1982), 284.

89. Hampshire, *Morality and Conflict*, 106.

90. See the discussions in Martin Heidegger, *Being and Time*, trans. John Macquarrie and Edward Robinson (New York: Harper & Row, 1962), esp. 67–71, 421–3; and Hubert L. Dreyfus, *Being-in-the-World: A Commentary on Heidegger's Being and Time, Division I* (Cambridge, Mass.: MIT Press, 1991).

91. Indeed, the notion that a whole which is to some extent integrated precedes the parts accounts, I would claim, not only for our perception of the ethically significant distinctions of our context, but for our perceptions *tout court*, and so our sensory perceptions as well. This would account for the neurologist Richard E. Cytowic's finding that synesthesia is normally latent in all human perceivers. See his *Synesthesia: A Union of the Senses* (New York: Springer Verlag, 1989); as well as his 'Synaesthesia: Phenomenology and Neuropsychology', in Simon Baron-Cohen and John E. Harrison (eds.), *Synaesthesia: Classic and Contemporary Readings* (Oxford: Blackwell, 1997). Cytowic's research, it seems to me, confirms the accounts that have been offered to us by Aristotle, Herder, and the hermeneuticist Maurice Merleau-Ponty. See Aristotle, *Aristotle's* De Anima*: Books II and III*, trans. D. W. Hamlyn (Oxford: Clarendon Press, 1968), 3. 2, 426^{b}8–427^{a}9; Herder, 'On the Origin of Language', 139–46; and Merleau-Ponty, *La Phénoménologie de la perception* (Paris: Gallimard, 1945), 264–5.

92. See the discussion in Dreyfus, *Being-in-the-World*, 68–9.

93. Hampshire, *Thought and Action*, 275.

94. For Hampshire, however, despite his self-declared affinities with Merleau-Ponty's hermeneutic phenomenology (ibid. 277), skills are still conceived of as a form of practice-free *thought*: 'The skilled use of language is an extreme case of condensed and unreconstructable thinking.' Hampshire, *Morality and Conflict*, 108.

95. See the discussion in Heidegger, *Being and Time*, 135–8.
96. Taylor, 'Rationality', in *Philosophy and the Human Sciences*, 141.
97. See John Kekes, *The Morality of Pluralism* (Princeton: Princeton University Press, 1993), 22, 188; and Galipeau, *Isaiah Berlin's Liberalism*, 59, 62.
98. Thus Berlin: 'The modes of thought of cultures remote from our own are comprehensible to us only to the degree to which we share some, at any rate, of their basic categories.' 'Historical Inevitability', in *Four Essays on Liberty*, 99.
99. See e.g. Walzer, *Interpretation and Social Criticism*, 45; Walzer, 'Nation and Universe', in Peterson (ed.), *Tanner Lectures on Human Values*, xi, 551; Walzer, 'Objectivity and Social Meaning', in Nussbaum and Sen (eds.), *Quality of Life*, 176; Hampshire, *Morality and Conflict*, 12, 165; and Hampshire, *Innocence and Experience*, 103.
100. Berlin, 'Introduction', in *Four Essays on Liberty*, p. xxviii.
101. Berlin and Jahanbegloo, *Conversations*, 109. See also Berlin, 'Pursuit of the Ideal', 10.
102. See e.g. Berlin, 'The Divorce between the Sciences and the Humanities', in *Against the Current*, esp. 98; Berlin, *Vico and Herder* (London: Hogarth Press, 1976); and Hampshire, *Innocence and Experience*, 44–8.
103. Berlin, 'Does Political Theory Still Exist?' in *Concepts and Categories*, 170.
104. Ibid. 168.
105. See Gadamer, *Truth and Method*, ii. i. 1–2. This reconstructive interpretive ideal goes back much further than Romanticism, however. For example, it was central to the Jewish *peshat* interpretive approach which emerged due to the influence of the rise of Islam in the 7th cent. See Edward L. Greenstein, 'Medieval Bible Commentaries', in Barry W. Holtz (ed.), *Back to the Sources: Reading the Classic Jewish Texts* (New York: Summit, 1984), 213–59.
106. See Taylor, 'Comparison, History, Truth', in *Philosophical Arguments*, 149–52.
107. See W. D. Ross, *The Right and the Good* (Oxford: Oxford University Press, 1963); and John McDowell, 'Virtue and Reason', *Monist*, 63/3 (1979), 331–50.
108. Taylor, 'What is Involved in a Genetic Psychology?', in *Human Agency and Language*, 140. Nussbaum, however, in the course of asserting that the list of goods she identifies must be open ended, advocates that we leave open the possibility of changes which entail 'subtracting some and adding others': 'Aristotelian Social Democracy', 219. That such changes are, for her, incrementalist (in that they do not necessitate altering the other goods on the list) is made clear by the fact that the above statement is immediately followed by a remark which refers to more holistic revisions as a distinctly separate matter.
109. See Ferdinand de Saussure, *Cours de linguistique générale*, ed. Charles Bully and Albert Sechehay (Paris: Payot, 1987).
110. See Taylor, 'Explanation and Practical Reason', in *Philosophical Argu-*

ments. This form of reasoning is described in the context of comparisons between whole traditions by MacIntyre in his *Whose Justice? Which Rationality?*, esp. chs. 18–20.

111. Aristotle, *The Politics*. 1253ª1.
112. Aristotle, *Nicomachean Ethics*. 1102ª1–3.
113. Hampshire, 'Justice is Conflict', 149.
114. Ibid. 148.
115. Quoted in Abrams, *Mirror and Lamp*, 173–4.
116. Plato, *Phaedo*, in *The Dialogues of Plato*, ii, 115 B.
117. Hampshire, *Morality and Conflict*, 116.
118. For Walzer, however, 'democratic speech' by which he means to refer to the negotiations fundamental to pluralist politics, has just such an 'adversarial quality': 'A Critique of Philosophical Conversation', 191.
119. Hampshire, 'Justice is Conflict', 20.
120. See e.g. Hampshire, *Morality and Conflict*, 12–13; and Hampshire, *Innocence and Experience*, 133.
121. Gadamer, *Truth and Method*, 126.
122. See Alan Megill, *Prophets of Extremity: Nietzsche, Heidegger, Foucault, Derrida* (Berkeley, Calif.: University of California Press, 1985), 21.
123. Taylor, 'What is Human Agency?', in *Human Agency and Language*, 40.
124. See the discussion in Taylor, *Sources of the Self*, 63–73.
125. See e.g. Taylor, 'Reply to Commentators', *Philosophy and Phenomenological Research*, 54/1 (Mar. 1994), 203–13, 204–5; and Taylor, 'Charles Taylor Replies', in James Tully (ed.), *Philosophy in an Age of Pluralism: The Philosophy of Charles Taylor in Question* (Cambridge: Cambridge University Press, 1994), 213.
126. See e.g. Taylor, *Sources of the Self*, part III.
127. See Peter Berger, 'On the Obsolescence of the Concept of Honour', in Stanley Hauerwas and Alasdair MacIntyre (eds.), *Revisions: Changing Perspectives in Moral Philosophy* (London: University of Notre Dame Press, 1983).
128. See James W. Fristrom and Michael T. Clegg, *Principles of Genetics*, 2nd edn. (New York: Chiron Press, 1988), 204, 462.
129. When Taylor himself refers to 'conceptual mutations' (in 'Interpretation and the Sciences of Man', in *Philosophy and the Human Sciences*, 55) or 'mutation' (in *Sources of the Self*, 315), I take him to be invoking only the interpretive sort of originality that is the product of the efforts of philosophers and critics. That he wishes to distinguish between this and the creative originality of the artist is clear from his statement that: 'The great epiphanic work can actually put us in contact with the sources it taps. It can *realize* the contact. The philosopher or critic tinkers around and shapes images through which he or another *might* one day do so. The artist is like the race-car driver, and we are the mechanics in the pit.' *Sources of the Self*, 512.

130. Leonard Cohen, 'Anthem', in *The Future* (Toronto: Sony Music Entertainment, 1992). See also Cohen, 'Democracy', ibid.; or see both reprinted in Cohen, *Stranger Music: Selected Poems and Songs* (London: Johnathan Cape, 1993), 373–4, 367–9.
131. Taylor, 'Introduction', in *Human Agency and Language*, 11.
132. See Taylor, *Sources of the Self*, chs. 23–4.
133. For arguments against even the coherence of such ambitions, see R. C. Zaehner, *Mysticism Sacred and Profane: An Inquiry into Some Varieties of Praeternatural Experience* (Oxford: Oxford University Press, 1967); and Martha Nussbaum, 'Transcending Humanity', in *Love's Knowledge: Essays on Philosophy and Literature* (Oxford: Oxford University Press, 1990), esp. 371–9.
134. T. S. Eliot, 'Sweeney Agonistes: Fragments of an Aristophanic Melodrama', in *Collected Poems: 1909–1962* (London: Faber & Faber, 1963), 131.
135. Taylor shares this assertion with pluralists. See e.g. Taylor, 'The Politics of Recognition', in *Philosophical Arguments*, 252–5; and Hampshire, *Innocence and Experience*, 138.
136. For Berlin, however, 'norms' and 'values' only 'justify'. Berlin and Jahanbegloo, *Conversations*, 113. And when Williams writes that it is for persons 'to decide how far they are prepared to adopt the perspective within which [a] justification counts' ('Moral Luck', in *Moral Luck*, 37) he is clearly supporting the pluralist position that it is possible to choose to grant no weight at all to the good behind the justification in question. Hermeneutics, however, goes beyond this conception in way that makes goods the bases of something more than what Williams has referred to as 'internal reasons' for action, though they cannot quite be captured by his notion of 'external reasons' either. See Williams, 'Internal and External Reasons', in *Moral Luck*.
137. Ludwig Wittgenstein, 'Wittgenstein's Lecture on Ethics', *Philosophical Review*, 74 (Jan. 1965), 3–26, 23.
138. Martha Nussbaum, *The Fragility of Goodness: Luck and Ethics in Greek Tragedy and Philosophy* (Cambridge: Cambridge University Press, 1986), 434 n. 65.
139. Williams e.g. stresses the clarity of those correct but 'morally disagreeable' decisions in his 'Politics and Moral Character', in Hampshire (ed.), *Public and Private Morality*, 61–2. Stocker does the same in his *Plural and Conflicting Values*, esp. 263.
140. 'The idea that there has been a moral cost itself implies that something bad has been done.' Williams, 'Moral Luck', 37.
141. See e.g. Walzer, 'Political Action: The Problem of Dirty Hands', 174. Though ultimately more rationalist than pluralist, it is worth pointing out that Ruth Barcan Marcus takes a similar position in her 'Moral Dilemmas and Consistency', in Christopher Gowans (ed.), *Moral Dilemmas* (Oxford: Oxford University Press, 1987), 198–9.

142. The Tragically Hip, 'Daredevil', in *Day for Night* (Toronto: MCA Records, 1994).

143. Though he is referring to a much less temporary condition than is often the case when it comes to facing a moral dilemma, this accords with Heinz Kohut's claim, a variation on one of Anna Freud's maxims, that 'a feeble, fragmented self will impinge on our awareness'. Kohut, *The Restoration of the Self* (New York: International Universities Press, 1997), 93.

144. Hampshire, *Morality and Conflict*, 158.

145. Walzer, 'The New Tribalism: Notes on a Difficult Problem', 171. See also Walzer, 'The Communitarian Critique of Liberalism', 21; Walzer, *Thick and Thin*, 82–104 (as well as the, in my opinion, insufficient qualification on p. 98); and Hampshire, *Morality and Conflict*, 152.

146. R. D. Laing, *The Divided Self: An Existential Study in Sanity and Madness* (London: Penguin, 1959).

147. See e.g. Kohut, *Restoration of Self*; Ernest S. Wolf, ' "Irrationality" in a Psychoanalytic Psychology of the Self', in Theodore Mischel (ed.), *The Self: Psychological and Philosophical Issues* (Oxford: Basil Blackwell, 1977); and Stanely B. Messer, Louis Sass, and Robert Woolfolk (eds.), *Hermeneutics and Psychological Theory: Interpretive Perspectives on Personality, Psychotherapy, and Psychopathology* (New Brunswick, NJ: Rutgers University Press, 1988), esp. chs. 8–10.

148. But not, of course, to the extent that we could speak of it as a unity, as in the organically unified conception that was championed by J. G. Hamann, one which became a focus of the German literary movement known as the *Sturm und Drang*. As Goethe described Hamann's central principle, 'everything that a man undertakes, whether it be produced in action or word or anything else, must spring from his whole united powers; all separation of powers is to be repudiated'. Berlin, 'Herder and the Enlightenment', in *Vico and Herder*, 203. See also Berlin, *The Magus of the North: J. G. Hamann and the Origins of Modern Irrationalism* (London: John Murray, 1993), 2–3 n. 2.

149. The notion of such an interior, 'microdialogue' of the self, one embodying a conflict of voices, has been explored by Mikhail Bakhtin in his *Problems of Dostoevsky's Poetics*, ed. and trans. Caryl Emerson (Minneapolis: University of Minnesota Press, 1984), esp. 74–5.

150. Deborah Tannen, *You Just Don't Understand: Women and Men in Conversation* (London: Virago, 1990), 282.

151. Gregory Bateson, 'Cultural Contact and Schismogenesis', in *Steps to an Ecology of Mind* (London: Paladin, 1972), 42.

152. Taylor has brilliantly highlighted the difficulties that can emerge from the dynamics of negotiation as regards the contemporary constitutional debate in Canada. On one side we have those Trudeauite federalists, who affirm a strong central government as a means of bringing the country closer together (analogous, perhaps, to the woman in the conflict above), while on the other are those *Québécois* nationalists who have been demanding

greater independence from Ottawa (our male role-player). Taylor has, rightly in my opinion, consistently objected to the ongoing compromise solution which amounts to nothing more than 'piecemeal accommodation in an atmosphere of mutual suspicion': *The Pattern of Politics* (Toronto: McClelland & Stewart, 1970), 142. See also Taylor, *Reconciling the Solitudes: Essays on Canadian Federalism and Nationalism* (Montreal: McGill-Queen's University Press, 1993).

NOTES TO CHAPTER 4

1. See Max Weber, 'Politics as a Vocation', in *From Max Weber: Essays in Sociology*, ed. and trans. H. H. Gerth and C. Wright Mills (London: Routledge, 1948), 117–28.
2. As in his *Innocence and Experience* (London: Allen Lane, The Penguin Press, 1989), esp. 170–7. Ch. 4 of Hampshire's *Morality and Conflict* (Oxford: Basil Blackwell, 1983) is entitled 'Morality and Pessimism'.
3. See Bernard Williams, 'Politics and Moral Character', in Stuart Hampshire (ed.), *Public and Private Morality* (Cambridge: Cambridge University Press, 1978).
4. Michael Walzer, 'Political Action: The Problem of Dirty Hands', *Philosophy and Public Affairs*, 2/2 (1973), 160–80, 165, 154.
5. Isaiah Berlin, 'Political Ideas in the Twentieth Century', in *Four Essays on Liberty* (Oxford: Oxford University Press, 1969), 11.
6. See e.g. Ruth Barcan Marcus, 'Moral Dilemmas and Consistency', in Christopher Gowans (ed.), *Moral Dilemmas* (Oxford: Oxford University Press, 1987).
7. Hampshire, *Innocence and Experience*, 74. Walzer has gone so far as to claim that there is a degree of 'hatred' towards each other inherent to groups in pluralism: 'Preface', in Jean-Paul Sartre, *Anti-Semite and Jew*, trans. G. J. Becker (New York: Schocken, 1995), p. xxiii. And, according to Raz: 'One of the difficulties in making multiculturalism politically acceptable stems from the enmity between members of different cultural groups, especially when they inhabit one and the same country. Such enmity is quite universal.' 'Multiculturalism: A Liberal Perspective', in *Ethics in the Public Domain* (Oxford: Oxford University Press, 1994), 163–4. As I will assert below, however, hatred is actually a sign that different ways of life share much more than the pluralist's drawing of solid conceptual lines between them allow.
8. Williams's lectures were presented as part of a seminar given jointly with Ronald Dworkin entitled 'Liberalism of Fear, Liberalism of Principle', at University College, Oxford, during Hilary Term, 1995.
9. Aeschylus, *The Oresteia*, trans. Robert Fagles (New York: Penguin, 1966), 109. Gadamer cites this maxim in his *Truth and Method*, 356.

10. Frye, 'Comedy', in Frye, Sheridan Baker, and George Perkins, *The Harper Handbook to Literature* (New York: Harper & Row, 1985), 110.
11. Northrope Frye, 'Historical Criticism: Theory of Modes', in *Anatomy of Criticism: Four Essays* (Princeton: Princeton University Press, 1957), 43.
12. See George Steiner, *The Death of Tragedy* (London: Faber & Faber, 1961).
13. Laurence Tribe, *Abortion: The Clash of Absolutes* (New York: Norton, 1990). In his book, Tribe goes no further than either looking to social and technological changes as a means of doing an 'end-run' around the conflict, or arguing that the 'absolutes' that constitute it, by virtue of their being associated with other, more 'contingent' values related to tradition, change, sex, and power, should be as open as these latter to compromise. Macedo also seems unable to go any further: *Liberal Virtues: Citizenship, Virtue, and Community in Liberal Constitutionalism* (Oxford: Clarendon Press, 1990), 72.
14. See Mason's discussion of 'the miscommunication thesis' in his *Explaining Political Disagreement* (Cambridge: Cambridge University Press, 1993), ch. 3.
15. A point missed by Berlin in his otherwise brilliant 'Rabindranath Tagore and Nationality', in *The Sense of Reality: Studies in Ideas and Their History*, ed. Henry Hardy (London: Chatto & Windus, 1996). In this piece, it seems to me, Berlin exaggerates the necessity of a nation being 'strong' if it is to obtain recognition, implying, as a result, that recognition is something which properly arises from within processes of either negotiation or force. 'Men seek recognition; rightly. They will not obtain it until they are strong.' Ibid. 263.
16. Regrettably, this fact seems to have escaped many Canadian federalists who, despite their increasing willingness to recognize Quebec as a 'distinct' or 'unique' society, continually fail to communicate that this is being done, not as a concession granted from within some constitutional bargaining session, but because they have come to truly understand that the province is the home of a nation. Of course, the aggressive tone employed by many *Québécois* nationalists has not helped matters either.
17. Luc Ferry and Alain Renault, *Philosophie politique 3: Des droits de l'homme à l'idée républicaine* (Paris: Presse Universitaires de France, 1985), 130; my translation.
18. Bernard Crick, *In Defence of Politics*, 4th edn. (London: Weidenfeld & Nicolson, 1992), 136, 154. However, Crick also refers to the 'mutual dependence' of certain values on each other, to the matter of how they are 'related'. Ibid. 204, 211. As he has also written, we should consider 'values together, in their social setting and in relation to each other'. Ibid. 222.
19. Bernard Crick, 'Procedural Values in Political Education', in Crick and Derek Heater, *Essays in Political Education* (Ringmer: Falmer, 1977), 113.
20. Crick, *In Defence of Politics*, 119. But then: 'Politics cannot embrace everything; but nothing can be exempted from politics entirely.' Ibid. 130.

21. This can be derived from Aristotle's response to the classic question: 'What if a benevolent genius could be found to act as dictator?' The answer of those who affirm political participation as a good-in-itself is not that such a person cannot be found, but that, regardless, he or she should be rejected. Crick, however, expresses sympathy for the reading that Aristotle's reply was that such person will not be found (ibid. 22–3). As I conceive of it, the background to the two positions is as follows. (i) With the first, one assumes that just political decision-making is a matter too complicated *by degree*, and so that, though we cannot say for certain that such an individual (or even computer) will never be found (or built), this seems extremely improbable. There is some justification for claiming that this is Aristotle's position, Aristotle's first (though not ultimate) choice for the ideal political regime being a kingship. See Aristotle, *The Politics* 1284^b. Note, however, the tension between this assertion and that other thrust in his work which seems to affirm politics as an intrinsic and not just instrumental good. (ii) With the second, the claim is that, *in principle*, no single individual could consistently come up with the right solutions to political conflicts. One reason for this is that political decision-making does not take place within a unified moral-political world, one in which answers that would fulfil the aspirations of all are always, at least in principle, reachable. To claim this is to claim that the need to turn to negotiated compromises between different groups or ways of life will sometimes be unavoidable. This is the position that is, more or less, upheld by both the pluralist and the patriot.

22. Ch. 7 of Crick's *In Defence of Politics* is entitled 'In Praise of Politics'.

23. Ibid. 7, 163, 169.

24. 'The debate never was, and never can be, one of nationalism versus political freedom. The problem, rather, is of the preservation of politics in a context overwhelmingly nationalistic.' Ibid. 90.

25. See Arendt, 'What is Freedom?', in *Between Past and Future: Six Exercises in Political Thought* (New York: World Publishing, 1961).

26. Benjamin Constant, 'De la liberté des anciens comparée à celles des modernes', in *De la liberté chez les modernes*, ed. Marcel Gauchet (Paris: Livre de Poche, 1980).

27. See Crick, 'Freedom as Politics', in *Political Theory and Practice* (Harmondsworth: Allen Lane, The Penguin Press, 1971), 57.

28. Ibid. 35.

29. Crick talks positively of the 'integration' of different cultures in *In Defence of Politics*, 232; refers to 'conciliation', ibid. 16, 28, 32, 55, 130, 172, 189; and to politics as either 'deliberative conciliation', ibid. 19, or 'creative compromise', in ibid. 134. He does, however, seem to use 'conciliation' and 'compromise' as synonyms, ibid. 30.

30. Ibid. 33; see also 117. For an interpretation of Plato's dialectics that, by downplaying the centrality accorded by more standard interpretations to his doctrine of the Forms, conceives of it as exemplifying hermeneutical conversation, see Hans-Georg Gadamer, *Plato's Dialectical Ethics:*

Phenomenological Interpretations Relating to the Philebus, trans. Robert
M. Wallace (London: Yale University Press, 1991), ch. 1.

31. Crick, 'Procedural Values in Political Education', 120.
32. See Crick, *In Defence of Politics*, 21–2. Recall the discussion of the
    comparatively 'non-naturalistic', historicized teleology of hermeneutics at
    ch. 3, s. IV(i).
33. Ibid. 24. See also ibid. 47. Crick also writes of how individuals can
    'grow' and societies 'improve' by virtue of a politics which exhibits a
    respect for truth. See Crick, 'Procedural Values in Political Education',
    119.
34. Crick, *In Defence of Politics*, 118.
35. Ibid. 171.
36. Ibid. 171 n. 2.
37. The Tragically Hip, introduction to 'New Orleans is Sinking', in *Another
    Roadside Attraction*, live concert performed in Landsdowne Park, Ottawa,
    Canada, 26 July 1998.
38. *In Defence of Politics*, 24, 18. Crick also argues that politics can lead to
    'consensus', ibid. 177.
39. Ibid. 33. I would add here that politics can never, by itself, get us there.
40. Ibid. 142.
41. Ibid. 185.
42. Charles Taylor, 'Modes of Civil Society', *Public Culture*, 3/1 (1990), 95–118,
    117.
43. See G. W. F. Hegel, *The Philosophy of Right*, trans. T. M. Knox (Oxford:
    Oxford University Press, 1942), esp. 155, 161–3, 168, 196–7, 201–3, 209, 266,
    281.
44. See Charles Taylor, *Hegel* (Cambridge: Cambridge University Press, 1975),
    537–46.
45. Taylor asserts that Hegel's distinction between state and civil society
    is too weak in his 'Hegel's Ambiguous Legacy for Modern Liberalism', in
    Drucilla Cornell, Michael Rosenfeld, and David Gray Carlson (eds.),
    Hegel and Legal Theory (London: Routledge, 1991), 75–6. Contrast this
    with a thinker such as Marx, whose antipolitics leads him to interpret it as
    too strong. See Marx, 'On the Jewish Question', in *Karl Marx: Selected
    Writings*, ed. and trans. David McLellan (Oxford: Oxford University Press,
    1977), esp. 47.
46. Taylor, 'Modes of Civil Society', 96. This has been evident both in
    some of his earliest, patriotic socialist writings, such as Taylor, 'A Socialist
    Perspective on the '70s', *Canadian Dimension*, 5/8 (Feb. 1969), 36–40,
    or *The Pattern of Politics*; as well as in his more recent, patriotic
    liberal work: e.g. 'Liberal Politics and the Public Sphere', in *Philo-
    sophical Arguments* (London: Harvard University Press, 1995), esp. 272.
    Crick, it should be noted, has remained an ardent patriotic socialist.
    See e.g. Crick, 'A Footnote to Rally Fellow Socialists', in *In Defence of
    Politics*.

47. Taylor, 'Liberal Politics and the Public Sphere', 279–80. A similar point is also made in Bellah *et al.*, *Habits of the Heart* (London: University of California Press, 1985), 212–18.
48. Taylor, 'Liberal Politics and the Public Sphere', 280.
49. See Taylor, 'Atomism', in *Philosophy and the Human Sciences*. As for how neutralism of the Kantian liberal variety can lead to social atomism and the kind of legitimation crisis that accompanies it, see William E. Connolly, *Appearance and Reality in Politics* (Cambridge: Cambridge University Press, 1981), ch. 4; and Michael Sandel, 'The Procedural Republic and the Unencumbered Self', in Shlomo Avineri and Avner de-Shalit (eds.), *Communitarianism and Individualism* (Oxford: Oxford University Press, 1992).
50. Taylor, 'Liberal Politics and the Public Sphere', 282–3. Or see Charles Taylor, *The Ethics of Authenticity* (Cambridge, Mass: Harvard University Press, 1991), 112–13.
51. Ibid. 110; my italics. See also Taylor, 'Irreducibly Social Goods', in *Philosophical Arguments*, 143–5.
52. See e.g. Taylor, 'The Diversity of Goods', in *Philosophy and the Human Sciences*; and Taylor, *Sources of the Self*.
53. Taylor, 'Leading a Life', in Ruth Chang (ed.), *Incommensurability, Incomparability, and Practical Reason* (Cambridge, Mass.: Harvard University Press, 1997), 183.
54. See the closing discussion of s. IV(i).
55. Peter Winch, *The Idea of a Social Science and its Relation to Philosophy*, 2nd edn. (London: Routledge, 1990), pp. xv–xvi. See also Ludwig Wittgenstein, *Philosophical Investigations*, 2nd edn, ed. G. E. M. Anscombe, Rush Rhees, and G. H. von Wright, trans. Anscombe (Oxford: Basil Blackwell, 1958), part I, ss. 65 ff; and Rush Rhees, 'Wittgenstein's Builders', in *Discussions of Wittgenstein* (London: Routledge & Kegan Paul, 1969), esp. 84.

NOTES TO CHAPTER 5

1. For, in such a view, as Taylor has written, when we take an instrumental stance towards something, 'we declare our separation from it, our moral independence': *Sources of the Self* (Cambridge, Mass.: Harvard University Press, 1989), 383.
2. See Bernard Williams, *Ethics and the Limits of Philosophy* (London: HarperCollins, 1985), 6–7, 174–96.
3. The exclusive use of the masculine pronoun here is no accident, as the ethic of heroism in classical republicanism has been mainly, though not exclusively, sexist. That is why those feminists who have turned to an unreformulated classical republicanism to support their visions of citizenship can do so only by completely ignoring its heroic dimensions. Mary Dietz

e.g. makes this error in her 'Context is All: Feminism and Theories of Citizenship', in Chantal Mouffe (ed.), *Dimensions of Radical Democracy* (London: Verso, 1992), esp. 75–6.

4. Homer, *The Iliad*, trans. Martin Hammond (Harmondsworth: Penguin, 1987), 6. 208, 134.

5. See Hannah Arendt, *The Human Condition* (Garden City, NY: Doubleday Anchor edn., 1958), 57.

6. The theatrical allusions here are no accident. For one thing, as Arendt has pointed out, the virtuosity of the political actor is meant to parallel that sort integral to the performing arts. See Arendt, 'What is Freedom?', in *Between Past and Future* (New York: World Publishing, 1961), 153–4. For another, glory here is understood to rely on the existence of an audience of the very sort assumed by classical conceptions of the theatre, i.e. of a *community* of persons sharing goods closely in common. The thrust stage of classical theatre, in which the stage juts out into the audience that sits around it, so they are unable to avoid catching sight of each other, is said to encourage a highly communal experience as well a critical focus, while the straight, proscenium arch model, used in cinemas and many modern theatres, encourages a much more individualistic and escapist affair for spectators. That is one reason why audiences of theatre may, as Eric Bentley has pointed out, partake of a qualitatively different experience from those of cinema, one productive of what he has referred to as 'a psychology of *we*': 'What is Theatre?', in *The Theatre of Commitment: And Other Essays on Drama in Our Society* (London: Methuen, 1954), 55–60.

7. For a discussion of the shift in classical Rome from this highly civic classical republican conception of law to the vision ascribed to the jurist Gaius, see J. G. A. Pocock, 'The Ideal of Citizenship since Classical Times', in Ronald Beiner (ed.), *Theorizing Citizenship* (Albany, NY: SUNY Press, 1995), esp. 29–45.

8. In this respect, as Arendt has pointed out, Aristotle is more Roman than Greek. See Arendt, *The Human Condition*, 173–5.

9. See Charles Secondat Montesquieu, *De l'esprit des lois*, i, ed. Laurent Versini (Paris: Gallimard, 1995), v. ii–iv. See also Niccolo Machiavelli, *The Discourses*, ed. Bernard Crick, trans. Leslie J. Walker (Harmondsworth: Penguin, 1970), iii. 47.

10. In Canada and the USA, there is a variation on the game in which a very small bean sack, called a 'hacky-sack', is used instead of a soccer ball.

11. Thucydides praises the fusion of the few and the many as found for a time in the Athenian constitution in his *History of the Peloponnesian Wars*, 8. 97; Plato refers to a mixture of governmental forms in his *Menexenus*, in *The Dialogues of Plato*, i, 238 cd; and in his *Laws*, in *The Dialogues of Plato*, 4. 691 d–692 c, 693 de, 701 e, 712 de; and Aristotle's ultimate (though not most preferred) choice is for a combination of aristocracy and democracy, as we see in his *The Politics*, 1266^{a}3–5. That this is not Aristotle's preference, his most favoured option being a straight kingship, seems to speak

against the interpretation that he affirmed political activity as an intrinsic good, and so puts his classical republican credentials into question. This is countered, however, by the fact that his ultimate choice seems to affirm the opposite extreme, its failure to include monarchical features leaving little room for 'the hero' in his political vision. For if that hero is to be a political actor, and not the contemplative philosopher of Book 10 of his *Nicomachean Ethics*, then it seems that there is no place for him. For when it comes to those who exhibit an exceptionally outstanding excess of virtue *vis-à-vis* other citizens, then, to the extent that this would place them above even the aristocratic hierarchy of the *polis*, Aristotle calls for such beings to be banished, since to him they can be but 'God[s] among human beings', and so cannot be governed by the laws of the city since 'they themselves are the law'. Aristotle, *The Politics*, 1284ª.

12. See Polybius, *The Histories*, iii, trans. W. R. Paton (London: William Heinemann, 1923), 6. 3–18.

13. These are some of the roles, and those responsible for fulfilling them, outlined in the Roman constitution as reported by Polybius. See ibid. 6. 11–14.

14. Ibid., esp. 6. 4. 2–4. 12, 10.

15. Ibid. 6. 11. 11. Polybius thus praises Lycurgus for having put together a constitution which '*united* in it all the good and distinctive features of the best governments'; my italics. Ibid. 6. 10. 6.

16. Ibid. 6. 8. 2–8. 3.

17. Aristotle, *The Politics*, 1290ª.

18. Ibid. 1301ᵇ–1303ª.

19. Ibid. 4. 11, 1295ª; and Aristotle, *Nicomachean Ethics*, 2. 6–9. As J. O. Urmson has pointed out, Aristotle's doctrine of the mean is *not* a doctrine of moderation, one in which extremes should be avoided. See Urmson, *Aristotle's Ethics* (Oxford: Basil Blackwell, 1988), 29. It thus should not, I would argue, be allied with any conception of practical reason which affirms compromising or the metaphor of 'balancing' as its base.

20. See Polybius, 6. 18. 1–18. 4. See also Machiavelli, *The Discourses*, ii. 25.

21. Ibid., 426; see also, i. 34, iii. 6.

22. Polybius, 6. 9. 12.

23. Aristotle, *The Politics*, 1279ª.

24. As M. J. C. Vile writes of the balanced constitution, 'the notion of a *balance* necessarily assume[s] a basis of *separation*': *Constitutionalism and the Separation of Powers* (Oxford: Clarendon Press, 1967), 99. Aristotle, however, comes out against the factions this implies in his *Politics*, 1296ª. With Polybius, the importance of appreciating that the parts of a mixed government are in no sense separate from each other is clear when he writes of how, to those who focused on the parts of the Roman constitution, it may have 'seemed' (Polybius, 6. 11. 12) that the three parts were independent and 'pure' (6. 12. 10), each 'appear[ing] to be entirely' (6. 13. 8) of a single form; in reality, however, 'none of the three is absolute' (6. 18. 7). As for his complementary discussion of the details of their 'union' (6. 18. 1), see 6. 15–17.

Machiavelli also comes out against any part of government being sovereign, a good example of which can be found in his *The Discourses*, 234.

25. On the influence of physics and mathematics on the political thought of the time, see George Clark, *The Seventeenth Century*, 2nd edn. (Oxford: Clarendon Press, 1947), 212–13. I was made aware of this source through a note in W. B. Gwyn, *The Meaning of the Separation of Powers* (New Orleans: Tulane University Press, 1965), 26 n. 3, though, despite his citation of Clark, as well as others who discuss the special emphasis on 'balancing' within 17th- and 18th-cent. political thought, Gwyn fails to make the distinction I am putting forward here between 'mixed' and 'balanced' governance. Others who have either blurred or wrongly distinguished between the two conceptions include Hannah Arendt, *On Revolution*, 2nd edn. (New York: Viking Press, 1965), 149; F. W. Walbank, *Polybius* (Berkeley: University of California Press, 1972), 150; J. G. A. Pocock, *The Machiavellian Moment: Florentine Political Thought and The Atlantic Republican Tradition* (Princeton: Princeton University Press, 1975), pp. viii, 197; Robert Dahl, *Democracy and its Critics* (London: Yale University Press, 1989), 24–7; and Richard Bellamy, 'The Political Form of the Constitution', in Bellamy and Dario Castiglione (eds.), *Constitutionalism in Transformation: European and Theoretical Perspectives* (Oxford: Blackwell, 1996), 28–35. 'Mixed' and 'balanced' governance are distinguished in ways compatible with that which I have put forward here, however, in Kurt von Fritz, *The Theory of the Mixed Constitution in Antiquity* (New York: Columbia University Press, 1954), esp. 186, 204–5, 217; and in Vile, *Constitutionalism*, 39, 68, 98–9. For more on how the fundamental place given to 'balancing' in much modern social and political thought has its origin as an import from the modern natural sciences, see Scott Gordon, *The History and Philosophy of Social Science* (London: Routledge, 1991), 71–4.

26. See Montesquieu, III. ii, vi–vii, x.

27. Ibid. XI. vi.

28. The New Testament was another important source, as Eric Auerbach shows in his *Mimesis*, trans. Willard R. Trask (Princeton: Princeton University Press, 1953), ch. 2.

29. There were, however, also those Renaissance Florentines, such as Giovanni Cavalcanti and Girolamo Savonarola, who affirmed a Christianized republicanism. See the discussion in Pocock, *The Machiavellian Moment*, ch. 4. For more on how these two ways of life have been combined, see Antony Black, 'Christianity and Republicanism: From St. Cyprian to Rousseau', *American Political Science Review*, 91/3 (Sept. 1997), 647–56. Polybius and Machiavelli, however, at least when they focused on the imperfectly founded republic that was their conception of classical Rome, had no need of a divinely inspired legislator to perform that founding, and so did not rely on a notion of a transcendent, sacred realm with which the idea of such a legislator is intrinsically linked.

30. As he himself puts it, a republic must try to avoid falling victim to the incessant flux of political life, in which everyone's fortunes always 'rise up or sink down' without ever being able to 'remain fixed'. *The Discourses* in *Machiavelli: The Chief Works and Others*, ed. and trans. Allan Gilbert (Durham, NC: Duke University Press, 1965), 210. See also Machiavelli, *The Discourses*, ed. Crick, 266. (Further citations of *The Discourses* will refer to the Crick edn.) Machiavelli also compares Fortune to a river which, when in flood, cannot be resisted and so sweeps all away, but against which, in fair weather, men can take the precautions of building embankments and dykes. See Machiavelli, *The Prince*, ed. Quentin Skinner and Russell Price, trans. Price (Cambridge: Cambridge University Press, 1988), ch. 25. And finally, to Arendt, republics can be built on promises which constitute 'islands of certainty in an ocean of uncertainty': *The Human Condition*, 220.

31. For classical republican references to the *polis* in this way, see e.g. Arendt, *On Revolution*, p. 20; Arendt, *On Violence* (London: Allen Lane, The Penguin Press, 1970), 78; or Pocock, *The Machiavellian Moment*, 145, 157.

32. See Taylor, 'Irreducibly Social Goods', in *Philosophical Arguments*, 139.

33. Locke e.g. refers to the unity of 'political society' (by which he means to refer to the state and civil society together) in his *Two Treatises of Government*, ed. Mark Goldie (London: Everyman, 1993), ii, 122, 159, 163–5, 172–3, 175–6, 178, 181. This is one of those fundamentals that can be traced back to Hobbes, as in his *Leviathan*, ed. C. B. Macpherson (Harmondsworth: Penguin, 1968), 220.

34. Indeed, according to Samuel Huntington, 'by the 1970s the debate was over, and Schumpeter had won': *The Third Wave: Democratization in the Late Twentieth Century* (London: University of Oklahoma Press, 1991), 5.

35. Joseph Schumpeter, *Capitalism, Socialism and Democracy*, 6th edn. (London: Unwin Paperbacks, 1987), 251.

36. Ibid. 252.

37. See Albert O. Hirschman, *The Passions and the Interests* (Princeton: Princeton University Press, 1977), 13–30.

38. Though not in their institutional thought, the concept of offices checking offices being limited to the Federalists' vision of a bicameral legislature, and not the whole governmental system. Federalist institutionalism was thus an exemplification—not of balanced government—but of the *functional* doctrine of the separation of powers, one which demanded not that different governmental departments should speak for different segments of society, but rather that they would address the different tasks of the whole society. See the discussion in Garry Willis, 'Introduction', to Alexander Hamilton, James Madison, and John Jay, *The Federalist Papers* (New York: Bantam, 1982), pp. xv–xvii (though note his misidentification of mixed for balanced government). Where a balancing of opposed forces is meant to come in for the Federalists is in their vision of the, to some extent, extra-state politics of conflicting factions.

39. There was anything but a smooth continuity here, however, 19th-cent. American political science being dominated by a highly monistic, state-centred approach. See John G. Gunnell, 'The Genealogy of American Pluralism: From Madison to Behavioralism', *International Political Science Review*, 17/3 (July 1996), 253–65, esp. 254–6.

40. The term is Gunner Myrdal's: *The Political Element in the Development of Economic Theory*, trans. Paul Streeten (London: Routledge & Kegan Paul, 1953), 54, 150. That Arendt can cite it approvingly is just one more indication of the vast differences between the 'common good' of classical republicanism and the 'public interest' of classical and neo-classical modern democracy. See Arendt, *The Human Condition*, 44 n. 36.

41. 'Si, quand le peuple suffisamment informé délibère, les Citoyens n'avoient aucune communications entre eux, du grand nombre de petites différences résulteroit toujours la volonté générale, et la délibération seroit toujours bonne.' Rousseau, *Du contrat social*, in *Œuvres complètes*, ed. Bernard Gagnebin and Marcel Raymond (Paris: Gallimard, 1964), II. iii.

42. This point is missed by Walzer in his overly pluralist interpretation of Rousseauian democracy. To Walzer, the fact that, when the people's will is mistaken, the Legislator, the figure Rousseau appoints as their guide, can deceive but not coerce them means that, for Rousseau, 'political legitimacy rests on will (consent) and not on reason (rightness)'. Walzer, 'Philosophy and Democracy', 385. But Rousseau's Legislator is not meant to participate in legitimate governance. Rather, his role is to assist people in getting out of the illegitimate state of legal and unequally distributed property, where they are considered to be but a collection of egoistic individuals, and into the transformed and legitimate state of the general will. Once there, there should be no need for his guidance because the general will does not make mistakes; the end that is the common good will be realized every time for 'la volonté générale est toujours droite et tend toujours à l'utilité publique'. Rousseau, *Du contrat social*, II. iii. We might say, then, that, for Rousseau, legitimacy rests on consent *and* rightness, on meeting the requirements of what he considers to be both the means *and* the ends of good governance. To him, people already granted their consent to end the state of war and establish the laws of property, but this was still far from enough to make for a legitimate regime: 'Telle fut, ou dut être l'origine de la Société et des Loix, qui donnérent de nouvelles entraves aux foible et de nouvelles forces aux riche, détruisirent sans retour la liberté naturelle, fixérent pour jamais la Loi de la propriété et de l'inégalité, d'une adroite usurpation firent un droit irrévocable, et pour le profit de quelques ambitieux assujétirent désormais tout le Genre-humain au travail, à la servitude et à la misére.' Rousseau, *Discourse sur l'origine de l'inégalité*, in *Œuvres complètes*, 178.

43. See Rousseau, *Du contrat social*, III. i.

44. Isaiah Berlin, 'The Originality of Machiavelli', in *Against the Current*, ed. Henry Hardy (Oxford: Oxford University Press, 1981), 75. See also Berlin,

'The Pursuit of the Ideal', in *The Crooked Timber of Humanity*, ed. Henry Hardy (London: John Murray, 1990), 7–8; and Stuart Hampshire, *Innocence and Experience* (London: Allen Lane, The Penguin Press, 1989), 162–8.

45. Plato, *The Republic*, 331 D.

46. Peter Berger refers to the neglect of motives of honour in Western law today in his 'On the Obsolescence of the Concept of Honour', in Hauerwas and MacIntyre (eds.), *Revisions*, esp. 172. The Tragically Hip make a similar point regarding revenge in particular in their song about the brother who was (unjustly, as the shame of the 'folks' below seems to indicate) convicted due to his murder of a rapist: 'See my sister got raped, so a man got killed, / Local boy went to prison, the man's buried on the hill. / Folks went back to normal when they closed the case, / But they still stare at their shoes when they pass our place.' The Tragically Hip, '38 Years Old', in *Up to Here* (Toronto: MCA Records, 1989).

47. The problem was often expressed in terms of how to restrain those great leaders who, while most effective during glorious military campaigns, found it difficult to live within the constraints necessary for politics. The reaction, as reported by Thucydides, of many Athenians to Alcibiades is a good example of this. See Thucydides, 6. 15; as well as Jacqueline de Romilly's study, *Alcibiade: Ou les dangers de l'ambition* (Paris: Fallois, 1995). A good summary of the various classical republican responses to this tension between heroism and civicism can be found in John Hope Mason, 'Creativity in Action: The Background to Machiavelli's "Lion" and "Fox"', in Hampsher-Monk (ed.), *Defending Politics*; Pocock gives a succinct account of how the tension asserts itself within Machiavelli's thought in his *The Machiavellian Moment*, 167; and Margaret Canovan, relying on Arendt's unpublished writings, has been able to show that Arendt, far from simply idealizing Athens, also worried that Athenian civicism inhibited the individual citizen's ability to act heroically: *Hannah Arendt: A Reinterpretation of Her Thought* (Cambridge: Cambridge University Press, 1992), 136 ff.

48. See Machiavelli, *The Discourses*, 105. In other places, however, it is Rome, in explicit contrast to Venice, that is referred to as 'perfect', as in Machiavelli, *The Art of War* in *The Portable Machiavelli*, ed. and trans. Peter Bondanella and Mark Musa (Harmondsworth: Penguin, 1979), 516.

49. See Machiavelli, *The Discourses*, 106–11; as well as Crick's 'Introduction', to the same edn., esp. 23–33; and Crick, 'Notes', ibid. 539 n. 51.

50. See e.g. Machiavelli, *The Discourses*, 110. Moreover, it was, to Machiavelli, nothing but the failure of the people and the nobles to put the common good of their republic first that was behind his native Florence's inability to match Rome's greatness. See Machiavelli, *History of Florence and of the Affairs of Italy: From The Earliest Times to the Death of Lorenzo the Magnificent*, trans. Istorie Fiorentine (New York: Harper & Brothers, 1960), III. i, 108–9.

51. For, to him, the citizens of even an imperfect republic should 'live without factions'. Machiavelli, *The Art of War*, 489. See also Machiavelli, *The Discourses*, 125, 130. Quentin Skinner is thus mistaken when he claims that Machiavelli approved of the presence of factions which, 'guided, as if by an invisible hand', were 'motivated entirely by their selfish interests' to check each other in a way beneficial for the health of the republic: *Machiavelli* (Oxford: Oxford University Press, 1981), 66. David Held, by following Skinner, is led to make the same anachronistic interpretation, one which leads both of them to repeat the all-too-common error of blurring mixed and balanced government. Ibid. 65; and Held, *Models of Democracy* (Oxford: Polity Press, 1987), 45.

52. Machiavelli, *The Discourses*, 114. Machiavelli also praises the quality of 'unity' (ibid. 143, 360, 480–1); and refers negatively to 'disunion' or 'division', (pp. 145, 478–80).

53. For classical republicans also sometimes assert that glory may arise from actions whose significance derives less from their role in conflict than from their extreme originality and inventiveness. This, I would claim, is the thrust of Arendt's vision of glory, and it is one that is appreciated even by Machiavelli, despite his considerable militarism. For in reference to 'what pertains to the arts', he asserts that 'in themselves they have so much lustre that time can scarce take away or add much to the glory which they themselves deserve'. Machiavelli, *The Discourses*, 266. I would contend, however, that there are important, indeed insurmountable, philosophical obstacles for the classical republican when it comes to making room for a glory based solely upon creativity, but that argument would take me too far afield here.

54. See Thucydides, 2. 41, p. 91. And Machiavelli refers to men who 'join together to commit an honourable act of evil'. Machiavelli, *The Art of War*, i. 492.

55. Psychological dramas are based on this 'enemy within' motif, a good example of which is Woody Allen's powerful film, *Another Woman* (Orion Pictures, 1988).

56. As e.g. in the case of the good samaritan who risks his or her life by diving in turbulent waters or entering a burning house, etc., to come to the aid of someone in peril. There is also said to be something glorious about capturing or controlling, and not just defeating, nature, as the figure of the heroic natural scientist attests.

57. That is to say, laying claim to great abilities is never enough, for glory comes only when the hero has actually succeeded in using them to defeat his or her opponents. That is why Machiavelli could praise only the 'qualities' of his friend Cosimo Rucellai, Rucellai having had reason on his deathbed to complain of Fortune's unkindness to him since 'his deeds did not materialize', meaning that, instead of being glorified, 'he knew that no one could say anything about him other than that a good friend had passed away'. Machiavelli, *The Art of War*, 485. Luck, then, can play an oddly asymmetri-

cal role when it comes to the hunt for glory, in that being unlucky may preclude even the most capable actor from succeeding, while being lucky does
not really detract from the praise that success brings. That is why heroes in
Homer, as A. W. H. Adkins has pointed out, were considered no less great
for being 'lucky' enough to have received the assistance of a god or goddess
in vanquishing an adversary. See Adkins, *From the Many to the One* (Ithaca,
NY: Cornell University Press, 1970), 26.

58. Indeed, as a friend of mine is fond of pointing out, it is difficult to be upset
with someone who is 'not even wrong'.

59. Arendt, *On Violence*, 70.

60. Joseph Schumpeter, *Capitalism, Socialism and Democracy*, 6th edn.
(London: Unwin Paperbachs, 1987), 269. Or, as Huntington puts it, a polity
is democratic 'to the extent that its most powerful collective decision
makers are selected through fair, honest, and periodic elections in which
candidates freely compete for votes and in which virtually all the adult
population is eligible to vote.' Huntington, *American Politics* (Cambridge,
Mass.: Harvard University Press, 1981), 7.

61. See Dahl, *Dilemmas of Pluralist Democracy* (London: Yale University
Press, 1982), 6; or *Democracy and its Critics* (London: Yale University
Press, 1989), 108–14, 129.

62. See Walzer, *Spheres of Justice*, 309–10.

63. Taylor makes a similar point in his 'Political Theory and Practice', in
Christopher Lloyd (ed.), *Social Theory and Political Practice* (Oxford:
Clarendon Press, 1983), 71.

64. Dahl, *Democracy and its Critics*, 124.

65. Ibid. 120.

66. Schumpeter, *Capitalism, Socialism and Democracy*, 245.

67. Dahl, *Democracy and its Critics*, 122.

68. Ibid. 101, 126–9.

69. Ibid. 129.

70. Ibid. 148, 195–209.

71. Ibid. 207.

72. Dahl, *Dilemmas of Pluralist Democracy*, 98.

73. Dahl, *Democracy and its Critics*, 129.

74. Ibid. 209.

75. For, as Taylor states, 'concepts of successful maturity are the basis of argu-
ments concerning how we should live': 'What is Involved in a Genetic
Psychology?' in *Human Agency and Language* (Cambridge: Cambridge
University Press, 1985), 162.

76. See Ch. 3, s. IV(ii).

77. In this they are echoed by those modern democrats who also assume that
a unity (though of a systematic rather than organic sort) underlies domestic politics, and so envision regimes as self-enclosed unities. Locke e.g.
maintains that governments remain in a state of nature in relation to each
other. See Locke, *Two Treatises*, 121–2, 189. This is shared by Rawls, who

announces at the outset of *A Theory of Justice* (Cambridge, Mass.: Harvard University Press, 1971), 8, that for his purposes society is viewed as a 'closed system isolated from other societies'.

78. See Machiavelli, *The Discourses*, i. 59, ii. 4, ii. 23. This is not to say that classical republicans such as Machiavelli or Arendt have no place for something like the *ius gentium*, that conception of international law which, for the Romans, was to be observed by all states. See Machiavelli, *The Discourses*, 368; or Canovan, *Hannah Arendt*, 221. But this is best understood, like the pluralist's universal minimal moral code, as the product of an 'overlapping' rather than a 'sharing' of certain basic notions of justice amongst states. For note how, with Machiavelli, regimes participating in a league never *integrate* into each other, as they always remain 'distinct' in an independent, separable sense, members of a 'confederation' rather than any sort of federation. See Machiavelli, *The Discourses*, 286.

79. One way to criticize it is to point out that although those who perform heroic deeds in battle are glorified by the community that benefits because of them, even those who have suffered defeat as a result can, at times, admit of a begrudging respect for the victors. After all as Machiavelli himself has written, 'virtue is praised and admired even in one's enemies': *The Discourses*, 253; see also pp. 181, 331. But if this is possible, then does it not mean that there is at least some virtue shared between regimes, and so that there should be a concomitant blurring of the sharp borders that the classical republican assumes lies between them?

80. Hampshire, *Innocence and Experience*, 74.

81. Weak pluralism is somewhat of an exception here. For example, Walzer's idea that there can be a consensus of understandings shared across the whole of a polity approaches, but does not reach, the patriotic assertion that all of a country's citizens may, indeed must, share in a public common good. For to the patriot that common good is, at base, constituted by practices rather than, as with Walzer, 'understandings', the latter term being much more mentalistic and so in keeping with the pluralist vision of goods as, at base, thin concepts. When it comes to societies where Walzer does not consider his theory of distributive justice applicable, however, these 'shared understandings' are, as with other pluralists, said to serve as but the bases of negotiations and not, as the patriot would have it, conversations over matters such as the 'problem of the unit'. See e.g. Walzer, 'The New Tribalism: Notes on a Difficult Problem', esp. 168, where he states that 'no theory of justice can specify the precise form of these arrangements. In fact, the forms are historically negotiated, and they depend upon shared understandings of what such negotiations mean and how they work.'

82. See e.g. Schumpeter, *Capitalism, Socialism and Democracy* 271.

83. See the discussion in Hirschman, *Passions and Interests*, 56–66.

84. Schumpeter, *Capitalism, Socialism and Democracy* 276.

85. Willis, 'Introduction', *Federalist Papers*, p. xvi.

86. Hannah Pitkin, *The Concept of Representation* (London: University of California Press, 1967), 125.
87. Both the 'expressivist' and 'instrumentalist' approaches to the interpretation of voting practices in contemporary political science can be said to be guilty of a too-great emphasis on voters as individuals. For a summary of these, see Richard Rose and Ian McAllister, 'Expressive versus Instrumental Voting', in Dennis Kavanagh (ed.), *Electoral Politics* (Oxford: Clarendon Press, 1992).
88. See Arendt's discussion of 'power' in her *On Violence*, ch. 2. And Taylor refers to something similar when he asserts the inadequacy of the modern democrat's politics of 'democratic will-formation' and calls on us to turn as well to a 'politics of democratic empowerment'. Taylor, *The Ethics of Authenticity* (Cambridge, Mass.: Harvard University Press, 1991), 118.
89. Rose and McAllister, however, fail to make this distinction in the course of pointing out that 'expressive' voting is consistent with any form of free elections. See Rose and McAllister, 'Expressive versus Instrumental Voting', 119.
90. On the idea that humans can have 'purposes' or 'concerns' while machines only 'objectives', see Hubert L. Dreyfus, *What Computers* Still *Can't Do: A Critique of Artificial Reason*, 3rd edn. (London: MIT Press, 1992), ch. 9.
91. Gadamer, *Truth and Method*, 279.
92. Crick, 'Procedural Values in Political Education', in Crick and Heater, *Essays in Political Education*, 122.
93. I write of those that 'tend' to do so recognizing that there are also many such groups which advocate a very wide range of policies, as Graham K. Wilson points out in his *Interest Groups* (Oxford: Basil Blackwell, 1990), 158.
94. This characterization certainly fits the brokerage conception of parties as found in Schumpeter, *Capitalism, Socialism and Democracy*, esp. 283.
95. Max Weber, *Economy and Society: An Outline of Interpretive Sociology*, ii, ed. Gunther Roth and Claus Wittich, trans. Ephraim Fischoff *et al.* (London: University of California Press, 1978), 1114. Weber discusses how this 'pure' type is watered down and 'fused' into the more routinized systems of modern representative democracy at pp. 1123–30.
96. Crick has noted that one of the meanings of 'action' is that of 'an irrational rebuttal of all reason and theory'. Crick, 'On Theory and Practice', in *Political Theory and Practice*, 26.
97. On the connection between charisma and psychopathology, see David Aberbach, *Charisma in Politics, Religion and the Media: Private Trauma, Public Ideals* (London: Macmillan, 1996).
98. As Berlin seems to hint when he writes, in a discussion of political judgement, that 'there is always the part played by pure luck—which, mysteriously enough, men of good judgement seem to enjoy rather more often than others'. Berlin, 'Political Judgement', in *The Sense of Reality*, 53.

99. As Weber famously did when he differentiated (perhaps too) sharply between 'charismatic' authority on the one hand, and what he identified as the 'rational' and 'traditional' forms of it on the other. See Weber, *Economy and Society*, i, part 1, ch. 3.
100. 'One who is incapable of participating or who is in need of nothing through being self-sufficient is no part of a city, and so is either a beast or a god.' Aristotle, *The Politics*, 1. 2. 14.
101. Think e.g. of Meursault in Albert Camus's *L'Étranger*, a character who seems to me to be a 'stranger' in just this sense, someone who is inspired to act in a certain way, though it can only be described as destructive rather than creative. Note how the scene in which he commits his fateful deed is rife with ocular metaphors and how, during his trial, he is accused by the prosecuting attorney of having 'rien d'humain' in him, of being truly 'monstrueux'. Camus, *L'Étranger* (Paris: Gallimard, 1957), 155, 157.

NOTES TO CHAPTER 6

1. See Milton Friedman, 'The Social Responsibility of Business', in Tom Beauchamp and Norman Bowie (eds.), *Ethical Theory and Business*, 5th edn. (Englewood Cliffs, NJ: Prentice-Hall, 1997).
2. See Adam Smith, *An Inquiry in the Nature and Causes of the Wealth of Nations*, i, ed. R. H. Campbell and A. S. Skinner (Oxford: Clarendon Press, 1976), 456.
3. Thus John R. Danely: 'Pluralism is so central to the Managerial perspective that the stakeholder model itself is pluralism writ small.' *The Role of the Modern Corporation in a Free Society* (Notre Dame, Ind.: University of Notre Dame Press, 1994), 236. See also Danely, 'Pluralism and Corporate Responsibility', in Joseph P. DeMarco and Richard M. Gox (eds.), *Philosophy in Context* (Cleveland: Cleveland State University Press, 1980).
4. In Berlin's case e.g. this translated into his tremendous admiration for US President Roosevelt and his New Deal policy. See Isaiah Berlin, 'President Franklin Delano Roosevelt', in *Personal Impressions*, ed. Henry Hardy (London: Hogarth Press, 1981). Will Hutton refers to stakeholding's Keynesian underpinnings in his 'The Stakeholder Society', in Hutton *et al.*, *Stakeholding and its Critics* (London: The IEA Health and Welfare Unit, 1997), 12–14.
5. See R. H. Coase, 'The Nature of the Firm', *Economica*, 4/16 (Nov. 1937), 386–405, esp. 388. For an interesting interpretation of this model, with the market as 'sea' being replaced with the metaphor of it as a chaotic blob or a wild rodeo bronco, the latter needing a skilful corporation to ride it, see David Bodanis, *Web of Words: The Ideas behind Politics* (London: Macmillan, 1988), ch. 6.

6. John Kay, *Foundations of Corporate Success: How Business Strategies Add Value* (Oxford: Oxford University Press, 1993), 33.

7. Committee for Economic Development, *Social Responsibilities of Business Corporations* (New York: CED, 1971), 16.

8. Ibid. 22.

9. See e.g. Adolph A. Berle and Gardiner C. Means, *The Modern Corporation and Private Property* (New York: Macmillan, 1932).

10. CED, *Social Responsibilities*, 31.

11. Porter and van der Linde, 'Toward a New Conception of the Environment-Competitiveness Relationship', *Journal of Economic Perspectives*, 9/4 (Fall 1995), 97–118, 98.

12. See Ch. 3, s. III.

13. Elaine Sternberg makes a point to this effect in her 'Stakeholder Theory: The Defective State it's in', in Hutton *et al.*, *Stakeholding and its Critics*, 76–7.

14. Lest there be any doubt that neo-classicists, at least those of the Chicago School, are limited to a strictly instrumental, profit-based conception of business ends, note this statement of Friedman's: 'Differences about economic policy among disinterested citizens derive predominantly from different predictions about the economic consequences of taking action . . . rather than from fundamental differences in basic values, differences about which men can only fight.' Friedman, 'The Methodology of Positive Economics', in *Essays in Positive Economics* (Chicago: University of Chicago Press, 1953), 5.

15. Kay, *Foundations of Corporate Success*, 35.

16. Ibid. 34.

17. See Danely, *Role of the Modern Corporation*, 229.

18. Kay, *Foundations of Corporate Success*, 182.

19. See Danely, *Role of the Modern Corporation*, 205.

20. See Max Weber, *The Protestant Ethic and the Spirit of Capitalism*, trans. T. Parsons (New York: Charles Scribner's Sons, 1958), 181–2.

21. Kay, *Foundations of Corporate Success*, 183. As Kay has put the matter elsewhere, 'There is something paradoxical here.' *The Role of Business in Society* (Oxford: Said Business School, University of Oxford, 1998), 16. See also Norman Bowie, 'The Profit-Seeking Paradox', in N. Dale Wright (ed.), *The Ethics of Administration* (Provo, Utah: Brigham Young University Press, 1988).

22. For there are those, as Weber has famously shown, who affirm it as an end-in-itself. See Weber, *Protestant Ethic.*

23. See Ch. 1, s. IV.

24. I take this to be an implication of Karl Polanyi's claims about money in his *The Great Transformation: The Political and Economic Origins of Our Time* (Boston, Mass.: Beacon Press, 1944), esp. 54, 196.

25. Richard M. Ebeling makes something like this claim in his 'What is a Price? Explanation and Understanding (with Apologies to Paul Ricoeur)',

in Don Lavoie (ed.), *Economics and Hermeneutics* (New York: Routledge, 1991).

26. This understanding of tools is, I think, what Rilke's reference to 'things' is all about in his 'The Temptation of the Saint', in *The Selected Poetry of Rainer Maria Rilke*, ed. and trans. Stephen Mitchell (New York: Vintage International, 1982), 105. For by describing these things as acting, or being acted upon, in strange ways, we are jarred into realizing that they are supposed to be used in some ways and not others, that is, that they are not 'pure' instrumental goods with wholly contingent relationships to the ends for which they are used.

27. See e.g. Kay, *Foundations of Corporate Success*, 185–6, 188–9.

28. Dreyfus, Flores, and Spinosa, *Disclosing New Worlds: Entrepreneurship, Democratic Action, and the Cultivation of Solidarity* (Cambridge, Mass.: MIT Press, 1997), 56.

29. See A. M. Honoré, 'Ownership', in A. G. Guest (ed.), *Oxford Essays in Jurisprudence* (Oxford: Oxford University Press, 1961).

30. It should be noted that Honoré equates this 'full' conception of ownership with 'liberal' ownership, this being the understanding that, to him, is *de facto* present in all modern societies with '*mature* legal systems' (my italics): ibid. 109. This reveals his (to me) unwarranted assumptions that, first, all modern societies must, ideologically speaking, be liberal societies and, second, that the liberal concept of ownership—despite his own qualifications to the contrary—is, in keeping with his subscription to a 'modernization' thesis, somehow more 'true' to the needs of all human beings than others for it 'can be explained by the common needs of mankind and the common conditions of human life'. Ibid. All this seems to me to fly in the face of the fact that— if I may be permitted some unsubstantiated assertions at this point—while Canadian political culture, for example, is at this time best interpreted as liberal, the American is conservative (with a dash of libertarianism), and the Scandinavian are democratic socialist. Honoré, I should add, also makes the pluralist assumption that the meaning of the concept of ownership is fixed and universalistic. As he writes (ibid.), 'the standard incidents of ownership do not vary from system to system in the erratic, unpredictable way implied by some writers but, on the contrary, have a tendency to remain constant from place to place and age to age.'

31. John Kay, 'The Stakeholder Corporation', in Gavin Kelly, Dominic Kelly, and Andrew Gamble (eds.), *Stakeholder Capitalism* (London: Macmillan, 1997), 129.

32. Ibid. 130.

33. Ibid. 131.

34. E.g. Herman E. Daly and John B. Cobb, Jr., *For the Common Good: Redirecting the Economy Toward Community, the Environment, and a Sustainable Future*, 2nd edn. (Boston, Mass.: Beacon Press, 1994) defends what I take to be a patriotic socialist/green/nationalist position; while

Jonathan Boswell, *Community and the Economy: The Theory of Public Co-Operation* (New York: Routledge, 1990) advances a patriotic socialism.

35. James Boyd White, 'How should we talk about Corporations?', *Yale Law Journal*, 94/6 (May 1985), 1416–25, 1424.

36. See Daly and Cobb, *Common Good*, 437.

37. Though Robert C. Solomon is right to caution us against paying excessive attention to corporate battles and the warrior virtues in business. See his *Ethics and Excellence: Cooperation and Integrity in Business* (New York: Oxford University Press, 1992), 23–4, 199–202, a work which alternates uneasily between making pluralist and hermeneutical/patriotic claims.

NOTES TO CHAPTER 7

1. See James Tully, *Strange Multiplicity: Constitutionalism in an Age of Diversity* (Cambridge: Cambridge University Press, 1995).

2. For a good account, see Kenneth Minogue, 'The History of the Idea of Human Rights', in Walter Laqueur and Barry Rubin (eds.), *The Human Rights Reader*, 2nd edn. (New York: Penguin Books, 1989).

3. See Joseph Raz, *The Morality of Freedom* (Oxford: Oxford University Press, 1986), ch. 7; and Galston, 'Practical Philosophy and the Bill of Rights', in Michael J. Lacey and Knud Haakonssen (eds.), *A Culture of Rights: The Bill of Rights in Philosophy, Politics, and Law–1791 and 1991* (Cambridge: Cambridge University Press, 1991), 216, 248, 254–7. Not all pluralists who write about rights adhere to the 'interest' approach. Steven Lukes e.g. is more attracted to Robert Nozick's conception of rights as 'side constraints', as well as to Ronald Dworkin's notion that rights defend an 'egalitarian plateau'. See, respectively, Lukes, 'Can a Marxist Believe in Human Rights?' in *Moral Conflict and Politics* (Oxford: Clarendon Press, 1991), 177; and Lukes, 'Five Fables about Human Rights', in Stephen Shute and Susan Hurley (eds.), *On Human Rights: The Oxford Amnesty Lectures 1993* (New York: Basic Books, 1993), 39. Lukes, however, distances himself from these two thinkers' neutralisms and asserts a more recognizably pluralist position when he claims that individual rights are only 'strongly prima facie' and so may, in some cases, be overridden: see 'Can a Marxist Believe in Human Rights?', 177–8.

4. For while Dworkin endorses, MacIntyre rejects, and Carol Gilligan is concerned with certain limitations of, rights, all three assume that to speak of rights is to speak of the rights of individuals. See Dworkin, *Taking Rights Seriously* (London: Duckworth, 1978); MacIntyre, *After Virtue*, 2nd edn. (Notre Dame, Ind.: University of Notre Dame Press, 1994), esp. 68–71; and Gilligan, *In a Different Voice: Psychological Theory and Women's Development*, 2nd edn. (Cambridge, Mass.: Harvard University Press, 1993).

5. See Raz, *Morality of Freedom*, 176, 180.

6. Ibid. 188.
7. Ibid. 181.
8. Ibid. 179.
9. Ibid. 171, 185.
10. Jeremy Waldron, 'Rights in Conflict', in *Liberal Rights* (Cambridge: Cambridge University Press, 1993), 212–13.
11. Ibid. 217. Raz discusses such conflicts in Raz, *Morality of Freedom*, 172, 181, 184.
12. See Waldron, *Liberal Rights*, 210–11, 215.
13. Raz, *Morality of Freedom*, 184.
14. Ibid.
15. Ibid.
16. Ibid. 184, 185.
17. Hampshire, *Morality and Conflict*, 115. See Ch. 3, s. II.
18. John Hardwig, 'Should Women Think in Terms of Rights?', *Ethics*, 94 (Apr. 1984), 441–55, 448. See also Peter Jones, *Rights* (New York: St Martin's Press, 1994), 208–9.
19. Waldron, 'When Justice Replaces Affection: The Need for Rights', in *Liberal Rights*, 373.
20. See Taylor, 'Why do Nations have to Become States?', in *Reconciling the Solitudes*, 48–54; and Taylor, 'Les Droits de l'homme: La Culture juridique', in Paul Ricoeur (ed.), *Les Fondements philosophiqes des droits de l'homme* (Paris: UNESCO, 1986).
21. Ibid.; and Taylor, 'Atomism', in *Philosophy and the Human Sciences*.
22. Raz, *Morality of Freedom*, 180, 176; my italics.
23. See T. Alexander Aleinikoff, 'Constitutional Law in the Age of Balancing', *Yale Law Journal*, 96/5 (Apr. 1987), 943–1005. For a different interpretation, see Mary Ann Glendon, *Abortion and Divorce in Western Law* (Cambridge, Mass.: Harvard University Press, 1987); and Glendon, *Rights Talk: The Impoverishment of Political Discourse* (New York: Macmillan, 1991). To Glendon, what makes American constitutionalism unique is that, rather than evoking the compromising of balancing, it has produced a type of rights talk which asserts certain individual rights as 'absolute' in the sense of being uncompromisable. Moreover, where, as I shall point out, Aleinikoff decries the rise of a constitutionalism of balancing, Glendon feels it necessary to call for a 'refining' of American rights discourse that would bring the USA more in line with the balancing approaches that she finds in other countries. In Glendon's works there is some concern expressed about the quality of dialogue in politics, as well as the odd mention of a role for persuasion in addition to compromise and negotiation. To the extent that she is gesturing here towards patriotic, and not just pluralist, concerns, then I find myself in sympathy with her work. But as I think that she is, overall, best interpreted as calling for a constitutionalism of pluralism over neutralism, the critique of rights talk that I am advancing here should be considered much more fundamental. The same point

can be made as regards Ronald Beiner, *What's the Matter with Liberalism?* (Berkeley, Calif.: University of California Press, 1992), ch. 4; and Paul M. Sniderman, Joseph F. Fletcher, Peter H. Russell, and Philip E. Tetlock, *The Clash of Rights: Liberty, Equality, and Legitimacy in Pluralist Democracy* (New Haven: Yale University Press, 1996), esp. ch. 8.

24. It can be interpreted as doing so by virtue of the 9th Amendment which states that 'The enumeration in the Constitution of certain rights shall not be construed to deny or disparage others retained by the people.' This can be understood to open the Bill up, meaning that the rights explicitly referred to in it cannot be considered uncompromisable when they conflict with certain others. Other such documents do this much more explicitly, as with the UN Universal Declaration on Human Rights (art. 29), the European Convention on Human Rights (arts. 8/2, 9/2, 10/2, 11/2, 15, 18), the Canadian Charter of Rights and Freedoms (s. 1), and the Basic Law of the Federal Republic of Germany (e.g. arts. 2 and 11).

25. Aleinikoff, 'Constitutional Law', 991–2.

26. Ibid. 984–5.

27. See Glendon, 'Rights in Twentieth-Century Constitutions', in Geoffrey R. Stone, Richard A. Epstein, and Cass R. Sunstein (eds.), *The Bill of Rights in the Modern State* (Chicago: University of Chicago Press, 1992), 520.

28. Hamilton, *The Federalist*, 84.

29. Hence my difficulty with some of the recent work of the pluralist William Galston: see his *Liberal Virtues*, ch. 10; and 'Liberal Virtues and the Formation of Civic Character', in Mary Ann Glendon and David Blankenhorn (eds.), *Seedbeds of Virtue: Sources of Competence, Character, and Citizenship in American Society* (New York: Madison Books, 1995).

30. Not that there has been much precedent for this so far, however. For as J. A. G. Griffith has written, 'In both democratic and totalitarian societies, the judiciary has naturally served the prevailing political and economic forces. Politically, judges are parasitic.' Griffith, *The Politics of the Judiciary*, 5th edn. (London: HarperCollins, 1997), 342. And according to Mark Tushnet, 'Is Judicial Review Good for the Left?', *Dissent* (Winter 1998), 70: 'Looking at Judicial review over the course of U.S. history, we see that the courts have regularly been more or less in line with what the dominant national political coalition wants. Sometimes the courts deviate a bit, occasionally leading to better political outcomes and occasionally leading to worse ones. Adapting a metaphor from electrical engineering, we can say that judicial review basically amounts to noise around zero. It offers essentially random changes, sometimes good and sometimes bad, to what the political system produces. Things would be different, of course, if we had better judges.'

An overly adversarial justice system, as is dominant especially in the Anglo-American world, is also to blame, as it ensures that conversation is virtually banned from the courtroom. On this matter and possible alternatives, see e.g. Jenny McEwan, *Evidence and the Adversarial System:*

The Modern Law (Oxford: Blackwell, 1992) regarding England; Franklin
D. Strier, *Reconstructing Justice: An Agenda for Trial Reform* (Chicago:
University of Chicago Press, 1994) concerning the USA; and the discussion of 'circle sentencing', deriving from Canadian aboriginal traditions,
in David Cayley, *The Expanding Prison: The Crisis in Crime and
Punishment and the Search for Alternatives* (Toronto: Anasi Press, 1998),
esp. 182–98.

31. See Ch. 5, s. IV.

32. In Canada, e.g., legislators have consistently voted against the return of
the death penalty, despite unwaveringly strong support for it in the public
opinion polls.

33. Robert Kroon, 'Let's Talk, Not Quarrel, About Rights', *International
Herald Tribune* (17 Mar. 1998), 4.

NOTES TO CHAPTER 8

1. See e.g. his discussion of the subject in John Rawls, *A Theory of Justice*
(Cambridge, Mass.: Harvard University Press, 1971), 501; and the some-
what different conception in Rawls, *Political Liberalism* (New York:
Columbia University Press, 1993), lecture 4.

2. 'When identities are multiplied, passions are divided.' Michael Walzer,
'The New Tribalism: Notes on a Difficult Problem', *Dissent* (Spring 1992),
171.

3. See Hans-Georg Gadamer, 'Hermeneutics as a Theoretical and Practical
Task', in *Reason in the Age of Science*, trans. Frederick G. Lawrence (Cambridge, Mass.: MIT Press, 1981). To the vast majority of political thinkers,
however, be they ancient or modern, because philosophy is conceived of
as, at base, theoretical rather than, with the hermeneuticist, as practical, it
has been the differences between philosophy and rhetoric that have
tended to receive emphasis. For classical republican and pluralist liberal
statements to this effect, see, respectively, J. G. A. Pocock, *The Machiavellian Moment* (Princeton: Princeton University Press, 1975), 58–9; and
Michael Walzer, 'Philosophy and Democracy', *Political Theory*, 1/3 (Aug.
1981), 379–99.

4. For a measured account, see Tony Kushner, *The Holocaust and the Liberal
Imagination* (Oxford: Blackwell, 1994).

5. See e.g. Jürgen Habermas, *Legitimation Crisis* (London: Heinemann,
1976); William E. Connolly, *Appearance and Reality in Politics*
(Cambridge: Cambridge University Press, 1981), ch. 5; or, regarding the
American context in particular, listen to REM, 'Ignoreland', in *Automatic
for the People* (New York: Warner Bros. Records, 1992).

6. See Alexis de Tocqueville, *De la démocratie en Amérique*, ii (Paris:
Gallimard, 1961).

7. See Connolly, *Appearance and Reality*, 139–40.

8. See Stanely K. Henshaw and Jennifer Van Vort, 'Abortion Services in the United States, 1991 and 1992', *Family Planning Perspectives*, 26 (1994), 100–6, 112; and Henshaw, 'Factors Hindering Access to Abortion Services', *Family Planning Perspectives*, 27/2 (Mar.–Apr. 1995), 54–9, 87. Recently, in Ontario, Canada, an anti-poverty coalition has taken to using the same tactics. See Margaret Philp, 'Poverty Crusade Gets Personal', *The Globe and Mail* (20 Sept. 1997), A1, A6.

9. For a recent typical example, see Albert O. Hirschman's discussion of the growing number of 'nondivisible', i.e. non-negotiable, conflicts: 'Social Conflicts as Pillars of Democratic Market Societies', in *A Propensity to Self-Subversion* (Cambridge, Mass.: Harvard University Press, 1995), esp. 244, 246.

10. Huntington, *American Politics: The Promise of Disharmony*. (Cambridge, Mass.: Harvard University Press, 1981).

11. See Hirschman, 'Social Conflicts', 248.

12. As in e.g. Mark Kingwell, *A Civil Tongue* (Philadephia: Pennsyhania State University Press, 1995); or see Nicholas Rescher, *Pluralism*, (Oxford: Clarendon Press, 1993), 173.

13. Hampshire, *Innocence and Experience*, 68.

14. I might mention here that Nussbaum fails to distinguish enough between friendship and romantic love, presenting the latter as but a concentrated version of the former. See Nussbaum, 'Love's Knowledge', in *Love's Knowledge* (Oxford: Oxford University Press, 1990), 274–80.

15. Crick makes this point in his *Basic Forms of Government* (London: Macmillan, 1973), 21. And, as Aristotle himself asserted, when judging the populations of city-states 'one should look not to their number but to their capacity'. Aristotle, *The Politics* 1326^a12.

16. See Fred D'Agostino, 'Ethical Pluralism and the Role of Opposition in Democratic Politics', *The Monist*, 73/3 (July 1990), 437–63.

17. Charles E. Lindblom, *Inquiry and Change: The Troubled Attempt to Understand and Shape Society* (London: Yale University Press, 1990), 289.

18. See Charles Taylor, *Sources of the Self* (Cambridge, Mass.: Harvard University Press, 1989), esp. 519.

19. Rescher, *Pluralism*, 4.

20. Isaiah Berlin and Ramin Jahanbegloo, *Conversations with Isaiah Berlin* (London: Peter Halban, 1992), 159.

Bibliography

Aberbach, David, *Charisma in Politics, Religion and the Media: Private Trauma, Public Ideals* (London: Macmillan, 1996).

Abrams, M. H., *The Mirror and the Lamp: Romantic Theory and the Critical Tradition* (Oxford: Oxford University Press, 1953).

Ackerman, Bruce, *Social Justice in the Liberal State* (New Haven, Conn.: Yale University Press, 1980).

Adkins, A. W. H., *From the Many to the One: A Study of Personality and Views of Human Nature in the Context of Ancient Greek Society, Values and Beliefs* (Ithaca, NY: Cornell University Press, 1970).

Aeschylus, *The Oresteia*, trans. Robert Fagles (New York: Penguin, 1966).

Aleinikoff, T. Alexander, 'Constitutional Law in the Age of Balancing', *Yale Law Journal*, 96/5 (Apr. 1987), 943–1005.

Allen, Woody, *Another Woman* (Orion Pictures, 1988).

Arblaster, Anthony, 'The Proper Limits of Pluralism', in Iain Hampsher-Monk (ed.), *Defending Politics: Bernard Crick and Pluralism* (London: British Academic Press, 1993).

Arendt, Hannah, *The Human Condition: A Study of the Central Dilemmas Facing Modern Man* (Garden City, NY: Doubleday Anchor edn., 1958).

—— 'What is Freedom?', in *Between Past and Future: Six Exercises in Political Thought* (New York: World Publishing, 1961).

—— *On Revolution*, 2nd edn. (New York: Viking Press, 1965).

—— *On Violence* (London: Allen Lane, The Penguin Press, 1970).

Aristotle, *Rhetoric*, trans. W. R. Roberts in *The Works of Aristotle*, xi, ed. W. D. Ross (Oxford: Clarendon Press, 1924).

—— *Nicomachean Ethics*, trans. Martin Ostwald (New York: Bobbs-Merrill, 1962).

—— *Aristotle's* De Anima: *Books II and III*, trans. D. W. Hamlyn (Oxford: Clarendon Press, 1968).

—— *The Politics*, trans. Carnes Lord (Chicago: University of Chicago Press, 1984).

Atkinson, Anthony B., and Stiglitz, Joseph E., *Lectures on Public Economics* (London: McGraw-Hill, 1980).

Auerbach, Eric, *Mimesis: The Representation of Reality in Western Literature*, trans. Willard R. Trask (Princeton: Princeton University Press, 1953).

Augustine, *Concerning the City of God Against the Pagans*, trans. Henry Bettenson (Harmondsworth: Penguin, 1972).

Bakhtin, Mikhail, *Problems of Dostoevsky's Poetics*, ed. and trans. Caryl Emerson (Minneapolis: University of Minnesota Press, 1984).

Barry, Brian, 'Social Criticism and Political Philosophy', *Philosophy and Public Affairs*, 19/4 (Fall 1990), 360–72.

Bateson, Gregory, 'Cultural Contact and Schismogenesis', in *Steps to an Ecology of Mind* (London: Paladin, 1972).

Baudelaire, Charles, 'Mon cœur mis à nu', in *Journaux intimes* (Paris: Les Éditions G. Crès et Cie, 1920).

Beiner, Ronald, *Political Judgement* (London: Methuen, 1983).

——*What's the Matter with Liberalism?* (Berkeley, Calif.: University of California Press, 1992).

——(ed.), *Theorizing Citizenship* (Albany, NY: SUNY Press, 1995).

Bellah, Robert N., Madsen, Richard, Sullivan, William M., Swidler, Ann, and Tipton, Steven M., *Habits of the Heart: Individualism and Commitment in American Life* (London: University of California Press, 1985).

Bellamy, Richard, *Liberalism and Modern Society* (Cambridge: Polity Press, 1992).

——'The Political Form of the Constitution: The Separation of Powers, Rights and Representative Democracy', in Bellamy and Dario Castiglione (eds.), *Constitutionalism in Transformation: European and Theoretical Perspectives* (Oxford: Blackwell, 1996).

Benjamin, Walter, 'Critique of Violence', in *One Way Street and Other Writings*, trans. Edmund Jephcott and Kingsley Shorter (London: NLB, 1979).

Bentham, Jeremy, *The Principles of Morals and Legislation* (Buffalo: Prometheus Books, 1988).

Bentley, Arthur F., *The Process of Government* (Chicago: University of Chicago Press, 1908).

Bentley, Eric, 'What is Theatre?', in *The Theatre of Commitment: And Other Essays on Drama in Our Society* (London: Methuen, 1954).

Berger, Peter, 'On the Obsolescence of the Concept of Honour', in Stanley Hauerwas and Alasdair MacIntyre (eds.), *Revisions: Changing Perspectives in Moral Philosophy* (London: University of Notre Dame Press, 1983).

Berle, Adolph A., and Means, Gardiner C., *The Modern Corporation and Private Property* (New York: Macmillan, 1932).

Berlin, Isaiah, 'Rationality of Value Judgements', in Carl J. Friedrich (ed.), *Nomos VII: Rational Decision* (New York: Atherton Press, 1964).

——*Four Essays on Liberty* (Oxford: Oxford University Press, 1969).

——*Vico and Herder* (London: Hogarth Press, 1976).

——'An Introduction to Philosophy', in Bryan Magee (ed. and interviewer), *Men of Ideas* (London: BBC, 1979).

——*Concepts and Categories: Philosophical Essays*, ed. Henry Hardy (Oxford: Oxford University Press, 1980).

——*Against the Current: Essays in the History of Ideas*, ed. Henry Hardy (Oxford: Oxford University Press, 1981).

—— 'President Franklin Delano Roosevelt', in *Personal Impressions*, ed. Henry Hardy (London: Hogarth Press, 1981).

—— *The Crooked Timber of Humanity: Chapters in the History of Ideas*, ed. Henry Hardy (London: John Murray, 1990).

—— and Ramin Jahanbegloo, *Conversations with Isaiah Berlin* (London: Peter Halban, 1992).

—— *The Magus of the North: J. G. Hamann and the Origins of Modern Irrationalism* (London: John Murray, 1993).

—— and Williams, Bernard, 'Pluralism and Liberalism: A Reply', *Political Studies,* 62/2 (June 1994), 306–9.

—— *The Sense of Reality: Studies in Ideas and their History*, ed. Henry Hardy (London: Chatto & Windus, 1996).

—— letter to Charles Blattberg, 19 March 1996.

Bernstein, Richard, *Beyond Objectivism and Relativism: Science, Hermeneutics, and Praxis* (Philadelphia: University of Pennsylvania Press, 1983).

Biddle, Francis, 'Necessity of Compromise', in R. M. MacIver (ed.), *Integrity and Compromise: Problems of Public and Private Conscience* (New York: The Institute for Religious and Social Studies, 1957).

Bird, Polly, *How to Run a Local Campaign* (Plymouth: Northcote House Publishers, 1989).

Black, Antony, 'Christianity and Republicanism: From St. Cyprian to Rousseau', *American Political Science Review*, 91/3 (Sept. 1997), 647–56.

Blake, William, 'On Homer's Poetry', in *Blake's Poetry and Designs*, ed. Mary Lynn Johnson and John E. Grant (London: W. W. Norton, 1979).

Blattberg, Charles, 'Political Philosophies and Political Ideologies', [forthcoming].

—— 'Athens and/or Jerusalem? Three Conceptions of Philosophy' [forthcoming].

Bodanis, David, *Web of Words: The Ideas behind Politics* (London: Macmillan, 1988).

Bohm, David, *Wholeness and the Implicate Order* (London: Routledge & Kegan Paul, 1980).

Bolt, Robert, *A Man for All Seasons: A Play of Sir Thomas More* (Oxford: Heinemann Educational Books, 1960).

Boswell, Jonathan, *Community and the Economy: The Theory of Public Co-Operation* (New York: Routledge, 1990).

Bowie, Norman, 'The Profit-Seeking Paradox', in N. Dale Wright (ed.), *The Ethics of Administration* (Provo, Utah: Brigham Young University Press, 1988).

Brandom, Robert B., *Making it Explicit: Reasoning, Representing and Discursive Commitment* (London: Harvard University Press, 1994).

Brody, Baruch, 'Pluralistic Moral Theory', *Revue internationale de philosophie*, 49/193 (Sept. 1995), 323–39.

Bruns, Gerald L., *Hermeneutics Ancient and Modern* (London: Yale University Press, 1992).

Buchanan, James, *The Limits of Liberty: Between Anarchy and Leviathan* (Chicago: University of Chicago Press, 1975).

Camus, Albert, *L'Étranger* (Paris: Gallimard, 1957).

Canovan, Margaret, *Hannah Arendt: A Reinterpretation of her Political Thought* (Cambridge: Cambridge University Press, 1992).

Cawson, Alan, *Corporatism and Political Theory* (Oxford: Basil Blackwell, 1986).

Cayley, David, *The Expanding Prison: The Crisis in Crime and Punishment and the Search for Alternatives* (Toronto: Anasi Press, 1998).

Christiansen, Lars, and Dowding, Keith, 'Pluralism or State Autonomy? The Case of Amnesty International (British Section): The Insider/Outsider Group', *Political Studies*, 62/1 (Mar. 1994), 15–24.

Clark, George, *The Seventeenth Century*, 2nd edn. (Oxford: Clarendon Press, 1947).

Clarke, Stanley G., and Simpson, Evan (eds.), *Anti-Theory in Ethics and Moral Conservativism* (Albany, NY: SUNY Press, 1989).

—— 'Introduction: The Primacy of Moral Practice', in Clarke and Simpson (eds.), *Anti-Theory in Ethics and Moral Conservativism* (Albany, NY: SUNY Press, 1989).

Coase, R. H., 'The Nature of the Firm', *Economica*, 4/16 (Nov. 1937), 386–405.

Cohen, Joshua, 'Review of *Spheres of Justice*', *The Journal of Philosophy*, 83/8 (Aug. 1986), 457–66.

—— 'Deliberation and Democratic Legitimacy', in Alan Hamlin and Philip Pettit (eds.), *The Good Polity: Normative Analysis of the State* (Oxford: Basil Blackwell, 1989).

Cohen, Leonard, *The Future* (Toronto: Sony Music Entertainment, 1992).

—— *Stranger Music: Selected Poems and Songs* (London: Johnathan Cape, 1993).

Coleridge, Samuel Taylor, *Biographia Literaria*, in *The Collected Works of Samuel Taylor Coleridge*, i, ed. James Engell and W. Jackson Bate (Princeton: Princeton University Press, 1983).

Collier, Robert Jacob, 'Holography and Integral Photography', *Physics Today*, 21/7 (July 1968), 55–63.

Collingwood, R. G., *The Principles of Art* (London: Oxford University Press, 1938).

Committee for Economic Development, *Social Responsibilities of Business Corporations* (New York: Committee for Economic Development, 1971).

Connolly, William E., *Appearance and Reality in Politics* (Cambridge: Cambridge University Press, 1981).

—— 'Identity and Difference in Liberalism', in Robert B. Douglass, Gerald M. Mara, and Henry S. Richardson (eds.), *Liberalism and the Good* (New York: Routledge, 1990).

—— *The Terms of Political Discourse*, 3rd edn. (Oxford: Martin Robinson, 1993).

Constant, Benjamin, 'De la liberté des anciens comparée à celles des modernes', in *De la liberté chez les modernes: Écrits politiques*, ed. Marcel Gauchet (Paris: Livre de Poche, 1980).

Cook, David, 'The Last Days of Liberalism', in Thomas Docherty (ed.), *Postmodernism: A Reader* (Hemel Hempstead: Harvester Wheatsheaf, 1993).

Cox, Andrew, 'Neo-Corporatism versus the Corporate State', in Cox and Noel O'Sullivan (eds.), *The Corporate State Tradition in Western Europe* (Aldershot: Edward Elgar, 1988).

Crick, Bernard, *Political Theory and Practice* (Harmondsworth: Allen Lane, The Penguin Press, 1971).

—— 'Introduction' and 'Notes', in Machiavelli, *The Discourses*, ed. Bernard Crick, trans. Leslie J. Walker (Harmondsworth: Penguin, 1970).

—— *Basic Forms of Government: A Sketch and a Model* (London: Macmillan, 1973).

—— 'Procedural Values in Political Education', in Bernard Crick and Derek Heater, *Essays on Political Education* (Ringmer: Falmer, 1977).

—— *In Defense of Politics*, 4th edn. (London: Weidenfeld & Nicolson, 1992).

Cytowic, Richard E., *Synesthesia: A Union of the Senses* (New York: Springer Verlag, 1989).

—— 'Synaethesia: Phenomenology and Neuropsychology', in Simon Baron-Cohen and John E. Harrison (eds.), *Synaesthesia: Classic and Contemporary Readings* (Oxford: Blackwell, 1997).

Dahl, Robert A., *A Preface to Democratic Theory* (Chicago: University of Chicago Press, 1956).

—— *Who Governs? Democracy and Power in an American City* (New Haven, Conn.: Yale University Press, 1961).

—— *Dilemmas of Pluralist Democracy: Autonomy vs. Control* (London: Yale University Press, 1982).

—— 'Rethinking *Who Governs?*: New Haven, Revisited', in Robert J. Waste (ed.), *Community Power: Directions for Future Research* (Beverly Hills, Calif.: Sage, 1986).

—— *Democracy and its Critics* (London: Yale University Press, 1989).

Daly, Herman E., and Cobb, Jr., John B., *For the Common Good: Redirecting the Economy Toward Community, the Environment, and a Sustainable Future*, 2nd edn. (Boston, Mass.: Beacon Press, 1994).

Danely, John R., *The Role of the Modern Corporation in a Free Society* (Notre Dame, Ind.: University of Notre Dame Press, 1994).

—— 'Pluralism and Corporate Responsibility', in Joseph P. DeMarco and Richard M. Gox (eds.), *Philosophy in Context* (Cleveland: Cleveland State University Press, 1980).

Daniels, Norman, 'Wide Reflective Equilibrium and Theory Acceptance in Ethics', *Journal of Philosophy*, 76 (Jan.–Dec. 1979), 256–82.

—— 'Introduction', in *Justice and Justification: Reflective Equilibrium in Theory and Practice* (Cambridge: Cambridge University Press, 1996).

Davidson, Donald, 'On the Very Idea of a Conceptual Scheme', in *Inquiries into Truth and Interpretation* (Oxford: Oxford University Press, 1984).

——'A Coherence Theory of Truth and Knowledge', in Alan Malachowski (ed.), *Reading Rorty* (Oxford: Basil Blackwell, 1990).

Dickens, Charles, *Dombey and Son* (Oxford: Oxford University Press, 1966).

Dietz, Mary, 'Context is All: Feminism and Theories of Citizenship', in Chantal Mouffe (ed.), *Dimensions of Radical Democracy: Pluralism, Citizenship, Community* (London: Verso, 1992).

Douglass, R. Bruce, Mara, Gerald M., and Richardson, Henry S. (eds.), *Liberalism and the Good* (New York: Routledge, 1990).

Dreyfus, Hubert L., 'Hermeneutics and Holism', *Review of Metaphysics*, 34 (Sept. 1980), 3–23.

——'Why Studies of Human Capacities Modeled on Ideal Natural Science can Never Achieve their Goal', in J. Margolis, M. Krauz, and R. M. Burian (eds.), *Rationality, Relativism and the Human Sciences* (Dordrecht: Martinus Nijhoff Publishers, 1986).

——*Being-in-the-World: A Commentary on Heidegger's* Being and Time, *Division I* (Cambridge, Mass.: MIT Press, 1991).

——'Heidegger's Hermeneutic Realism', in David R. Hiley, James F. Bohman, and Richard Shusterman (eds.), *The Interpretive Turn: Philosophy, Science, Culture* (London: Cornell University Press, 1991).

——*What Computers* Still *Can't Do: A Critique of Artificial Reason*, 3rd edn. (London: MIT Press, 1992).

——Flores, Fernando, and Spinosa, Charles, *Disclosing New Worlds: Entrepreneurship, Democratic Action, and the Cultivation of Solidarity* (Cambridge, Mass.: MIT Press, 1997).

Dworkin, Ronald, 'Liberalism', in Stuart Hampshire (ed.), *Public and Private Morality* (Cambridge: Cambridge University Press, 1978).

——*Taking Rights Seriously* (London: Duckworth, 1978).

——and Walzer, Michael, 'Spheres of Justice: An Exchange', *The New York Review of Books* (21 July 1983).

——*A Matter of Principle* (Cambridge, Mass.: Harvard University Press, 1985).

Eagleton, Terry, *Literary Theory: An Introduction* (Oxford: Basil Blackwell, 1983).

Ebeling, Richard M., 'What is a Price? Explanation and Understanding (with Apologies to Paul Ricoeur)', in Don Lavoie (ed.), *Economics and Hermeneutics* (New York: Routledge, 1991).

Eliot, T. S., 'Sweeney Agonistes: Fragments of an Aristophanic Melodrama', in *Collected Poems: 1909–1962* (London: Faber & Faber, 1963).

Elster, Jon, 'The Market and the Forum: Three Varieties of Political Theory', in Elster and Aanund Hylland (eds.), *Foundations of Social Choice Theory* (Cambridge: Cambridge University Press, 1986).

Femia, Joseph V., 'Complexity and Deliberative Democracy', *Inquiry*, 39/3–4 (Dec. 1996), 359–97.

Ferry, Luc, and Renault, Alain, *Philosophie politique 3: Des droits de l'homme à l'idée républicaine* (Paris: Presse Universitaires de France, 1985).

Foucault, Michel, 'Polemics, Politics, and Problematizations: An Interview with Michel Foucault', in Paul Rabinow (ed.), *The Foucault Reader* (New York: Pantheon, 1984).

Freeden, Michael, *Rights* (Milton Keynes: Open University Press, 1991).

——'Political Concepts and Ideological Morphology', *The Journal of Political Philosophy*, 2/2 (1994), 140–64.

——*Ideologies and Political Theory: A Conceptual Approach* (Oxford: Oxford University Press, 1996).

Friedman, Milton, 'The Social Responsibility of Business', in Tom Beauchamp and Norman Bowie (eds.), *Ethical Theory and Business*, 5th edn. (Englewood Cliffs, NJ: Prentice-Hall, 1997).

——'The Methodology of Positive Economics', in *Essays in Positive Economics* (Chicago: University of Chicago Press, 1953).

Fristrom, James W., and Clegg, Michael T., *Principles of Genetics*, 2nd edn. (New York: Chiron Press, 1988).

Fritz, Kurt von, *The Theory of the Mixed Constitution in Antiquity: A Critical Analysis of Polybius' Political Ideas* (New York: Columbia University Press, 1954).

Frye, Northrope, 'Historical Criticism: Theory of Modes', in *Anatomy of Criticism: Four Essays* (Princeton: Princeton University Press, 1957).

——'Comedy', in Frye, Sheridan Baker, and George Perkins, *The Harper Handbook to Literature* (New York: Harper & Row, 1985).

Gadamer, Hans-Georg, 'Hermeneutics as a Theoretical and Practical Task', in *Reason in the Age of Science*, trans. Frederick G. Lawrence (Cambridge, Mass.: MIT Press, 1981).

——*Truth and Method*, trans. Joel Weinsheimer and Donald G. Marshall, 2nd edn. (New York: Crossroad, 1989).

——*Plato's Dialectical Ethics: Phenomenological Interpretations Relating to the Philebus*, trans. Robert M. Wallace (London: Yale University Press, 1991).

Gagnon, Alain G., and Tanguay, A. Brian, 'Introduction', in Gagnon and Tanguay (eds.), *Canadian Parties in Transition*, 2nd edn. (Scarborough: Nelson, 1996).

Galipeau, Claude J., *Isaiah Berlin's Liberalism* (Oxford: Clarendon Press, 1994).

Gallie, W. B., 'Essentially Contested Concepts', *Proceedings of the Aristotelian Society*, 56 (1956), 167–98.

Galston, William, *Liberal Purposes: Goods, Virtues, and Diversity in the Liberal State* (New York: Cambridge University Press, 1991).

——'Practical Philosophy and the Bill of Rights', in Michael J. Lacey and Knud Haakonssen (eds.), *A Culture of Rights: The Bill of Rights in Philosophy, Politics, and Law–1791 and 1991* (Cambridge: Cambridge University Press, 1991).

——'Liberal Virtues and the Formation of Civic Character', in Mary Ann Glendon and David Blankenhorn (eds.), *Seedbeds of Virtue: Sources of*

Competence, Character, and Citizenship in American Society (New York: Madison Books, 1995).

Gauthier, David, *Morals by Agreement* (Oxford: Clarendon Press, 1986).

Geertz, Clifford, 'Thick Description: Toward an Interpretive Theory of Culture', in *The Interpretation of Cultures* (New York: Basic Books, 1973).

Geison, Gerald L., *The Private Science of Louis Pasteur* (Princeton: Princeton University Press, 1995).

Gilligan, Carol, *In a Different Voice: Psychological Theory and Women's Development*, 2nd edn. (Cambridge, Mass.: Harvard University Press, 1993).

Glendon, Mary Ann, *Abortion and Divorce in Western Law* (Cambridge, Mass.: Harvard University Press, 1987).

——*Rights Talk: The Impoverishment of Political Discourse* (New York: Macmillan, 1991).

—— 'Rights in Twentieth-Century Constitutions', in Geoffrey R. Stone, Richard A. Epstein, and Cass R. Sunstein (eds.), *The Bill of Rights in the Modern State* (Chicago: University of Chicago Press, 1992).

Gordon, Charles, and Mailman, Stanley, *Immigration Law and Procedure* (New York: Matthew Bender, 1993).

Gordon, Scott, *The History and Philosophy of Social Science* (London: Routledge, 1991).

Grant, Wyn, 'Introduction', in Grant (ed.), *The Political Economy of Corporatism* (London: Macmillan, 1985).

Gray, John, 'On Negative and Positive Liberty', in *Liberalisms: Essays in Political Philosophy* (London: Routledge, 1989).

—— 'What is Dead and what is Living in Liberalism?', in *Post-Liberalism: Studies in Political Thought* (London: Routledge, 1992).

—— *Enlightenment's Wake: Politics and Culture at the Close of the Modern Age* (London: Routledge, 1995).

—— *Isaiah Berlin* (London: HarperCollins, 1995).

Greenstein, Edward L., 'Medieval Bible Commentaries', in Barry W. Holtz (ed.), *Back to the Sources: Reading the Classic Jewish Texts* (New York: Summit, 1984).

Grey, Thomas C., 'The First Virtue', *Stanford Law Review*, 25/286 (Jan. 1973), 286–327.

Griffith, J. A. G., *The Politics of the Judiciary*, 5th edn. (London: HarperCollins, 1997).

Gunnell, John G., 'The Genealogy of American Pluralism: From Madison to Behavioralism', *International Political Science Review*, 17/3 (July 1996), 253–65.

Gutmann, Amy (ed.), *Multiculturalism and 'The Politics of Recognition'* (Princeton: Princeton University Press, 1992).

—— 'Justice across the Spheres', in David Miller and Michael Walzer (eds.), *Pluralism, Justice, and Equality* (Oxford: Oxford University Press, 1995).

Gwyn, W. B., *The Meaning of the Separation of Powers* (New Orleans: Tulane University Press, 1965).

Habermas, Jürgen, *Knowledge and Human Interests*, trans. Jeremy J. Shapiro (London: Heinemann, 1972).

——*Legitimation Crisis*, trans. Thomas McCarthy (London: Heinemann, 1976).

——*The Theory of Communicative Action*, trans. Thomas McCarthy, 2 vols. (Boston, Mass.: Beacon Press, 1984 and 1987).

——*The Structural Transformation of the Public Sphere: An Inquiry into a Category of Bourgeois Society*, trans. Thomas Burger (Cambridge: Polity Press, 1989).

Hanson, Donald W., 'The Meaning of "Demonstration" in Hobbes's Science', *History of Political Thought*, 11/4 (Winter 1990), 587–626.

Hamilton, Alexander, Madison, James, and Jay, John, *The Federalist Papers* (New York: Bantam, 1982).

Hampsher-Monk, Iain (ed.), *Defending Politics: Bernard Crick and Pluralism* (London: British Academic Press, 1993).

Hampshire, Stuart (ed.), *Public and Private Morality* (Cambridge: Cambridge University Press, 1978).

——*Thought and Action*, 2nd edn. (London: Chatto & Windus, 1982).

——*Morality and Conflict* (Oxford: Basil Blackwell, 1983).

——*Innocence and Experience* (London: Allen Lane, The Penguin Press, 1989).

——'Nationalism', in Edna and Avishai Margalit (eds.), *Isaiah Berlin: A Celebration* (London: Hogarth Press, 1991).

——'Justice is Conflict: The Soul and the City', in Grethe B. Peterson (ed.), *The Tanner Lectures on Human Values,* xix (Salt Lake City: University of Utah Press, 1998).

Hardwig, John, 'Should Women Think in Terms of Rights?', *Ethics*, 94 (Apr. 1984), 441–55.

Hegel, G. W. F., *The Philosophy of Right*, trans. T. M. Knox (Oxford: Oxford University Press, 1942).

——*Hegel's Logic*, trans. William Wallace (Oxford: Oxford University Press, 1975).

Heidegger, Martin, *Being and Time*, trans. John Macquarrie and Edward Robinson (New York: Harper & Row, 1962).

——'The Thing', in *Poetry, Language, Thought*, trans. Albert Hofstadter (New York: Harper & Row, 1971).

Held, David, *Models of Democracy* (Oxford: Polity Press, 1987).

Henshaw, Stanley K., 'Factors Hindering Access to Abortion Services', *Family Planning Perspectives*, 27/2 (Mar.–Apr. 1995), 54–9, 87.

Henshaw, Stanley K., and Van Vort, Jennifer, 'Abortion Services in the United States, 1991 and 1992', *Family Planning Perspectives*, 26 (1994), 100–6, 112.

Heracleitus, *The Art and Thought of Heracleitus*, ed. Charles H. Kahn (Cambridge: Cambridge University Press, 1979).

Herder, Johann Gottfried, 'Essay on the Origin of Language', trans. Alexander

Gode, in Jean-Jacques Rousseau and Herder, *On the Origin of Language* (London: University of Chicago Press, 1966).

Hesse, Mary, *Revolutions and Reconstructions in the Philosophy of Science* (Bloomington, Ind.: Indiana University Press, 1980).

Hirschman, Albert O., *The Passions and the Interests: Political Arguments for Capitalism Before its Triumph* (Princeton: Princeton University Press, 1977).

—— 'Social Conflicts as Pillars of Democratic Market Societies', in *A Propensity to Self-Subversion* (Cambridge, Mass.: Harvard University Press, 1995).

Hobbes, Thomas, *Leviathan*, ed. C. B. Macpherson (Harmondsworth: Penguin, 1968).

Holmes, Stephen, 'The Permanent Structure of Anti-Liberal Thought', in Nancy Rosenblum (ed.), *Liberalism and the Moral Life* (Cambridge, Mass.: Harvard University Press, 1989).

Homer, *The Iliad*, trans. Martin Hammond (Harmondsworth: Penguin, 1987).

Honig, Bonnie, *Political Theory and the Displacement of Politics* (London: Cornell University Press, 1993).

Honoré, A. M., 'Ownership', in A. G. Guest (ed.), *Oxford Essays in Jurisprudence* (Oxford: Oxford University Press, 1961).

Howard, Michael, 'Walzer's Socialism', *Social Theory and Practice*, 12/1 (Spring 1986), 103–13.

Humboldt, Wilhelm von, *On Language: The Diversity of Human Language-Structure and its Influence on the Mental Development of Mankind*, trans. Peter Heath (Cambridge: Cambridge University Press, 1988).

Hume, David, *An Inquiry Concerning Human Understanding*, in *On Human Nature and the Understanding*, ed. Antony Flew (London: Collier-Macmillan, 1962).

Huntington, Samuel P., *American Politics: The Promise of Disharmony* (Cambridge, Mass.: Harvard University Press, 1981).

—— *The Third Wave: Democratization in the Late Twentieth Century* (London: University of Oklahoma Press, 1991).

Husserl, Edmund, 'On the Theory of Wholes and Parts', in *Logical Investigations*, ii, trans. J. N. Findlay (London: Routledge & Kegan Paul, 1970).

Hutton, Will, 'The Stakeholder Society', in Hutton *et al.*, *Stakeholding and its Critics* (London: The IEA Health and Welfare Unit, 1997).

Jones, Peter, *Rights* (New York: St Martin's Press, 1994).

Jordan, Grant, 'The Pluralism of Pluralism: An Anti-Theory?', in Jeremy J. Richardson (ed.), *Pressure Groups* (Oxford: Oxford University Press, 1993).

Joyce, James, *Finnegans Wake* (Harmondsworth: Penguin, 1978).

Kay, John, *Foundations of Corporate Success: How Business Strategies Add Value* (Oxford: Oxford University Press, 1993).

—— 'The Stakeholder Corporation', in Gavin Kelly, Dominic Kelly, and Andrew Gamble (eds.), *Stakeholder Capitalism* (London: Macmillan Press, 1997).

—— *The Role of Business in Society: Inaugural Lecture* (Oxford: Said Business School, University of Oxford, 1998).

Kekes, John, *The Morality of Pluralism* (Princeton: Princeton University Press, 1993).

Kelso, William Alton, *American Democratic Theory: Pluralism and its Critics* (Westport, Conn.: Greenwood Press, 1978).

Kingwell, Mark, *A Civil Tongue: Justice, Dialogue, and the Politics of Pluralism* (Pennsylvania: Pennsylvania State University Press, 1995).

Knopff, Rainer, and Morton, F. L., *Charter Politics* (Scarborough: Nelson Canada, 1992).

Kocis, Robert, *A Critical Appraisal of Sir Isaiah Berlin's Political Philosophy* (Lampeter: Edwin Mellen Press, 1989).

Kohut, Heinz, *The Restoration of the Self* (New York: International Universities Press, 1977).

Kroon, Robert, 'Let's Talk, Not Quarrel, About Rights', *International Herald Tribune* (17 Mar. 1998).

Kuhn, Thomas, *The Structure of Scientific Revolutions*, 2nd edn. (Chicago: University of Chicago Press, 1970).

—— 'Reflections on my Critics', in Imre Lakatos and Lan Musgrave (eds.), *Criticism and the Growth of Knowledge* (Cambridge: Cambridge University Press, 1970).

—— 'Notes on Lakatos', in Roger C. Buck and Robert S. Cohen (eds.), *PSA 1970, in Memory of Rudolf Carnap* (Dordrecht: D. Reidel, 1971).

—— 'Mathematical versus Experimental Traditions in the Development of Physical Science', in John Rajchman and Cornel West (eds.), *Post-Analytic Philosophy* (New York: Columbia University Press, 1985).

Kushner, Tony, *The Holocaust and the Liberal Imagination: A Social and Cultural History* (Oxford: Blackwell, 1995).

Kymlicka, Will, *Liberalism, Community and Culture* (Oxford: Clarendon Press, 1989).

—— *Contemporary Political Philosophy: An Introduction* (Oxford: Clarendon Press, 1990).

Laing, R. D., *The Divided Self: An Existential Study in Sanity and Madness* (London: Penguin, 1959).

Larmore, Charles, *The Morals of Modernity* (Cambridge: Cambridge University Press, 1996).

Laurence, Margaret, *The Diviners* (Toronto: MacClelland & Stewart, 1974).

Lévinas, Emmanuel, *Autrement qu'être ou au-delà de l'essence* (The Hague: Martinus Nijhoff, 1974).

Lindblom, Charles E., *Politics and Markets: The World's Political-Economic Systems* (New York: Basic Books, 1977).

—— *Inquiry and Change: The Troubled Attempt to Understand and Shape Society* (London: Yale University Press, 1990).

Locke, John, *Two Treatises of Government*, ed. Mark Goldie (London: Everyman, 1993).

Lukes, Steven, 'Can a Marxist Believe in Human Rights?', in *Moral Conflict and Politics* (Oxford: Clarendon Press, 1991).

—— 'Five Fables about Human Rights', in Stephen Shute and Susan Hurley (eds.), *On Human Rights: The Oxford Amnesty Lectures 1993* (New York: Basic Books, 1993).

McDowell, John, 'Virtue and Reason', *Monist*, 63/3 (1979) 331–50.

McEvoy, James, *The Philosophy of Robert Grosseteste* (Oxford: Clarendon Press, 1982).

McEwan, Jenny, *Evidence and the Adversarial System: The Modern Law* (Oxford: Blackwell, 1992).

MacIntyre, Alasdair, *After Virtue: A Study in Moral Theory*, 2nd edn. (Notre Dame, Ind.: University of Notre Dame Press, 1984).

—— *Whose Justice? Which Rationality?* (London: Duckworth, 1988).

—— 'Epistemological Crises, Dramatic Narrative and the Philosophy of Science', in Stanely G. Clarke and Evan Simpson (eds.), *Anti-Theory in Ethics and Moral Conservatism* (Albany, NY: SUNY Press, 1989).

—— 'Moral Dilemmas', *Philosophy and Phenomenological Research*, 50 (supp., Fall 1990), 367–82.

—— 'A Partial Response to my Critics', in John Horton and Susan Mendus (eds.), *After MacIntyre: Critical Perspectives on the Work of Alasdair MacIntyre* (Notre Dame, Ind.: University of Notre Dame Press, 1994).

McLennan, Gregor, *Pluralism* (Buckingham: Open University Press, 1995).

MacPherson, C. B., *The Political Theory of Possessive Individualism: Hobbes to Locke* (Oxford: Oxford University Press, 1962).

Macedo, Stephen, *Liberal Virtues: Citizenship, Virtue, and Community in Liberal Constitutionalism* (Oxford: Clarendon Press, 1990).

Machiavelli, Niccolo, *History of Florence and of the Affairs of Italy: From the Earliest Times to the Death of Lorenzo the Magnificent*, trans. Istorie Fiorentine (New York: Harper & Brothers, 1960).

—— *The Discourses* in *Machiavelli: The Chief Works and Others*, ed. and trans. Allan Gilbert (Durham, NC: Duke University Press, 1965).

—— *The Discourses*, ed. Bernard Crick, trans. Leslie J. Walker (Harmondsworth: Penguin, 1970).

—— *The Art of War*, in *The Portable Machiavelli*, ed. and trans. Peter Bondanella and Mark Musa (Harmondsworth: Penguin, 1979).

—— *The Prince*, ed. Quentin Skinner and Russel Price, trans. Price (Cambridge: Cambridge University Press, 1988).

Malachowski, Alan (ed.), *Reading Rorty* (Oxford: Basil Blackwell, 1990).

Malter, Henry, 'Personifications of Soul and Body', *Jewish Quarterly Review*, NS 2/4 (Apr. 1912), 453–79.

Man, Paul de, 'The Rhetoric of Blindness: Jacques Derrida's Reading of Rousseau', in *Blindness and Insight: Essays in the Rhetoric of Contemporary Criticism*, 2nd edn. (London: Routledge, 1983).

Mandel, Michael, *The Charter of Rights and the Legalization of Politics in Canada*, 2nd edn. (Toronto: Thompson Educational Publishing, 1992).

Marcil-Lacoste, Louise, 'The Paradoxes of Pluralism', in Chantal Mouffe (ed.), *Dimensions of Radical Democracy: Pluralism, Citizenship, Community* (London: Verso, 1992).

Marcus, Ruth Barcan, 'Moral Dilemmas and Consistency', in Christopher Gowans (ed.), *Moral Dilemmas* (Oxford: Oxford University Press, 1987).

Marx, Karl, *Capital: A Critical Analysis of Capitalist Production*, i, ed. Frederick Engels, trans. Samuel Moore and Edward Aveling (Moscow: Foreign Languages Publishing House, 1958).

—— *Economic and Philosophical Manuscripts* in *Karl Marx: Early Writings*, ed. and trans. Tom B. Bottomore (London: C. A. Watts & Co., 1963).

—— 'On the Jewish Question', in *Karl Marx: Selected Writings*, ed. and trans. David McLellan (Oxford: Oxford University Press, 1977).

—— letter to Friedrich Adolph Sorge, 19 Oct. 1877, in *Karl Marx, Frederick Engels: Collected Works*, xxxxv (London: Lawrence & Wishart, 1991).

Mason, Andrew, *Explaining Political Disagreement* (Cambridge: Cambridge University Press, 1993).

Mason, John Hope, 'Creativity in Action: The Background to Machiavelli's "Lion" and "Fox"', in Ian Hampsher-Monk (ed.), *Defending Politics* (London: British Academic Press, 1993).

Megill, Allan, *Prophets of Extremity: Nietzsche, Heidegger, Foucault, Derrida* (Berkeley, Calif.: University of California Press, 1985).

Merleau-Ponty, Maurice, *La Phénoménologie de la perception* (Paris: Gallimard, 1945).

Messer, Stanley B., Sass, Louis, and Woolfolk, Robert (eds.), *Hermeneutics and Psychological Theory: Interpretive Perspectives on Personality, Psychotherapy, and Psychopathology* (New Brunswick, NJ: Rutgers University Press, 1988).

Miller, David, 'Political Theory', in Miller *et al.* (eds.), *The Blackwell Encyclopedia of Political Thought* (Oxford: Basil Blackwell, 1987).

—— *Market, State, and Community: Theoretical Foundations of Market Socialism* (Oxford: Clarendon Press, 1989).

—— 'Equality', in G. M. K. Hunt (ed.), *Philosophy and Politics: Supplement to Philosophy 1989* (Cambridge: Cambridge University Press, 1990).

—— 'Distributive Justice: What the People Think', *Ethics*, 102/3 (Apr. 1992), 555–93.

—— 'Complex Equality', in Miller and Michael Walzer (eds.), *Pluralism, Justice, and Equality* (Oxford: Oxford University Press, 1995).

—— and Walzer, Michael (eds.), *Pluralism, Justice, and Equality* (Oxford: Oxford University Press, 1995).

Minogue, Kenneth, 'The History of the Idea of Human Rights', in Walter Laqueur and Barry Rubin (eds.), *The Human Rights Reader*, 2nd edn. (New York: Penguin, 1989).

Montesquieu, Charles Secondat, *De l'esprit des lois*, i, ed. Laurent Versini (Paris: Gallimard, 1995).

Moon, J. Donald, *Constructing Community: Moral Pluralism and Tragic Conflicts* (Princeton: Princeton University Press, 1993).

Mouffe, Chantal (ed.), *Dimensions of Radical Democracy: Pluralism, Citizenship, Community* (London: Verso, 1992).

Murdoch, Iris, 'The Idea of Perfection', in *The Sovereignty of Good* (New York: Routledge & Kegan Paul, 1970).

Myrdal, Gunner, *The Political Element in the Development of Economic Theory*, trans. Paul Streeten (London: Routledge & Kegan Paul, 1953).

Narveson, Jan F., 'Rawls on Equal Distribution of Wealth', *Philosophia*, 7 (1977), 281–92.

Newman, Otto, *The Challenge of Corporatism* (London: Macmillan, 1981).

Nicholls, David, *Three Varieties of Pluralism* (London: Macmillan Press, 1974).

Nietzsche, Fredrich, *On the Genealogy of Morals*, trans. Walter Kaufmann and R. J. Hollingdale (New York: Random House, 1967).

Nozick, Robert, *Anarchy, State, and Utopia* (New York: Basic Books, 1974).

Nussbaum, Martha, '*Psuchē* in Heraclitus, I', *Phronesis*, 17 (1972), 1–16.

—— *The Fragility of Goodness: Luck and Ethics in Greek Tragedy and Philosophy* (Cambridge: Cambridge University Press, 1986).

—— 'Aristotelian Social Democracy', in R. Bruce Douglass, Gerald M. Mara, and Henry S. Richardson (eds.), *Liberalism and the Good* (New York: Routledge, 1990).

—— *Love's Knowledge: Essays on Philosophy and Literature* (Oxford: Oxford University Press, 1990).

—— 'Non-Relative Virtues: An Aristotelian Approach', in Nussbaum and Amartya Sen (eds.), *The Quality of Life* (Oxford: Clarendon Press, 1993).

—— and Sen, Amartya (eds.), *The Quality of Life* (Oxford: Clarendon Press, 1993).

Oakeshott, Michael, *On Human Conduct* (Oxford: Clarendon Press, 1975).

Philp, Margaret, 'Poverty Crusade Gets Personal', *The Globe and Mail* (20 Sept. 1997), A1, A6.

Pitkin, Hannah, *The Concept of Representation* (London: University of California Press, 1967).

—— *Wittgenstein and Justice: On the Significance of Ludwig Wittgenstein for Social and Political Theory* (London: University of California Press, 1972).

Plant, Raymond, *Modern Political Thought* (Oxford: Basil Blackwell, 1991).

Plato, *The Dialogues of Plato*, trans. Benjamin Jowett, 4th edn., i and iv (Oxford: Oxford University Press, 1953).

—— *The Republic*, trans. Allan Bloom (New York: Basic Books, 1968).

Pocock, J. G. A., *The Machiavellian Moment: Florentine Political Thought and the Atlantic Republican Tradition* (Princeton: Princeton University Press, 1975).

—— 'The Idea of Citizenship since Classical Times', in Ronald Beiner (ed.), *Theorizing Citizenship* (Albany, NY: SUNY Press, 1995).

Polanyi, Karl, *The Great Transformation: The Political and Economic Origins of Our Time* (Boston, Mass.: Beacon Press, 1944).

Polanyi, Michael, *The Tacit Dimension* (New York: Anchor Books, 1966).

Polybius, *The Histories*, iii, trans. W. R. Paton (London: William Heinemann, 1923).

Popper, Karl, *The Logic of Scientific Discovery* (London: Hutchinson, 1959).

——*Conjectures and Refutations: The Growth of Scientific Knowledge* (London: Routledge & Kegan Paul, 1961).

Porter, Michael E., and van der Linde, Claus, 'Toward a New Conception of the Environment–Competitiveness Relationship', *Journal of Economic Perspectives* 9/4 (Fall 1995), 97–118.

Quine, Willard, *Word and Object* (Cambridge, Mass.: MIT Press, 1960).

——*Ontological Relativity and Other Essays* (New York: Columbia University Press, 1969).

——'Two Dogmas of Empiricism', in *From a Logical Point of View: 9 Logico-Philosophical Essays*, 2nd edn. (London: Harvard University Press, 1980).

——'On the Very Idea of a Third Dogma', in *Theories and Things* (Cambridge: Harvard University Press, 1981).

——'Let me Accentuate the Positive', in Alan Malachowski (ed.), *Reading Rorty* (Oxford: Basil Blackwell, 1990).

Rawls, John, *A Theory of Justice* (Cambridge, Mass.: Harvard University Press, 1971).

——*Political Liberalism* (New York: Columbia University Press, 1993).

Raz, Joseph, *The Morality of Freedom* (Oxford: Oxford University Press, 1986).

——'Multiculturalism: A Liberal Perspective', in *Ethics in the Public Domain: Essays in the Morality of Law and Politics* (Oxford: Oxford University Press, 1994).

Reicher, Klaus, 'Fragment and Totality', in Bonnie Kime Scott (ed.), *New Alliances in Joyce Studies* (London, Associated University Presses, 1988).

REM, 'Ignoreland', in *Automatic for the People* (New York: Warner Bros. Records, 1992).

Rescher, Nicholas, *Pluralism: Against the Demand for Consensus* (Oxford: Clarendon Press, 1993).

Rhees, Rush, 'Wittgenstein's Builders', in *Discussions of Wittgenstein* (London: Routledge & Kegan Paul, 1969).

Rilke, Rainer Maria, *The Selected Poetry of Rainer Maria Rilke*, ed. and trans. Stephen Mitchell (New York: Vintage International, 1982).

Romilly, Jacqueline de, *Alcibiade: Ou les dangers de l'ambition* (Paris: Fallois, 1995).

Rorty, Richard, 'The Contingency of Language', in *Contingency, Irony, and Solidarity* (Cambridge: Cambridge University Press, 1989).

——'The Priority of Democracy to Philosophy', in *Objectivity, Relativism and Truth: Philosophical Papers*, i (Cambridge: Cambridge University Press, 1991).

Rose, Richard, and McAllister, Ian, 'Expressive versus Instrumental Voting', in Dennis Kavanagh (ed.), *Electoral Politics* (Oxford, Clarendon Press, 1992).

Rosenblum, Nancy (ed.), *Liberalism and the Moral Life* (Cambridge, Mass.: Harvard University Press, 1989).

Ross, W. D., *The Right and the Good* (Oxford: Oxford University Press, 1963).

Rousseau, Jean-Jacques, *Œuvres Complètes*, ed. Bernard Gagnebin and Marcel Raymond (Paris: Gallimard, 1964).

Russell, Bertrand, *The Philosophy of Logical Atomism*, ed. David Pears (La Salle, Ill.: Open Court, 1985).

Ryan, Alan (ed.), *The Idea of Freedom: Essays in Honour of Isaiah Berlin* (Oxford: Oxford University Press, 1979).

Ryle, Gilbert, *Collected Papers*, ii (London: Hutchinson & Co., 1971).

Sandel, Michael, *Liberalism and the Limits of Justice* (Cambridge: Cambridge University Press, 1982).

——'The Procedural Republic and the Unencumbered Self', in Shlomo Avineri and Avner de-Shalit (eds.), *Communitarianism and Individualism* (Oxford: Oxford University Press, 1992).

Sartori, Giovanni, 'Guidelines for Concept Analysis', in Sartori (ed.), *Social Science Concepts: A Systematic Analysis* (Beverly Hills, Calif.: Sage, 1984).

Sartre, Jean Paul, *L'Existentialisme est un humanisme* (Paris: Gallimard, 1996).

Saussure, Ferdinand de, *Cours de linguistique générale*, ed. Charles Bully and Albert Sechehay (Paris: Payot, 1987).

Schedler, Andreas (ed.), *The End of Politics? Explorations into Modern Antipolitics* (London: Macmillan, 1997).

Scholem, Gershom G., *Major Trends in Jewish Mysticism*, 3rd edn. (New York: Schocken, 1954).

Schumpeter, Joseph, *Capitalism, Socialism and Democracy*, 6th edn. (London: Unwin Paperbacks, 1987).

Shelley, Percy Bysshe, *Hellas*, in *Shelley's Poetry and Prose*, ed. Donald H. Reiman and Sharon B. Powers (London: W. W. Norton, 1977).

Siedentop, Larry, 'Two Liberal Traditions', in Alan Ryan (ed.), *The Idea of Freedom* (Oxford: Oxford University Press, 1979).

Skinner, Quentin, *Machiavelli* (Oxford: Oxford University Press, 1981).

——*The Foundations of Modern Political Thought, ii. The Age of Reformation* (Cambridge, Cambridge University Press, 1978).

Smith, Adam, *An Inquiry in the Nature and Causes of the Wealth of Nations*, i, ed. R. H. Campbell and A. S. Skinner (Oxford: Clarendon Press, 1976).

Smith, Martin J., 'Pluralism, Reformed Pluralism and Neopluralism: The Role of Pressure Groups in Policy-Making', *Political Studies*, 38/2 (June 1990), 302–22.

Sniderman, Paul M., Fletcher, Joseph F., Russell, Peter H., and Tetlock, Philip E., *The Clash of Rights: Liberty, Equality, and Legitimacy in Pluralist Democracy* (New Haven: Yale University Press, 1996).

Solomon, Robert C., *Ethics and Excellence: Cooperation and Integrity in Business* (New York: Oxford University Press, 1992).

Solzhenitsyn, Alexander, *One Day in the Life of Ivan Denisovitch*, trans. Ralph Parker (London: Victor Gallancz, 1963).

Steiner, George, *The Death of Tragedy* (London: Faber & Faber, 1961).

Sternberg, Elaine, 'Stakeholder Theory: The Defective State it's in', in Will Hutton *et al.*, *Stakeholding and its Critics* (London: The IEA Health and Welfare Unit, 1997).

Stocker, Michael, *Plural and Conflicting Values* (Oxford: Clarendon Press, 1990).

Strier, Franklin D., *Reconstructing Justice: An Agenda for Trial Reform* (Chicago: University of Chicago Press, 1994).

Tamir, Yael, *Liberal Nationalism* (Princeton: Princeton University Press, 1993).

Tannen, Deborah, *You Just Don't Understand: Women and Men in Conversation* (London: Virago, 1990).

Taylor, Charles, 'A Socialist Perspective on the '70s', *Canadian Dimension*, 5/8 (Feb. 1969), 36–40.

——*The Pattern of Politics* (Toronto: McClelland and Stewart, 1970).

——*Hegel* (Cambridge: Cambridge University Press, 1975).

——'Action as Expression', in Cora Diamond and Jenny Teichman (eds.), *Intention and Intentionality: Essays in Honour of G. E. M. Anscombe* (Brighton: Harvester Press, 1979).

——'Understanding Human Science', *Review of Metaphysics*, 34 (Sept. 1980), 25–38.

——'Political Theory and Practice', in Christopher Lloyd (ed.), *Social Theory and Political Practice* (Oxford: Clarendon Press, 1983).

——*Human Agency and Language: Philosophical Papers 1* (Cambridge: Cambridge University Press, 1985).

——*Philosophy and the Human Sciences: Philosophical Papers 2* (Cambridge: Cambridge University Press, 1985).

——'Les Droits de l'homme: La culture juridique', in Paul Ricoeur (ed.), *Les Fondements philosophiqes des droits de l'homme* (Paris: UNESCO, 1986).

——'The Hermeneutics of Conflict', in James Tully (ed.), *Meaning and Context: Quentin Skinner and his Critics* (Cambridge: Polity, 1988).

——'Balancing the Humours: An Interview with Charles Taylor', *The Idler* (Nov.–Dec. 1989).

——*Sources of the Self: The Making of the Modern Identity* (Cambridge, Mass.: Harvard University Press, 1989).

——'The Rushdie Controversy', *Public Culture*, 2/1 (Fall 1989), 118–22.

——'Modes of Civil Society', *Public Culture*, 3/1 (Fall 1990), 95–118.

——'Hegel's Ambiguous Legacy for Modern Liberalism', in Drucilla Cornell, Michel Rosenfeld, and David Gray Carlson (eds.), *Hegel and Legal Theory* (London: Routledge, 1991).

——*The Ethics of Authenticity* (Cambridge, Mass.: Harvard University Press, 1991).

——'Modernity and the Rise of the Public Sphere', in Grethe B. Peterson (ed.), *The Tanner Lectures on Human Values*, xiv (Salt Lake City: University of Utah Press, 1993).

——*Reconciling the Solitudes: Essays on Canadian Federalism and Nationalism* (Montreal: McGill-Queen's University Press, 1993).

Taylor, Charles, 'Charles Taylor Replies', in James Tully (ed.), *Philosophy in an Age of Pluralism: The Philosophy of Charles Taylor in Question* (Cambridge: Cambridge University Press, 1994).

——'Reply to Commentators', *Philosophy and Phenomenological Research*, 54/1 (Mar. 1994), 203–13.

——*Philosophical Arguments* (London: Harvard University Press, 1995).

——'Leading a Life', in Ruth Chang (ed.) *Incommensurability, Incomparability, and Practical Reason* (Cambridge, Mass.: Harvard University Press, 1997).

The Tragically Hip, '38 Years Old', in *Up to Here* (Toronto: MCA Records, 1989).

——'Daredevil', in *Day for Night* (Toronto: MCA Records, 1994).

——'Gift Shop', in *Trouble at the Henhouse* (Toronto: MCA Music, 1996).

——introduction to 'New Orleans is Sinking', in *Another Roadside Attraction*, live concert performed in Landsdowne Park, Ottawa, Canada, 26 July 1998.

Thucydides, *History of the Peloponnesian Wars*, ed. W. Robert Conner, trans. Richard Crawle (London: Everyman, 1993).

Tocqueville, Alexis de, *De la démocratie en Amérique*, ii (Paris: Gallimard, 1961).

Todorov, Tzvetan, *Théories du symbole* (Paris: Seuil, 1977).

Tribe, Laurence, *Abortion: The Clash of Absolutes* (New York: Norton, 1990).

Truman, David, *The Governmental Process* (New York: A. A. Knopf, 1951).

Tully, James, *Strange Multiplicity: Constitutionalism in an Age of Diversity* (Cambridge: Cambridge University Press, 1995).

Turner, Stephen, *The Social Theory of Practices: Tradition, Tacit Knowledge and Presuppositions* (Cambridge: Polity, 1994).

Tushnet, Mark, 'Is Judicial Review Good for the Left?', *Dissent* (Winter 1998).

Urmson, J. O., *Aristotle's Ethics* (Oxford: Basil Blackwell, 1988).

Vanderbeke, Dirk, 'Physics, Rhetoric, and the Language of *Finnegans Wake*', in R. M. Bollettieri Bosinelli, C. Marengo Vaglio, and C. van Boheemen (eds.), *The Languages of Joyce* (Amsterdam: John Benjamins, 1992).

Vile, M. J. C., *Constitutionalism and the Separation of Powers* (Oxford: Clarendon Press, 1967).

Volozhyn, Rabbi Hayyim de, *L'Âme de la vie: Nefesh hahahyyim*, trans. Benjamin Gross (Paris: Éditions, Verdier, 1986).

Walbank, F. W., *Polybius* (Berkeley, Calif.: University of California Press, 1972).

Waldron, Jeremy, *Liberal Rights: Collected Papers 1981–1991* (Cambridge: Cambridge University Press, 1993).

Wallach, John R., 'Contemporary Aristotelianism', *Political Theory*, 20/4 (Nov. 1992), 613–41.

Walzer, Michael, 'Political Action: The Problem of Dirty Hands', *Philosophy and Public Affairs*, 2/2 (1973), 160–80.

——'Pluralism in Political Perspective', in Stephan Thernstrom (ed.),

The Politics of Ethnicity (Cambridge, Mass.: Harvard University Press, 1980).

——'Philosophy and Democracy', *Political Theory*, 1/3 (Aug. 1981), 379–99.

——*Spheres of Justice: A Defense of Pluralism and Equality* (New York: Basic Books, 1983).

——'Liberalism and the Art of Separation', *Political Theory*, 12/3 (1984), 315–30.

——'Introduction', in Isaiah Berlin, *The Hedgehog and the Fox: An Essay on Tolstoy's View of History* (New York: Simon & Schuster, 1986).

——'Justice Here and Now', in Frank S. Lucash (ed.), *Justice and Equality Here and Now* (Ithaca NY: Cornell University Press, 1986).

——*Interpretation and Social Criticism* (Cambridge, Mass.: Harvard University Press, 1987).

——'Socializing the Welfare State', in Amy Gutmann (ed.), *Democracy and the Welfare State* (Princeton: Princeton University Press, 1988).

——'Citizenship', in Terence Ball, James Farr, and Russell L. Hanson (eds.), *Political Innovation and Conceptual Change* (Cambridge: Cambridge University Press, 1989).

——'Flight from Philosophy', *Times Literary Supplement* (2 Feb. 1989), 42–4.

——*The Company of Critics: Social Criticism and Political Commitment in the Twentieth Century* (London: Peter Halban, 1989).

——'The Good Life', *New Statesman and Society* (6 Oct. 1989).

——'A Critique of Philosophical Conversation', *The Philosophical Forum*, 21/1–2 (Fall–Winter 1989–90), 182–96.

——'Nation and Universe', in Grethe B. Peterson (ed.), *The Tanner Lectures on Human Values*, xi (Salt Lake City: University of Utah Press, 1990).

——'The Communitarian Critique of Liberalism', *Political Theory*, 18/1 (Feb. 1990), 6–23.

——'The Minimalist', in *The New Republic* (22 Jan. 1990), 39–41.

——'Comment', in Amy Gutmann (ed.), *Multiculturalism and 'The Politics of Recognition'* (Princeton: Princeton University Press, 1992).

——'The Civil Society Argument', in Chantal Mouffe (ed.), *Dimensions of Radical Democracy: Pluralism, Citizenship, Community* (London: Verso, 1992).

——'The New Tribalism: Notes on a Difficult Problem', *Dissent* (Spring 1992), 165–71.

——'Exclusion, Injustice, and the Democratic State', *Dissent* (Winter 1993), 56–64.

——'Objectivity and Social Meaning', in Martha Nussbaum and Amartya Sen (eds.), *The Quality of Life* (Oxford: Clarendon Press, 1993).

——'Multiculturalism and Individualism', *Dissent* (Spring 1994), 185–91.

——*Thick and Thin: Moral Argument at Home and Abroad* (Notre Dame, Ind.: University of Notre Dame Press, 1994).

——'Are there Limits to Liberalism?', *New York Review of Books* (19 Oct. 1995).

Walzer, Michael, 'Preface', to Jean-Paul Sartre, *Anti-Semite and Jew: An Exploration of the Etiology of Hate*, trans. George J. Becker (New York: Schocken, 1995).

——'Response', in David Miller and Walzer (eds.), *Pluralism, Justice, and Equality* (Oxford: Oxford University Press, 1995).

——*On Toleration* (New Haven, Conn.: Yale University Press, 1997).

——'Pluralism and Social Democracy', *Dissent* (Winter 1998).

Warnke, Georgia, *Justice and Interpretation* (Cambridge: Polity, 1992).

Weber, Max, 'Politics as a Vocation', in *From Max Weber: Essays in Sociology*, ed. and trans. H. H. Gerth and C. Wright Mills (London: Routledge, 1948).

——*The Protestant Ethic and the Spirit of Capitalism*, trans. Talcott Parsons (New York: Charles Scribner's Sons, 1958).

——*Economy and Society: An Outline of Interpretive Sociology*, ii, ed. Guenther Roth and Claus Wittich, trans. Ephraim Fischoff *et al.* (London: University of California Press, 1978).

Weinsheimer, Joel, *Gadamer's Hermeneutics: A Reading of* Truth and Method (New Haven, Conn.: Yale University Press, 1985).

White, James Boyd, 'How should we Talk about Corporations? The Languages of Economics and of Citizenship', *Yale Law Journal*, 94/6 (May 1985), 1416–25.

Wiggins, David, 'Deliberation and Practical Reason', in Amélie Oksenberg Rorty (ed.), *Essays on Aristotle's Ethics* (London: University of California Press, 1980).

Wilber, Ken (ed.), *The Holographic Paradigm and Other Paradoxes* (Boston, Mass.: New Science Library, 1985).

Williams, Bernard, 'Politics and Moral Character', in Stuart Hampshire (ed.), *Public and Private Morality* (Cambridge: Cambridge University Press, 1978).

——'Ethical Consistency', in *Problems of the Self: Philosophical Papers, 1956–1972* (Cambridge: Cambridge University Press, 1981).

——*Moral Luck: Philosophical Papers 1973–1980* (Cambridge: Cambridge University Press, 1981).

——*Ethics and the Limits of Philosophy* (London: HarperCollins, 1985).

——'Saint-Just's Illusion', in *Making Sense of Humanity: And Other Philosophical Papers 1982–1993* (Cambridge: Cambridge University Press, 1995).

Williamson, Peter J., *Varieties of Corporatism* (Cambridge: Cambridge University Press, 1985).

Willis, Garry, 'Introduction', in Alexander Hamilton, John Madison, and John Jay, *The Federalist Papers* (New York: Bantam, 1982).

Winch, Peter, *The Idea of a Social Science and its Relation to Philosophy*, 2nd edn. (London: Routledge, 1990).

Wittgenstein, Ludwig, *Philosophical Investigations*, 2nd edn., ed. G. E. M. Anscombe, Rush Rhees, and G. H. von Wright, trans. Anscombe (Oxford: Basil Blackwell, 1958).

——'Wittgenstein's Lecture on Ethics', *Philosophical Review*, 74 (Jan. 1965), 3–26.

——*On Certainty*, ed. G. E. M. Anscombe and G. H. von Wright, trans. Anscombe and Denis Paul (Oxford: Blackwell, 1979).

Wolf, Ernest S., ' "Irrationality" in a Psychoanalytic Psychology of the Self', in Theodore Mischel (ed.), *The Self: Psychological and Philosophical Issues* (Oxford: Basil Blackwell, 1977).

Zaehner, R. C., *Mysticism Sacred and Profane: An Inquiry into Some Varieties of Praeternatural Experience* (Oxford: Oxford University Press, 1967).

Index